Understanding Peace

Understanding Peace: A Comprehensive Introduction fills the need for an original, contemporary examination of peace that is challenging, informative, and empowering. This well-researched, fully documented, and highly accessible textbook moves beyond fixation on war to highlight the human capacity for nonviolent cooperation in everyday life and in conflict situations. After deconstructing numerous ideas about war and explaining its heavy costs to humans, animals, and the environment, discussion turns to evidence for the existence of peaceful societies. Further topics include the role of nonviolence in history, the nature of violence and aggression, and the theory and practice of nonviolence. The book offers two new moral arguments against war, and concludes by defining peace carefully from different angles and then describing conditions for creating a culture of peace. *Understanding Peace* brings a fresh philosophical perspective to discussions of peace, and also addresses down-to-earth issues about effecting constructive change in a complex world. The particular strength of *Understanding Peace* lies in its commitment to reflecting on and integrating material from many fields of knowledge. This approach will appeal to a diverse audience of students and scholars in peace studies, philosophy, and the social sciences, as well as to general-interest readers.

Michael A. Fox is Emeritus Professor of Philosophy at Queen's University, Canada.

D0920690

Understanding Peace
A Comprehensive Introduction

Michael Allen Fox

Routledge
Taylor & Francis Group

NEW YORK AND LONDON

First published 2014
by Routledge
711 Third Avenue, New York, NY 10017

and by Routledge
2 Park Square, Milton Park, Abingdon, Oxon OX14 4RN

Routledge is an imprint of the Taylor & Francis Group, an informa business

© 2014 Taylor & Francis

The right of Michael Allen Fox to be identified as author of this work has been asserted by him/her in accordance with sections 77 and 78 of the Copyright, Designs and Patents Act 1988.

All rights reserved. No part of this book may be reprinted or reproduced or utilized in any form or by any electronic, mechanical, or other means, now known or hereafter invented, including photocopying and recording, or in any information storage or retrieval system, without permission in writing from the publishers.

Trademark Notice: Product or corporate names may be trademarks or registered trademarks, and are used only for identification and explanation without intent to infringe.

Library of Congress Cataloging-in-Publication Data

Fox, Michael Allen, 1940 May 7–
Understanding peace : a comprehensive introduction / by
Michael A. Fox. — 1 [edition].
    pages cm
  Includes bibliographical references and index.
  1. Peace. I. Title.
B105.P4F69   2013
303.6'6—dc23
2013020485

ISBN: 978-0-415-71569-0 (hbk)
ISBN: 978-0-415-71570-6 (pbk)
ISBN: 978-1-315-88013-6 (ebk)

Typeset in Minion Pro
by Apex CoVantage, LLC

Printed and bound in the United States of America by
Edwards Brothers Malloy

The earth is too small a planet and we too brief visitors for anything to matter more than the struggle for peace.

—Coleman McCarthy, *I'd Rather Teach Peace* (2007)

I am certain that after the dust of centuries has passed over our cities, we, too, will be remembered not for victories or defeats in battle or in politics, but for our contribution to the human spirit.

—John F. Kennedy, *remarks on behalf of National Cultural Center which would come to bear his name, 29 November 1962; inscribed on wall of John F. Kennedy Center for the Performing Arts, Washington, DC*

To Jason, Tim, Zoé, Ava, and Hannah.
And to all children, present and future,
including their own, with the hope that
they may live in a more peaceful world.

Contents

Acknowledgments

I would like to thank all those who have helped me develop my ideas on peace over the years. They include students in courses I have taught on the philosophy of peace at Queen's University, Kingston, Ontario, Canada, and various members of Concerned Philosophers for Peace, Philosophers for Peace (and Prevention of Nuclear Omnicide), and the Peace and Justice Studies Association. Brian Byrne and Robin Fox kindly agreed to vet my entire manuscript, and I cannot thank them enough for their astute observations and suggestions, which have been of great benefit to me and to the quality of this book. Leo Groarke assisted me in thinking through the earliest stage of this project. Steven Mitchell put forward the idea that peace needs to be "sold"—which I at first rejected, then later found useful for framing my argument in the Introduction. Tom Bristow first proposed that I submit my manuscript to Routledge, and persuaded me to do so. I also owe a debt of gratitude to several other individuals who have inspired me and/or helped me work my way through specific issues, roadblocks, and decisions about the structure and content of the book: Marty Branagan, Peter Erskine, Ken Fraser, Adam Harris, Russell Hogg, Louise Noble, Lynne Rienner, John Scott.

A special thanks is due to Diana Francis, whose very clear, reasoned, forceful, and impassioned writing on war inspired the pacifist arguments presented in Chapter 3.

My editors at Routledge, Felisa Salvago-Keyes, Andrew Beck, and John Downes-Angus have been very helpful and encouraging. I am grateful for their support. My thanks also go to the rest of the Routledge team for their efforts to make this book a success. To the anonymous reviewers of my manuscript, thank you for your votes of approval and good suggestions.

Research for this book was conducted primarily at the University of New England, Armidale, New South Wales, Australia, which provided me with a much-appreciated adjunct appointment and access to essential facilities, and to a lesser extent at the beautiful Library of Congress in Washington, DC.

An earlier version of the Introduction appeared, under the title "Thinking About Peace Today," in the *Journal of Sociology and Social Welfare* 38 (2011), pp. 15–36. The material on compassion in Chapter 5 first appeared as "Compassion and Peace" in *Philosophy Now* #80 (August/September 2010), pp. 28–9. The editors of these journals have kindly allowed this content to be included here. Bruce Bonta has generously agreed to the usage of his ideas in the diagram "Features of a Peaceful Society" in Chapter 2.

Preface

This book has three main goals: to explain the fundamentals of peace in a clear and accessible manner within a secular framework; to show that peace in the world is possible; and to argue that where war is concerned, we are not using our brains effectively in the interest of survival and flourishing. Peace is not a great mystery. We know to a large extent what we need to do to realize it. But there is no simple recipe for motivating people to do what they ought to do and can do—which is essentially to choose the path of intelligence and nonviolent coexistence. By appealing to everyone's sense that peace is desirable, *Understanding Peace: A Comprehensive Introduction* aims to stimulate greater interest in peace as well as creative thinking and action to help promote it. But it is also necessary to address a prevailing kind of skepticism that suggests peace is only an elusive dream of humankind, and this is done here by arguing that we have the resources, individually and collectively, to make peace a realistic objective that is worth working toward.

A few central questions will occupy our attention: Why does war crowd out peace in our consciousness of the world? What is peace anyway? What is the human potential for peace? How can it best be promoted? If we can get a grip on peace by answering questions of this kind, then we will be well situated to do things that will help bring it about. While we must not ignore the serious threats to peace that exist today, we can empower ourselves by seeing that we do indeed have choices; that we are actually developing some of the ideas and tools needed for peace to become a reality; and that we are therefore not destined, as a species, to a gloomy future of violent responses to inter-human problems, destructive confrontation, perhaps even self-annihilation.

This book is written without the use of the first-person "I." The reason for this is that I, the author, want you, the reader, to join with me in considering certain relevant evidence, reasoning through a set of problems and arguments, and trying out (or trying on) certain assumptions and intuitions to see where they might lead. So when you encounter the personal pronoun "we," as above, this is meant to encourage you to share a particular point of view—to be part of this "we"—and to acknowledge that we are all indeed in the same boat, as reflected by a certain issue, position, or judgment. I hope that this approach resonates with you as you go along and that I have identified some important beliefs and values we hold in common as fellow beings on this endangered planet.

The plan of the book is as follows. Since peace needs to dethrone war, a reversal of the usual emphasis is needed: *Peace, not war, must be our primary focus and central concept.* The Introduction aims to overcome the widespread preoccupation with war and resistance to thinking about peace that exist today. The strategy here is to deconstruct attitudes that promote war and myths of war, then to examine and reject negative assessments of humans' capacity for peaceful behavior. Wide-ranging costs of war and war-preparedness are also exposed. The Introduction concludes with a list of "Home Truths" (beliefs that invite universal assent), from which a constructive conversation on peace might begin.

Chapter 1 reflects on the ways in which historical accounts help shape a cultural outlook where war appears to be a permanent and integral part of the human condition. The antidote to this "militarist" historical narrative is an alternative story that clarifies the significant role of nonviolence in human affairs, and that provides examples from various eras and parts of the world to explain how nonviolence shapes history. A contribution to this alternative story is offered here.

The war mentality assumes that, given a certain conception of human nature, war is here to stay. Chapter 2 provides a more optimistic view of our species and of how we can and do get along with one another—and have done so for millennia. Through an examination of, and commentary on, numerous studies of peaceful societies, we learn important and positive lessons about the human capacity for nonviolent living. This chapter also discusses some new ideas about evolution that feature cooperative interrelationships, both nonhuman and human.

Discussions of war and peace cannot avoid adopting an ethical perspective. Some moral arguments about war start from the premise that war is unavoidable in certain circumstances, and end with prescriptions governing how wars can legitimately be started and then conducted in an ethically acceptable manner. Chapter 3 analyzes and rejects the foregoing approach, epitomized by the "just war tradition," and introduces two new arguments against war. These arguments demonstrate that (i) war undermines and violates the basic premise of morality; and (ii) war negates the extension of morality to other species and nature, to both of which we owe important obligations. The conclusion drawn from these arguments is that war is fundamentally immoral. Some critical objections to this outcome are examined and put aside.

"Violence," "aggression," and "nonviolence" are indispensable terms for describing human behavior of various types, and they are of central concern to peace theorists. These concepts are investigated in Chapter 4. After considering how best to understand violence and aggression, and the difference between them, we explore the meaning of nonviolence. Being nonviolent, it is argued, does not mean being quietly resigned and passive, but rather being actively self-assertive in certain ways. This perspective teaches us that there are different forms of nonviolence, and that nonviolence can be a potent force for change.

Peace, relative to war, is an unfamiliar notion. Yet peace possesses a rich variety of meanings, many of which we already identify with. Chapter 5 explores these dimensions of meaning, and then incorporates peace and peacefulness into an overall outlook on life. In the course of this discussion, attention is turned to compassion, an attribute that is a key component of morality and of peace. This chapter highlights, in addition, the "will to peace"—a strong and motivating desire that exists beneath the surface in people. Some evidence in support of positing this psychological phenomenon is reviewed and evaluated, which enables the characterization of peace as a way of life.

Chapters 6 and 7 define what the nature and scope of a culture of peace might be, and examine how one can be created. Since peace is a process to the same extent as, or even more than, anything else, it requires continuous cultivation and monitoring. There are many trends in global affairs the individual can do little to influence, except very indirectly. However, there are all kinds of activities and behaviors that will help build a better world. Among these are nonviolent conflict management, everyday peaceful conduct, and showing respect for human rights. Even how we treat the natural environment and members of other species count significantly in this regard. Within this larger context, we also come to appreciate education as a vital agent of change across the range of issues pertaining to the creation of a peaceful form of life. Chapter 7 concludes with an account of the gradual emergence of a global outlook for humanity, which is a pivotal event in the development of a universal peace-consciousness.

Understanding Peace argues that peace is central to a constructive and comprehensive view of our place in the world, and that realizing peace is a function of self-examination, choice, and commitment. Arguments do not necessarily change the way things are in the world, much as we might wish they could. But at least they show us where certain beliefs and behaviors will lead us, and if we do not like what we see, we can find the strength and determination to choose a different direction. This is the beginning of constructive change. Those who would like to bring about peace, and to experience and live in a more peaceful world, have formidable opponents—not tin-pot dictators, terrorists, the military-industrial complex, international arms dealers, and greedy capitalists. These are there all right, but none of them, nor even all of them combined, are the main issue. The main issue is clinging to the status quo and thinking inside the box. What box? The box confining us to an outlook that prescribes military solutions to human problems, as though such solutions really work, a view that convinces us we cannot do any better. However, when we gain insights into the nature of peace and our potential for peaceful living, these can help energize our quest to bring about positive transformations that will make the world a better place. Everyone has a part to play in accomplishing this great human project, and everyone stands to benefit from it.

Diagrams

Introduction: Thinking about Peace Today

The only alternative to coexistence is codestruction.

—Jawaharlal Nehru, first prime minister of
independent India (1947–64)

You can no more win a war than you can win an earthquake.

—Jeannette Rankin, first woman elected to the United States
Congress (1916), and a lifelong pacifist who voted
against entry into both World Wars

We seem always ready to pay the price for war. Almost gladly we give our time and our treasure—our limbs and even our lives—for war. But we expect to get peace for nothing.

—Peace Pilgrim, adopted name of Mildred Norman Ryder (1908–81),
spiritual teacher, nonviolence advocate, and peace prophet,
who for twenty-eight years walked for peace across
North America, *Peace Pilgrim: Her Life and
Work in Her Own Words* (1992)

1. THE OBSTACLE OF WAR

How we think about the world determines the ways we act in it; this is obvious to most people, most of the time. But there are more subtle levels on which the relationship between thinking (including the holding of beliefs, attitudes, and values) and action (as well as inaction) calls out for investigation and exposure to the clarifying light of day. Thinking about peace and war is a case of this kind.

1

War versus Peace

Peace and war are uncomfortable and restless opposites. The meaning of each, in a way, depends on how we understand the other, and yet each makes its own independent claims for our attention. A fresh look at both is called for, because dangerous forms of militarism that abound in the world today prevent improvements in the quality of human life, and indeed cast a cloud over the future of the planet; as a consequence, the need for a new dialogue *about* peace and *for* peace has never been greater. War is, of course, just one of many pressing global issues of our time. Richard Smalley, a Nobel Prize-winning chemist also known as "the father of nanotechnology," lists the following ten problems (in descending order) as the crucial challenges facing humanity: energy, water, food, environment, poverty, terrorism and war, disease, education, democracy, population.[1] But a moment's reflection will convince us that these are interconnected by virtue of their mutual impacts. War, and in particular its complex causes, are related to most, if not all, of the other nine factors on this list. And peace is related to all ten. It follows that we must keep in mind a holistic view of war and peace, as we go along.

Some of the best thinking about humans as social and political beings has been devoted to peace. However, a far greater amount has undoubtedly been devoted to war. Indeed, war hovers, like some abstract entity, over the surface of daily life and, tragically often enough, occupies the surface itself. When war is not "hot" in one's own region or in some geographical area nearby, it seems guaranteed to be going on elsewhere in the world. But even where no active conflict is raging, war consumes many resources while biding its time and exercising its metaphorical presence—as in the sentence you are now reading. War, as it appears and reappears on the stage of human life, is reflected in everyday discourse not only as a metaphor but also as a paradigm for conscientious, constructive action. (And the language of war figures prominently in the way we speak and report on everyday events, with words like "ammunition," "battle," "bombshell," "fallout," "minefield," "onslaught," "shoot down," and "trenches" being commonly employed.) Taking a closer look, campaigns to improve the human lot, as everyone is aware, are often characterized as: "war on poverty," "war against climate change," "war on hunger," "war against HIV/AIDS," "war on child abuse," and so on. "The [US] federal government needs to build a public health defense system that can wage and win a War on Asthma," declared a report issued by the Pew Environmental Health Commission in 2001, which added that, in order to accomplish this, it would be necessary to "develop and deploy a '911 Force' at the Centers for Disease Control and Prevention" in Atlanta.[2] A *Newsweek* magazine cover photograph of

Hillary Rodham Clinton as US Secretary of State accompanies the announce-ment of the cover story: "Hillary's War." Inside, the reader learns with bewil-derment that, ironically, this article is really about "her most heartfelt mission: to put women and girls at the forefront of the new world order."[3]

For over a decade, the "war on terror" was a headline news event almost daily, and this ill-considered concept licensed a spectrum of illegal and im-moral behaviors—from systematic lying by elected leaders to the dark excesses of Abu Ghraib and Guantánamo, which are comparable to wartime crimes of the past. Think you've heard it all? You haven't. Surfing the crest of the war on terror wave, the Civil Aviation Authority of Australia declared "war on error"—an educational "roadshow" aimed at reducing pilot mistakes.[4] Politi-cal contests and picayune squabbles between rival candidates are so frequently portrayed as "wars" that this way of talking barely raises an eyebrow anymore. But there really is no limit to the absurdly elastic use of this term: A well-known newsstand magazine shouts out the title of a report on innovative light-ing technology: "The Light Bulb Wars."[5]

War is free for the taking in lots of ways. Some say that, in contrast, peace has to be "sold"—that there is a problem of "marketing peace" to those who know little and maybe think less about it, or else are just downright skeptical of the whole idea. Why should there be a problem of this kind? It seems very puzzling. But let us accept the premise and see where we can go from there. Peace scholar David Cortright remarks that "Throughout history the cause of peace has been on trial, standing like a forlorn defendant before the court of established opinion, misunderstood and maligned on all sides."[6] Cortright's reflection suggests that the answer to the "why" question posed a moment ago can be framed as follows: Peace is an unfamiliar and poorly understood con-cept and reality. Perhaps it has been too seldom experienced—or in the case of some people, hardly tasted at all. Learned observers note that there have been fewer inter-state wars in recent times; that democracies do not go to war with one another; and that war as a useful extension of national policy and means of pursuing political objectives is a thing of the past. For instance, one author writes that "The obsolescence of the old kind of war and of the old kind of citizen readiness for military sacrifice is a world-wide phenomenon."[7] Another asserts, paradoxically, that "War has almost ceased to exist."[8] Perhaps so; but this does not prevent wars from occurring in abundance, and increasingly, they are intrastate civil wars, guerrilla-led insurgencies, explosions of ethnic violence, criminal power-struggles, proxy wars, or some combination of these, in which ordinary civilians are defenseless targets of "militias, paramilitaries, warlords and armies seeking control of resources through depredation, terror and force."[9] Global governance specialist Mary Kaldor calls these "new wars," and describes them as "a new type of organized violence, . . . a mixture of war, organized crime and massive violations of human rights"; she adds that they utilize "tactics of terror and destabilization that are theoretically outlawed by the rules of modern warfare."[10]

Seeing beyond War

Because war is such a familiar part of human life, past and present, and peace, by contrast, occupies the shadows, the position we are in is that if we want to bring peace out into the open in order to think clearly about it, we first have to get past being captivated by thoughts about war. The second step is to try seeing the world from the standpoint of peace rather than war. This amounts to an epistemological and ethical reversal of sorts, inasmuch as we must not only foreground peace as the norm in human life and war as the aberration, but also seek to define the positive attributes of peace, placing it in the position of primacy, instead of viewing peace as merely the negation or derivative opposite of war. Subsequent chapters (especially Chapter 5) will bring this approach into the light of day.

Getting beyond war requires us to move past some pretty formidable and influential ideas. But before we confront these, a definition of "war" is needed. This is important not only in the interest of a logical progression of ideas, but also because we will then know better what it is that we need to put aside in order to grasp what peace means. The meaning of war adopted here is the following: *War is a situation or process of openly hostile (and generally armed) struggle between two or more organized groups whose premeditated intention is to inflict damage and/or death upon each other's members and destroy each other's territory in the interest of achieving a desired end.*[11] A qualification is in order: *In the case of an aggressive invasion by one side of the other's territory, the latter may lack this premeditated intention and have the primary goal of repelling the invader in order to protect its people and territory.*[12] A particular war may be identified by its symbolic, ideological, economic, historical, and political features, which are in turn related to its causes, and also determine its overall character as a form of conflict. The proposed definition provides a useful paradigm for understanding war in the literal sense, with secondary or metaphorical usages of the term being more distantly related to its primary meaning.

Now, what are the ideas about war that must be overthrown? There are many: that war brings out the best qualities in men; that it is a "manly art"; that it makes men out of boys; that a nation comes of age through armed conflict, its defining moment being some famous battle or a particular war; that the most honorable way in which one can serve one's country (or group) is by shedding blood for it. Both masculinity and patriotism, in relation to war, are complex, multifaceted social constructs that require a great deal of care to unpack.[13] Some consider that dying in war is made not only acceptable, but even desirable and glorious, owing to their beliefs about rewards awaiting heroes in the afterlife. None of these ideas has served humanity well—rather, just the opposite. They have led us blindly into more and more wars, genocides, arms races, and ultimately, to the constant state of war-readiness we find ourselves in today—a kind of "unending war," as some observers have labeled our contemporary situation. Deep-seated beliefs about war have cost our species and the planet hugely in terms of both the casualties and consequences of armed conflict and the resources consumed by war-preparedness. What is it all for? Are we stuck forever within cultures of violence, fear, and war? Do we lack the intelligence, will, moral fiber, and sense of world community to find better ways of conducting our affairs? Is it in our genes to be warriors? Is there something specifically wrong with how males are biologically constituted or socialized that leads to war? Do conditions that seem to drive human beings to war keep arising and periodically need to be dealt with? Are there forces in history with their own irresistible momentum that cause brutal clashes between groups and nations? Or, on the other hand, are there perhaps many valuable templates already in existence for building relationships, negotiation strategies, trust, and modes of behaving that can provide alternatives to war and even terrorism? As Australian Prime Minister Kevin Rudd pondered in 2008, on the ninetieth anniversary of Armistice Day, "Is war our permanent condition? Must every generation go through war to be reminded why there should be no war? Or can we dare to do something different, can we dare to think something different?"[14] The questions pile up like the dead and maimed that humans continue to produce in armed confrontations.

Many have raised these questions and more, wondering whether human beings are fatefully warlike and locked into perennial cycles of mortal combat. To be sure, no one can claim to have complete answers to the hardest questions about war because abundant areas of uncertainty still persist in our knowledge about our own species. Even if we could gather together all of the world's psychologists and psychiatrists, it is unlikely they could explain everything we need to know in order to create a world free from war and violent conflict. But we can try to move forward with the insights we have achieved and the tools we possess for understanding and promoting the factors that make peace possible, with the aim of stimulating new and different thought and feeling processes that may promise better choices in the future than those made in the past and present.

2. WAR MYTHS

In keeping with the commitment to examine and overcome barriers that block thinking about peace, it will be useful to expose some myths. Eighteenth-century philosopher and political theorist John Locke assigned himself the task of "removing some of the rubbish that lies in the way to knowledge."[15] In a similar spirit, deconstructing the myths of war will enable a better profile of peace to emerge. Of course, the existence of myths alone does not explain the war phenomenon. A monocausal account could never do justice to the complexities of war or the particularities of any given conflict, and no attempt will be made here to provide a comprehensive explanation of why wars occur. That would be an entirely different and very ambitious project.[16] But whatever else might be said about war, it lives in the domain of myth, and this applies both to the factors that help bring it about and to those that create and sustain ideas such as that of the "demonic enemy." As psychologist Lawrence LeShan points out, war brings about a shift from the normal or "sensory mode" of perceiving reality to a "mythic mode"[17] with a logic of its own. Journalist Chris Hedges, who has reported on-the-scene from numerous wars, explains this "logic": "The enduring attraction of war is this: Even with its destruction and carnage, it can give us what we long for in life. It can give us purpose, meaning, a reason for living. Only when we are in the midst of conflict does the shallowness and vapidness of much of our lives become apparent. . . . And war is an enticing elixir. It gives us resolve, a cause. It allows us to be noble. And those who have the least meaning in their lives . . . are all susceptible to war's appeal."[18] Looking back at his own experience of war's addictive allure, Hedges adds, "The chance to exist for an intense and overpowering moment, even if it meant certain oblivion, seemed worth it in the midst of war—and very stupid once the war ended."[19] The great popular philosopher and pacifist Bertrand Russell expressed a similar view in a book published in 1917: "If men's actions sprang from desires for what would in fact bring happiness, the purely rational argument against war would have long ago put an end to it. What makes war difficult to suppress is that it springs from an impulse, rather than from a calculation of the advantages to be derived from war."[20] But what neither Hedges nor Russell acknowledges about war, however, is that *we have to find meaning there*—especially those who have fought in them—in order to keep a grip on sanity and personal integrity. This is a task that challenges everyone: combat soldiers, because of the horrors they face and the lethal actions required of them; their commanders, because of the horrors they are responsible for perpetrating; and the rest of us, because we are complicit in these horrors (they are done in our name). Nor do these authors confront the fact that some combatants (most would say a small minority) love war too much, that is, actually enjoy killing,[21] and that war corrupts ordinary morality at a very deep level (as discussed in the antiwar arguments of Chapter 3).

War also thrives on symbolism and imaginative associations, and it has been remarked, in this vein, that: "Wars commence in our culture first of all, and we kill each other in euphemisms and abstractions long before the first . . . missiles have been launched. . . . The deformed human mind is the ultimate doomsday weapon. . . ."[22] Partly because of these myths and subconscious connections, historian Jeremy Black cautions that in studying wars, past or present, "Rather than focusing on individual conflicts, it is more important to understand the values that made compromise unacceptable, force appear necessary and even desirable, and war seem crucial to identity and self-respect."[23]

The Illogic of War

If we step back from all of this and think carefully for a moment, the total absurdity of war readily shows itself. In conventional wars, soldiers who have no prior relationship to one another, and who, as individuals, have no reason for animosity toward one another, are given the job of killing one another—if at all possible, and however possible, no questions asked. They are expected and commanded to participate not just in killing, but in mass killing. (Of course, war makes not only anonymous strangers into enemies, but also fathers and sons, brothers, other relatives, friends, and neighbors.) And after the killing is over—maybe a year later, maybe a decade or two—they can be friends and even close allies in various ventures. As Jean-Jacques Rousseau maintains, "War is not . . . a relationship between man and man, but between state and state, in which individuals become enemies only by accident. . . ." As soon as the vanquished surrender, "ceasing to be enemies or agents of the enemy, they become simply men again, and there is no longer any right over their lives."[24] In short, after a war is over (strange as it may seem), enemy combatants are transformed once again into beings whose full moral status is magically restored to them.

From another standpoint, the unfolding of war goes like this: "We have issues with one another that have historically fermented. We each claim to be innocent and to be grievously wronged by the other. Both of us have hatreds that need avenging. We have patriotic zeal, so do you. So let's unleash as much destruction on one another as possible and see who survives best. The winner gets to dictate the terms of peace." The conditions under which unconventional wars are fought may vary from these models, but there is not a great deal of difference in their basic dynamics. Certain nagging questions push themselves forward here: How is it that, in the face of manifest absurdities, the patterns of war-making are so hard to abandon? How are soldiers (insurgents, terrorists, and so on) conditioned to do what they do? These are long stories, which we will not go into here; suffice it to say for the moment that many—if not all—of the answers are supplied by well-known and readily available research studies on the social construction and politics of masculinity, group identity and loyalty formation, patriotism, authority structures, indoctrination techniques, propaganda (principally, seeing the enemy as the personification of a despised ideology or value-set), fear-mongering, xenophobia, and attitudes toward the use of violence. But war is sustained as well by myths that weave their way through many of the foregoing sociocultural elements. These myths we will now examine.

Six Myths about War

Myth #1. According to one prominent fabrication about war that everyone will recognize, *the history of humankind is equivalent to the story of great deeds done by famous rulers and leaders (mostly men) and the wars they have prepared for and fought.* Peace, viewed from this standpoint, consists of the dull, uneventful periods in between wars that are unworthy of examination. (The book section of a large local chain store contains a shelf labeled "History/War." And where might one find a shelf marked "Peace"? The question answers itself.) Aside from begging questions about the nature of peace, peace as a desirable goal, and the best avenues by which to reach a peaceful world, the outlook just described neglects the positive phenomenon of peaceful everyday interactions that predominate among humans, as well as the perspective that the full story of humanity cannot be written without reference to the actions and ways of life of average people throughout the ages. Kenneth Boulding points out that "In all nations, even in democratic societies, the decision-making power with regard to war and peace is highly concentrated, though it is always to some extent modified by the fear of possible consequences to the decision maker."[25] This already opens up a gap between two alternative stories of humankind: what we might call, on the one hand, the "outstanding figures and their exploits" story, and, on the other, the story of history "as forged by ordinary people and unsung heroes." Each represents part of the whole truth and we would therefore be foolish to choose one over the other. But as Boulding also notes, "Even when two countries are at war, a large part of the behavior of the inhabitants is totally unrelated to the war—sleeping, eating, making love, having children, producing civilian goods, and so on. . . . I am convinced it is in the field of what I have called nonconflict—working, producing, buying and selling, learning, thinking, worshipping, loving, procreating—that the mainstream of the human race goes on."[26] We will return to examine many of these themes concerning history, war, peace, and everyday life in the following chapters.

Myth #2. Closely related to this first myth is a second one, with an ancient lineage. In the dim and more recent past, it would look like this: *The venerated leader is a great and fearless warrior.* Today's version would be toned down but would still express the same belief, perhaps in a manner closer to the following: "A satisfactory head of government will have a good inventory of modern weapons at his or her disposal, and must possess the will to use them (but of course only 'when necessary')." The state of the world could be vastly improved if the principle by which leaders were chosen read instead: "A great national leader has a first-class understanding of international affairs and other cultures, compassion, trust in his or her own citizenry, and excellent communication, negotiating, and peace-building skills."

Myth #3. There is also the myth that *wars solve human problems and advance interests more effectively than other kinds of engagements.* The fact that wars are recurrent should by itself show that (with a very few, debatable exceptions) they do not solve problems, or at best, do so only temporarily and partially, while sowing the seeds for narrow-minded nationalism, inter-group hatred, revenge-seeking, defective political arrangements and boundaries, and therefore, for future incidents of violence and armed conflict. At the end of the day, communication, respectful coexistence, and sometimes even forgiveness and reconciliation, are the only ways to bury hostilities with finality. As one social scientist observes, "What all wars have in common is the unmistakable moral lesson that homicide is an acceptable, even praiseworthy, means to certain ends."[27] (More on this in Chapter 3.) But following this go-nowhere teaching can only yield negative results: Aggression begets more aggression; violence, more violence; and war, more war, if they remain unchecked by negotiation and nonviolent resolution. Surely bitter experience has taught us that there is no "war to end war"—or has it?

There are those who argue that war is sometimes needed in order to make peace possible. But it is at least as plausible to claim that peace, when fully developed makes war impossible, or at least very much less likely to occur. The beneficial impacts of peace are wider and deeper than any gains resulting from war. That is common knowledge. However, it is also documented in a more empirical fashion. For example, in a series of case studies, historian Ian Bickerton focuses on the aftermath of war looked at from a perspective twenty-five years on, and turns up these sobering findings:

> The inescapable and tragic conclusion one reaches is that it is hard to tell who won and who lost the war. . . . [M]ost of the assumptions about the benefits of victory in

warfare are either exaggerated or simply false. . . . [M]ilitary victory rarely guarantees compliance by the defeated belligerent, nor does it act as a deterrent against further outbreaks of war. Victors rarely achieve the international, political or military stability they seek. Power and coercion are highly transitory in international relations. Territorial arrangements are almost always short lived. The goal of the victorious party of transforming the defeated party's domestic political system and social values is hardly ever successful. . . . The postwar reconstruction of the defeated party far exceeds projected costs. . . . In addition . . . the postwar economic benefits that flow from victory rarely match prewar expectations. In other words, when examined a generation later, it can be seen that the victor's triumphs on the battlefield yield little long-term value.[28]

Bickerton's research covers a period ranging from the Napoleonic Wars of the early nineteenth century through the two world wars of the last century and beyond. One might be forgiven for thinking that a simple cost-benefit calculation based on inductive inference from past experience (call it gambling odds, if you prefer) would be sufficient to deter political leaders from waging war. Unfortunately, it does not. More advanced alien social scientists from another planet, studying our own, would probably be astonished at the shortsightedness we "rational beings" display in regard to war.

Myth #4. Another associated myth is that *wars—or "military operations" that perpetrators seek not to have thought of as wars, invasions, or acts of aggression—are undertaken (always) "in defense of" shared ideals and a cherished way of life.* On the contrary, historical examples show that in warfare, economic, class, and other factors are often front and center, and that private political aspirations, the jingoism of particular interest groups, and various ideological factors are rife. Some writers have pointed out that the greatest enthusiasm for war usually comes from those who do not have to fight in them, but send others to do their dirty work for them. While it is simplistic and one-dimensional to argue that in all wars the poor and disadvantaged serve the interests of the rich and powerful, a stark slogan from the First World War—"A bayonet is a weapon with a worker on both ends"—makes us wonder whether this perspective might contain a significant grain of truth. (Some studies of the Vietnam War and of the contemporary US armed services support the perspective in question.[29] And a recent empirical analysis shows that "Americans who have died in Afghanistan are disproportionately white and Native American working-class young people with no more than a high school education."[30]) Widespread opposition to, and public demonstrations against, the Vietnam War and the Iraq War, both in America and abroad, also bring into focus the question of whose values, interests, and political judgments were driving these conflicts. Furthermore, as the wartime record shows, and some post-9/11 events confirm, basic human rights and civil liberties may get trampled even by those nations claiming to be their staunchest guardians.

The values identified with war are of course always laden with patriotic references to one's own nation and its singular destiny. An interesting example, taken from the Australian popular media, is an advertisement for "Tea from a Time When Men Were Willing to Fight for a Cause." Tea, of course, in the British tradition, is as homey, comforting, and essential to daily life as you can get, in good times or in bad. The tea company in question "contributes to . . . support the families of diggers [soldiers] who have given their lives for our country."[31] And who can possibly not want to donate to that? But looking deeper, notice that the main headline suggests several hidden meanings: Men who lost their lives in past wars were one and all doing so for a (presumably just) cause that they did not question. Men were once willing to fight and die for such a cause—but probably are not now, having lost their backbone and their clear moral sense of right and wrong. War is the proper way to take a stand when values are under serious threat. A real man is prepared to answer the call obediently when it comes from those in authority. Further deconstruction would no doubt disclose additional nuances of meaning. We see here how so simple a thing as a cup of tea can be used to conjure up images and emotion-charged associations that promote war.

Myth #5. By virtue of a closely related kind of myth-making, *historical conflicts, through a complex process, become transformed into a fixed part of national identity and infused with various quasi-religious attributes.* Historian George L. Mosse describes how this happens as follows, in relation to the two world wars of the twentieth century: "The myth of war experience was designed to mask war and to legitimize the war experience; it was meant to displace the reality of war. The memory of war was fashioned into a sacred experience which provided the nation with a new depth of religious feeling, putting at its disposal ever-present saints and martyrs, places of worship, and a heritage to emulate."[32] We can all recognize how this flight of fancy echoes today in our own national consciousness and practices of remembrance.[33] In addition, as Noah Richler observes, countries such as the United States and Canada, which are hungry for heroes in uncertain times, tend to venerate people in uniform, regardless of what they accomplish while wearing it. According to the official line, no soldier ever "dies in vain," and it is unpatriotic to think otherwise. (Many cenotaphs are dedicated "To our glorious war dead.") This is why more troops are committed to lost causes that leaders lack the courage to identify as such, or as having been a mistake in the first place. Meanwhile,

everyday civilian heroes, who hold families and society together, teach our
difficult children, create the culture we enjoy, or put themselves at considerable risk to work for peace and human rights, are largely ignored and unher-
alded.[34] Among others, this last group comprises members of the Nonviolent
Peaceforce, Peace Brigades International, UN Volunteers, Witness for Peace,
Médecins Sans Frontières, Nonviolence International, Christian Peacemaker
Teams, Amnesty International, and Human Rights Watch. Many of these organizations operate in zones of active hostility, protecting people, helping to
enforce existing agreements, and monitoring and publicizing human rights
violations.

Myth #6. A final myth to be considered here is the widely held view
that *human nature is inherently aggressive and warlike.* Because it is so well-
established that many consider it proven beyond doubt, we will consider
Myth #6 in greater detail. The claim it embodies appears in two forms: (1) War
is an inseparable and permanent feature of our biological endowment; and
(2) Even though war is biologically rooted in us and essential to our development as a species, we may have begun to evolve beyond it.

Here is an example of outlook (1): "War in humans is similar to war in
other creatures, primates, social insects, etc. War has always been a means
of weeding out weak groups, of redistributing resources among humanity, of
driving evolution and adaptability. Unless we develop the economic tools to
achieve redistribution without violence, violence will always be the natural
and 'reasonable' final solution of those who find themselves to be stronger, yet
who have less resources than others."[35] This is a curious assemblage of ideas:
war as part of our biological makeup (comparably to other animals); Social
Darwinism (war as assuring that the fittest survive); fact (war as an economic
tool); sociobiology (war as enhancing the victors' gene pools); and yet faith in
freedom of choice (the possibility of developing nonviolent means of resource
redistribution). Concerning the internal contradiction here between biological determinism and freedom to select another path for humanity, several decades ago, Ludwig von Mises, a prominent member of the Austrian school
of economics and arch-defender of capitalism and liberalism, observed the
following: "We may also assume that under the conditions of earlier ages the
inclination for aggression and murder was favorable to the preservation of
life. . . . However, [as a being of reason,] man has made his choice. . . . He has
entered upon the way toward civilization, social cooperation, and wealth. . . .
Wars, civil wars, and revolutions are detrimental to man's success in the struggle for existence because they disintegrate the apparatus of social cooperation."[36] This is an entirely plausible and more consistent hypothesis, which, as
we shall see in a moment, accords well with recent empirical research. It also

directs our attention toward the second outlook: that although war is biologically rooted in us, and essential to our evolution, we may have evolved beyond it.

A widely held theory "suggests [that] the cooperative skills we've had to develop to be effective warriors have turned into the modern ability to work towards a common goal."[37] Some might infer that such a perspective is perhaps merely another vaguely disguised glorification of war, a coopting of our peaceful instincts by a view about our inborn (biologically determined) aggressiveness. However, it would be a mistake to draw this conclusion, given that the theory in question stems from research findings in a number of fields that converge toward a consensus. More importantly, it tells us that although cooperative tendencies evolved from warlike ones, they have subsequently taken on a life of their own and now play a real, independent role in human affairs. Looking at the theory in this manner helps us to avoid endorsing the fallacious belief that the way things once were can tell us how they will be, ought to be, or even must be. What has occurred or might have occurred during the distant (and not so distant) past life of our species is a very unreliable and not necessarily desirable guide to how things might be or should be. This is because humans are capable of choice, rational reflection and analysis, and hence also of change. Unless one accepts some form of rigid determinism, no biological or anthropological account can provide everything we require in order to understand the past or plan for the future. Not only this, but humans at present are actually showing signs of being able to control their own future evolution. ("Being able," of course, does not entail that we are yet willing to take on the task in a responsible manner, and to use this potential wisely.) While some aspects of human nature may be relatively constant, our species is noteworthy for having reinvented itself many times over. As current brain research on "neuroplasticity" keeps demonstrating, humans are not so "hardwired" into stereotypical patterns of thinking and response as many suppose.[38] And we should not neglect to record here that many human actions already undertaken to change the way things are done in the world serve as examples of nonviolent cooperation. We will take a closer look at a number of these in later chapters.

A century ago, William James, psychologist, philosopher, confirmed pacifist, and proponent of the idea that humanity exists in a state of unending war, confidently proclaimed—as if it were a truism needing no argumentative or empirical support—that "Our ancestors have bred pugnacity into our bone and marrow, and thousands of years of peace won't breed it out of us."[39] But, as we have seen above, this view is being challenged on both historical and scientific grounds. Many scholars now support the argument that war is a sociopolitical construct and that it has come to be seen as "inevitable" only within the modern state system (and even more recently, in relation to the so-called security state[40]). And if the once-scorned idea that "environment can alter heredity" eventually takes hold,[41] this will open up still further the possibilities for changing human behavior for the better—if we so choose.

We can now begin to see more clearly that evolutionary traits revealed in the human past do not license inferences about the inevitability of war and other forms of violent conflict in the future. The claim that "war is in our genes" should therefore be rejected, as Chapters 2 and 4 will argue in greater detail. Leaving aside possible supplements to the theory of natural selection, a growing body of evidence tends toward the conclusion that, even if humans' evolution into peaceful beings is not guaranteed, it is equally apparent that war cannot simply be rationalized as a kind of "biological compulsion."[42] Furthermore, inasmuch as belief in the inevitability of something tends to make that thing inevitable (a self-fulfilling prophecy), we need to be on guard against any such belief for it negates humans' decision-making capacity and consequently the ability to change the course of events in which they are involved.

It is extremely significant that the myth of humans' innate aggression has been coopted many times as a propaganda tool for creating a mood that favors war. One notable example is the work of Friedrich von Bernhardi, a German general who states, in his influential 1941 book *Germany and the Next War*, that "aspirations for peace . . . threaten to poison the soul of the German people," and that "War is a biological necessity. . . . It gives a biologically just decision, since its decisions rest on the very nature of things."[43] This shabby reasoning, of course, contributed to the mythology that sustained Germany's ill-fated determination to succeed in World War II.

A very different kind of German thinker, the brilliant Enlightenment philosopher Immanuel Kant, advanced a very different and much more subtle theory about war. According to Kant,

> war itself requires no particular motivation, but appears to be ingrained in human nature and is even valued as something noble; indeed, the desire for glory inspires men to it, even independently of selfish motives. Consequently, *courage in war* (among American Indians as well as during Europe's chivalric period) is judged to be of immediate and great worth not only *during war* (as is reasonable), but also in order that *war might be*, and often war is begun only as a means to display courage. As a result, an intrinsic worth is bestowed on war, even to the extent that philosophers, unmindful of that Greek saying, "War is a bad bet because it produces more evil people than it eliminates," have praised it as having a certain ennobling influence on mankind.[44]

This is a perceptive and interesting blend of two views: the belief that humans are innately warlike and the idea (mentioned above) that war has the magic transformative power to actualize the finest aspects of human nature. Kant concedes a certain amount of truth to both views; but it is of far greater importance to notice that the context in which he discusses them—his justly celebrated essay on "perpetual peace"—builds a strong argument on behalf of a rational arrangement of mutual interests by which nations can restrain these tendencies in order to abolish war.

The outcome of all this is that we needn't be frightened of the theory that war has developed cooperative skills in our species. Let us assume that war *has* done so, rather than struggle in resignation against admitting the possibility. Many other activities have also undoubtedly codeveloped these same skills. And the conclusion we ought therefore to reach is that while the route we have followed to this end is in some ways unfortunate, the cooperative skills now exist and can be used and developed creatively in novel settings. Cooperation is as biologically based as is the tendency toward violent aggression. In this respect, as in many others, the future does not have to resemble the past, with ourselves as mere passive and despairing onlookers. On the contrary, it can be consciously and conscientiously fashioned by us, and this provides grounds for hope that we will do so. And we may add, as a warning to ourselves about the urgency of the matter, that *if* evolution has made us (men in particular) fearful, suspicious, jealous, and hateful of one another, *then* further evolution had better change us so we are no longer like that—otherwise we will not survive as a species.

Many writers, such as Hedges (cited in the previous section), affirm that war produces a strong sense of common purpose and solidarity. This assertion should not be either scorned or dismissed lightly.[45] Acknowledgment of this fact motivated James to introduce the important idea of a "moral equivalent of war,"[46] that is, some participatory activity or activities that are capable of yielding the same beneficial outcomes for humanity as does war. While James's (and Kant's) accounts express the masculinist bias of their times, they nevertheless make an important point by directing our attention to the rewards and emotional outlets often attributed to war. Fortunately, ongoing research is providing evidence that alternative activities can produce the same effects.[47] (See further discussion of this idea in Chapter 6, section 6.6, "Everyday Peaceful Conduct and Alternatives to Violence.") But, in the end, the question remains whether, for the vast majority of humans of both sexes (the dead, injured, maimed, and all noncombatants), this is the most relevant issue. Given the fragile state of the world today and the costs of war (see the next section), as one group of psychologists remarks, "peace cannot wait until all the data are in."[48]

Another perspective that tends to foster pessimism about our species' warlike nature is Freud's theory of the "death instinct." First conceived by the philosopher Empedocles (c. 495–435 BCE) in ancient Greece, this idea appeared in Freud's *Beyond the Pleasure Principle* (1920) and was developed in several of his later works. Most of Freud's early students and followers rejected the theory, with the notable exception of Melanie Klein, but renewed interest in it has been stimulated by French psychoanalysts Jacques Lacan and Jean Laplanche. Philosopher Richard Boothby, an expert on Lacan, contends that the death instinct is "the darkest and most stubborn riddle posed by the legacy of psychoanalysis."[49]

In "Analysis Terminable and Interminable" (1937), Freud argues that there are "unmistakable indications of the presence of a power in mental life which we call the instinct of aggression or of destruction according to its aims, and which we trace back to the original death instinct of living matter."[50] The death instinct enters the scene primarily to explain neurosis, masochism, certain kinds of dreams, and other phenomena as surrogate forms of self-punishment or self-eradication, and human psychic life then comes to be understood as the site of a struggle between "Eros" (the life instinct) and "Thanatos" (the death instinct). Eros includes impulses that "seek to preserve and unite," and the death instinct, those that are motivated by hatred and that "seek to destroy and kill." Yet, Freud insists, each is equally "essential" to our makeup.[51] In an intriguing way that he could not have foreseen, he was on to something important. It is now known not only that aggression in the face of perceived threats to our well-being has a biological basis, so too do altruism, empathy, anger control, and cooperation.[52] The expression of these is then further modified and refined by culture, as we will see in Chapters 2 and 4.

Which of these tendencies will triumph in the human species? Freud recognized this as a pressing question, and eventually postulated that the death drive threatens to overwhelm the life drive in each of us (rather than the reverse, or some equilibrium state being reached). Against this background, he then characterizes civilization as the precarious process whereby humans learn to sacrifice raw expression of instinctual drives in favor of stability, sociability, and the rule of law. Instinctual energies are rechanneled into other avenues of endeavor, and although social disintegration and war are constant disruptive tendencies within the human condition, Freud paradoxically envisions the possibility that all of us may even become pacifists one day.[53]

Freud's death instinct has not gained much traction in psychoanalysis or the social sciences generally, but it certainly appears to have passed into the everyday and literary forms of imagination as a way of capturing our predicament, and references to a "collective death wish" are not uncommon in popular culture. This is entirely understandable in view of the persistence of warfare and violence as means of settling disputes and conflicts of various sorts, dealing with offenses and exacting revenge, using nefarious strategies

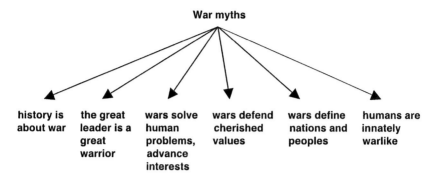

Figure 0.1 War Myths

for advancing vested interests, and the like; the manufacture and proliferation of high-tech weapons and weapons of mass destruction; and the burgeoning of cultural products concerned with death, destruction, torture, terror, the symbolism of death and aggression, an apocalyptic future, and so on. One might likewise be forgiven for pondering the reality of a collective death wish, given the everyday neglectful behavior of human beings toward their own kind; the indiscriminate killing of one another that prevails in armed conflicts; and our abuse of the biosphere as a whole—that support system on which our continued survival so delicately depends.

Whether the idea of a universal death instinct in humans belongs within the realm of fact or fantasy will not be judged here. However, as even its arch-theorist realized, we must resist entrapment by its deterministic tone; for we can only act meaningfully when choosing our own destiny as a species, and this entails addressing and taking charge of both the best and the worst in us. Once again, this insight beckons us toward the study of peace as an alternative pathway for humanity.

A bit of reflection on all of the myths discussed above makes it apparent that they are interlocked in a pattern of thinking that promotes war and the resort to armed hostilities for addressing human problems. Similarly, they are mutually reinforcing. We must relinquish their hold on us in order to view peace as accurately as we are able.[54]

3. THE COSTS OF WAR

The devastating effects of war in the modern world are well known to those who have either experienced them directly or learned about them indirectly, which includes pretty much all of us. The same goes for the nonproductive effects of aggressive violence at the individual and group levels. It will nonetheless advance our investigation of peace if we confront a few facts and figures. To start with, as Cortright correctly argues, "the permanent mobilization for war that emerged in the wake of World War II reinforced the predisposition of political leaders to use military force and created greater institutional capacities to intervene in the affairs of other countries."[55] Superpowers and other major powers among nations have followed this route numerous times in postwar decades, because adherence to militarized policy "devalued diplomatic approaches."[56] While this is no doubt true, there are contrasting tendencies including, and inspired by, the United Nations, which provide hope for the present and future.

Preparing for War

War-preparedness is very costly, as we all know, and it inspires the mind-set that "We've paid for all this stuff, so we'd better use it" (to justify the cost to taxpayers and legislators); or "We might as well use it" (because it can be used, needs to be tried out, and so on). Besides, with a huge arsenal at one's disposal, there is the temptation to deal with every recalcitrant regime in a military fashion. During the Cold War, there was also the motivation to "Use it or lose it," exacerbated by fears of being on the receiving end of a nuclear first strike. This belief arguably caused much of the stress and social anxiety of that era for leaders and citizenry alike, although fortunately the ultimate weapons were never launched.

Annual global military expenditures in 2012 were estimated by the Stockholm International Peace Research Institute at 1.75 trillion US dollars. Notwithstanding a small decrease from 2011, "the global total was still higher in real terms than the peak near the end of the cold war." Close to 40 percent of the world's military spending is accounted for by the United States alone.[57] In contrast, the UN estimates that it could operate for sixty-seven years on the current world global military budget.[58] This is the "big picture" cost of *war-preparedness*.

It sometimes looks as if there is not much distance, when all is said and done, between the slogans "If you want peace, prepare for war" (which many say and believe) and "War is Peace" (which you may recognize from George Orwell's novel *1984*).[59] While the first is supposedly "what history teaches" (that deterrence prevents war), the second (although intended to display an obvious contradiction) is the message projected by cultures of violence as they constantly ready themselves for armed hostilities. One might be forgiven for thinking that there is an inevitable development from the first view to the second.

Meanwhile, the gross disparity between the world's rich and poor continues, and it is appalling by any measure. Peace and development activist and author

Vijay Mehta observes that "This emphasis on militarism stands in sharp contrast to the social deficit of humanity."[60] It is easy to see what he means when close to one billion people in the world today are malnourished (one in seven, and about the same as the number who are defined as living in extreme poverty).[61] Each year, an estimated 2.6 million children (an average of 300 per hour) die of malnutrition, and 170 million people suffer from stunted development owing to chronic malnutrition.[62] So, a reasonable conclusion to draw is that diversion of a substantial portion of the massive military costs borne by nations today into solving global problems of living, by means other than the use of deadly force and threats, is money better spent in the name of common humanity (promoting global well-being), and also in the interest of finding solutions to our mutual security issues. With specific reference to the United States, the National Priorities Project, an Internet resource, invites viewers to see how tax dollars spent on defense (including weapons development) could alternatively be allocated to socially beneficial programs—nationally, by state, by congressional district, and by city, town, or county.[63]

The trade-off of alternative outputs, determined by some investment choice, is known in economics as its "opportunity cost." Thus, the labor, productivity, goods produced, and social benefits sacrificed in favor of investing in military items and operations collectively count as the opportunity cost of war-preparation. One of the most high-profile figures to articulate, as well as lament, this opportunity cost was Dwight Eisenhower, Supreme Commander of Allied Forces in Europe during World War II and US president from 1953 to 1961. In a 1953 speech, he stated: "Every gun that is made, every warship launched, every rocket fired signifies, in the final sense, a theft from those who hunger and are not fed, those who are cold and are not clothed. This world in arms is not spending money alone. It is spending the sweat of its laborers, the genius of its scientists, the hopes of its children. . . . This is not a way of life at all, in any true sense. Under the cloud of threatening war, it is humanity hanging from a cross of iron. . . . Is there no other way the world may live?"[64] Eisenhower gives examples such as the number of schools that could be built for the cost of producing one long-range bomber, which have not been included here since they are outdated; but the reader can easily imagine or actually fill in the blanks in today's terms.[65] To these effects can be added the impact of military expenditures in terms of suppressing international development.[66] Finally, also to be considered in the overall picture of losses would of course be the opportunity cost to both one's own country and to those of adversaries that flow from actually using weapons in wartime, which we will get to in a moment.[67]

Military expenditures (even in "peacetime") arguably have beneficial effects for a nation's economy in relation to employment and the development of new products and technologies. Examples of the latter (spin-off effects of defense research) are provided by the Internet, the Global Positioning System, clothing for inhospitable climates, and medical research and applications of various kinds (for instance, penicillin, blood transfusion, regeneration of tissues). Projects of national consolidation during armed conflict and of transformation afterwards are also stimulated by war, as are high-quality cultural products, such as films, novels, pictorial art, photography, and musical compositions.[68] In addition to these benefits, soldiers of many nations contribute regularly to civilian rescue and rebuilding efforts and humanitarian relief operations. But the point is that, when an economy comes to be largely or substantially centered on weapons research, design, and manufacture, and the preparations for war (strategic planning, maintenance and deployment of armed forces, and so on), it then faces the danger—about which Eisenhower also famously warned—of becoming controlled by a "military-industrial complex," and of now depending on war-oriented expenditures to keep itself vital and growing. However, this state of affairs returns us to the opportunity cost problem, because an economy of this type and scale "is geared toward war, producing goods that destroy use value (bombs, bullets, land mines, etc.)."[69] This statement takes a little unpacking. If we understand by "use value" what classical economic theory describes as "the want-satisfying power of a commodity"[70] (or more simply, the capacity to satisfy wants and needs), then weapons obviously destroy this in abundance when employed in battle. Not only that, but leaving aside the question whether weapons of war are in any meaningful sense "commodities" or have any "want-satisfying power," they arguably also destroy use value by displacing needed commodities that might have been produced instead of them. In addition to all this, the employment benefits noted earlier are open to question; for it has been shown that one billion US dollars could create 27.6 percent more jobs through tax cuts stimulating personal consumption; 47.4 percent more in clean energy; 69 percent more in health care; and 150.9 percent more in education.[71] Another example, from South Africa, reveals that the vast amount spent since 2000 on jet fighter planes that were not needed and are largely disused could have funded the construction of two million houses or the creation of ten million low-skill jobs.[72] In a world where unemployment rates are soaring, we should learn from these illustrations and urgently reconsider our priorities.

Making War and War's Lingering Effects: General Observations

The "big picture" cost of *actual warfare* cries out for examination as well. Notwithstanding opportunity cost arguments pro and con, the cost of conducting war is wholly disproportionate to the investment in human well-being that good sense would prescribe, and opens up an all-consuming, bottomless pit of financial burden. In addition to the expenditures that are dictated by the decision to go to war, the problem of monetary cost is further exacerbated by the fact that during the period of engagement, "new vested interests emerge dependent upon the political economy of the war itself"; more crudely put, "Violence spawns a host of groups who benefit directly from its continuation."[73] These factors generate a self-sustaining momentum that makes it difficult to de-escalate armed conflict or, in many cases, to envision a meaningful timeline for achieving either strategic or peaceful objectives.

Over 1.4 trillion dollars has been spent on the US-led wars in Iraq and Afghanistan from 2001 to early 2013, according to one source.[74] This unfathomable sum does not include several major factors: costs to other countries participating in the coalition; costs borne by individual taxpayers, service people and their families; loss of government services reduced or suspended owing to military expenditures; and future costs such as medical care for veterans and interest on the national debt incurred by deficit financing.[75] The Costs of War Project of the Watson Institute for International Studies at Brown University estimates US military engagements in Iraq, Afghanistan, and Pakistan since 2001 have claimed more than 330,000 lives, and cost nearly four trillion dollars, not including interest on borrowing to fund these conflicts (with additional costs accruing to ongoing actions in Yemen). Veterans' care and other future costs may bring the total closer to six trillion dollars.[76] Many further costs will likely never be fully known: costs to the citizens of these other countries; costs borne by neighboring countries that have had to deal with refugees and other spillover effects; and the collateral damage that is intangible, difficult to verify or quantify, and far-reaching—such as increased hatred and anger toward the United States and its allies; the use of Iraq and other countries as terrorist training arenas; assaults on civil liberties and international law; fanning the flames of other conflicts; further destabilization of the Middle East and Pakistan; and aggravation of personal risk for international travelers.

It is typical of warfare to have a large range of costs (including unintended ones) and "invisible," intangible effects that roll out for decades afterwards. As Oliver Ramsbotham, Tom Woodhouse, and Hugh Miall report, "The typical civil war puts development into reverse, reducing pre-war incomes in directly affected countries by 15 per cent on average, and reducing growth in neighbouring countries on average by 0.5 per cent per annum. . . . These effects tend to persist after the fighting is over, and the resulting maldevelopment and institutional deformation raises the risk of the conflict being renewed."[77] Speaking of psychological rather than economic impacts, James Tyner states that "Long after the fighting has stopped, the treaties have been signed, and the militaries demobilized, the legacies of violence endure: the sights, sounds, smells, and other sensations of conflict remain part of many people's everyday lives. The 'post' traumatic events are all too real and continue to affect both the survivors and their relatives for years and even decades. In fact, there is no 'post' in trauma, for the mental anguish of violence extends beyond war."[78] With reference to genocidal civil wars of recent times, peace studies specialist Helen Ware and her colleagues describe a situation in which "the generations of those left behind . . . face a world where there is no safety, no security, no human warmth, no rules any more." They add that "however poor a country is, war makes it more impoverished. This occurs not just through the destruction of roads, schools, clinics and homes but also through the loss of people—'human capital'—as those with skills are killed, caught up in the military or flee the country. Most importantly there is impoverishment through the destruction of bonds between people and their willingness to help each other."[79]

A More Detailed Look at the Effects of War on People

To make this picture more concrete, here is a tragic testimonial from someone trapped and frozen by the brutal Mozambique civil war (1977–92), which took a million lives and resulted in five times that number of displaced and/or injured persons:

> "We have arrived here from all over, scattered victims of Renamo [the externally funded anti-government rebel movement] violence. Everyone has lost everything they had. Their homes were burned, their goods stolen, their crops destroyed, their family members slaughtered. Even those that managed to run often ran in different directions from the rest of their families, and today do not know if the rest are alive or dead. Many have been through this cycle more than once, having fled to a 'safe area' only to be attacked again. Me, this is my third relocation. I do not know where most of my family is. Maybe we will be attacked yet again—we hear Renamo passing by here at night. It is difficult to find the will to plant crops and tend children when it may all be taken from us tonight, and maybe we will not survive this time. The worst of it is the way this attacks our spirits, our very selves. Everyone here thinks: 'Before this I knew who I was, I farmed the land that my father farmed, and his ancestors before him, and this long line nurtured the living. I had my family that I fathered, and I had my house that I built, and the goods that I had worked for. I knew who I was because I had all of this around me. But now I have nothing, I have lost what makes me who I am. I am nothing here.'"[80]

What we witness in this passage is that the experience of war deeply affects the sense of self and personal identity, and there is nothing more basic than this, spiritually and psychologically, nothing more vital to a sense of meaningful existence.

Closely related to the above is an additional "background effect" of war, the psychological toll on active-duty soldiers and the lingering impact upon veterans—which constitutes collateral damage to victor and vanquished alike. In 2012, there were more deaths by suicide than by combat among American soldiers actively deployed around the world.[81] Notwithstanding the fact that the US Defense Department oversees 900 suicide prevention programs, the annual number of military suicides has dramatically risen between 2001 and 2012.[82] Although addressing suicidal tendencies is a matter of acute crisis intervention that calls for the most earnest duty-of-care response, the underlying idea of patching up soldiers so that they can return to service as more efficient fighting machines must be seriously questioned—just as the legitimacy and sanity of war itself must be questioned.

The problem of suicide among actively serving military personnel is mirrored by the appalling number of veterans who have committed suicide (see Chapter 4, section 4.2, "The Limitations of Violence"). Up to 20 percent of service personnel returning from the wars in Afghanistan and Iraq suffer from post-traumatic stress disorder (PTSD); child and spousal abuse among veterans are on the increase. But perhaps more alarming still is the fact that nearly 60 percent of those treated at veterans' hospitals in the United States are veterans of a war that ended more than four decades ago. "Even as Vietnam veterans now enter their 60s and begin to die off," it is reported, "the number seeking P.T.S.D. treatment is growing."[83] Leaving aside the monetary cost of veterans' payouts of all kinds (for the United States alone, around 44.7 billion US dollars in 2009), one can easily see that a terrible price is being paid by those who have fought in these wars.[84] Claude Anshin Thomas, a highly decorated Vietnam combat veteran, went through an extended period of PTSD, including depression and self-destructive behavior, and then became a Buddhist monk and peace activist in order to rehabilitate himself and atone for his acts of killing in the war. His testimony is quite revealing:

> There was no "after the war" for me. My life, as a survivor of Vietnam, was an ongoing war. I isolated myself more and more from other people, took more and more drugs, and lived more and more on the fringes of society.... My involvement in this war has scarred me in many ways. It scarred my body, it scarred my heart, it scarred my soul. The reality of this war lives with me today. It doesn't go away. There is no sense in trying to hide it, because war does not go away.[85]

As writer Matthieu Aikins succinctly observes, "The problem is, becoming good at war often involves becoming bad at peace."[86]

A study conducted by the American Medical Association adds further testimony to what has already been given here. It found that after fourteen years of civil war in Liberia, 44 percent of the adult population suffered from the symptoms of PTSD.[87] PTSD, it now appears, is simply TSD, an affliction which may indifferently occur with the events that cause it, or afterwards, or both.

There seems to be little doubt that war veterans also commonly suffer from what is now being called "moral injuries."[88] They do so because of the ambiguous campaigns they find themselves embroiled in and the onerous split-second decisions they are compelled to make in order to carry out their missions, stay alive, or protect their comrades. But, as Chapter 3 will show, moral injury is nothing new, since the very nature of war is such that it requires participants to engage in deeply immoral, senseless, unredeemable acts that fragment the self in ways that are often permanent.

In a further recent development, autopsies performed on deceased American veterans from the Iraq and Afghanistan wars have begun to reveal a high incidence of chronic traumatic encephalopathy (CTE), a degenerative condition of the brain likely caused, in their case, by the concussive effects of shock waves from explosives.[89] In the event of this diagnosis being correct, there is no treatment or cure for the condition, which compounds the problem of rehabilitation still further.

Another related and "invisible" or little reported, little thought-about effect of war is its impact on women and children, who traditionally, as well as today, bear many of the costs of armed conflict, having always been regarded as among the spoils of war and as instruments for humiliating the enemy.[90] Rape is one of the most universal and egregious forms of human rights violation during periods of armed conflict, as is well known. This crime was widely committed both during World War II and for years afterwards in occupation zones.[91] Victims of rape who physically survived the Rwandan genocide in 1994 (when the UN failed to intervene) were psychologically destroyed.[92] The civil war that tore apart the Democratic Republic of the Congo from 1998 onwards (also known as the Second Congo War) has been called "the world's deadliest conflict since World War II."[93] This horrible war is "forgotten" by (or perhaps even unknown to) most of us, notwithstanding the involvement of seven countries, and a toll of 5.4 million dead and 1.5 million people internally displaced or made refugees. While children comprise 19 percent of the population, they represent 47 percent of the fatalities.[94] In addition, an estimated 200,000 women and girls have been raped or sexually brutalized.[95] The BBC reports that "Despite a peace deal and the formation of a transitional government in 2003, people in the east of the country remain in terror of marauding militia and the army."[96] The reason for this has largely to do with control of a lucrative trade in minerals—abundant in the Congo—used in the manufacture of electronic devices. Many, and possibly most of us have one or more such devices made from these so-called "conflict minerals," although the United States and the European Union are trying to legislate an end to this trade.[97] In addition to all of this, UNESCO states that "as many as 250,000 child soldiers—some as young as eight years old, are involved in more than 20 conflicts around the world. Children are used as combatants, messengers, spies, porters, cooks, and girls in particular are forced to perform sexual services. Some are forcibly recruited or abducted; others are driven to join by poverty, abuse and discrimination."[98] These abandoned young people have had their childhood stolen and pose vast post-conflict rehabilitation problems.

Israel's invasion of Gaza that began in late December 2008 also illustrates many of the disturbing effects that violent conflict has on children. In this operation, more than 1,400 people were killed, a large majority of whom were noncombatants, and more than 5,300 injured. In excess of 5,000 homes were destroyed or severely damaged, another 16,000 "moderately damaged," and subsequent importation of essentials "has been insufficient to meet the needs of the 1.5 million people trapped inside the Gaza Strip."[99] Estimates of total damage range up to two billion US dollars and above. The UN Committee on the Rights of the Child has stated: "In particular, the Committee is deeply disturbed by the psychological effects on children in Gaza resulting from [Israel's 2008–09] Operation 'Cast Lead' and the lack of assistance for these children. The Committee is furthermore concerned over the lack of adequate programmes for rehabilitation of children who have been victims of anti-personnel mines."[100] (In general, it has been found that "Among the consequences of war, the impact on the mental health of the civilian population is one of the most significant,"[101] with children, not surprisingly, standing out as especially vulnerable.) A recently study shows that 65 percent of young people in Gaza suffer from PTSD.[102] These are children who have grown up in a situation of continuous conflict and whose future looks extremely bleak. The current living situation in Gaza continues being dire, with no signs of improvement on the horizon.[103] Most recently, the UN has declared that by 2020 Gaza will cease to be a "liveable place."[104]

Children have also borne great physical and psychological damage from the civil war in Syria that began in 2011. Thousands have fled to Jordan, many having to make it on their own, without their parents.[105] This intolerable situation, in which the UN is blocked from intervening by some of its own members, is creating a generation that will be scarred for life and yet will also have to rebuild the country one day.

One can include as well among the "invisible" costs of war the destruction or theft of people's cultural heritage, by which they define themselves. Many examples could be cited, such as the massive damage caused to the Parthenon (and its contents) in Athens in 1687, when the Venetians attacked the Ottoman Turks, who were using the building as a gunpowder depot, first blowing this up, then later looting whatever remained that was of value;[106] the plundering of art collections in occupied countries by Napoleon and later the Nazis; fire-bombing of the city of Dresden—one of the classic art capitals of Europe—by the Allies in World War II; the pillaging of Iraq's National Museum treasures by unknown individuals after the fall of Saddam Hussein; and the 2013 burning and theft of priceless Islamic manuscripts in Timbuktu, Mali by jihadist insurgents.

The Damage War Causes to the Environment and Animals

A further frequently ignored or overlooked legacy of war is its environmental impact. According to geographer Joni Seager, "Militaries are the world's biggest environmental vandals, whether at war or in peace. . . . [T]he environmental costs of militarized peace bear suspicious resemblance to the costs of war."[107] But, beyond generalities, let us briefly consider a few cases to illustrate what she is referring to.

Across large areas of the globe, landmines and other "explosive remnants of war" have killed and maimed countless victims, and continue doing so. Incredibly, an average of 250 tons of unexploded weaponry (including toxic gas canisters)—century-old leftovers from World War I—is still unearthed every year by farmers in Flanders, Belgium.[108] According to one source, "There are between 70 and 80 million landmines in the ground in one-third of the world's nations. They cost as little as $3 to produce, but as much as $1000 to remove."[109] Apart from the many deaths caused by undetonated ordnance, Tyner notes that "There are an estimated 473,000 landmine survivors in the world, . . . many of whom require lifelong medical care and assistance. This demand creates a huge *economic* burden on both households and societies, many of which are ill-prepared and ill-equipped to rebuild after war."[110] Studies have also reported the deadly toll of these devices on elephants, brown bears, snow leopards, tigers, gazelles, mountain gorillas, as well as sheep, cattle, and goats; countries affected include Croatia, Bosnia, India, Libya, Rwanda, Mozambique, Afghanistan, and Cambodia. In Myanmar (Burma) and Angola, anti-tank mines have been used by poachers deliberately to kill endangered animals that are highly valued in illegal world trade. Not only do landmines take lives, they also shut down agricultural and other land uses because of fear of their veiled omnipresence. This effect is significant in Angola, Sudan, Somalia, and Mozambique.[111] Another environmental impact has to do with radioactive products. As is reliably reported, practices for handling nuclear waste during the Cold War (1945–89) ranged from cavalier to criminally irresponsible. Consider the following:

> Future generations will also be confronted with the realization that throughout the Cold War, both the Soviet Union and the United States, in particular, gave relatively low priority to the problem of the storage and disposal of radioactive wastes. In the United States alone, nuclear waste has accumulated at 120 sites; this includes approximately 55,000 tons of high-level waste from civilian reactors and 15,000 tons from nuclear weapons production. . . . And, similar to the dumping of chemical weapons following the Second World War, Soviet officials simply discarded *tons* of radioactive materials into the northern waters of Europe.[112]

The consequences of this sorry tale will be played out over centuries, if not millennia, with the various life-forms (including our own) that depend on a healthy environment paying the price.

It is worth stating here, too, that the specter of "nuclear winter" (atmospheric occlusion) that haunted the Cold War period will continue to be a realistic possibility as long as nuclear weapons exist. A report by the Physicians for Social Responsibility (based on several other current sources) states that "The number of people threatened by nuclear-war induced famine would be well over one billion,"[113] owing to the impact on agriculture alone. While the nuclear winter scenario first studied was the hypothetical outcome of an all-out conflict between the United States and the USSR, this report highlights what might be expected to result from "just" a regional nuclear war between India and Pakistan, underlining the urgent need for the elimination of these weapons worldwide.

During the Gulf War (1990–91), Saddam Hussein's Iraqi forces deliberately "dumped approximately one million tons of crude oil [from Kuwait] into the Persian Gulf"; and "Crude oil was also spilled into the desert, forming oil lakes covering 50 square kilometers. In due time the oil percolated into underground aquifers."[114] The effects on wildlife, sea-dwelling food sources, and human health were predictably vast. And, immediately after this war, Saddam Hussein created an "ecological disaster" by draining the marshes at the confluence of the Tigris and Euphrates Rivers, in order to crush the Shi'ite opponents of his regime seeking sanctuary there.[115]

Meanwhile, Coalition air attacks on Iraqi installations released quantities of nerve gas into the Tigris River, and "Soon after the ceasefire was signed, U.N. observers declared this salient river dead."[116] At the time, it was reported that bombing campaigns in Iraq "consume 12 million gallons of fuel a day," and that the number of bombs dropped on Iraq and Kuwait "is generally believed to exceed what was used in all of World War II."[117] In addition to obvious military targets, "Croplands, barns and grain silos were . . . attacked, along with irrigation floodgates that caused vast incursions of seawater into southern Iraq, killing crops and permanently salting farmland."[118] A group of scientific researchers, in the conclusion of their article, starkly notes that "The Iraqi occupation and the subsequent armed conflict devastated the terrestrial environment of Kuwait."[119] As a postscript to this case study, it is worth taking note that "According to the Arab Monetary Fund, the Iraqi occupation of Kuwait and the war to reverse it cost the region some \$676 billion"—not counting the environmental destruction just described.[120]

The preceding account represents only a slice of the actual or suspected environmental damage resulting from this particular war alone. Recovery and rehabilitation of regional ecosystems have been a long-term process and some good outcomes are claimed.[121] In the larger context, there are ongoing discussions in the literature aimed at defining accountability for ecological damage in wartime and at developing guidelines intended to help limit negative environmental consequences during future military operations.[122] It is important to observe here that the issue is not whom we should blame for starting a particular conflict; who did the most damage; whether recovery and rehabilitation are viable after technologically advanced warfare; or whether policies to restrict environmental destruction in wartime can be framed (in the spirit of just-war doctrine). The point is simply that war and a healthy planet are totally incompatible states of affairs.

Finally, a little-known, barely discussed impact of war is the cost to nonhuman animals. This includes, most significantly, the injury and death of animals in zones of active conflict and the use of animals for military research in peacetime. Arguably, medical advances have been achieved through military animal research. However, leaving aside questions about whether such beneficial research could be (or is already) covered in the civilian arena, and whether animal research should be condoned in general, the real issue here is whether it is morally acceptable to subject animals to harmful, extremely painful, and lethal experiments in order to advance knowledge of the techniques of warfare—for example, research on the effects of chemical, biological, laser, and nuclear weapons, microwaves, gunshot wounds, and the most deadly pathogens and diseases.[123] A further problem is that military research, being secret, lacks adequate (or any) oversight and ethics review. In the United States and the United Kingdom, a continuous struggle for accountability has been going on for decades. Even when animals are not themselves the subjects of experiments, they may still be casualties of military research. For example, according to the US Navy's own environmental impact statement, whales and dolphins may be harmed up to 2.8 million times during the Navy's proposed 2014–18 sonar and explosives testing program, due to effects on their hearing and habitat.[124] Animals are also the casualties, in great abundance, of actual warfare, whether serving in combat-related roles or as by-standing "collateral damage" (pets and livestock).[125] The total number of horses alone killed in World War I, for example, was 500,000 according to one estimate.[126] Next to nothing is written into international law concerning this matter.

Costs of War

War-preparedness

> **financial burden**
> **opportunity costs**

Conducting war

> **cost of ordnance, military operations**
> **opportunity costs**

War damage

> **death and injury to combatants and noncombatants**
> **psychological trauma to combatants and noncombatants**
> **economic impact**
> **widespread destruction of all types**
> **harm to fabric of society**
> **destruction and theft of cultural heritage**
> **explosive remnants and toxic wastes**
> **harm to human coexistence**
> **effects on noninvolved nations and other international repercussions**
> **harm and death to animals**

Reflecting on the Costs of War

Bickerton remarks that "The ravages of war can never be accurately quantified, but what we can say is that modern warfare results in an appalling number of (principally civilian) deaths, and produces immense destructiveness. Wars no longer end with surrender ceremonies and tickertape parades. They end in a fog of ambiguity, and it is easier to discern what's been sacrificed than what's been gained."[127] Some of these costs have been documented above, but only a very small sample has been extracted from a vast sea of misery and ruinous waste. Even so, it is not difficult to draw reliable general conclusions. As American politician and military veteran Ron Paul has written, "The cost of war is always more than anticipated. If all the costs were known prior to the beginning of a war, fewer wars would be fought."[128] This assessment may be too optimistic, as it assumes a level of rationality tragically often bracketed out of the equation that leads to war-making. Nevertheless, Paul's conclusion that "Most wars could be avoided with better diplomacy, a mutual understanding of minding one's own business, and respect for the right of self-determination" shines forth as a truth we would all do well to memorize and implement.

4. WHY WE NEED PEACE

Although world military expenditures declined for several years after 1988 (the post-Cold War period), by 2008, they had regained the 1988 level and have risen more or less annually ever since.[129] The end-of-Cold War "peace dividend" that many believed would give a big boost to nonmilitary spending in the United States and elsewhere disappointingly did not eventuate. Given the level of violence in the world today, as well as the squandering of resources and human potential that war and war preparations represent, there is an acute need for peace everywhere. A new world peace dividend must be created as an act of collective willpower. (US President Barack Obama in fact promised one in the second electoral debate of 16 October 2012; he said it would follow the end of US engagement in Iraq and Afghanistan. The reader can judge whether this happens.) War and preparations for war are bad for all living things— socially, economically, environmentally, and in terms of survival and basic well-being. Peace, by contrast, we have observed, has many benefits. These can best be appreciated by means of a brief initial overview.

One way to gain this perspective invokes the concepts of "negative peace" and "positive peace," as they are commonly called. (These ideas are discussed in detail in Chapter 5.) The claim made here is that we can readily discern what peace has to offer under both of these headings. Negative peace refers to the absence of war and violent hostilities. This includes, or may include, the cessation of armed conflict, the ending of territorial occupation, the withdrawal and decommissioning of armaments and armed forces, and arms limitation and other kinds of treaties, amnesties, and the like. Negative peace offers relief or freedom from war, which is an essential prerequisite for the resumption and continuation of normal everyday life. Clearly, negative peace, if maintained, offers the benefits of security, repatriation, rebuilding, and reconciliation. It does not take learned peace scholars, though, to make us realize that this is only part of the story, and here is where positive peace enters the picture.

Figure 0.2 Advantages of peace

Positive peace typically unfolds within the domain of options opened up by
negative peace and reveals what can be accomplished therein. We may call this
"real peace" because it embraces all the processes and projects out of which
a better world can emerge. Here we see that peace yields many valuable advantages that war and preparation for war grossly diminish or eliminate, and
that rational choice would clearly seem to favor. Examples are: replacement of
tension-driven rhetoric (what former Canadian Prime Minister Pierre Trudeau
called "megaphone diplomacy") by less alienating and more constructive
forms of discourse; greater scope for developing healthy, cooperative relations
among nations and peoples; the chance to improve national infrastructures,
education, and other human resources; the prospect of dismantling forms of
structural violence (such as poverty, hunger, and social or religious repression)
and institutional violence (such as discriminatory laws, harsh imprisonment,
unequal access to health care, and police brutality) and redirecting effort to
the creation of equality and equal opportunity; the chance to focus more carefully on environmental issues and even to exploit the potential for evolving international environmental cooperation as a means to build sustainable global
peace; the opening up of possibilities for personal transformation (so-called
"inner peace"); and, in general, the encouragement to think about alternative
ways of coexisting that have not been conceived of or tried out before. Peace
is not an easy path, for the reason that very entrenched psychological traits
and habits stand in the way; but beyond any doubt, the rewards are worth the
effort. We can agree, at a minimum, to "give peace a chance" in the following
spirit: Not trying to change things will guarantee that they do not change; trying has at least a chance of success.

5. THE APPEAL OF PEACE

Social anthropologist Donald Tuzin argues that peace is a "spectre" that lurks
in the background of human experience and expectations.[130] Historian Michael

Howard writes that: "Peace may or may not be 'a modern invention' but it is certainly a far more complex affair than war."[131] If so, then maybe peace, after all, does not need to be "sold" so much as allowed to reveal itself to us. In this sense, informing ourselves concerning what peace might be all about is the first step toward achieving a peaceful world. Guided by the objective just stated, this Introduction ends with a series of observations labeled "Home Truths," which reinforce the reflections offered above on why we need peace. Specifically, the statements that follow are intended to be expressions of common sense and shared concern that invite a more detailed consideration of peace by each of us.

Home Truths

- All members of our species (not to mention other species) have a common interest in survival.
- Humans have survived evolution thus far because of their social (including caring and nurturing) behavior as well as their biologically rooted communication skills and empathetic and cooperative tendencies, rather than because of their aggressive and violent tendencies.
- Security (a sense of safety and a positive quality of life) is a common interest of all human beings. Nationally, security signifies territorial integrity, the preservation and flourishing of certain values and ways of life, as well as self-sufficiency in defensive strategies and economic, energy, and resource matters. At the personal level, security embraces a safe and healthy natural and social environment, well-being, a decent standard of living, meaningful employment, adequate housing, freedom of expression, participation in decision-making processes that affect one's life, a sense of belonging and recognition (a sense of mattering)—and for children, being loved, looked after, and educated.[132]
- If we (no matter whom the word "we" designates) have basic security needs, then it is fair to assume that this is also true of everyone else (every other "we," whether a loose collection of individuals, an identifiable group, or a nation). In a cosmopolitan community (a rapidly changing world, created by "globalization"), such as the one that exists today, security cannot be unilaterally or militarily assured. The vulnerability of every individual, group, and nation is increasingly apparent, but so too is the benefit of working together to solve the problems faced by humanity. Given that security (on various levels) is desirable, reducing levels of vulnerability becomes a paramount goal for everyone and must become a joint project.

- It is better (easier in practice, and more effective, economical, and conducive to mutual security and well-being) to realize interests and achieve goals by nonviolent rather than by violent means. It is better to avoid or prevent violent conflict than to manage or resolve it after the fact, just as it is better to prevent any kind of damage from happening in the first place than to have to repair it.

- True security entails attempting to remove or reduce the causes of war and violent conflict, many of which are well-known or obvious, even if not equally well understood—for example, poverty, historical inequalities and injustices, colonialism, lack of access to resources, abuse of power, unfair trade practices, unsustainable development, unethical exploitation of markets and foreign economies, violation and undermining of international law, lack of trust, aggressive foreign relations, proliferation of weaponry, inability to see beyond narrow self-interest or national interest, lack of cooperation in defining and solving common problems.

- Armed conflict cannot continue indefinitely without destroying what is being fought for. In the end, it must give way to communication and learning how to coexist. Focusing on the latter processes instead of the former is less painful all around and offers greater positive benefits to all concerned.

- Notwithstanding what we constantly imbibe from the media, everyday human life is largely based on peaceful transactions, which, in normal circumstances, we build upon, either instinctively or deliberately.

Pondering the above statements and others like them might just help to clear a space within which a constructive conversation about peace can occur—one that invites all interested persons to become involved. Either we will end war and preparations for war, or they will end us. Ending them, therefore, is not just a choice, it is also an imperative. Discussion of what peace is, and of how we can obtain and develop it, must therefore be kept at the forefront of public dialogue and discussions of social welfare.

NOTES TO INTRODUCTION

1. Richard E. Smalley, "Top Ten Problems of Humanity for Next 50 Years," Energy and Nano Technology Conference, Rice University, 3 May 2003.
2. Pew Environmental Health Commission, "Attack Asthma: Why America Needs a Public Health Defense System to Battle Environmental Threats," 2001; http://healthyameri cans.org/reports/files/asthma.pdf.
3. Gayle Zemach Lemmon, "The Hillary Doctrine," Newsweek, 14 March 2011, pp. 46ff.

4. Margo Marchbank, "The War on Error," *Flight Safety (Australia)*, 67 (March–April, 2009), p. 8.

5. John Herrman, "The Light Bulb Wars," *Popular Mechanics*, September 2011, pp. 96–102.

6. David Cortright, *Peace: A History of Movements and Ideas* (Cambridge, UK: Cambridge University Press), p. 1.

7. Martin Woollacott, "Friends Reunited" (review of James Sheehan, *The Monopoly of Violence* [see footnote 91 below]), *The Guardian*, 19 January 2008; http://www.guardian.co.uk/books/2008/jan/19/politics1.

8. John E. Mueller, "War has Almost Ceased to Exist," *Political Science Quarterly* 124 (2009), pp. 297–321. See also John E. Mueller, *The Remnants of War* (Ithaca, NY: Cornell University Press, 2004).

9. Oliver Ramsbotham, Tom Woodhouse, and Hugh Miall, *Contemporary Conflict Resolution: The Prevention, Management and Transformation of Deadly Conflicts*, 2nd ed. (Cambridge, UK: Polity Press, 2008), p. 138. Note, too, as war historian Jeremy Black cautions, "It is possible that low-intensity warfare will be that which is most common in the future, but, equally, across much of the world there is no effective restraint on the ambitions and activities of states, and the continued combination of issues over which to dispute, and bellicose leaderships, may lead to serious levels of warfare between regular forces" (*Why Wars Happen* [London: Reaktion Books, 1998], p. 235).

10. Mary Kaldor, *New and Old Wars: Organized Violence in a Global Era*, new ed. (Cambridge, UK: Polity Press, 2001), back cover.

11. This definition, it will be noticed, states that combatants are "generally armed." The reason is that unarmed hand-to-hand fighting between groups should also be able to count as war. The intentionality of war in the given definition is underlined by anthropologist Raymond Kelly (who, like most authors, defines war as armed combat): "One of the key features of war is that the deaths of other persons are envisioned in advance and this envisioning is encoded in the purposeful act of taking up lethal weapons" (Raymond C. Kelly, *Warless Societies and the Origin of War* [Ann Arbor: University of Michigan Press, 2000], p. 4).

12. My thanks to Ken Fraser for pointing this out.

13. For a very good brief discussion, see Joane Nagel, "War," in *International Encyclopedia of Men and Masculinities*, ed. Michael Flood et al. (London: Routledge, 2007), pp. 626–9.

14. Kevin Rudd, commemorative address at Remembrance Day service, The Australian War Memorial, Canberra, 11 November 2008; http://pmrudd.archive.dpmc.gov.au/node/5479.

15. John Locke, "Epistle to the Reader," in *An Essay Concerning Human Understanding* (1690), abridged and ed. Raymond Wilburn (London: J. M. Dent & Sons, 1947), p. xxiii.

16. There are many good books on this subject, for example: Bertrand Russell, *Why Men Fight: A Method of Abolishing the International Duel* (New York: Century, 1917); Seyom Brown, *The Causes and Prevention of War* (New York: St. Martin's Press, 1987); Geoffrey Blainey, *The Causes of War*, 3rd ed. (New York: Free Press, 1988); W. B. Gallie, *Understanding War* (London: Routledge, 1991); Greg Cashman, *What Causes War?* (New York: Macmillan/Lexington, 1993); Hidemi Suganami, *On the*

Causes of War (New York: Oxford University Press, 1996); Black, *Why Wars Happen*; Steven Le Blanc and Katherine E. Register, *Constant Battles: Why We Fight* (New York: St. Martin's Press, 2003); Lowell Tollefson, *What Is War? Philosophical Reflections about the Nature, Causes, and Persistence of Wars* (Lincoln, NE: iUniverse, 2007); David Sobek, *Causes of War* (Cambridge, UK: Polity Press, 2008); Richard Ned Lebow, *Why Nations Fight: Past and Future Motives for War*, reissue ed. (Cambridge, UK: Cambridge University Press, 2010); Thomas Lindemann, *Causes of War: The Struggle for Recognition* (Colchester, Essex: European Consortium for Political Research Press, 2011).

17. Lawrence LeShan, *The Psychology of War: Comprehending Its Mystique and Its Madness*, enlarged ed. (New York: Helios Press, 2002).

18. Chris Hedges, *War Is a Force That Gives Us Meaning* (New York: Anchor Books, 2003), pp. 3–4. Philip Caputo has explored the allure of war in detail in *A Rumor of War* (New York: Holt, Rinehart and Winston, 1977).

19. Hedges, *War Is a Force*, p. 5.

20. Russell, *Why Men Fight*, p. 80.

21. See, for example, J. Glenn Gray, *The Warriors: Reflections on Men in Battle* (New York: Harcourt, Brace, 1970); Sönke Neitzel and Harald Welzer, *Soldaten: On Fighting, Killing, and Dying*, trans. Jefferson Chase (New York: Alfred A. Knopf, 2012).

22. E. P. Thompson, cited by Barrie Zwicker, "Journalism and the Bomb," in *Sources: A Directory of Contacts for Editors, Reporters and Researchers in Canada*, Summer 1983, p. 7.

23. Black, *Why Wars Happen*, p. 242.

24. Jean-Jacques Rousseau, *The Social Contract* (1762), trans. Christopher Betts (Oxford: Oxford University Press, 1994), bk. I, chap. iv, pp. 51, 52.

25. Kenneth E. Boulding, *Stable Peace* (Austin: University of Texas Press, 1978), p. 20.

26. Boulding, *Stable Peace*, pp. 27, 90.

27. Dane Archer, *Violence and Crime in Cross-National Perspective* (New Haven, CT: Yale University Press, 1984), p. 66.

28. Ian Bickerton, *The Illusion of Victory: The True Costs of War* (Carlton, VIC: Melbourne University Press, 2011), pp. ix, 205–6.

29. See, for example, Christian G. Appy, *Working-Class War: American Combat Soldiers and Vietnam* (Chapel Hill: University of North Carolina Press, 1993); David M. Halbfinger and Steven A. Holmes, "A Nation at War: The Troops—Military Mirrors a Working-Class America," *New York Times*, 30 March 2003; http://www.nytimes.com/2003/03/30/us/a-nation-at-war-the-troops-military-mirrors-a-working-class-america.html?pagewanted=all&src=pm.

30. Michael Zweig, Michael Porter, and Yuxiang Huang, "American Military Deaths in Afghanistan, and the Communities from Which These Soldiers, Sailors, Airmen, and Marines Came," Center for Study of Working Class Life, October 2011; http://www.stonybrook.edu/workingclass/publications/Casualty%20study%20main%20report%20Oct%202011.pdf.

31. Advertisement for Billy Tea, *Sydney Morning Herald*, 21–22 January 2012, p. 17.

32. George L. Mosse, *Fallen Soldiers: Reshaping the Memory of the World Wars* (New York: Oxford University Press, 1990), p. 7.

33. David Rieff argues that "remembrance may be the friend of justice but it is rarely the friend of peace" (*Against Remembrance* [Carlton, VIC: Melbourne University Press, 2011], p. 105). By this, he means that remembrance may help us bear in mind what we owe to past generations, but dwelling on it may prevent moving forward, beyond the conditions that cause war.

34. See Noah Richler, *What We Talk about When We Talk about War* (Fredericton, NB, Canada: Goose Lane Editions, 2012).

35. A. Coyne, commentary on Jonathan Schell, *The Unconquerable World: Power, Nonviolence, and the Will of the People* (New York: Metropolitan Books, 2003). Retrieved from Amazon.com (customer reviews).

36. Ludwig von Mises, *Human Action: A Treatise on Economics*, 3rd rev. ed. (Chicago: Henry Regnery, 1966), pp. 172, 176.

37. Bob Holmes, "Born to Fight, Evolved for Peace," *New Scientist* 2682 (15 November 2008), p. 8.

38. See Norman Doidge, *The Brain That Changes Itself: Stories of Personal Triumph from the Frontiers of Brain Research* (New York: Viking Penguin, 2007); Lise Eliot, "Girl Brain, Boy Brain?" *Scientific American*, 8 September 2009; http://www.scientificamerican.com/article.cfm?id=girl-brain-boy-brain&page=3.

39. William James, "The Moral Equivalent of War" (1910), in *William James: Writings 1902–1910*, ed. Bruce Kuklick (New York: Library of America, 1987), p. 1283.

40. See Jack Nelson-Pallmeyer, *Brave New World Order: Must We Pledge Allegiance?* (Maryknoll, NY: Orbis Books, 1992).

41. See Oliver Burkeman, "Why Everything You've Been Told about Evolution Is Wrong," *The Guardian*, 19 March 2010; http://www.guardian.co.uk/science/2010/mar/19/evolution-darwin-natural-selection-genes-wrong?INTCMP=SRCH.

42. John Horgan, "The End of War," *New Scientist* 2715 (4 July 2009), pp. 36–9.

43. Friedrich von Bernardi, quoted in Ashley Montagu, *The Nature of Human Aggression* (New York: Oxford University Press, 1976), p. 273.

44. Immanuel Kant, *To Perpetual Peace: A Philosophical Sketch* (1795), in Immanuel Kant, *Perpetual Peace and Other Essays on Politics, History, and Morals*, trans. Ted Humphrey (Indianapolis: Hackett, 1983), p. 123 (emphasis in original).

45. See Martin Van Creveld, *The Culture of War* (New York: Presidio Press, 2008) for a detailed discussion of this point.

46. James, "Moral Equivalent of War."

47. See LeShan, *Psychology of War*; Rachel MacNair, *The Psychology of Peace: An Introduction*, 2nd ed. (Santa Barbara, CA: Praeger, 2012); Daniel J. Christie, Richard V. Wagner, and Deborah Du Nann Winter, eds., *Peace, Conflict, and Violence: Peace Psychology for the 21st Century* (Upper Saddle River, NJ: Prentice-Hall, 2001).

48. Deborah Du Nann Winter, Daniel J. Christie, Richard V. Wagner, and Laura B. Boston, "Conclusion: Peace Psychology for the Twenty-First Century," in Christie, Wagner, and Winter, eds., *Peace, Conflict, and Violence*, p. 366.

49. Richard Boothby, *Death and Desire: Psychoanalytic Theory in Lacan's Return to Freud* (New York: Routledge, 1991), p. 1.

50. Sigmund Freud, *Analysis Terminable and Interminable* (1937), trans. Joan Riviere, in *Standard Edition of the Complete Psychological Works of Sigmund Freud*, ed. James Strachey, vol. 23 (London: Hogarth Press and Institute of Psycho-Analysis, 1964), p. 243.

51. Sigmund Freud, *Why War?* (1933), trans. James Strachey, in *Standard Edition*, ed. Strachey, vol. 22 (1964), p. 209.

52. They are grounded, for example, in neural circuits of the amygdala and ventromedial prefrontal cortex of the brain, and governed by biochemicals such as oxytocin, produced by the hypothalamus. (My appreciation to Brian Byrne for pointing this out to me [personal communication, 30 July 2012].)

53. Freud, *Why War?* p. 215.

54. For further discussion of these and other myths of war, see David Swanson, *War Is a Lie* (Charlottesville, VA: davidswanson.org, 2010).

55. Cortright, *Peace*, p. 155.

56. Cortright, *Peace*, p. 123.

57. Stockholm International Peace Research Institute (SIPRI), "World Military Spending Falls, but China, Russia's Spending Rises, says SIPRI," 15 April 2013; http://www.sipri.org/media/pressreleases/2013/milex_launch.

58. United Nations, "Questions and Answers . . . Image and Reality . . . about the UN"; http://www.un.org/geninfo/ir/index.asp?id=150.

59. "If you want peace, prepare for war": saying found in various ancient texts, for example Publius Flavius Vegetius Renatus, *De Re Militari* (4th–5th century CE), bk. 3. "War is Peace": motto inscribed on the "Ministry of Truth" building in George Orwell's futuristic novel *1984*, bk. 1, chap. 1.

60. Vijay Mehta, "The Price of Peace—Bread or Bombs: Reducing Weapons for Giving Peace a Chance"; http://www.arcuk.org/pages/vj_price_of_peace_bread_or_bombs.htm.

61. World Hunger Education Service, "2012 World Hunger and Poverty Facts and Statistics"; http://www.worldhunger.org/articles/Learn/world%20hunger%20facts%202002.htm#Number_of_hungry_people_in_the_world.

62. Jay Rayner, "Malnutrition: the Hidden Crisis," *Guardian Weekly*, 24 February–1 March 2012, p. 1.

63. National Priorities Project (n.d.), "Cost of War"; http://costofwar.com.

64. Dwight David Eisenhower, "The Chance for Peace," speech given to the American Society of Newspaper Editors, 16 April 1953; http://harpers.org/archive/2007/11/hbc-90001660.

65. A convenient tool with which to begin this exercise is the National Priorities Project's "Cost of War" indicator, referenced in note 63 above.

66. See Control Arms Campaign's report *Guns or Growth? Assessing the Impact of Arms Sales on Sustainable Development*; http://www.oxfam.org/sites/www.oxfam.org/files/Guns_or_Growth_0.pdf.

67. The following interesting argument suggests that there is but one way in which the economic losses engendered by war can be offset by its economic gains: "[T]he only way war can bring the countries involved in it any economic benefit is through the

destruction of lives and property that are having a negative effect on a nation's economy, such as the lives of an oppressive totalitarian dictator and his enforcers and any records these oppressors may have been keeping on their subjects in order to blackmail them. War brings no other kind of net economic benefit to the combatants, and therefore any argument in favor of having a war based on the premise that war will stimulate productivity is fallacious because the premise is false; going to war will invariably decrease that nation's net productivity" ("Parable of the Broken Window," *Wikipedia*, http://en.wikipedia.org/wiki/Parable_of_the_broken_window).

68. I owe this point to Russell Hogg (personal communication, 17 August 2012).

69. Kent D. Sheffield, *From War to Peace: A Guide to the Next Hundred Years* (Jefferson, NC: McFarland, 2011), pp. 12–13.

70. See http://www.economictheories.org/2008/07/adam-smith-theory-of-value.html.

71. Robert Pollin and Heidi Garrett-Peltier, "The U.S. Employment Effects of Military and Domestic Spending Priorities: An Updated Analysis," Political Economy Research Institute (PERI), University of Massachusetts-Amherst, 2009, p. 5; http://www.peri.umass.edu/fileadmin/pdf/published_study/spending_priorities_PERI.pdf.

72. Andrew Feinstein, "The Shadow World," *New Internationalist* 448 (December 2011), p. 22.

73. Ramsbotham, Woodhouse, and Miall, *Contemporary Conflict Resolution*, pp. 88, 161.

74. National Priorities Project, "Cost of War."

75. National Priorities Project, "Cost of War."

76. Watson Institute for International Studies, Brown University, "Costs of War" (2013 report); http://costsofwar.org.

77. Ramsbotham, Woodhouse, and Miall, *Contemporary Conflict Resolution*, p. 73.

78. See James A. Tyner, *Military Legacies: A World Made by War* (New York: Routledge, 2010).

79. Helen Ware, ed., et al., *The No-Nonsense Guide to Conflict and Peace* (Oxford: New Internationalist, 2006), pp. 114, 116.

80. Statement made by "A middle-aged man in a beleaguered village of deslocados in the southern part of Mozambique"; cited by Carolyn Nordstrom, *A Different Kind of War Story* (Philadelphia: University of Pennsylvania Press, 1997), p. 184.

81. Ed Pilkington, "US Forces Hit by Rising Wave of Suicides," *Guardian Weekly*, 8–14 February 2013, p. 10.

82. Jacqueline Garrick, Acting Director of the Defense Suicide Prevention Office, "Statement before the Subcommittee on Military Personnel of the House Armed Services Committee Concerning Update on Military Suicide Prevention," 6 March 2013; available at: http://docs.house.gov/meetings/AS/AS02/20130321/100277/HHRG-113-AS02-TTF-GarrickJ-20130321.pdf.

83. Michael Winerip, "Generation B: Vietnam's Damage, Forty Years Later," *New York Times*, 6 September 2009, p. 2.

84. See, for example, Nancy Sherman, *The Untold War: Inside the Hearts, Minds, and Souls of Our Soldiers* (New York: W.W. Norton, 2010); Ronald Glasser, *Broken Bodies,*

Shattered Minds: A Medical Odyssey from Vietnam to Afghanistan (Palisades, NY: History Publishing, 2011); John Cantwell, *Exit Wounds: One Australian's War on Terror* (Melbourne: Melbourne University Press, 2012).

85. Claude Anshin Thomas, *At Hell's Gate: A Soldier's Journey from War to Peace* (Boston: Shambhala, 2004), pp. 29, 34.

86. Matthieu Aikins, "Mental Combat," *Popular Science*, March 2013, p. 46.

87. Tamasin Ford, "Battle for War-scarred Minds," *Guardian Weekly*, 19–25 October 2012, p. 44. The AMA study was conducted in 2008.

88. See James Jeffrey, "The Lonely Soldier and the Moral Scars of War," *The Guardian*, 17 February 2013; http://www.guardian.co.uk/commentisfree/2013/feb/17/lonely-soldier-moral-scars-war. See also Kevin Sites, *The Things They Cannot Say: Stories Soldiers Won't Tell You about What They've Seen, Done or Failed to Do in War* (New York: Harper Perennial, 2013).

89. Nicholas D. Kristof, "Veterans and Brain Disease," *New York Times*, 25 April 2012; http://www.nytimes.com/2012/04/26/opinion/kristof-veterans-and-brain-disease.html?hp.

90. See Ann Jones, *War Is Not Over When It's Over: Women Speak Out from the Ruins of War* (New York: Metropolitan Books, 2010); Elizabeth D. Heineman, ed., *Sexual Violence in Conflict Zones: From the Ancient World to the Era of Human Rights* (Philadelphia: University of Pennsylvania Press, 2011); John K. Roth and Carol Rittner, *Rape: Weapon of War and Genocide* (St. Paul, MN: Paragon House, 2012).

91. James Sheehan, *The Monopoly of Violence: Why Europeans Hate Going to War* (London: Faber and Faber, 2008), pp. 140–1.

92. Ware, ed. et al., *No-Nonsense Guide to Conflict and Peace*, p. 114.

93. Anup Shah, "Global Issues: The Democratic Republic of Congo" (updated 21 August 2010); http://www.globalissues.org/article/87/the-democratic-republic-of-congo.

94. Shah, "Democratic Republic of Congo"; Peter Beaumont, "Years of Congo Conflict Etched on a Refugee Village Chief's Face," *The Guardian/The Observer*, 21 March 2010; http://www.guardian.co.uk/world/2010/mar/21/congo-refugees-fear-un-pullout.

95. War Child organization, "The Conflict in the Congo"; http://www.warchild.org.uk/issues/conflict-in-democratic-republic-of-congo.

96. BBC News, "Democratic Republic of Congo profile," 13 October 2011; http://www.bbc.co.uk/news/world-africa-13283212; see also Ian Birrell, "Congo once more descends into chaos," *Guardian Weekly*, 30 November–6 December 2012, pp. 18–19. See also page 243, footnote 40.

97. Aarushi Nigam, "Does Your Mobile Fund Wars?" *Times of India*, 12 November 2011; http://timesofindia.indiatimes.com/entertainment/hollywood/news-interviews/Does-your-mobile-fund-wars/articleshow/10702762.cms.

98. UNICEF, "Child Soldiers"; http://www.unicef.org.au/Discover/News/March-2012/Child-Soldiers-in-Uganda.aspx?gclid=CLDN2JmXhrACFYY3pAodgCnnjw.

99. Palestinian Centre for Human Rights, "23 Days of War, 928 Days of Closure: Life One Year after Israel's Latest Offensive in the Gaza Strip," 27 December 2008–18 January 2009," p. 13; http://www.pchrgaza.org/files/Reports/English/pdf_spec/23-days.pdf.

100. United Nations Committee on the Rights of the Child (4 March 2010), *Convention on the Rights of the Child* (CRC/C/OPAC/ISR/CO/1), 4 March 2010, point 37; http://unispal.un.org/UNISPAL.NSF/0/2CE67BFD6C6BDAFD852576E800601CB6.

101. R. Srinivasa Murthy and Rashmi Lakshminarayana, "Mental Health Consequences of War: A Brief Review of Research Findings," *World Psychiatry*, 5/1 (2005), pp. 25–30; http://www.ncbi.nlm.nih.gov/pmc/articles/PMC1472271.

102. Chris McGreal, "Undying Hatred in Gaza Combat Zone," *Guardian Weekly*, 30 November–6 December 2012, p. 6.

103. See United Nations, Office for the Coordination of Humanitarian Affairs, Occupied Palestinian Territory, "Five Years of Blockade: The Humanitarian Situation in the Gaza Strip," June 2012; http://www.ochaopt.org/documents/ocha_opt_gaza_blockade_factsheet_june_2012_english.pdf.

104. "Gaza 'Will Not be Liveable by 2020'—UN Report," BBC News, 27 August 2012; http://www.bbc.co.uk/news/world-middle-east-19391809.

105. Harriet Sherwood, "Dispossessed and Afraid: Children Who Bear the Brunt of the War," *Guardian Weekly*, 5–11 October 2012, pp. 10–11.

106. In 1954, the international community enacted a Convention for the Protection of Cultural Property in the Event of Armed Conflict, at The Hague; see http://www.icrc.org/ihl.nsf/FULL/400. This gives an indication that attitudes toward this matter have undergone important change; however the use of indiscriminate firepower and looting, as well as weapons of mass destruction, still pose a huge threat to the preservation of valuable cultural objects.

107. Joni Seager, "Foreword," in William Thomas, *Scorched Earth: The Military's Assault on the Environment* (Philadelphia: New Society, 1995), p. xi.

108. ABC (Australia), 7:00 p.m. television news, 23 April 2013.

109. United States Campaign to End Landmines, 2011; http://www.uscbl.org/about-landmines.

110. Tyner, *Military Legacies*, p. 81 (emphasis in original).

111. The foregoing account is based on Tyner, *Military Legacies*, pp. 88–9.

112. Tyner, *Military Legacies*, pp. 140, 143 (emphasis in original).

113. Ira Helfand, on behalf of International Physicians for the Prevention of Nuclear War and Physicians for Social Responsibility, *Nuclear Famine: A Billion People at Risk—Global Impacts of Limited Nuclear War on Agriculture, Food Supplies, and Human Nutrition* (Somerville, MA: IPPNW; Washington, DC: PSR, 2012); available at: http://www.psr.org/nuclear-weapons/nuclear-famine-report.pdf.

114. S. M. Enzler, "Environmental Effects of Warfare: The Impact of War on the Environment and Human Health" (September 2006), p. 1; http://www.lenntech.com/environmental-effects-war.htm.

115. International Review, "Iraq's Ecological Disaster," 12 February 2003; http://www.int-review.org/terr36a.html.

116. Thomas, *Scorched Earth*, p. 123.

117. John Kifner, "War in the Gulf: Logistics; from Bombs to Burgers, Gulf War Involves Biggest Supply Effort Ever," *New York Times*, 4 February 1991, p. 1; http://www.nytimes.com/1991/02/04/world/war-gulf-logistics-bombs-burgers-gulf-war-involves-biggest-supply-effort-ever.html.

118. Thomas, *Scorched Earth*, p. 124.

119. Samira A.S. Omar, Ernest Briskey, Raafat Misak, and Adel A.S.O. Asem, "The Gulf War Impact on the Terrestrial Environment of Kuwait: An Overview," in *The Environmental Consequences of War: Legal, Economic, and Scientific Perspectives*, ed. Jay E. Austin and Carl E. Bruch, (Cambridge, UK: Cambridge University Press, 2000), p. 336.

120. Michael Renner, *Budgeting for Disarmament: The Costs of War and Peace*, Worldwatch Paper 122 (Washington, DC: Worldwatch Institute, 1994), p. 11.

121. See Omar, Briskey, Misak, and Asem, "Gulf War Impact," pp. 332–5; Richard Porter, "Marsh Flooding Brings New Life to Iraq's 'Garden of Eden,'" BBC News, 1 June 2013; http://www.bbc.co.uk/news/magazine-22706024.

122. See Austin and Bruch, eds., *Environmental Consequences of War*; Jurgen Brauer, *War and Nature: The Environmental Consequences of War in a Globalized World* (Lanham, MD: AltaMira Press, 2009).

123. See, for example, New England Anti-Vivisection Society, "Military Research"; http://www.neavs.org/research/military.

124. Miguel Llanos, "Navy Raises Sonar Impact on Whales, Dolphins Dramatically," NBC.com, 11 May 2012; http://usnews.nbcnews.com/_news/2012/05/11/11659008-navy-raises-sonar-impact-on-dolphins-whales-dramatically?lite.

125. See, for example, Susy Pryde, "Guest Post: The Animal Casualties of War," The Solution for a Better World, 8 March 2010; http://thesolution.org.nz/2010/03/08/guest-post-the-animal-casualties-of-war.

126. Sheehan, *Monopoly of Violence*, p. 81.

127. Bickerton, *Illusion of Victory*, p. xi.

128. Ron Paul, "The Hidden Costs of War," June 16, 2005, p. 1; http://www.antiwar.com/paul/?articleid=6330.

129. SIPRI, "World Military Expenditure, 1988–2012"; http://www.sipri.org/research/armaments/milex/sipri-military-expenditure-database.

130. Donald Tuzin, "The Spectre of Peace in Unlikely Places: Concept and Paradox in the Anthropology of Peace," in *A Natural History of Peace*, ed. Thomas Gregor (Nashville: Vanderbilt University Press, 1996), pp. 3–33.

131. Michael Howard, *The Invention of Peace: Reflections on War and International Order* (New Haven: Yale University Press, 2000), pp. 1–2.

132. Robert J. Burrowes suggests a definition of security that is even more wide-reaching: "Security, then, is a condition of certainty regarding the ongoing viability of the ecological, political, economic, social, and psychological circumstances necessary for all individuals and identity groups, as well as the Earth and all its species, to satisfy their needs, to live in harmony, and to survive indefinitely" (*The Strategy of Nonviolent Defense: A Gandhian Approach* [Albany: State University of New York Press, 1996], p. 149). See also Frances Moore Lappé, "Could Our Deepest Fears Hold the Key to Ending Violence?" *YES! Magazine*, 19 April 2013; available at: http://www.commondreams.org/view/2013/04/19–2.

Part I

Beyond the War Mentality

1

Historical Narrative and the Presupposition of Violence

There was never a good war, or a bad peace.

—Benjamin Franklin, letter to Sir Joseph Banks, president of
the Royal Society, 27 July 1783

Peace has its victories no less than war, but it doesn't have as many monuments to unveil.

—Frank McKinney ("Kin") Hubbard (1868–1930), American
journalist, cartoonist, and humorist

[I]t is the lot of all myths to creep gradually into the confines of a supposedly historical reality, and to be treated by some later age as unique fact with claims to historical truth.

—Friedrich Nietzsche, *The Birth of Tragedy out of the Spirit of Music*,
sec. 10

1.1. HISTORY AS A CONFLICT ZONE

History and Truth

Accounts of the past single out parts of the human story that historians perceive as worth telling or somehow obligatory to tell, which are then told from a certain standpoint or standpoints—temporal, cultural, topical, and so on. Nobel Prize author V. S. Naipaul correctly observes that "There must always be certain things that drop out of history. Only the broadest movements and

45

themes can be recorded. All the multifarious choppings and changings, all the individual hazards and venturesomeness, and failures, cannot be recorded. History is full of mysteries. . . . Certain things are lost. . . ."[1] But a more specific problem about history also calls for our attention. As the description of a recent historiographical volume states, "Every piece of historical writing has a theoretical basis on which evidence is selected, filtered, and understood."[2] One prominent historian asserts that "it is apparent that the past impinges on many people and no single group has exclusive possession of it. It is also apparent that the historian plays a vital role in assisting occupancy."[3] Many may find these sorts of ideas unfamiliar, and perhaps a bit odd and unsettling. We are inclined to believe that there is knowledge, on the one hand, and everything else, on the other. We are likewise predisposed to think that if a reputable or learned authority, such as a historian, tells us something against the background of his or her expertise, then that must be the way it is. But we learn as we grow older that these assumptions cannot necessarily be relied upon or even, more radically, that the foundation on which they rest is either very shaky or eroded beyond repair. Living in a postmodern age of increasing skepticism about conclusive statements of any kind makes it quite difficult to cling to reassuring certainties and to resist the idea that "truth" might itself be a fiction, or at any rate a will-o'-the-wisp, an unattainable goal even in principle.

Although there is no possibility of historians stepping outside of their own era and system of beliefs, there are nevertheless those who would speak of studying the past as a way of "objectively" getting at the "facts" about it, and of aiming to ascertain what it "really means"—all very loaded and frequently ill-defined notions. Yet for each of these historians, there are probably at least as many others who ask, "Who owns history?";[4] or decry "the discipline's relentless focus on the experience of white men only";[5] or assert that only the victorious get to write the "definitive" account of an event or age; or observe that historical writing in a certain area is beset by "history wars," "ethnocentrism," "mythmaking," "fabrication," "political correctness," "left-wing" or "right-wing" agendas, and more. Recent books include telling title phrases or chapter headings such as these: "whitewashing war," "history as weapon," "history on trial," and "lies my teacher told me."[6] Summing up the variety of problems raised by the writing of history, a professor of the discipline rhetorically asks, "Who determines which history is 'anointed' as the 'true' history?"[7]

In addition to this more "innocent" dilemma, there is the comparatively daunting one of correcting deliberately falsified and/or "official" versions of the history of a particular country, ethnic group, or time period. There is also the little-known history of those who have been *displaced by history*—for example, the victims of colonialism and various diasporas around the world.[8]

It begins to look as if the past cannot escape being an assemblage made from the (or rather someone's) standpoint in the present, and so history-telling is in danger of coming to resemble virtual reality, personal memoir, or opinion piece more than fact.[9]

Yet in spite of these confronting ideas about the construction of historical narratives, history is indispensable because it defines who we have been, are, and may yet be; expresses the significance of our collective actions; and helps us understand how to come to terms with what we have done and propose to do. Historical narrative is a tool for finding our way, our place in the scheme of things—even for identifying what "the scheme of things" is. And historians do strive to focus on and stay faithful to certain "facts," although, as it has been said, "No historian . . . treats every fact equally."[10] But because history is a defining form of cultural reference, misusing it to specify reality (or some part of it) as one sees fit, or as certain vested interests, prevailing cultural values, or traditions require, is a serious matter. Aside from the influences and underlying factors that may govern historical interpretation, there is a sort of inertia, too, that propels it along, unless and until it meets with opposition. Newton's First Law of Motion applies to ideas as well as to objects.

A Common View of History

Whatever perspective one takes on the issues briefly reviewed above, it must be observed that standard versions of history, as most people have been taught it, revolve around the great deeds and ambitions of famous (mostly male) rulers and the wars they have fought (see Introduction, "War myths," Myth #1). Ambrose Bierce put the point humorously in his *Devil's Dictionary*: "History, *n*. An account mostly false, of events mostly unimportant, which are brought about by rulers mostly knaves, and soldiers mostly fools."[11] More precisely, one could say that the "engines" of history are usually seen as economic power, invention, technology, religion, growing populations, environmental resources, ideas, and war, with all of these factors either directly or indirectly serving the last—war. Of course, these are generalizations, and they are in no way intended to obscure recognition that many worthy historical studies of specific cultural trends and tendencies do not fit this pattern, just as some accounts of the past, like Howard Zinn's *A People's History of the United States*,[12] do emphasize the role played by the actions of ordinary and even obscure individuals and movements. However, our interest here is in capturing what has most generally been presented as "history" or "world history" and therefore what most readily comes to mind when these words are mentioned.[13]

The reader will perhaps have noticed, too, that absent from the above list of the factors that shape history is *cooperation* (discussed in Chapter 2). Historical accounts do acknowledge some forms of cooperation, for example, military treaties, alliances, and foreign aid. Yet cooperation plays a much more fundamental role in history, which is only superficially captured in such partnerships as these.

Lively controversies in Australia and Canada underline the kinds of concerns raised so far. In Australia, some historians have charged that the history taught in schools is being militarized, and war glorified and romanticized; others declare in response that students are being exposed to different dimensions of war and are being encouraged to examine military interpretations of history critically.[14] In Canada, Conservative Prime Minister Stephen Harper committed 28 million dollars to commemorating the hundredth anniversary of the War of 1812, which is, in his words, "the beginning of a long and proud military history in Canada." Reflecting on Harper's decision, historian Ian McKay and journalist Jamie Swift acerbically suggest that Canada's forthcoming observance of the World War I centenary (in 2014) will likely "romanticize that ghastly spasm of ineptitude in the service of a 'Birth of a Nation' story, all the while airbrushing out its incalculable costs."[15] Many historians dispute, in any case, whether the War of 1812 accomplished anything significant by its military campaigns—though it might alternatively be celebrated for the peace treaty that banned warships permanently from the Great Lakes and established the longest undefended border in the world, between the United States and Canada.

1.2. CONSTRUCTING, REVISING, AND CONTROLLING HISTORY

The Power of Historical Accounts and their Manipulation

Even though most historians do their job conscientiously and with a scholarly respect for the truth, there clearly are false and deceptive historical accounts. These can have deadly consequences when they play a role in *causing* real wars. Historian Glenda Sluga contends that in the destruction of Yugoslavia that occurred in the 1990s, historians played a key role in creating an environment in which ethnic conflict seemed inevitable:

> To some degree, the new wars between (depending on when and where) individuals whose motives were reduced to their collective assignations as Serbs or Croats or "Muslims" or Bosnians or Albanians or Macedonians, were conceived of, or imagined, with the help of commentators in the press and on television, as well as in the universities,

as extensions of older wars. But they were also wars fought to affirm a particular version of those past wars and of past and present injustices. The sides that coalesced into
ethno-religious groupings did so as a result of the ways in which historical narratives
were invoked.[16]

To be fair, however, one should reflect here that history can be abused not
only by those who write it, but also by those who regard it uncritically or who
appropriate it for their own ends. The past is not reconstructed by historians
alone. And, clearly, historians cannot be held responsible for all the distortions
people make of their narratives. In wartime and peacetime alike, politicians,
demagogues, and other opinion-shapers try to mold the public's perception of
the reality of world affairs, in order to create constituencies of their own.

Disturbing though the Yugoslavian example is, there is nothing especially
unique about it. John Quigley shows, for instance, how US administrations
have manufactured and manipulated historical reasons for starting wars since
the end of World War II, public opinion falling into place accordingly.[17] Negative images of the enemy and doublespeak are devices also typically mar-
shaled in support of war-preparedness and war-making.[18] These are but a few
of the means that have been at the disposal of war propagandists throughout
the ages.

Perhaps it should come as no surprise, then, that narratives of the past are
contested, inasmuch as no one "owns" history; furthermore, as Michel Fou-
cault has carefully shown, the control of information flow and of the interpretation of events are power games. John Pilger, a prominent journalist, author,
and filmmaker, points out that in the modern world, any effort to control history in order to advance a political agenda crucially depends on "the media as
its transmitter and amplifier."[19] This includes actively or passively endorsing
official governmental outlooks and policies, while effectively silencing others.
Leading up to the Iraq War, against which there were large-scale demonstrations worldwide, Christopher Leahey remarks, "The media failed to challenge
the Bush Administration's pronouncements, seek out alternative sources of
information, provide space for dissenting voices, and portray the dangers and
complexity of war."[20] Leahey, a public school teacher, also shows how in the
United States, critical consideration of wars past and present is perceived as
crossing the line into forbidden terrain and is stifled by blinkered "corporate
textbooks" and conservative school boards that yield to interest groups and
self-proclaimed guardians of patriotism. Examining how world history textbooks cover the Vietnam War, he relates that "none of them devote a single
sentence to the 504 civilians killed at My Lai and My Khe." He also finds that
among American history textbooks, "Only 5 of the 12 . . . mention the My

Lai massacre. When it is mentioned, several textbooks ignore or minimize the cover-up, dehumanize the victims, and treat the massacre as an isolated event. . . ." Not only this, but even though "the alleged [1964] attacks of August 4 [on US warships in the Gulf of Tonkin] are now widely known by historians to have been a fabrication" used to rationalize President Lyndon Johnson's decision to massively escalate the war, high school textbooks have not yet caught up with the fact.[21] Here we have an example of the history profession divided against itself. But the real point is that adulterated historical accounts of war can actually have important repercussions for policy, international stability, and the amount of suffering unleashed upon the world.

Salvaging History

Pilger's analysis focuses on war correspondents who, as narrators of contemporary history, have been all-too-willing and unreflective accomplices in deceiving their audiences about the reasons for war, the nature of war, what really occurs on the ground, how events are actually unfolding, and in reinforcing the myths of war examined in the Introduction. Media censorship imposed by political and military entities is a serious issue, of course; but Pilger believes that this issue betrays a fear of the truth, which people have a right to know, and that the obligation of war reporters is to somehow find a way to convey the truth. "[A]nd the truth of war is the grotesque. It is trees hanging with the body parts of children. It is people going insane before your eyes. It is terrified soldiers with their trousers full of shit. It is human damage that runs through countless families: civilians and soldiers. That's war. The coverage of war should be this eyewitness but it should also try to tell us the *why*. That means journalists not colluding but investigating."[22] Philosopher David Livingstone Smith makes the same point (but without specific reference to journalists): "War is mangled bodies and shattered minds. It is the stomach-churning reek of decaying corpses, of burning flesh and feces. It is terrible beyond comprehension, but it is not *senseless*. Wars are purposeful. They are fought for resources, lebensraum, oil, gold, food, and water or peculiarly abstract and imaginary goods like God, honor, race, democracy, and destiny."[23] Thus do we glorify war. But Smith denies that wars are senseless because there are reasons why they are fought, and believes that we can (and should) seek for explanations of their occurrence. (Whether such "reasons" might not in general be stand-ins or disguises for other motivators, or inseparable from emotional factors, is additionally worthy of investigation.[24])

The question raised by these authors concerns not only people's right to know the unvarnished truth, but also to understand the worst about what humans are capable of, perhaps with the faint hope that precious resources of all types might not continue to be squandered on war in our name if we were well-informed about what we are buying into (a possibility considered in the Introduction as well). Needless to say, how people are trained and encouraged to see the world will determine how they act in it. As Spanish-American philosopher George Santayana famously declared, "Those who cannot remember the past are condemned to repeat it."[25] Therefore, any change in attitudes about war and peace, including the willingness to wage and support wars, depends upon an open, vibrant, broadly based critical scrutiny of events that have taken place and that are happening now.

Some theorists argue that transparency concerning opposed viewpoints on history, and vigorous debate of them, are not on the agenda, at least not in the mainstream media, controlled as they are by giant, often politically biased corporate interests. Such outlets function, wittingly or unwittingly, as propaganda machines, according to political analysts like Edward S. Herman and Noam Chomsky. To take just one small example out of their complex and detailed study of the media, these authors argue that "as long as illegalities and violations of democratic substance are confined to marginal groups or distant victims of U.S. military attack, or result in a diffused cost imposed on the general population, media opposition is muted or absent altogether."[26] While one may despair about the fate of the truth in the face of the considerable evidence and data that back up such claims, encouragement can be derived from the fact that hard-hitting books like theirs help to remedy the deficiencies of reportage from within the larger publishing industry.

1.3. NONVIOLENCE IN HISTORY MADE VISIBLE: (I) GENERAL CONSIDERATIONS

In addition to issues surrounding the presence of war in currently unfolding, recent, and past history, and the treatment of specific wars by some historians and the media, there is another quite significant problem: the overall neglect in historical narratives of nonviolence as a formative influence in world affairs. This is tied in obvious ways to the general emphasis on wars and strategies of warfare, and to other specific biases, and it has the most serious ramifications for the understanding and practice of peace—for the evolution of a peaceful world. This is so because to the extent that we characterize the past as the product of violent acts, so too shall we be likely to project this as our image of the present and future. There is therefore a pressing need to highlight nonviolence in history in order to counteract this imbalance of perspectives and open up the possibility of a different kind of future.

Locating Nonviolence and Peace in History

Two views, in particular, require to be challenged. The first, allied with the standard perception of world history discussed earlier, is that the story of the past is the story of war, or that war occupies a far more vast period of history overall than does peace. Historian Keith Hopwood remarks that "ancient societies . . . rested entirely on an agrarian base, exploited either by staid farmers or large-scale rentier landlords. In neither case, without profound social change or extreme technological progress, was increased production possible. Expanding population, or simply naked greed, inevitably found its expression in war. Peace might break out from time to time; it was eminently desirable, but not normal."[27] This outlook gains expression in an epigram offered by nineteenth-century philosopher Arthur Schopenhauer, a penetrating observer of human psychology and the human condition: "History shows us the life of nations and can find nothing to relate except wars and insurrections; the years of peace appear here and there only as short pauses, as intervals between the acts."[28] But one might demand to know, in response, whether this statement merely signals a defect in history, as normally written, or rather is meant to represent how things really are (or at least have been) in the story of humanity. Either way, what has been need not necessarily determine the future, as explained in the Introduction ("War Myths," Myth #6) and in Chapter 2, section 2.3 ("Human Universals"). More specifically, one can challenge the principles of selectivity that underlie such a perspective. What counts as a war in a particular time and place? Was the whole world at war, or only those states or entities deemed (perhaps owing to a Eurocentric bias, for example) to be "makers of history" in that era? And might it be the case that the definition of "peace" utilized here to make a definitive judgment is just "negative peace" (the absence of war), rather than something much broader that can geographically coexist with war, or contextualize it in such a way that we might even see a given war as an aberration from the peaceful norm?[29] Beyond this, could it be that our very concept of "history" is shaped to an inordinate degree by the (dubious) belief that aggression and violence prevail in human nature? (This last issue will be considered fully in Chapters 2 and 4.)

The second related view to be confronted and, if possible surmounted, is that peaceful periods of history—and by extension, peaceful means of making history—are uneventful; that peace and nonviolent moments in history are simply uninteresting and hence not worth wasting time over by including them in a larger account of the past. One of the characters in Thomas Hardy's play *The Dynasts* observes that "War makes rattling good history; but Peace is poor reading."[30] Well, *is* peace "poor reading"? Certainly a lot depends on what kind of reading you like, and more pertinently, what kind you are conditioned to accept as likable and therefore preferable. But bear in mind that a large part of the shift to a peaceful world must be a willingness to break out of old habits and preconceptions—about both war and peace. Indeed, a premise of this book is that while war is pretty familiar to most of us through the study of history, ceremonies of remembrance, displays of military paraphernalia, personal experience, a steady diet of media reports, and other sources, and while violence seems to be everywhere and is often glorified, peace is a relative stranger in our midst. Looking around, as Schopenhauer did (see above), one might even suppose that peace exists not so much "in our midst" as in the guise of a fringe-dweller. But, as we shall see, an alternative interpretation is possible. Cutting to the chase, a short tour through the literature of peace and the history of nonviolence reveals a very different sort of terrain and provides grounds for a judgment radically different from the one espoused above by the character in Hardy's play.

Let us have it out in the open, then: *Peace is an interesting and vital phenomenon to learn about; and the history of nonviolence in human affairs is informative, fascinating, eye-opening, and inspiring.* These points have been clearly demonstrated by a growing body of contemporary work of a scholarly and/ or documentary nature.[31] While nonviolence and peace have been actively and widely portrayed, celebrated, and promoted by literature and the arts, we will stick here to a few examples of the historical approach to our subject. In reviewing this material, we should bear in mind the observation (suggested previously in this chapter) that "What historians do best is to make connections with the past in order to illuminate the problems of the present and the potential of the future."[32] If war counts as a "problem of the present," as it surely must, and nonviolence and peace are to be found in "the potential of the future," as the text you are now reading tries to convince you, then a nonviolent perspective on history unquestionably deserves our fullest attention.

1.4. NONVIOLENCE IN HISTORY MADE VISIBLE: (II) SOME EXAMPLES

Revolutions

One might be forgiven for wondering whether revolutions could ever serve as examples of nonviolent history-in-the-making. Are they not, after all, bloody affairs almost by definition? Well, yes and no. Some are and some are not. Furthermore, it all depends on the focus of attention and on a realization that, while there are such identifiable mega-events as revolutions, each consists of many smaller events. Not only that, but there is room for argument about which of the smaller events was (or were) the most decisive. And here especially nonviolence comes to the fore.

Peace historian David Cortright records that "Latin America's indigenous communities . . . struggled over the centuries to resist assimilation by Spanish conquerors and national governments, often through nonviolent methods of mass noncooperation. In recent decades numerous Latin American social movements have utilized nonviolent action to overcome repression, end military dictatorship, and defend human rights."[33] At the time this chapter was being written, hundreds of indigenous protestors in Ecuador were on a two-week march from the Amazon rain forest to the capital, Quito, in order to demonstrate their opposition to "large-scale mining projects" they believe "will contaminate water and force people off their land."[34] These nonviolent struggles span several centuries, with, of course, mixed results. But what this slice of history shows is that the very survival and way of life of some ethnic groups in the world crucially depend on nonviolence, which indicates the existence here of a very significant source of untold stories.

It is almost a cliché of historical hindsight that revolutions occur first in the minds and hearts of people before blood is ever shed. But, in order to gauge the truth of this claim, one must respectfully listen to the judgment of history-makers like John Adams and Abraham Lincoln, both of whom argued in this manner. According to Adams, "The [American] revolution was in the minds of the people, and in the union of the colonies, both of which were accomplished before hostilities commenced."[35] Lincoln later affirmed that "The Union . . . was formed in fact by the Articles of Association of 1774."[36] Jonathan Schell observes that these perspectives focus on "the process by which ordinary people withdrew cooperation from the British government and then, well before even the Declaration of Independence, set up their own governments in all the colonies."[37] This is not to deny that smaller or micro-events of another sort—specific military campaigns and battles—were important, which of course they were, in cementing the gains that had been made by nonviolent strategies and actions. But the point is to interrogate the prevailing assumption that the larger or macro-event we call "the American Revolution" was "won" or "forged" only by violent means. While one cannot truthfully represent this revolution as wholly the product of nonviolence, at the same time, to conceptualize it entirely in terms of bloody armed conflict is to grossly distort the transformation that occurred, by eradicating the vital role that nonviolent activity played in creating a significant historical moment. And, looking back from the vantage-point of 1839, abolitionist and nonviolence advocate Charles K. Whipple provocatively declared: "We should have attained independence as effectually, as speedily, as honourably, and under very much more favourable conditions, if we had not resorted to arms."[38]

Nonviolence and Transformation

We can go on from here to acknowledge examples of historical change that are either totally or almost exclusively owing to nonviolent actions. And these should be thought about within the context of the claim, documented by Schell, Cortright, Mark Kurlansky, Elise Boulding, Gene Sharp, and others (see Bibliography), that a vast reservoir of "people power" tactics has been built up and refined over many centuries, honed by trial and error, and applied peacefully in all kinds of settings. Michael Karlberg suggests, in a reversal of perspectives, that "a proper accounting might reveal that, throughout much of history, meaningful social reform has been achieved primarily through non-adversarial means, while adversarial strategies have absorbed enormous amounts of human energy and generated significant attention yet yielded few lasting results."[39] Many of these nonviolent contributions lie well concealed within the pages of history, if they show up there at all.

In a landmark history of peace, Antony Adolf surprises us, for instance, with the suggestion that "Contrary to popular and even some academic beliefs, it may be the Middle Ages more than any other single period that has shaped modern peace principles and practices, notably by innovations in treaty-making and through the *modus vivendi* of monasticism, but in other ways as well."[40] This is in Western culture. In non-Western culture, the League of Peace and Power provides a further example: an alliance of Mohawks, Oneidas, Onondagas, Cayugas, and Seneca of northeastern North America, which "endures to this day as one of the oldest forms of participatory democracy on earth."[41] Its "Great Law of Peace" (or "Great Binding Law") was created somewhere between 900 and 1600 BCE, according to different estimates, and is described as "the world's oldest living constitution."[42] (The Tuscarora nation joined the compact in 1722.) A number of researchers have argued, over the past four decades, that some of the founders of American democracy (notably Benjamin Franklin and James DeLancy, the acting governor of New York in 1754) met with and sought council from members of this association[43] (known as the Iroquois Confederacy, Iroquois League, or Six Nations) in which, among other things, women had personal liberty, significant political and economic power and control, and a leading role in education of the young (the Iroquois were also matrilineal societies). While the thesis concerning the League's influence on the shaping of the American republic has been keenly debated by scholars, a 1988 US congressional resolution acknowledges and confirms it.[44]

Jumping over several centuries, we find instances of nations that have for lengthy periods conducted their affairs on the world stage from a position of neutrality, and/or have not engaged in any warfare, such as Sweden (since 1814), Switzerland (since 1815), Brazil (since the 1870s), and Iceland (excepting the brief "Cod War" confrontations with the UK in the 1950s and 1970s, since 1256).[45] Costa Rica, with a background of colonial occupation and twentieth-century dictatorships, has become a world capital of peace, having abandoned its army in 1949, and thereafter flourished as a modern democracy, economy, and leader in environmental protection. In fact, a 2001 study found twenty-seven countries without armies and, "In addition, at least eighteen dependent territories or geographical regions are demilitarized by agreement with the sovereignty-claiming country such as the Aland Islands of Finland, or by international treaty, including Antarctica and the Moon."[46]

Twentieth-Century Events

Recent history has revealed numerous instances in which nonviolent means of bringing about change have proved not just effective, but decisive. The successful movement for the independence of India (1949), led by Mohandas Gandhi (see Chapter 4, section 4.5, "Strategic [or Transformative] Nonviolence"), is the most straightforward example, while in South Africa, nonviolent methods (such as strikes and boycotts) and isolation by the international community were crucial factors in achieving a breakthrough—the abandonment of apartheid in the early 1990s. The fall of the Soviet Union offers a complex and interesting case, which deserves closer examination.

A commonplace view in the West on the collapse of the Soviet Union is that "capitalism (or the free market) defeated communism"; that "Reagan and Thatcher triumphed over Gorbachev." Those who subscribe to this piece of erroneous historical interpretation conveniently forget, first of all, that some form of communism still prevails in China, comprising a mere fifth of humanity, as well as North Korea, Vietnam, Laos, and Cuba. But, more importantly, they also overlook or fail to credit two crucial factors: President Mikhail Gorbachev's conciliatory and tension-reducing behavior during the Cold War, and the nonviolent protest movements that incrementally and ultimately ended the Soviet Union by making government power unviable in Russia's satellite states. Concerning the first factor, Cortright notes that "Gorbachev ordered a halt to Soviet underground nuclear testing in August 1985. This bold initiative, coinciding with the fortieth anniversary of the Hiroshima bombing, placed enormous pressure on the Reagan administration and the West." There followed a series of such initiatives from both sides, including "the unilateral demobilization of US tactical nuclear weapons from ships and submarines and the removal and dismantling of nuclear artillery and short-range missiles in Europe," undertaken by President George H. W. Bush. There is no doubt that the hawk-like stance of both Presidents Ronald Reagan and Bush were significantly toned down and their energies channeled into more productive pathways by the need to respond to Soviet arms reductions. These instances of de-escalation exhibit what Cortright calls "the power of positive reciprocity," and he rightly observes that "Disarmament initiatives and strategic concessions from the Soviet Union proved decisive in easing political tensions and reducing the dangers of the East-West nuclear stand-off."[47] Arguably, these moves and counter-moves and the flexible, forward-looking attitudes of Gorbachev created an environment in which the revolutionary momentum of 1989 in Eastern Europe could prevail. But even if one rejects or downplays his contribution, the mutual force reductions Gorbachev began stand as a prime example of the nonviolent approach to political conflict resolution in action.

An interesting bit of background to the above is that when the Soviet army rolled into Czechoslovakia two decades earlier, "[Czech leader Alexander] Dubček urged his people not to resist, despite the fact that the Czech army was considered the best in the Warsaw Pact. When the world saw the Soviet Union invade one of its closest allies, and saw its tanks stared down by unarmed students, its defeat had already begun. Mikhail Gorbachev, . . . years later, after his country had collapsed, agreed that nothing was ever the same after the 1968 invasion."[48] Here we see, once again, strong evidence of the power of nonviolence and its ability to influence the course of history. The changes it brings about may emerge slowly, but they are no less decisive for that slowness.

As already mentioned, the second neglected factor in the collapse of Soviet-style communism was the wave of resistance movements that swept Eastern Europe from 1980 onward. The Solidarity labor movement was founded in Poland in that year and, in spite of various setbacks and repressive responses, the tide of change it inspired led eventually to its participation and victory in the 1989 national parliamentary elections, followed by the formation of Eastern Europe's first noncommunist government. During 1989 and 1990, a rapid succession of demonstrations, popular uprisings, formation of opposition groups, general strikes, and civil disobedience precipitated the overthrow of regimes in Hungary, Bulgaria, Czechoslovakia, Romania, and East Germany (followed by the dismantling of the Berlin Wall and the reunification of Germany). Of these events, the only revolution marked by violence was in Romania. In 1991, the Soviet Union was dissolved and fifteen nations, including Russia, declared their independence. There followed the abandonment of communist government in Yugoslavia and Albania in 1990–92, and in other countries further afield.[49] Major catalysts to these events were Gorbachev's attempts at new policies of political openness and economic reform, and his declaration of noninterference in the sovereignty of other states.[50]

During this same period, nonviolent protest also resulted in the overthrow of Ferdinand Marcos in the Philippines. Marcos, elected president in 1965, later used martial law and other ways of usurping power in order to establish an oppressive regime and, at the same time, to enrich himself, his cronies, and selected foreign companies. Political imprisonment and torture became commonplace. The nonviolent movement against Marcos was sparked by the 1983 assassination of his leading political opponent, Benigno ("Ninoy") Aquino, Jr., who had declared, "I have concluded that revolution and violence exact the highest price in terms of human values and human lives in the struggle for freedom. In the end there are really no victors, only victims. . . . I have decided to pursue my freedom struggle through the path of nonviolence, fully cognizant that this may be the longer and more arduous road."[51] With an already well-developed Marxist guerrilla army in the country and this shocking murder, the course of events might have been expected to turn toward violent civil war and more repression. But instead, a nonviolent movement was born and spread through education in nonviolence conducted by international experts in the field and the clergy.

Marcos called a presidential election for 1986 in which he was challenged by Cory Aquino, the widow of the dead opposition leader. Several hundred nuns risked their lives to guard polling stations and ensure a fair election, but they could not prevent all irregularities from occurring. Marcos emerged as the "certified" winner, and was just about to be endorsed as such by parliament, when suddenly "thirty young computer workers involved in the official vote count left their posts . . . to protest the deliberate posting of dishonest returns. That daring act ended any credibility still enjoyed by the official returns."[52] Marcos decided to steal the election nevertheless. The Catholic Church, the minister of defense, and part of the army turned against him, supported in street rallies by huge numbers of civilians from all walks of life, from the poor to orders of nuns to the wealthiest members of society. In a moment of high drama, tanks and armed personnel carriers were confronted at point-blank range by nuns in prayer and an old woman in a wheelchair.[53] More military defections and other incidents of courageous defiance followed, eventuating in Marcos's fleeing the country and Ms. Aquino's taking over as president.

A Glimpse of the Twenty-First Century

In early 2011, massive but peaceful and persistent street demonstrations during the "Arab Spring" brought down the governments of Tunisian President

Zine El-Abidine Ben Ali, who fled the country, and Egyptian President Hosni Mubarak, who yielded to public protests calling for his resignation which had occurred daily for more than a fortnight. In Egypt, the military turned against the regime and sided with the citizens seeking civil liberties and democratization. In Algeria, a two-decades-long state of emergency was ended. In Libya, armed rebels, supported by NATO airstrikes, deposed and later killed ruler Muammar Gaddafi, clearing the way for a transition to democratic government. Leaders in Iraq and Sudan chose not to seek reelection, and other protest movements in the Middle East and North Africa are ongoing and have achieved mixed results, some having been met with a violent response from those in power. Egypt's political landscape has become polarized and bloody since its democratically elected Morsi government was ousted by the military in July 2013. Certainly it is too early to pass judgment on this period with finality (or on the results of any other nonviolent change of regimes discussed earlier), but the gains of nonviolence in action are already substantial.

1.5. A POSTSCRIPT ON NONVIOLENCE IN HISTORY

Nonviolence on Trial

In his 2009 Nobel Peace Prize acceptance speech, US President Barack Obama declared that "A non-violent movement could not have halted Hitler's armies."[54] This old chestnut is meant to be the ultimate refutation of the belief that nonviolence is the most effective and therefore best way to confront and overcome violence and repression. (It is not even *a* way to do so, according to those who take this approach.) The subtext of Obama's remark appears to be that if a strategic or tactical approach cannot solve *all* problems, then it cannot solve *any*. But the fallaciousness of such a statement is so manifest that it needs no refutation; for if this were the case, then any plan of action that can be named would deserve consignment to the rubbish bin of history. None works in every instance and—not to be downplayed—the record of success for violent methods in achieving their objectives is anything but cause for celebration. (More on this topic can be found in the Introduction and Chapter 4.) Beyond this point, however, it is worth noting that every counterfactual claim about the past is equally unverifiable and irrefutable. It must be assumed that President Obama chooses his words very carefully. Notice then that he says not just that a nonviolent movement *would not* have stopped Hitler, but that it *could not* have achieved this end. However, in principle, we do not and cannot know whether anything that might have been tried in history would (or would not) and therefore could (or could not) have produced a different result—simply because we cannot rerun the past in order to find out. Any opinion on the matter, then, is sheer speculation. But observe that this cuts both ways: There is no basis for judging whether nonviolence could not have halted Hitler *or* that it could have. Neither critics nor proponents of the case for nonviolence, then, can gain any leverage from speculating on what might have been, but wasn't. So this debate is a nonstarter, whether one is an advocate of nonviolence, a skeptic, or even a proponent of violence.

Putting nonviolence on trial in the manner of Obama is also problematic in another sense. This is because the question: "Could nonviolence have stopped Hitler?" is open to more than one interpretation. If it is taken to mean (as Obama obviously intended): "Could forms of nonviolent resistance have defeated the Nazi juggernaut in battle or in the midst of its rolling over weaker countries?" then the incontestable answer would seem to be: "No, certainly not." But if instead the question being asked is rephrased in this way: "Could Hitler's rise to power have been thwarted by nonviolent campaigns?" then the answer is not so apparent; the only thing we do know is that this tactic wasn't tried in any ongoing, large-scale manner. (This is an instance of a bigger issue: Nonviolence cannot be written off as an inadequate or failed response to particular human problems if it has not been tried as a means to solving them.) Now we cannot replay the events of Hitler's rise to power, any more than we can replay those of World War II, in order to test an alternate hypothesis about history. However, there is one further interpretation of our question that *does* provide some room for argument: "Could nonviolent strategies have made a difference to the pursuit of Hitler's war aims?" And the reason why it leaves room for argument is that not only *could* they have done so, they *actually did* do so. Therefore, let us look for a moment at the historical record for a few examples of what was accomplished by nonviolence against Nazism during World War II.

Nonviolence against Nazism

Even though various plots to assassinate Hitler failed, there were several incidents in which high-ranking military officers and regional administrators either ignored or deliberately neglected to pass orders through the chain of command so that the orders would not be carried out. For instance, "*Reichskommissar* Erich Koch of the Ukraine was directed by the East Ministry on September 7, 1942, to seize all Jewish and other abandoned property and to use former Ukrainian officers and civil servants for the job. Koch, however, ignored the order and on March 16, 1943, informed Alfred Rosenberg [his superior] that the decree was a 'political and organizational impossibility.'"[55]

Hitler's armies invaded Denmark with ease in 1940, the Danish government having wisely decided not to resist. The story of what happened after that is not unequivocal. The Danish government went through stages of surrender to occupying forces, collaboration, cooperation (in the hopes of shielding citizens from harsh measures), resistance to Nazi demands, and, in some instances, and increasingly over time, refusal to carry them out. King Christian X vowed, in the face of a German death-threat, that he would himself remove any swastika flag flown over Amalienborg Castle in Copenhagen, with the result that it never was. In spite of the fact that Danes were conscripted into pro-Nazi fighting units and compelled to produce war materiel for the Germans, a steady rise in underground activities, protests, general strikes, and other forms of noncooperation and unarmed defiance made the occupation of Denmark a difficult task for Hitler's soldiers and administrators, especially when the Germans were facing defeats elsewhere in Europe in the later years of the war. Danish acts of sabotage were also widespread, and these cannot be counted as examples of nonviolence. But certainly there are things that do count, such as underground newspapers, nationwide strikes (notwithstanding curfews, lethal reprisals, and periods of martial law), as well as the hiding and clandestine nighttime ferrying of more than 7,000 Danish Jews to safety in neutral Sweden during 1943–44. As Peter Ackerman and Jack Duvall reflect, "If the Nazis, the cruelest killing machine in the [twentieth] century's history, could be kept off balance by Danish schoolboys, amateur saboteurs, and underground clergymen, what other regime should ever be thought invulnerable to nonviolent resistance?"[56] Even though Danish noncooperation did not end the war, stop Hitler in his tracks, expel the Nazis from Denmark, or perhaps even make that big a difference in the overall scheme of things, it is plainly true that much more was achieved by nonviolent resistance there than could ever have been achieved by the suicidal slaughter of the Danish army on the battlefield.

French historian and political scientist Jacques Sémelin, who has carefully studied nonviolent resistance to the Nazis, writes that "The rescue of the Jews owes its success to the strength of this social cohesion among the Danish population." He adds that it was "one of the most remarkable events of the war."[57] Nonviolent methods also saved many Jews from deportation to concentration camps from Bulgaria, Romania, France, Belgium, and Finland. Many Jews were deported from these countries, but many others were spared that fate by the actions of their fellow citizens. In one striking episode, after an official Nazi deportation order was issued for Bulgarian Jews, a leading prelate of that country helped defeat it when he publicly vowed to conduct a "campaign of civil disobedience including personally lying down on the railroad tracks before the deportation trains, if the planned operation was carried out."[58]

Sémelin relates that German generals interviewed after the war revealed that they had experienced bafflement and frustration when confronted by nonviolent resistance movements.[59]

Even from within the heart of Nazi Germany (Berlin) at the worst period (1943), a small success story concerning nonviolent activism can be reported. After the extermination of most German Jews, Hitler's regime proceeded to imprison at their workplaces Jews who had non-Jewish spouses. Women whose husbands were among the missing began a protest vigil outside the incarceration center, vocally demanding their release. Only a handful of women at first, the demonstration soon attracted hundreds more. As is well documented: "In spite of the interventions of the Berlin police and the SS brigade, who threatened to shoot into the crowd, the protests continued. The police managed to disperse the group, but it gathered again every day. From February 27 to March 5, 1943, in the coldest weather, this group of women, joined by up to 600 men, protested in the streets of Berlin until their spouses were released, starting on March 6."[60] We can never know how well similar protests—had there been any—would have fared, nor whether, if they had come early enough, they might have stopped Hitler in his tracks, or at any rate scuttled his "final solution" of the "Jewish problem." But it is intriguing to imagine the possibility of wholly different outcomes than those unfortunate ones that constitute part of the history of this sorry period.

Psychologist Philip Zimbardo argues that the potential for performing both evil actions and heroic good deeds resides within each of us, and that how we choose to react to situations we find ourselves in determines which we decide for.[61] (Of course, we can also choose to do nothing when facing a challenge.) The reasons for these choices are not clearly understood. But Zimbardo asserts that in spite of all the horrors humans perpetrate on their own kind, heroic good deeds are commonplace, as we see in the above examples of nonviolent resistance to the Nazis.

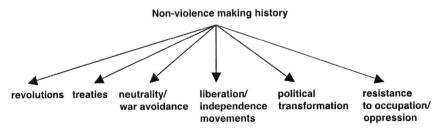

Figure 1.1 Nonviolence making history

A Different Perspective on History

The general point of this chapter can now be stated quite simply. While history as a narrative is open to various kinds of abuse, bias, and distortion, our main concern has been its lack of attention to the role that nonviolent actions have played in shaping major events. This is not an issue about what might have occurred, could have occurred, or would have occurred if diverse scenarios had developed differently. Nor is it one of neglecting to record the history of nonviolence, for that has been thoroughly done by numerous scholarly authors. As well, an ongoing file of nonviolent contributions to history is being maintained by the International Center on Nonviolence.[62] Finally, it is not about disputing the fact that wars have importantly shaped the course of history. Rather, it is an issue about failing to assign any weight at all—much less the weight that is due—to the actual, positive contributions of nonviolence in the continuing story of humanity. The aim here has been to remedy this fault.

NOTES TO CHAPTER 1

1. V. S. Naipaul, *A Turn in the South* (London: Picador, 2011), p. 86.
2. Product description for Kathleen Troup and Anna Green, eds., *The Houses of History: A Critical Reader in Twentieth-Century History and Theory* (New York: New York University Press, 1999). Retrieved from Amazon.com.
3. Stuart Macintyre, "Introduction," in *The Historian's Conscience: Australian Historians on the Ethics of History*, ed. Stuart Macintyre (Melbourne: Melbourne University Press, 2004), p. 14.
4. For example, Eric Foner, *Who Owns History? Rethinking the Past in a Changing World* (New York: Hill and Wang, 2003).
5. Marilyn Lake, "On History and Politics," in *Historian's Conscience*, ed. Macintyre, p. 104.
6. Christopher R. Leahy, *Whitewashing War: Historical Myth, Corporate Textbooks, and Possibilities for Democratic Education* (New York: Teachers College Press, 2010); James W. Loewen, "Introduction: History as Weapon," in *Teaching What Really Happened: How to Avoid the Tyranny of Textbooks and Get Students Excited about Doing History* (New York: Teachers College Press, 2009); Gary B. Nash, Charlotte Crabtree, and Ross E. Dunn, *History on Trial: Culture Wars and the Teaching of the Past* (New York: Vintage Books, 2000); James W. Loewen, *Lies My Teacher Told Me: Everything Your American History Textbook Got Wrong*, rev. ed. (New York: Touchstone, 2007).
7. See, for example, Erna Paris, *Long Shadows: Truth, Lies, and History* (New York: Bloomsbury USA, 2002).
8. See Dione Brand, *A Map to the Door of No Return* (Toronto: Random House Canada, 2001).
9. See Christopher Butler, *Postmodernism: A Very Short Introduction* (Oxford: Oxford University Press, 2002), pp. 32–6.

10. Martha Howell and Walter Prevenier, *From Reliable Sources: An Introduction to Historical Methods* (Ithaca, NY: Cornell University Press, 2001), p. 84.

11. Ambrose Bierce, *The Enlarged Devil's Dictionary*, ed. Ernest Jerome Hopkins (London: Victor Gollancz, 1967), p. 134.

12. Howard Zinn, *A People's History of the United States* (New York: Harper Perennial, 2010).

13. This may be more a statement about how history is taught than about how it is written today, for as Howell and Prevenier observe, "After World War II . . . historians mined the archives for facts about social life—the family, health, poverty. More recently, the history of what the French call mentalités (attitudes, patterns of thought, culture in its most general sense) has become a central concern of the profession. . . ." (*From Reliable Sources*, p. 85).

14. Anna Clark, *History's Children: History Wars in the Classroom* (Sydney: University of New South Wales Press, 2008); Marilyn Lake and Henry Reynolds, *What's Wrong with Anzac? The Militarisation of Australian History* (Sydney: University of New South Wales Press, 2010). See also extensive critical comments on these books by Robert Lewis in customer reviews of Lake and Reynolds at Amazon.com.

15. Ian McKay and Jamie Swift, "What's Wrong with Celebrating the War of 1812?" ActiveHistory.ca, 16 May 2012; http://activehistory.ca/2012/05/whats-with-celebrating-the-war-of-1812.

16. Glenda Sluga, "Whose History?" in *Historian's Conscience*, ed. Macintyre, pp. 135–6.

17. John B. Quigley, *The Ruses for War: American Interventionism Since World War II* (Amherst, NY: Prometheus Books, 2007).

18. See Michael Allen Fox, "The Nuclear Mindset: Motivational Obstacles to Peace," in *Nuclear War: Philosophical Perspectives*, ed. Michael Allen Fox and Leo Groarke, 2nd ed. (New York: Peter Lang, 1987), pp. 113–29.

19. John Pilger Interview, *New Internationalist* 438 (December 2010), p. 26.

20. Leahey, *Whitewashing War*, p. 1.

21. Leahey, *Whitewashing War*, pp. 88, 92, 64. See also Bill Bigelow, "Camouflaging the Vietnam War: How Textbooks Continue to Keep the Pentagon Papers Secret," *GOOD Magazine*, 18 June 2013; http://www.good.is/posts/camouflaging-the-vietnam-war-how-textbooks-continue-to-keep-the-pentagon-papers-secret.

22. John Pilger Interview, pp. 26–7.

23. David Livingstone Smith, *The Most Dangerous Animal: Human Nature and the Origins of War* (New York: St. Martin's Griffin, 2007), p. 7.

24. See, for example, Jonathan Mercer, "Emotional Beliefs," *International Organization* 64 (2010), pp. 1–31. I am grateful to Louise Noble for drawing my attention to Mercer's work.

25. George Santayana, *The Life of Reason; Or, The Phases of Human Progress*, 5 vols. (New York: Charles Scribner's Sons, 1905), v.1: *Reason in Common Sense*, p. 284.

26. Edward S. Herman and Noam Chomsky, *Manufacturing Consent: The Political Economy of the Mass Media* (New York: Pantheon Books, 1988), p. 300.

27. Keith Hopwood, "Peace in the Ancient World," in *World Encyclopedia of Peace*, ed. Javier Perez De Cuellar and Young Seek Choue, 2nd ed. (Dobbs Ferry, NY: Oceana, 1999), vol. 4, p. 216.

28. Arthur Schopenhauer, "Additional Remarks on the Doctrine of the Suffering of the World," *Parerga and Paralipomena: Short Philosophical Essays*, trans. E. F. J. Payne (Oxford: Oxford University Press, 1974), vol. 2, chap. XI, sec. 150.

29. This point is inspired by an observation of Antony Adolf's in *Peace: A World History* (Cambridge, UK: Polity Press, 2009), p. 1.

30. Thomas Hardy, *The Dynasts: An Epic-Drama* (London: Macmillan, 1978), pt. I, act 2, sc. 5, p. 88.

31. See, for example, James C. Juhnke and Carol M. Hunter, *The Missing Peace: The Search for Nonviolent Alternatives in United States History*, 2nd ed. (Kitchener, ON, Canada: Pandora Press, 2004); Maciej Bartkowski, ed., *Recovering Nonviolent History: Civil Resistance in Liberation Struggles* (Boulder, CO: Lynne Rienner, 2013).

32. Joyce Appleby, Lynn Hunt, and Margaret Jacob, "Telling the Truth about History," in *The Postmodern History Reader*, ed. Keith Jenkins (London: Routledge, 1997), p. 216.

33. David Cortright, *Peace: A History of Movements and Ideas* (Cambridge, UK: Cambridge University Press, 2008), pp. 12–13.

34. "Ecuador Indigenous Protestors March against Mining," BBC News, 8 March 2012; http://www.bbc.co.uk/news/world-latin-america-17306228.

35. John Adams, *The Works of John Adams* (Boston: Little, Brown, 1956), vol. 10, p. 180. This theme is explored further by Walter H. Conser, Jr. in "The United States: Reconsidering the Struggle for Independence, 1765–1775," in *Recovering Nonviolent History*, ed. Bartkowski, chap. 16.

36. Abraham Lincoln, cited by Mario Cuomo, *Lincoln on Democracy* (New York: HarperCollins, 1990), p. 204.

37. Jonathan Schell, *The Unconquerable World: Power, Nonviolence, and the Will of the People* (New York: Metropolitan/Owl Books, 2003), pp. 161–2.

38. Charles K. Whipple, *Evils of the Revolutionary War* (Boston: New England Non-Resistance Society, 1839), p. 2.

39. Michael Karlberg, *Beyond the Culture of Contest: From Adversarialism to Mutualism in an Age of Interdependence* (Oxford: George Ronald, 2004), p. 183.

40. Adolf, *Peace: A World History*, p. 103 (emphasis in original).

41. "Deganawidah (Wyandor [Huron]) (fl. 1100–1150)," in *The Encyclopedia of Native American Legal Tradition*, ed. Bruce E. Johansen (Westport, CT: Greenwood Press, 1998), p. 81.

42. Joseph Bruchac, ed., *Native Wisdom* (San Francisco: HarperSanFrancisco, 1995), p. 19.

43. "Albany Plan of Union (1754)," in *Encyclopedia of Native American Legal Tradition*, ed. Johansen, pp. 11–13.

44. 100th Congress, 2nd Session, H. Con. Res. 331, 4 October 1988; http://www.senate.gov/reference/resources/pdf/hconres331.pdf.

45. Although Iceland belongs to NATO, "it is the only NATO country with no standing military of its own" ("Background Note: Iceland," US State Department, Bureau of European and Eurasian Affairs, 8 November 2011; http://www.state.gov/r/pa/ei/bgn/3396.htm).

46. Glenn D. Paige, *Nonkilling Global Political Science*, 2nd ed. (LaVergne, TN: Xlibris, 2007), p. 45. See also Christophe Barbey, "Nonmilitarisation and Countries without

Armies," in Joám Evans Pim, ed., *Nonkilling Security and the State* (Honolulu: Center for Global Nonkilling, 2013), pp. 153–76.

47. Cortright, *Peace*, pp. 153–4.

48. Mark Kurlansky, *Nonviolence: The History of a Dangerous Idea* (London: Jonathan Cape, 2006), p. 172.

49. "Revolutions of 1989," *Wikipedia*; http://en.wikipedia.org/wiki/Revolutions_of_1989# Poland.

50. Peter Ackerman and Jack Duvall, *A Force More Powerful: A Century of Nonviolent Conflict* (New York: Palgrave, 2000), p. 427.

51. Benigno Aquino, Jr., statement to US House of Representatives Subcommittee on Asian and Pacific Affairs, 23 June 1983; cited by Ronald J. Sider, *Non-Violence: The Invincible Weapon?* (Dallas: Word Publishing, 1989), p. 57.

52. Sider, *Non-Violence*, p. 62.

53. Sider, *Non-Violence*, p. 66.

54. Barack Obama, Nobel Prize acceptance speech, 10 December 2009; available at: http://www.whitehouse.gov/the-press-office/remarks-president-acceptance-nobel-peace-prize.

55. Gene Sharp, *The Politics of Nonviolent Action* (Boston: Extending Horizons Books, 1973), p. 323 (emphasis in original).

56. Ackerman and Duvall, *Force More Powerful*, p. 231.

57. Jacques Sémelin, *Unarmed Against Hitler: Civilian Resistance in Europe, 1939–1943*, trans. Suzan Husserl-Kapit (Westport, CT: Praeger, 1993), pp. 153, 154.

58. Frederick B. Chary, *The Bulgarian Jews and the Final Solution (1940–1944)* (Pittsburgh: University of Pittsburgh Press, 1972), p. 90.

59. Sémelin, *Unarmed Against Hitler*, p. 120.

60. Sémelin, *Unarmed Against Hitler*, p. 143.

61. Philip Zimbardo, *The Lucifer Effect: How Good People Turn Evil* (New York: Random House, 2007).

62. See International Center on Nonviolent Conflict, "Nonviolent Conflict"; http://www.nonviolent-conflict.org.

Peaceful Societies and Human Potential

Don't tell me peace has broken out. . . .

> —Bertolt Brecht, *Mother Courage and Her Children*

To jaw-jaw is always better than to war-war.

> —Winston Churchill, remarks at a White House luncheon, 26 June 1954

War is not a primordial biological "curse." It is a cultural innovation, an especially vicious, persistent meme, which culture can help us transcend.

> —John Horgan, "No, War Is Not Inevitable," *Discover*, June 2012

2.1. A FUTURE WITHOUT WAR?

Grounds for Discouragement and Optimism

The future unfolds from our thoughts about the present, and our hopes hang on estimating the chances that events will take a certain course. And what we think about in this respect depends very much on the input of information we receive daily. On a single morning, during the writing of this chapter, the following news items were reported:

- Lone US soldier in the province of Kandahar, Afghanistan, leaves his base in predawn hours, invades local citizens' homes, and kills sixteen, including women and children, creating huge waves of hatred against Americans.

- Russia and China continue to block UN action on Syria, where thousands of rebels and noncombatants have died in assaults by the Assad regime's military machine. Diplomat Kofi Annan leaves Syria, having failed in his initial attempt to mediate the conflict.
- Israeli warplanes attack Gaza for the fourth day as Palestinians fire rockets into Israel. Twenty-five Palestinians are killed, and eighty, including eight Israelis, are wounded.
- Death squads in Iraq target gay men and teenagers dressed and styled to imitate American "emo" subculture. Between sixty and two hundred believed murdered in recent years, and Shi'ite militias circulate additional "hit lists."
- Suicide bomber kills fifteen and wounds thirty at a funeral in northwest Pakistan. His apparent target: an anti-terrorist politician who escapes unharmed.[1]

When we hear such dismal news, peace seems impossibly beyond grasp, and a feeling of despair and helplessness seeps into our consciousness, in spite of ourselves.

But what you *do not* typically find in the media headlines are stories like this:

- "The international target to halve the number of people without access to safe drinking water was met five years before the 2015 deadline, the UN announces. Between 1990 and 2010 more than 2 billion people gained access to improved drinking water sources."[2]
- "[T]he World Bank has announced that . . . the global target of cutting by half the proportion of people living in extreme poverty was achieved in 2010. In addition, the number of people living in extreme poverty has also declined in all regions of the world, including in Africa where challenges are greatest. . . ."
- "[T]he world has made progress in driving down tuberculosis, with 40 percent fewer deaths compared to 1990, and global malaria deaths have declined by nearly a third over the past decade."
- "[Globally] we now see near parity in primary education between girls and boys."
- "[W]e have achieved the MDG [Millennium Development Goals] target of significantly improving the lives of at least 100 million slum dwellers— ten years in advance of the 2020 deadline."[3]
- UNICEF announces that the global infant mortality rate has nearly halved since 1990.[4]

- "Never in history have the living conditions and prospects of so many people changed so dramatically and so fast," says the UN's 2013 Human Development Report.[5] A commentator notes that "Today, millions of people around the world are living longer, healthier, freer, safer and more prosperous lives than ever before in human history—and we have the data to prove it."[6]

- Meanwhile, Liberia reelects the first female head of state in Africa, Ellen Johnson Sirleaf (2011). Thailand elects first female prime minister, Yingluck Shinawatra (2011). Denmark elects first female prime minister, Helle Thorning-Schmidt (2011). Malawi elects first female president, Joyce Banda (2012). South Korea elects first female president, Park Geun-hye (2012). Canada now has six women premiers/territory heads of government, including the first openly gay premier (Kathleen Wynne, elected in Ontario, 2013). In addition, since 2009, women have either been elected, appointed, or have succeeded to the position of president, prime minister, or premier in Australia, Bangladesh, Bermuda, Brazil, Costa Rica, Finland, Guinea Bissau, Iceland, Jamaica, Kosovo, Krgyzstan, Lithuania, Mauritius, Serbia, Sint Maarten, Slovakia, Switzerland, and Trinidad and Tobago. Fatou Bensouda of Gambia is appointed the first female chief prosecutor of the International Criminal Court (2012). Nkosazana Dlamini-Zuma is elected first female head of African Union (2012). The current managing directors of the World Bank and the International Monetary Fund are both women (Caroline Anstey and Christine Lagarde, respectively).

- Ecuador rises from economic chaos to unprecedented new prosperity.[7] Rwanda achieves impressive gains in economic recovery and social development since the 1994 genocide, with women playing a key role, including world-leading majority representation in parliament.[8] Sierra Leone, after ten years of civil war, registers the world's highest growth rate (35 percent), as its diamond trade is freed from criminal control.[9] Hopes rise for Somalia with installation of its first functional government since 1991, adoption of a new constitution, routing of militant Islamists, and return of expatriates.[10]

- Guinea worm disease, a parasitic infection formerly affecting millions in the world's poorest areas, is on the verge of becoming the second disease (after smallpox) to be completely eradicated.[11]

- The 2012 London Olympic Games make history by being the first in which women are represented on the team of every participating country.

It is an interesting question to ponder, why these accomplishments, advances, and success stories are not featured in loud and clear terms on radio, TV, and in the press. Much has been spoken about the sensationalism and negativism of the media, which will not be reiterated here. Suffice it to say that we are seriously shortchanged by neglect of positive news, and that this has an equally serious impact on our ability to think about peace and the prospects for peace and peaceful progress. As one observer remarks, for example, "Africa's progress. . . . [is] far removed from the usual stereotypes presented by much of the media and their allies in the aid lobby. They offer simplistic images of death and destruction, ignoring the complex realities of a continent encompassing 54 countries and 30 million square kilometers in which life is becoming more peaceful and prosperous."[12]

Do human beings have the ability to bring about a peaceful world and to live in a sustainable state of nonviolent coexistence with one another? This is a great unknown—perhaps the greatest there is in human affairs. And it might be easy to assume that a negative answer to our question is obvious. The global *Conflict Barometer 2012* of the Heidelberg Institute for International Conflict Research, for instance, reveals "the highest number of violent conflicts ever observed." While high levels of violence characterize a large proportion of political conflicts studied by the Institute, many go on nonviolently, or with only sporadic violence.[13] Nevertheless, the findings of this study suggest a fairly dismal prognosis for world peace. But a broader perspective is needed in order to come to any sensible judgment on the matter of where things might be heading—especially if we want to try to gain a sense of optimism and encouragement. (See also Chapter 7, pages 277–9.)

Several authors have argued, in contrast to the above assessment, that, as measured by objective criteria, wars and war casualties are on the decline in the present age. Although some confine this claim to wars between nations, international relations professor Joshua Goldstein has recently defended it in a more general fashion:

> the last decade has seen *fewer war deaths* than any decade in the past 100 years. . . . Far from being an age of killer anarchy, the 20 years since the Cold War ended have been an era of rapid progress toward peace. . . . The last conflict between two great powers, the Korean War, effectively ended nearly 60 years ago. The last sustained territorial war between two regular armies, Ethiopia and Eritrea, ended a decade ago. Even civil wars, though a persistent evil, are less common than in the past; there were about a quarter fewer in 2007 than in 1990. If the world feels like a more violent place than it actually is, that's because there's more information about wars—not more wars themselves. . . . When U.S. forces come home from the current wars . . . there will be fewer U.S. troops deployed around the world than at any time since the 1930s.[14]

The Geneva Declaration on Armed Violence and Development asserts that, although armed conflict has declined, civil armed violence is on the increase, while the Human Security Report Project affirms a decline in international armed conflicts and the death toll that they claim.[15] Even more importantly, the Project discloses that "Peace agreements today are more stable than is usually assumed. And conflicts that restart in the wake of peace agreements that break down still see a dramatic reduction—some 80 percent, on average—in annual battle-death tolls. Peace agreements, in other words, succeed in saving lives even when they 'fail.'"[16]

One ought, of course, to reserve judgment in the face of such apparently contradictory evaluations (Heidelberg Institute vs. the rest, for example). But if we focus on the prevalence of *nonviolent conflicts* (some of which get resolved, others of which are ongoing), there has to be some room for hope. Attitudes tolerant of and conducive to war have become more open to critical examination and rebuttal, and meanwhile, international peacekeeping and various conflict-resolution efforts increasingly make their mark. Of course, terrorist activities continue, there are seemingly intractable hostilities in certain places, global armaments expenditures are soaring (as we saw in the Introduction), and fears grow of armed struggles over resources, territories, and international influence. How these problems will be dealt with is unpredictable, but this should not blind us to the beacons of hope that exist.

The Secret Peace, by Jesse Richards, builds on statistics showing positive worldwide historical and contemporary developments in peace, technology, health, the alleviation of poverty, and other areas, which are seldom highlighted by the mainstream media. Much of the case he makes depends upon showing how significantly better off people are today in general (worldwide) than ever before, as measured by numerous criteria of the quality of life. According to Richards' account, "peace is on its way. . . . [and] for much of the world, peace is already here."[17] Of course, a lot depends on what is meant by "peace," as we'll see later on, but one can hardly not sit up and take note of such findings.

Another encouraging sign comes from a landmark book by psychologist Steven Pinker, which documents the decline of violence over many centuries. *The Better Angels of Our Nature* is a monumental and detailed study, more than 800 pages in length; and, having barely appeared in print, it had already created controversy and attracted both lavish praise and strong negative criticism. Debate over it will no doubt continue for some time, but Pinker's thesis is intriguing in a major way:

> Believe it or not—and I know that most people do not—violence has declined over long stretches of time, and today we may be living in the most peaceable era in our species' existence. The decline, to be sure, has not been smooth; it has not brought violence down to zero; and it is not guaranteed to continue. But it is an unmistakable development,

visible on scales from millennia to years, from the waging of wars to the spanking of children.[18]

His explanation for this phenomenon, backed up by many statistics, cites changes in human settlement, sociopolitical organization, ethical ideas, and other factors as converging toward the general reduction of violence in the world.

Former US president, philanthropist, and ambassador-at-large Bill Clinton, in a *Time* magazine cover story, lays out "the case for optimism" by describing five factors making for a better world: the impact of mobile phones on equality; construction of health-care systems in developing countries; the growth of green energy; the advancement of women; and future planning that involves a broad spectrum of interests. He draws attention to many examples of cooperation between governments, the private sector, NGOs, and grassroots activists.[19]

Meanwhile, some authors are making the case for a materially better future for everyone. Matt Ridley explains, in *The Rational Optimist*, that human specialization and the ability to engage in trade for mutual advantage have spurred progress throughout the ages.[20] These factors will continue to improve the human condition indefinitely into the future. In *Abundance*, Peter Diamandis and Steven Kotler attempt to show how a combination of universally accessible technology, innovation, philanthropic generosity, and investment will bring about a new world of peace and plenty.[21]

Disturbing Trends and Prospects for Change

Thinking about the future (and preparing for it today) must take into account other realities as well, in particular, trends that have the potential to degrade the quest for peace and security in people's lives. One is the increase in world population. In 2012 the UN revised its estimate of future population growth, based on a "medium variant" (middle-of-the-pack) projection, and now states that the likely global population in 2050 will be 9.6 billion (a one-third increase over the present level).[22] The total could be higher or lower, and could continue rising, subject to several variables (fertility rates, life expectancy, and infant mortality in different countries, for example). The UN figures are not indisputable; however, what is certain is that there will be a major jump in world population over the present century, with a huge impact on "the ability to provide food, water, energy, education and employment for millions of people in the world's poorest nations."[23]

An unsettling trend that is also underway is the development of robot war machines and the proliferation of cyberwar.[24] Automated devices (such as vending machines) have been with us for a long time, as have computer-assisted activities (like aircraft autopiloting) and computer-controlled applications initiated by human decisions (heat-seeking missiles, for example). Robotic machines (including nano-devices now being conceived) offer benefits, to be sure, in areas like dangerous missions (such as clearing minefields, searching for survivors in mining accidents, or handling radioactive materials), delicate types of surgery, accident-prevention systems in passenger cars, and elsewhere. Many types of robotic and computer-assisted or computer-controlled inventions are already at work in war—drone aircraft, remotely operated car searchers, and disarmers of improvised explosive devices being well-established instances. What is most worrying, though, is the advent of autonomous systems, designed to act in situations where time does not allow for human intervention. "Autonomous systems . . . perform much more complex tasks by taking thousands of readings from the environment. These translate to a near-infinite number of input states, which must be processed through lengthy computer code to find the best possible outcome. Some believe it is the same basic method we use to make decisions ourselves," says one author.[25] These are the robots of the not-too-distant future, some artificial-intelligence researchers believe, and they present the possibility of machines that are beyond the control of their inventors, both in their performance and perhaps also in relation to the use of their own powers, although others profess skepticism about their feasibility and/or likelihood of running completely amok. On the positive side, it has been suggested that robotic systems might be programmed with an "artificial conscience" to make better, more consistently ethical decisions than do humans in difficult circumstances of engagement.[26] Science writer and futurist Jon Turney maintains that whatever kinds of robots will be deployed next in armed combat, "Battle robots that actually work would make wars easier to wage, and thus more tempting to enter." He also points out that "the arrival of robots on the battlefield continues the long-running trend of distancing users of weapons from the consequences," which is arguably one of the most serious developments in modern warfare.[27]

Spying and sabotage are nothing new, of course, but what the world is experiencing in the arena of cyberwar is forms of these old practices that can be conducted remotely and unaccountably, like robotic warfare, and also without detection or at any rate anonymously. The era that is unfolding has been labeled "the first global electronic arms race," and the targets are a foreign country's "infrastructure and economy"[28] (for example, financial markets, public transportation systems, power grids, corporate databases). (Also in this category could be placed WikiLeaks-style use of restricted electronic documents for the purposes of political exposé and public humiliation/punishment of governments, and hacking in support of self-selected causes by the group Anonymous.) As has been known for a long time, "the control of information is critical to determining which side wins a war";[29] what is not so clear yet is whether cyberwar has the capacity to become full-scale war in its own right. The United States, the United Kingdom, and Australia claim somewhere between hundreds and millions of hacking attempts on their treasury, defense, and other computer systems, and consideration is being given, in the United States at any rate, to retaliation by means of military force against the most serious forms of cyberattack.[30] Fears have also been raised that terrorists or other entities could one day "use cybertrickery to co-opt . . . weapons systems, perhaps including nuclear arms."[31] It is difficult to tell where all of this is going, but the short-term signs are mostly ominous. (An exception is "cyberwar games" in which the United States and China are currently engaging, in an attempt to reduce mutual suspicions and risks of future conflict. Russia and the United States also plan to use secure communications "in the effort to ensure that misperceptions in cyberspace do not escalate to full hostilities."[32])

The integrity of the Internet is a much larger issue, even than that of cyberwarfare. Efforts to limit access to the Internet in certain ways continue to be tried out in some countries, and are discussed openly in others. But while such proposals are perhaps well-intentioned in a few contexts (such as limiting the availability of child pornography and hate propaganda online), they quickly run aground on doubts about their likelihood of working at all, let alone achieving the desired result, on the one hand, and concern over the right to freedom of expression and information, on the other. The latter issue has become especially pointed in view of the important role electronic communications have played in contemporary dramas such as the "Arab Spring" uprisings in the Middle East and North Africa.

There is an inherent momentum to technology. Not that it is a law unto itself or a force we cannot control, but there is a certain mentality among humans, operating sometimes consciously, sometimes only semiconsciously, that says in effect that ends which can be advanced via technological innovations will, should, or must be pursued. The results of this process have proven both beneficial and unfortunate. (Not only that, but destructive and constructive outcomes are often intertwined; as noted in the Introduction, inventiveness that begins with military applications in mind also produces certain dividends for society at large.) The focus here, however, is on the negative implications of pursuing inventions and discoveries that, so far as can be judged, have no apparent goal other than to expand the repertoire of violent and harmful means to achieve political ends. And the worry is whether we will decide (or perhaps at a later stage, even can decide) to control them.

An imponderable in relation to the technology of possible future wars is whether things like robots and cyberwar possess net advantage or disadvantage for those who utilize them. Why? Because when "breakthroughs" in war-making technology appear on the scene, not only one but many countries eventually gain the same or a similar capacity, which negates the original strategic and tactical benefit of having them, and may even lead to a stalemate where their use is unthinkable and, consequently, where the desirability of negotiations to curtail their use becomes apparent. This situation has been evident, most notably, in the case of nuclear weapons. To be sure, the logic of events suggested here does not close out the danger that someone might nevertheless utilize a new technology for self-aggrandizement, but it does open up the possibility that other avenues to resolving conflict might evolve that do not depend on innovations in methods of destruction. At least we can hope that human decision-makers, learning as they go, can be moved in this direction and will eventually see more clearly the positive side of doing so.

It would seem evident, then, that in order to think about a future without war, we must be able to posit the possibility of people changing—of their calling a halt to policies and practices that perpetuate war as a central feature of human life, and to projects that develop new war-making skills and endlessly drain off economic and human resources in the service of war, creating further insecurities for everyone. But why should we entertain the idea that humans *are* capable of this kind and magnitude of change, of being motivated to change, or even of being interested in changing, in order to avoid future war? Where can we look for inspiration and reassurance about these matters? The short answer is: to *what makes us human*. Accordingly, the rest of this chapter explores widely gathered information about human societies, as well as fresh thinking about human nature and evolution. The extent of peacefulness prevailing in everyday circumstances will also be considered.

2.2. EARLY HUMANS AND WAR

There is a considerable body of research on the origins of war and on peaceful societies. The field is in a certain amount of turmoil because of conflicting judgments about human nature and about the evidence available from which knowledge of the dim past can reasonably be constructed. Riane Eisler's *The Chalice and the Blade* created a stir in the 1980s owing to its argument that prehistoric peoples (before approximately 5000 BCE) organized themselves according to peaceful, "partnership" principles. She hypothesizes that they were female-positive, more egalitarian than not, and respectful of the natural world around them. Examples are the early Neolithic culture of Çatal Hüyük (in what is now Turkey) and that of Minoan Crete, which flourished from about 6000 BCE until it came under Greek rule around 1450 BCE. Archaeological support for Eisler's thesis is drawn from wall paintings in which the absence of warlike imagery is striking; from artifacts indicating worship of female deities, from burial sites in which nonhierarchical practices prevail, and from other data. Somewhere in the neighborhood of 7,000 years ago, she asserts, things began to change for various, not clearly understood reasons, and "dominator" societies started to emerge. These were (and are) based on perceptions of male superiority, ruthless exploitation of the environment, male deities, and hierarchical organization. Warfare features prominently among these groups and becomes more lethal over time. Eisler's estimate of the period when war emerged gains support from the work of anthropologist Raymond Kelly, who believes available evidence entails that "earlier hunter-gatherer societies were warless and that the Paleolithic (extending from 2,900,000 to 10,000 B.P.) was a time of universal peace. Warfare then originates rather abruptly."[33]

In a very comprehensive study of war, political scientist Azar Gat offers a contrasting assessment. He maintains that "the evidence suggests that hunter-gatherers in their evolutionary natural environment and evolutionary natural way of life, shaped in humankind's evolutionary history over millions of years, widely engaged in fighting among themselves."[34] While this may be so, we also need to consider whether what counts as war in those remote times may have been quite different from the image war conjures up today. In one respect, this obviously has to be the case, since population numbers are much greater now, and the technology of killing and wounding and laying waste is much better perfected. For example, the research team of Jean Guilaine and Jean Zammit assert, in relation to prehistoric periods, "Primitive warfare operates on lower numbers, often involving individual volunteers who are not 'specialists' and have no elaborate strategic plan. It tends to take the form of confrontation, with no authority figure on either side, and participants are undisciplined and unorganized. . . . The word 'war' should be understood in its most general sense here—the sense is not one of armed conflict but rather of bloody clashes between small groups, raids carried out on neighboring parties, ambush attacks, and even individual murders."[35] Anthropologist Lawrence Keeley, however, presents an opposing view: "that warfare was extremely frequent in nonstate societies, and that tribal societies often mobilized for combat very high percentages of their total manpower. . . . Primitive warfare is simply total war conducted with very limited means. . . . Therefore, it comes as a shock to discover that the proportion of war casualties in primitive societies almost always exceeds that suffered by even the most bellicose or war-torn modern states."[36]

Now one might ask: "Isn't war, war after all, however frequently and in whatever shape or form we encounter it?" Probably the most sensible short answer is "Yes." Consequently, no attempt will be made here to deny that war (however understood) did take place in prehistory. Although it would be useful for the argument of this book to be able to do so, or at least to take an agnostic position on the matter, the wiser course is to concede that the evidence of war as a recurrent preoccupation of human life stretches back several millennia. Modern warfare can then be seen as the development of violent conflict, shaped and aggravated by various factors such as the rise of the state, technology, political, economic, and territorial ambitions, and so forth. In spite of this concession, however, there is a significant difference between finding solid (or at least very suggestive) evidence of war in human prehistory and claiming that humans are innately warlike creatures, as even Keeley points out.[37] Historian Arther Ferrill, who sounds a similarly cautious note, judges that "the evidence is too scanty" at present to settle anthropologists' long-standing dispute over whether the various *Australopithecine* ancestors of modern *Homo sapiens* were warlike or peaceful.[38] That being said, he maintains that "Prehistoric warfare . . . was as independently important in early society as the discovery of agriculture, the development of proto-urban settlements and the emergence of organized religious systems."[39] Even so, Ferrill confesses, "There is in fact until the final stages of the Palaeolithic Age [roughly 12,000–8,000 BCE] no conclusive evidence that any of the so-called prehistoric tools or hunting weapons were used against man at all. . . . The cave paintings . . . reflect very little evidence of warfare or of advances in weapons technology."[40] And, if we wish to reach really far back into our natural origins, we will find additional grounds for thinking that *Homo sapiens* is not predetermined to be a warlike species. Frans de Waal, who has distinguished himself as one of the world's leading primatologists, records that humans are genetically closer to bonobos, which are totally unwarlike, than we are to chimpanzees, which do engage in violent and lethal intraspecies skirmishes.[41] Thus, we *seem* to go full circle back to Eisler's claim that ancient societies were not warlike, and that war emerged as a feature of human behavior only relatively recently, and for reasons poorly known or understood.

Yet we need to tread lightly here, as is revealed by a closer look at the problems inherent in scientific study of the past, which limit the conclusions that can be drawn concerning the prevalence (or lack) of war many millennia ago. Anthropologist Leslie Sponsel asserts that "As in the case of the palaeontological record, so with the archaeological record, lack of evidence is not proof of absence."[42] Now this clearly cuts both ways: Absence of evidence for warlike ways in prehistoric cultures does not by itself demonstrate these cultures' peacefulness, any more than the lack of signs of peaceful living demonstrates the cultures' warlike ways. Sponsel observes, for instance, that "Some apparent fortifications may actually be retention walls. . . . Some rock art depicting fighting may be ritualistic reflections of shamanistic visions rather than documenting ordinary reality. . . ." But it is equally the case that "Weapons and fortifications of organic material are unlikely to be preserved archaeologically, except under very special climatic, geological, or other circumstances. . . ." Furthermore, "Nonmaterial aspects of warfare such as political and diplomatic processes are not preserved in the archaeological record. . . ."[43] The same issue is highlighted by Guilaine and Zammit, when they observe that "Ancient warfare and, in particular, short-lived battles and conflicts rarely left any trace in terms of material evidence." For this reason, their guarded judgment on the past is that "even if the presence of violent behavior in the Upper Paleolithic era can be confirmed, all interpretations of this behavior remain speculative, particularly where the earliest periods of human existence are concerned."[44] Anthropologist Walter Goldschmidt simply concludes that "The ethnographic data gives those who believe warfare to be an 'unnatural' excrescence as little comfort as it does the biological determinists."[45]

While some researchers clearly affirm the prevalence of warfare in human prehistory and others hold a more speculative and tentative position on the matter, a divergent school of thought maintains that there is at least as much evidence for societies that live (or have lived) peacefully most of the time (with war unknown or merely an unpleasant, occasional interlude), as there is for the hypothesis that war is the normal human condition. We will look at some of these views in the next section.

2.3. HUMAN UNIVERSALS

Are humans more or less the same everywhere and at all periods of time? This question could not even get a serious hearing, except from very rare individuals, until relatively recently. And what would it imply if we do share universal characteristics and capacities? Philosopher Kwame Anthony Appiah imaginatively suggests that anthropologists who studied other cultures in the early days of their science had to paint an interesting picture of the strange peoples they encountered in order to justify their difficult endeavors. So they "didn't usually come back with a report whose one-sentence summary was: they are pretty much like us. And yet of course they had to be. They did, after all, mostly have gods, food, language, dance, music, carving, medicines, family lives, rituals, jokes, and children's tales. They smiled, slept, had sex and children, wept, and, in the end, died."[46] As contemporary anthropologist Donald E. Brown confirms, concerning members of his profession, human universals are "similarities that they rely upon at every turn in order to do their work."[47]

The Malleability of Human Beings

A very old controversy concerns the question whether human nature is fixed or flexible, predetermined or self-chosen. While some researchers try to score points in the "nature vs. nurture" debate, others, like the existentialists, cast doubt on the entire tendency of positing such a thing as "human nature" at all. Probably the truth lies somewhere between the immutable-or-amorphous polarity of views on what it is to be human. (For this reason, we might better say that qualities and endowments of various sorts belong to "humanity" or the "human repertoire" rather than to "human nature.") Settling the issue whether it is appropriate to attribute a nature or essence to human beings goes far beyond the aims of this book. However, what we can usefully do here is to consider and reflect upon some relatively recent insights that lean in the direction of encouraging us to affirm that humans can determine what they want to be, given what they are as a species.

We might best begin with the 1986 Seville Statement on Violence, drafted and promulgated by an important group of international scholars, representing diverse fields of the human sciences and related disciplines.[48] Although the statement is a manifesto rather than a detailed and referenced study, it is backed by the force of a vast amount of research conducted by its signatories and others. The gist of this document is that *human beings are not genetically predestined to be either warlike or violent*. Although the Seville Statement is regarded by some as contentious, it was endorsed by the American Psychological Association, and this endorsement represents an encouraging sign that solid scientific findings favor the malleability of human nature view (defended earlier in the Introduction), as opposed to what we might call the "determinist/warist" perspective. One recent piece of research that is relevant to this discussion shows that "DNA, once held to be the unchanging template of heredity, now appears subject to a good deal of environmental change; considered to be identical in all cells and tissues of the body, there is growing evidence that somatic mosaicism is the normal human condition. . . ."[49] This finding suggests that even DNA is modifiable by one's life circumstances, and that "somatic mosaicism"—having "two or more genetic or cytogenetic cell lines within the cells of the body ([which] may or may not include the germline cells)"[50]—is the statistical norm for our species. While this does not disprove the claim that war is "in our genes," it certainly makes even greater room for the possibility of rearing and educating people to be nonviolent and peaceful rather than violent and bellicose.

We have already seen, in the Introduction, that cooperation probably both aided in and was developed by war as our species evolved. We saw there too that tendencies toward aggressive violence and toward more life-affirming behaviors (such as caring and nurturing) are both "part of what it is to be human," and have been such for as long as we can trace back our species' lineage. It follows that there is nothing particularly threatening to human freedom in the idea that evolution helps to make us what we are. For it does not do so entirely, and if we have the will, we can determine its very course in a number of important ways—choosing to be peaceable and recognizing the survival advantage of peacefulness being outstanding among them.

2.4. THE EXISTENCE OF PEACEFUL SOCIETIES

Peter Kropotkin: "Mutual Aid"

With these thoughts in mind, we can turn to a discussion of peaceful societies and the role of peace in everyday life. We are so accustomed to thinking about war rather than peace, and to assuming that the former, not the latter, is the usual condition of human beings, that it comes as a startling revelation to hear that there have been, and still are, fundamentally peaceful peoples inhabiting the same Earth as we. An early classic to make a mark in this field of investigation is *Mutual Aid*, by Russian prince, scientist, and revolutionary activist Peter Kropotkin, which appeared in 1902, but was serialized a decade earlier.[51] While most of this work is concerned with cooperation as a formative influence, alongside competition, in the evolution of many species, Kropotkin devotes chapters to reciprocal assistance and support as features of life in medieval cities and in several ethnic groups just beginning to be studied in his time.

Margaret Mead: "War Is an Invention"

The next milestone was an important essay by anthropologist Margaret Mead, titled "Warfare Is Only an Invention—Not a Biological Necessity" (1940). Mead remarks that those who believe war is inevitable fall into three groups: one that sees war as rooted in human biology; a second that identifies war as a product of sociopolitical conditions (such as the rise of the state, competition for land and resources, and class systems); and a third that identifies frustration of basic human drives by culture as exploding into war. The first group urges that the only hope for avoiding war lies in finding substitute activities to harness aggression, while the second argues for the creation of new structures and institutions that can alleviate the causes of war, and the third offers no specific answer or recommendations (at least in Mead's version of it). These views, as we have discovered, have their representatives in today's debates over war and peace. Mead's contrasting opinion is that war "is an invention like any other of the inventions in terms of which we order our lives."[52] The reason she offers is twofold: (a) For all human practices, however universal they appear to be (such as marriage and the use of fire), there must have been a time before which they did not exist and at which they were discovered or "invented"; and (b) There are present-day cultural groups which still lack the very idea of war, whether aggressive or defensive in character.[53] With respect to the latter point, Mead observes that just because a concept of war is absent among a certain people, it does not follow that they are completely peaceful and nonviolent. Indeed, she claims, with reference to the Eskimo culture, "The personality necessary for war, the circumstances necessary to goad men to desperation are present, but there is no war."[54]

Why is there sometimes war and sometimes not, under the same cultural and psychological conditions? Mead ventures to suggest that the balance is tipped toward war only when it is understood to be a possible means of dealing with particular conflicts of interest, and when masculinity has been so constructed that going to war is acceptable, laudatory, and recognized and sanctioned as a means to certain ends. Her conclusion, then, is that war can be ended if humans come to see it as "a defective social institution," and if a new "invention" can be proposed to take its place. But, as she rightly points out, in order for there to be a new invention of the required sort, we must first liberate our thinking to allow for its emergence—by rejecting the inevitability of war. The remarkable thing here is that in only a few pages, Mead has managed to weave together some of the most important antiwar ideas and to mount an impressive argument against the self-fulfilling prophecy inherent in supposing that humans are genetically predestined to engage in campaigns of mutual destruction.

Science journalist John Horgan, reflecting on Mead's theory seventy years later, contends that "War is both underdetermined and overdetermined. That is, many conditions are sufficient for war to occur, but none are necessary. Some societies remain peaceful even when significant risk factors are present, such as high population density, resource scarcity, and economic and ethnic divisions between people. Conversely, other societies fight in the absence of these conditions." In support of his claim, Horgan states that "Analyses of more than 300 societies in the Human Relations Area Files, an ethnographic database at Yale University, have turned up no clear-cut correlations between warfare and chronic resource scarcity."[55] To be sure, this leaves an explanatory vacuum, because, if true, there is no general account capable of specifying both the necessary and sufficient conditions of war. Innumerable volumes have been written on the causes of war (see Introduction, footnote 16), but the main conclusion to be drawn here must be that wars need to be explained on a case-by-case basis. (And a complicating factor in all of this, identified by a number of anthropologists, is that war often spreads owing to the need of nonwarring societies to defend themselves from warring ones.) As Winslow Myers points out, "The immediate causes of war through the ages are multiple and complex enough to fill many bookshelves with scholarly analysis. . . . What is harder to see is the universality of the thinking that leads to war, to see it in history and to see it in ourselves. . . . The root cause of war is this old, and now obsolete, mental division of the world into 'us' and 'them.'"[56] But it is just as crucial to note that individual accounts are also required in order to explain the ways of organizing, the myriad solutions to common human problems, and the underlying beliefs that make some societies peaceful. We have already looked at some shared beliefs ("Home Truths") in the Introduction that might constitute part of the foundation for peace. How a culture of peace might be conceived and constructed will be examined in detail in Chapters 6 and 7.

Kelly agrees that there have been (and are) peaceful societies, which are not always characterized by nonviolence, and that war is a later development (beginning in the Near East about 7,500 BCE, he estimates). But he offers a more nuanced argument concerning the emergence of war in some of these. Reflecting on the results of a range of studies, Kelly concludes, "These findings very strongly suggest that the origin of war—in the sense of the initiation of warfare in a sociocultural context where it did not previously exist—entails a transition from one form of collective violence to another, rather than a transition from peaceful nonviolence to lethal armed conflict."[57] This does not of course invalidate Mead's view that war is an invention; for, as both she and Kelly acknowledge, the transition in question has to be accounted for, and Mead could posit that it arises from a new stratum of ideas created over time by the collective imagination of the group, or perhaps by the myths and laws framed by the group's elders. That hypothesis would be difficult, but presumably not impossible, to verify. A further complication arises from the fact that the kind of invention Mead refers to might occur at the unconscious level, as does much creative cultural transformation. If such a transformation takes place unconsciously and, as it were, out of sight, then how can it possibly be changed? The position taken in this book is that part of the path to a peaceful world is determined by the sort of activity conducted above in the Introduction: In that chapter, widely shared ideas and emotional responses related to war and the dominant ("hegemonic") discourse about it—all of which generally go unacknowledged and unexamined—are illuminated and deconstructed, with the aim of neutralizing their influence and thereby opening up new avenues for change. In a similar fashion, the unexamined assumptions of classism, racism, sexism, ageism, and speciesism have come increasingly under scrutiny, with an impact that is personal, cultural, and historical in significance.

More Recent Research

The argument on behalf of peaceful human groups has been advanced by a number of other authors too within the past forty years. Matthew Melko, for example, in *52 Peaceful Societies* (1973), charts the field from ancient times to the present. His fifty-two societies had to meet two criteria: They needed to be societies "without war, revolution, or other physical conflicts among men"; and they had to belong to "a historical period of more than a century in which a clearly discernible political area was generally peaceful."[58] As with any compilation of this type, there are bound to be problems of methodology, including those that concern definitions, evidence gathering, lack of adequate (or any) historical records of a relevant sort, and the like, which Melko forthrightly acknowledges. Yet his conclusions are nonetheless striking. The collection he assembles comprises ancient kingdoms of the Nile Valley, Greek and Iranian civilizations, European entities of the Middle Ages, South Asian and East Asian societies from premedieval times to the eighteenth century, and a selection of modern countries in different regions up to the present. Certain groups that no longer live together in the same geographical area (such as Quakers and Mennonites) are allowed to be included, however, because they meet all or nearly all of the other conditions. Some classifications might be challenged, as might be the judgment that a society qualifies as peaceful even when it is waging a foreign war; but Melko makes his point nonetheless. His conclusion is certainly worth weighing carefully: "Peace is a fact, not a vision. It is ubiquitous, incessant, normal. Peace prevails in most places at most times."[59]

Research librarian Bruce Bonta, in *Peaceful Peoples* (1993), takes a bibliographic approach to this topic, cataloguing and carefully describing 438 publications on the subject of his book's title. These items largely support the judgment that the peoples in question are peaceful, but where scholarly opinion is divided, both sides are represented. Bonta explains that

> Peacefulness, for the purposes of this bibliography, is defined as a condition whereby people live with a relatively high degree of interpersonal harmony; experience little physical violence among adults, between adults and children, and between the sexes;

have developed workable strategies for resolving conflicts and averting violence; are committed to avoiding violence (such as warfare) with other peoples; raise their children to adopt their peaceful ways; and have a strong consciousness of themselves as peaceable.[60]

This is a very useful summary, as it helps one to gain an understanding of peace as a way of life, a topic we will explore more fully in Chapters 5 and 6. The definition would have additional force if the ideas of respect, dignity, and equality had been woven into it, but arguably "a relatively high degree of interpersonal harmony" includes these at least to some degree, even if not explicitly.

Elise Boulding, a well-known sociologist and peace scholar, offers a broad contemporary perspective on peaceful societies. In *Cultures of Peace* (2000) she takes a worldwide overview of utopian experiments, peace organizations, and "the practice of peacemaking skills that actually exist in every society."[61] These peacemaking skills are found in many areas of daily life. (See "Peace in Everyday Life," in section 2.6 later in this chapter, and "Everyday Peaceful Conduct and Alternatives to Violence," in Chapter 6, section 6.6.) Boulding also considers "the behavioral dynamics of peaceableness" in various communities, including four tribal societies: the Inuit (Canada), Mbuti (Zaire), Zuni (US), and Arapesh (New Guinea).[62]

In *Beyond War: The Human Potential for Peace* (2007), Douglas Fry, an anthropologist and authority on aggression and conflict resolution, stresses that anthropology (with the aid of history) paints a large panorama of human activity and achievement which, if examined with the utmost care, provides hope for the future:

A macroscopic view suggests that humans have the *capacity* to replace the institution of war with international conflict resolution procedures to ensure justice, human rights, and security for the people of the world—social features that are sorely underdeveloped in the current international war system. . . . Such a macroscopic anthropological perspective, spanning evolutionary time and cross-cultural space, is considerably broader than most current-day political perspectives. It can provide novel insights about the possibilities of achieving and maintaining peace.[63]

Fry's examples of peaceful societies, summarized in an appendix, total seventy-four and are spread out over every continent. He comments, succinctly, that "The list is far from exhaustive."[64]

Is there an exhaustive list? Even though it was published earlier, Johan M. G. van der Dennen's magisterial and massive two-volume study, *The Origin of War* (1995) must surely come close to capturing this title. Notwithstanding the fact that van der Dennen takes issue with the criteria according to which some previous authors have classified societies as peaceful, he experiences little trouble compiling his own list of 518 "primitive peoples claimed to be highly unwarlike (war reported as absent or mainly defensive)" and another 290 among whom there is "allegedly mild, low-level and/or ritualized warfare."[65] He supplies literally thousands of research references, dating from the mid-nineteenth century to the present, in order to shore up his individual assessments. Van der Dennen suggests that "There is no need to postulate a Beast Within to explain the evolutionary origin of war."[66] His thesis, by contrast, is that "war evolved as a facultative [or "opportunistic"] male reproductive (or parental investment) strategy"—one that is dependent upon cultural, geographical, and other factors.[67] Finally, he concludes, "Warring behavior is confined to typically highly-social and 'brainy' species, cognitively capable of establishing relatively long-term polyadic coalitions, mainly Hominidae and Panidae [the Great Apes]. This, at least partially, explains why warfare emerged so (relatively) late in evolution and why it is so conspicuously absent in mammals generally."[68] Let us assume, for the sake of argument, that van der Dennen's hypothesis about the biological evolution of war is correct. It would seem to follow that in today's world, where "reproductive strategies" have changed due to human choice and altered cultural norms, or perhaps have even become haphazard or nonexistent, the underlying conditions for war in the biological sense are overridden. Therefore, it is logical to judge that the focus of attention must now shift to different—social and political—causes of war and ways to mitigate or eliminate them.

The Lesson Learned: War Is Not Inevitable

The selection of works on peaceful societies we have looked at is only a sample of what is available. All of this material constitutes an impressive database. Even the most hardened skeptic about the human capacity for peaceful living would have to pause and reconsider in the face of such evidence. Although the existence of peaceful societies, either today or at some time in the past, neither proves that our species is progressing toward peacefulness nor refutes the belief that war has always been part of human life, it does present an explanatory dilemma for advocates of the "inevitability of war" doctrine. For if the evidence cited cannot be denied or undermined, then the choice appears to be either to abandon (or seriously modify) that doctrine, or else show how it is compatible with there being so many apparently peaceful societies. Defenders of the inevitability doctrine, it must be said, have thus far failed to do any of these things convincingly. Keeley, after critically evaluating several studies of

Figure 2.1 Features of a peaceful society

peaceful societies, concludes: "Thus pacifistic societies seem to have existed at every level of social organization, but they are extremely rare and seem to require special circumstances."[69] This strikes one as an excessively parsimonious interpretation of the evidence provided by other qualified observers. But even on Keeley's account, the possibility of identifying peaceful social arrangements remains open, and such an inquiry therefore continues to be instructive.

Politics professor and peace specialist Seyom Brown writes that "The existence of even very few societies in which physical violence (actual or threatened) is virtually absent would call into question the theory of a strong innate predisposition to violence in the human species." But this does not mean that in such societies "there is a strong 'instinct for peace', as it were, that operates without social inducement"; rather, in these groups, "everywhere there are socializing devices to constrain and deflect such violent inclinations."[70] In other words, peace, like violence and war, is a product of cultures and the dynamics of reinforcement or social learning that are prominent in them.

2.5. WHAT DOES A REAL-LIFE PEACEFUL SOCIETY LOOK LIKE?

Some Examples

It is impossible to distill an essence or simple recipe for "peacefulness" from examples of societies that do not go to war. Yet a great deal of worthwhile information can be acquired by studying them. To provide some idea of what is discussed in the volumes covered in the previous section, we will first consider an essay on "Two Paths to Peace: Semai and Mehinaku Nonviolence," by anthropologists Thomas Gregor and Clayton Robarchek.[71] This report is of special interest because it concerns still-living societies and offers a comparison of peaceful cultures as they actively go about their business. The two groups of interest—the Semai of Malaysia and the Mehinaku Indians of Brazil—are both "small-scale tropical-forest societies" surrounded by warlike neighbors.[72] The Semai live in autonomous villages and consider themselves equals. "Such commonly 'masculine' qualities as bravery, strength, and aggressiveness have no special value to the Semai," these authors tell us.[73] Peace for the Semai is a function of rigorous self-control and internalized fear of committing acts of violence. " '[G]oodness' is defined positively in terms of the nurturance of the group, while 'badness' is defined negatively in terms of aggressiveness, violence, and other behaviors inimical to affiliation. These normative ideals are largely realized in behavior: most Semai are generous, unassuming, unassertive, nonaggressive, and, above all, nonviolent."[74] According to another study, "the Semai are known to give gifts to one another as a form of peacemaking. They have no formal governmental or judicial system and tend to rule themselves through public consensus. . . . When major disputes arise, they resolve them by holding a meeting (bcaraa') at the home of one of the community members. They will stay for as long as it takes to explore the cause of the problem and what should be done about it."[75] (This is a not uncommon method of dispute resolution among peaceful peoples.) Food sharing is a highly important feature of this culture and springs partly from a sense of extreme vulnerability in the world and partly from a codependency mind-set.

The Mehinaku, on the other hand, operate with a sexual hierarchy, are more overtly emotional, engage in competitive sport, interact pragmatically with outside tribes, and embed peaceful relations within community regulatory structures rather than within inhibitions controlling the individual psyche. For example, "Prestige is awarded those who avoid conflict; there are currently no roles for warriors; religious sanctions inhibit aggression; and methods of disciplining children discourage displays of anger."[76] Mehinaku are "outgoing, optimistic, and friendly," dramatically and sexually self-expressive, place value on personal property, and have a strong sense of responsibility for their personal welfare.[77] While both Semai and Mehinaku societies have elaborate practices for avoiding confrontations, settling disputes, and preventing outbreaks of violence within the group, ritualized violence occurs episodically among the Mehinaku.

What is particularly striking about these two examples is that they demonstrate quite clearly the role cultural conditioning plays in determining whether a society is either cooperative and peaceful or aggressive and warlike. Psychologist Ervin Staub notes simply that "Since aggressive men . . . view toughness and strength as masculine ideals, they have to be tough and strong to fulfill their need for a positive identity. Feeling empathy and concern for people, except perhaps some intimates, will not fulfill their need for a positive identity. Increasing their empathy would not constitute a desirable 'expansion of the self' for these individuals."[78] So the cultural response to this, in the interest of peacefulness, would seem to be twofold: finding ways to express "masculine virtues," like toughness and strength, in nonaggressive, non-"macho," nonviolent ways, and valorizing qualities like cooperation, empathy, and mutual problem-solving. The Semai and the Mehinaku provide instructive examples of how these dynamics work.

An additional, quite striking example is provided by the following discussion of a warless African society:

> [W]hen members of the Mbuti (or Bambuti) people, a forest hunting and gathering society in Congo, experience conflict, they settle it quickly, often with the use of laughter. A member of the community may serve in the role of defuser, creating a comic diversion. This may include jokes, ridicule, mime, or humorous antics in which he tries to refocus the conflict on himself and start everyone laughing. This enables the community to move forward. When Mbuti engage in conflict—usually resulting from disputes over sex, food, territory, theft, or personality that have nothing to do with the institution of war—they seem to have a way of dissipating problems before they become serious. Having no formal method for resolving problems, the Mbuti do not tend to pass judgment on each other. When someone has engaged in a "bad" action, counterproductive to community needs, he or she may be punished. Usually disputes are settled through debate or mild individual fighting; sometimes ostracism occurs.[79]

Who would have thought that laughter—even though unquestionably a human universal—could be enlisted in the service of serious peacemaking and reconciliation? This case surely proves beyond doubt that the creative scope of human peacebuilding activities is virtually unlimited.

Peacemaking and Peacekeeping

The answer, then, to the question "What does a peaceful society look like?" is: "No one thing." The above examples cannot be judged as typical, since no other society is exactly like them; yet neither are they completely atypical, because there is a discernible logic in these societies' individual and group behaviors that serves to stimulate solution-strategies for emotions and situations which could otherwise spill over into violent confrontation—strategies that are in fact comparable to those found elsewhere in the human domain. The upshot is simply that pieces of the peace puzzle fall into place when we take care to examine on-the-scene reports from qualified scientists.

In addition, several overall conclusions can be drawn from studies such as the one by Gregor and Robarchek discussed above. To begin with, unless a very restrictive and unrealistic definition is applied, societies that count as peaceful will be seen to contain conflict, aggressive behavior, and even acts of violence, which need to be carefully interpreted and kept in perspective. Second, we can see that there are degrees and types of peaceful living arrangements, some of which are more successful at maintaining peace in certain respects and contexts, while others succeed better in different respects and contexts. Third, maintaining peace involves constantly renewed dedication to the norms that define the society. This is another way of saying that peace is a process (see Chapter 5), not a static state of affairs. When we hold cultures of peace up as presenting a desirable alternative to those of war and violence, we are addressing some of the most deeply engrained behaviors and attitudes of the latter, which are aggravated by the emotional overlay they carry. For a society to change from being warlike to being peaceful is quite a radical development; such a change cannot occur overnight and must be a gradual process. It should also be recognized that maintaining peace in any interpersonal system depends on a balancing act involving various sacrifices, compromises, and trade-offs. Such a social system is no different in this respect from one in which war is prominent. However, what is revealed here is that fundamental choices are being made within each system, expressing the group's intention to define its collective self-interest in completely different ways. Fourth, the question "Why peace?" is at least equally lively and open for further investigation as is the well-worn question "Why war?" Any simplistic formulas are to be avoided, however tempting. Goldschmidt gloomily warns, for instance, that "The literature on the peacemaking process among tribal peoples offers no model for coping with our own problems of endemic international conflict. The practices they display are obvious; the means are meager; and the results discouraging."[80] What makes any given peaceful society work as such is a matter both complex and deep, as well as being relative to time, place, language, world-view, and other factors. An account of how it came to be that way is sometimes attainable, but an understanding of how it perpetuates itself may require much further work. However, in the final analysis Gregor and Robarchek express the powerfully suggestive precept that "peace systems, if they are to survive, must be sustained by antiviolent values."[81]

The Benefits of Studying Peaceful Societies

This last observation deserves emphasis. The nature of war has altered greatly over the ages, in several respects. First, there have been many transformative changes wrought by innovations in weaponry (such as long bows, firearms, dynamite, tanks, aircraft, and guided missiles), tactical and strategic ideas, communication and detection devices, propaganda, and so on. The industrialization of weapons production during the past two centuries and into the present is also a striking factor, as is the quantum leap represented by the invention of nuclear weapons. And today's wars do not fit the model of a statically entrenched or barely moving, regimented confrontation over largely insignificant territory, but instead, take place in urban and rural areas with civilians being pawns unwillingly located at the center of the conflict zone. Frequently, these conflicts are "proxy wars" fought on behalf of, and funded by, external interests, possibly even involving mercenaries, or tribal wars, or drug-funded territorial struggles, and so on. (See also Chapter 3, section 3.3, "Further Critical Reflections on the Just War Concept.") As numerous commentators have pointed out, probably at least half of all war casualties now are people who used to be designated as "noncombatants" (as in classical just war doctrine), though sadly this category has become next to meaningless. Large numbers are also forced to collaborate or, in some cases, either just killed outright, raped, coopted, or conscripted. Torture and other cruelties are widespread in these dirty wars, which are often deemed "small-scale," but are far from being minor to those whose lives are torn apart by them. All of this may incline one to express cynicism about the value of studying peaceful societies, which seem so far removed from present-day realities in many places on Earth. Yet as we have learned from a brief look at these societies, there are ways of working out conflicts—inevitably part of human life though they are—that can provide clues for the rest of us. The argument for preserving species diversity on our planet has been stated in this way: All existing species "represent . . . successful sets of solutions to a series of biological problems, any one of which could be immensely valuable to us in a number of ways."[82] In like manner, all existing peaceful societies—and for that matter, all societies, period—represent solutions from which important lessons, both positive and negative, can be learned. And one clear message from all of this is that the evidence provided by studies of peaceful societies yields much that is worth sifting through and learning from, in the quest for our own strategies of survival.

2.6. PEACE IN EVERYDAY LIFE

Most people in the world go about their daily affairs peacefully and live in peace with one another. (See also Chapter 6, section 6.6, "Everyday Peaceful Conduct and Alternatives to Violence.") When reading this statement, qualifications immediately come to mind: "Yes, but what about those living in war or conflict zones, situations of oppression, grinding poverty, and so on? Surely these people don't live in peace, either with others or within themselves?" Of course, there are exceptions to any generalization, but nevertheless, for far the greatest number of us, the initial claim remains true. While a large percentage of the global population lives in need and below any decent standard of minimum income, most do not. As everyone feels intuitively, peace has various levels of meaning (as shown in Chapter 5), so a decision has to be made whether persons existing in a state of need or under constant threat of violence can be said to be living in peace in any true sense. Perhaps for many of them, the answer, sadly, is that they do not. But it might be argued that even for the greater number of people so described, most daily interactions are still peaceful, to the extent that these are under their own control. Elise Boulding observes that "Sometimes the peace culture has been a hidden culture, kept alive in the cracks of a violent society" and even in conflict zones,[83] which illustrates that the resources they represent are always available to be drawn upon if there is the will to do so. For instance, in the Israel-Palestinian Territory region, there are numerous grassroots movements and NGOs working for peace and common understanding, often at the family and community level, and even at significant risk to themselves. A few examples are: Neve Shalom/ Wahat al-Salam (Oasis of Peace), Ta'ayush (Arab-Jewish Partnership), Parents Circle-Families Forum (Palestinian Israeli Bereaved Families for Peace), The Villages Group: Cooperation in Israel-Palestine, Middleway—Compassionate Engagement in Society, Windows: Channels for Communication, Machsomwatch (Women against Occupation and for Human Rights), Combatants for Peace, Arab-Hebrew Theatre, Hand in Hand, and Jerusalem Link.

Characteristics of Daily Peacefulness

Fry develops the picture of peacefulness in everyday life from an anthropologist's experienced perspective:

> In actuality, one can travel from continent to continent and personally observe hundreds of thousands of humans interacting nonviolently. Even if searching for conflict, an observer may find people talking over their differences, ridiculing a rival, persuading and coaxing someone, and perhaps arguing. An observer also may find people negotiating solutions to their disputes, agreeing to provide compensation for damages, reaching compromises, while perhaps also reconciling and forgiving one another, all without violence, within families and among friends, neighbors, associates, acquaintances, and strangers. In contrast to violence, such pervasive human activities rarely make the news. . . . Additionally, time and again, individuals from various cultures simply walk away from conflict. . . .[84]

This excerpt yields crucial insight into who and what we are as human beings: basically decent and caring, self-interested to be sure, but likewise very
motivated to keep our lives in balance, implicitly recognizing that we have to
negotiate and earn this state of equilibrium by constructive interaction with
others—even those whom we may not know or like especially well. We understand that we are sometimes in the wrong, that we cannot have everything
tailored to our own personal wants, that give-and-take and respectful awareness of others' needs are vital ingredients of all relationships.

Boulding's feminist sensibility leads her to amplify the consideration of
peacefulness in everyday life by drawing attention to a different selection of
human attributes:

> Where do we find these behaviors, these peace culture resources? In the recurring cycles,
> rhythms, and rituals of human celebration, with its feasting, singing, dancing, and shar-
> ing of gifts. In the reproductive cycles of human partnering, of birthing, of family main-
> tenance as the years go by, and the completion of dying—in the cycles that bind people
> together across kin groups. In the succession of woundings and healings of human bod-
> ies as they move through life's dangers in those cycles. In the labor to produce suste-
> nance from the earth. In the daily round of trade, the barter and exchange of goods and
> services. And, perhaps most wonderful of all, in human play—the playing of games, the
> play of artistic creation, the play of the mind in the pursuit of knowledge.[85]

Our attention is directed here, in a remarkably succinct, poetic, and focused way, to many fundamental practices that not only define what it is to
be human, but also to what makes cultures identifiably what they are, as well
as to activities that give life meaning and purpose in general. Boulding ingeniously grounds everyday peace within a framework comprising human self-
expression, the regular activities and rituals in which we all participate, and
the outer limits of life itself.

Trust

Underlying the attributes and endeavors discussed so far are human propensi-
ties for sociability, communication, and trust. At the most elementary level,
we trust one another; and, in fact, we must do so. To do otherwise is to cripple
oneself as an agent, like a paranoiac person who, by contrast, trusts no one.
There is a common saying that trust has to be earned, and indeed it does. But
trusting one another, as we do, implies that even where it has not been directly
earned, we give each other the benefit of the doubt with respect to this matter
because we feel that trust is generally a better investment in our (individual

and mutual) welfare than mistrust. Children may be trusting by nature, but for adults things are of a different order. Based on past experience, we judge that trust has a higher probability of producing favorable results in relation to our own individual freedom of action and safety, in interactions with others, than does the withholding of trust.

To explain this, let us look a little more closely at trust in everyday life, assuming a society that is free of ongoing armed conflict. Walking out on the street in order to go anywhere, we take it for granted that we will not be killed or assaulted or injured by objects (whether under human control or not). The same applies in workplaces, shops, and schools, on public transportation or driving our cars, at major events, in intimate relationships, and so on. If we are "street smart" (in the widest sense of the term), we do not always trust absolutely (or perhaps never do) without supporting evidence, or against contrary evidence that should warn us of danger; but, in general, we proceed on the assumption that there are positive grounds for trust. Why is this? It is because we believe that—at least on a superficial level—most people are of good will and in control of themselves, and are not looking for excuses to vent anger and act out their frustrations on us by harmful means. Unless we have reason to think otherwise, we will adhere to this principle and act accordingly. There is no cause to speak of naivety here; we all learn as we go, but we start out as trusting beings because it is advantageous to be this way and because trust is usually rewarded by trust in kind, as well as by friendliness and other forms of human generosity of spirit.

The Prevalence of Peacefulness

It follows from all of this that humans are perhaps much more peaceful (or "peace-loving," if you prefer) than we are inclined to give ourselves credit for. As Fry points out above, we receive a very heavy dose of violence and mayhem through the media, whereas the good news is seldom considered newsworthy at all.[86] The fact is that peace tends to be overlooked in its everydayness, owing to our preoccupation with the disruptive and the discordant, which get privileged as the norm. Peacefulness then becomes the abnormal condition. However, this is a profound mistake that inverts the truth: *Peacefulness is precisely our normal condition.* Even where the conditions for peacefulness are absent, as discussed earlier, the human potential for it still exists, and then should inspire anyone who can, to try working for remedies for those situations in which it is lacking.

2.7. COOPERATION AND COEVOLUTION

Thinking about peace in everyday life requires no special training and, once we have done it, the conclusions we reach seem almost like stating the obvious or appealing to common sense. But some scientists and scholars have delved into the psychological and behavioral background of our disposition to act peacefully, and we will now consider a few of their findings.

The Origins of Cooperation

While human beings frequently portray themselves as selfish and genetically driven to seek self-aggrandizement aggressively, this is far from the whole picture. In the Introduction, it was noted that cooperation has played as vital a role in human evolution as aggression, and considerable attention has been devoted in recent times to understanding how cooperation originates and how it works. Anthropologist Bruce Knauft stresses that "Widespread cooperation and exchange of information among diffuse networks of unrelated as well as related individuals are central to social functioning in all known human societies. . . . [M]ost people do follow rule-of-thumb rules of social cooperation much, perhaps most, of the time. . . . This cooperative disposition has been rigorously documented under experimental conditions in the absence of self-interested payoffs. . . ."[87] It may be necessary to repeat here that talking about cooperation as a deeply embedded human trait in no way excludes recognizing either our self-interested side (whether explained in terms of reproductive advantage or otherwise) or aggression as an innate human tendency. But what it does exclude is any method of marginalizing cooperation or explaining it away.

Much of the work of anthropologists like Knauft is directed toward making a case for viewing human societies as more cooperative and culture-centered than is allowed for by the reductionist accounts influenced by sociobiological and Hobbesian views of human nature that held sway for a greater part of the twentieth century. Yet even within that research environment, biologists W. D. Hamilton and Robert Trivers demonstrated forms of altruism within nonhuman species.[88] And because altruism is not uniquely human, it is therefore unsurprising to find it in humans.

Recent and ongoing research by comparative and developmental psychologist Michael Tomasello and others shows that human children are innately cooperative. From as early as twelve months old, prelinguistic children exhibit helpful behavior and engage in cooperative activities as well. While these

tendencies are reinforced and refined later on by socialization, they are not initially caused by it but instead arise during the course of normal development.
Tomasello notes that humans are both self-centered and other-regarding: "All
viable organisms must have a selfish streak; they must be concerned about
their own survival and well-being or they will not be leaving many offspring.
Human cooperativeness and helpfulness are, as it were, laid on top of this self-
interested foundation."[89]

Tomasello mentions that one of the leading problems in evolutionary theory today is how to reconcile altruism with selfishness, since altruism does not,
on the surface of things, appear to enhance an organism's reproductive advantage. We needn't get into this controversy here, except to acknowledge that according to Tomasello (who sidesteps the issue himself), a more significant fact
about human beings is that their lives together are characterized by mutuality:
We forge joint projects and work toward common goals; "shared intentionality" presides over these projects and is represented by the pronoun "we."[90]
Again, these claims are supported by a sizable body of ingenious research on
very young children. "Collaborative activities," Tomasello hypothesizes (such
as those involved in obtaining food), arose early in human evolution and per-
sisted because of their obvious survival benefits (in terms of hunting success
rate, adequate group nourishment, and so forth).[91]

Wider Spheres of Cooperation

Tim Flannery, writer, scientist, and explorer, argues quite simply that cooperation (which involves elements of empathy, altruism, and compromise) is a
universal phenomenon in nature, and a concept without which we could not
understand how the biosphere has developed on this planet. "It's not that living things chose to cooperate," Flannery states, "but that evolution has shaped
them to do so."[92] Cooperation is the strategy for species survival and the key
to explaining it. Extrapolating from this concept, Flannery posits a process
of "coevolution," a sort of mega-trend, the results of which can be seen everywhere: "Natural selection that is triggered by interactions between related
things is called coevolution. It can act at every level, from that of individual
amino acids to entire organisms, and it may not be just a property of life, but
something far more profound."[93] Likewise, biologist and mathematician Martin Nowak has described mechanisms of cooperation that "apply to all manner of organisms, from amoebas to zebras (and even, in some cases, to genes
and other components of cells)," but he also points out that "humans are the
most cooperative species."[94] Nowak has constructed mathematical models of

the ways in which cooperation evolves. As these reports indicate, there can no longer be any doubt that cooperation has a biological foundation. Perhaps one day, science will be able to shed light on ways to maximize human cooperation.

Along the lines of Flannery's speculation above, Lee Smolin, a theoretical physicist, has attempted to apply the idea of natural selection to the evolution of possible universes. We need not go into that, but it is challenging to encounter a perspective on ideas like competition and cooperation that, for a change, comes from a thinker outside of the life sciences. Smolin writes that "While popular accounts of evolution have often stressed competition, looking at the plethora of different ways species have invented to live, it seems that an important theme of evolution might instead be the ability of the process to invent new ways of living, in order to minimize the actual competition among the different species."[95] The point here is not to posit some kind of "invisible hand" guiding evolution, but rather to give a novel overview of it—to model natural selection as having an alternative logic to it. Again, the accent is on *co-evolution*, as opposed to the usual understanding of natural selection as being a function of reproductive advantage in the "struggle for survival."

Cooperation, then, is a very basic impulse throughout the natural world and perhaps beyond. Like other impulses, it can be used for good or ill; but the more we understand our own species as a product of cooperation, and that cooperation is essential for survival, the greater is the likelihood of our learning to work together toward common ends. As well, the greater is the likelihood of our coming to appreciate cooperative interdependence among species as the key to sustainability.

2.8. SOME TENTATIVE CONCLUSIONS

We can now attempt to bring all of these stimulating and constructive ideas together in the following points.

2.8.1.   While many insist that the future has already arrived, this is only a picturesque way of stating that change (especially in various technologies) occurs amazingly fast—often bringing transformations that people do not have time to process and react to. Although there are planners who make it their business to forecast future scenarios and whose decisions have the potential to affect all of our lives, in an important sense, the future is still in the future, or is still open, and short of an ultimate cataclysm, it cannot be used up. The point here is, once again, that the path of responsibility for everyone is to avoid buying into—or trying to implement—self-fulfilling prophecies.

Both personally and collectively, we need to take hold of the future rather than treat it as some sort of autonomously developing, uncontrollable monster.

2.8.2.   No firm inferences can be made from nonhuman (especially Great Ape) behaviors to human ones; but so far as the best research indicates, human morality, moral emotions, and cooperative behavior have evolutionary roots among other, closely related species. Charles Darwin asserted "that any animal whatever, endowed with well-marked social instincts, the parental and filial affections being here included, would inevitably acquire a moral sense or conscience, as soon as its intellectual powers had become as well, or nearly as well-developed, as in man."[96] Research that is current has established the presence of kinship ties, reciprocity and justice, altruism, and forms of sexual morality in nonhumans.[97]

2.8.3.   Disagreement among anthropologists about the prevalence or absence of war and violence in prehistory should caution us not to draw any hasty inferences about this part of our past. In fact, the path of prudence here would be to draw no firm conclusions at all. However, what matters most is the lessons we can glean from historical examples, modern science, and disciplined reflections on human nature, both past and present. So far as all this goes, we can say that humans have both violent/aggressive and cooperative/caring/compassionate tendencies, and that probably all people naturally possess these, but in varying and modifiable proportions. (See more detailed discussion of this in Chapter 4.) This is already an important conclusion to have reached, for if true, it indicates two things: (a) that conflict will always be with us, but can potentially be resolved in different (more or less harmful and damaging) ways; and (b) that there are choices we can make (among methods of education, role-modeling, socio-economic environments, and so on) that will maximize our peaceful and nonviolent tendencies and minimize the opposing ones.

2.8.4.   We must take care not to project upon other societies—and even more so onto humanity in general—a warlike image that may only be a reflection of our own present society and its values. For this feeds into the problem of turning war into a human destiny and defeats the opportunity to learn from open-minded encounters with different ways of living and resolving conflict.

2.8.5.   Perhaps most importantly, as acute observers from the time of French essayist Michel de Montaigne (1533–92) to the present have reported, human beings are more alike than they are different, once we get below surface variations of belief and cultural practice. There is therefore no basis for attitudes of either superiority or animosity toward others in the human family, and there are no rational grounds for a generalized suspicion or fear of them. As Flannery comments, "Nothing is as challenging to such a belief as meeting the 'other' on an equal footing. There is as much diversity of thought, mannerism, and emotion in a small New Guinean village as there is in the entire world, and in this commonality lies the foundations of our universal human civilization, as well as its hopes for a future."[98] Remaining receptive and nonjudgmental toward others and toward new information is as essential to peace as it is to any other human endeavor.

NOTES TO CHAPTER 2

1. ABC (Australia) 7:00 a.m. radio news, 12 March 2012.
2. "Safe Water Targets Met," *Guardian Weekly*, 16–22 March 2012, p. 2 (buried in a small box).
3. UN Secretary General Ban Ki-moon, "Secretary-General's Remarks at Press Conference on Millennium Development Goals," 8 March 2012; http://www.un.org/sg/offthecuff/index.asp?nid=2255.
4. "Child Deaths: UNICEF Says Global Mortality Rates Fall," BBC News, 12 September 2012; http://www.bbc.co.uk/news/world-19581433.
5. United Nations Development Programme, *Human Development Report 2013: The Rise of the South—Human Progress in a Diverse World*, p. 11; available at: http://hdr.undp.org/en. Additional support for this conclusion comes from the Oxford Poverty and Human Development Initiative's Global Multidimensional Poverty Index (MPI) 2013; http://www.ophi.org.uk.
6. Michael Cohen, "World Is Making Very Clear Progress," *Guardian Weekly*, 5–11 April 2013, p. 18. See also Dan Roberts, "Extreme Poverty Could Be Wiped out by 2030, World Bank Estimates Show," *The Guardian*, 2 April 2013; http://www.guardian.co.uk/business/2013/apr/02/global-poverty-wiped-out-world-bank.
7. Jayati Ghosh, "Banana Republic No Longer," *Guardian Weekly*, 27 January–2 February 2012, p. 29.
8. John Rwangombwa, "Rwanda Can Be Proud of Its Economic Progress," *Wall Street Journal*, 10 February 2012; http://online.wsj.com/article/SB10001424052970203824904577212704208216364.html; Palash R. Ghosh, "Rwanda: The Only Government in the World Dominated by Women," *International Business Times*, 3 January 2012; http://www.ibtimes.com/rwanda-only-government-world-dominated-women-213623.
9. Monica Mark, "Diamonds Shine with Promise," *Guardian Weekly*, 22–28 June 2012, p. 31.
10. David Smith, "Somalis Awaken to a Fresh Dawn," *Guardian Weekly*, 24–30 August 2012, pp. 1–2.
11. Alyssa A. Botelho, "Sustained Action Sees off Painful Parasite," *Guardian Weekly*, 7–13 September 2012, p. 46. See also Afua Hirsch, "The Road Back to Africa," and various authors, "Faces of Change," *Guardian Weekly*, 14–20 September 2012, pp. 25–8.

12. Ian Birrell, "Our Image of Africa Is Hopelessly Out of Date," *Guardian Weekly*, 31 August–6 September 2012, p. 19.

13. Heidelberg Institute for International Conflict Research, *Conflict Barometer 2012*; available at: http://www.hiik.de/de/konfliktbarometer/pdf/ConflictBarometer_2012.pdf.

14. Joshua S. Goldstein, "Think Again: War (World Peace Could Be Closer Than You Think)," *Foreign Policy*, Sept./Oct. 2011 (emphasis in original); http://www.foreignpolicy.com/articles/2011/08/15/think_again_war?page=full. See also Joshua S. Goldstein, *Winning the War on War: The Decline of Armed Conflict Worldwide* (New York: Dutton, 2011).

15. Geneva Declaration on Armed Violence and Development; http://www.genevadeclaration.org/the-geneva-declaration/what-is-the-declaration.html; Human Security Report Project, *Human Security Report 2009/2010*; available at: http://www.hsrgroup.org/human-security-reports/20092010/text.aspx.

16. Human Security Report Project, *Human Security Report 2012*, p. 13; available at: http://www.hsrgroup.org/human-security-reports/2012/text.aspx.

17. Jesse Richards, *The Secret Peace: Exposing the Positive Trend of World Events* (New York: Book & Ladder Press, 2010), p. 4.

18. Steven Pinker, *The Better Angels of Our Nature: Why Violence Has Declined* (New York: Viking/Penguin, 2011), p. xxi.

19. Bill Clinton, "The Case for Optimism," *Time*, 1 October 2012, pp. 18–23.

20. Matt Ridley, *The Rational Optimist: How Prosperity Evolves* (London: Fourth Estate, 2010).

21. Peter H. Diamandis and Steven Kotler, *Abundance: The Future Is Better Than You Think* (New York: Free Press, 2012).

22. United Nations, "Press Conference by Population Director on Revised World Population Prospects," 13 June 2013; http://www.un.org/News/briefings/docs/2013/130613_Population.doc.htm.

23. Hania Zlotnick, UN director of population research, cited by Bill Varner, "World Population Forecast to Hit 10.1 Billion by 2100, UN Says"; http://www.bloomberg.com/news/2011–05–03/world-population-forecast-to-hit-10–1-billion-by-2100-un-says.html.

24. Other trends that are "underway" (but not discussed here) include the development of space, biological, and chemical weapons.

25. Jon Cartwright, "Rise of the Robots and the Future of War," *The Observer*, 21 November 2010; http://www.guardian.co.uk/technology/2010/nov/21/military-robots-autonomous-machines.

26. See Ronald C. Arkin, *Governing Lethal Behavior in Autonomous Robots* (Boca Raton, FL: Chapman & Hall/CRC, 2009).

27. Jon Turney, *The Rough Guide to the Future* (London: Rough Guides, 2010), p. 250; see also Chris Cole, "Rise of the Drones," *New Internationalist* 488 (December 2011), pp. 24–5.

28. "Cyberwar," *Australian Science Illustrated* 13 (September/October 2011), pp. 58, 59; Paul Harris, "Age of Cyberwar Dawns," *Guardian Weekly*, 1–7 March 2013, pp. 1, 10. See also Jonathan W. Greenert, "Imminent Domain," *U.S. Naval Institute Proceedings*

Magazine 138/12 (December 2012); available at: http://www.usni.org/magazines/proceedings/2012–12/imminent-domain.

29. "Cyberwar," p. 60.

30. Tom Leonard, "'Cyber Attacks Are an Act of War': Pentagon to Announce New Rules of Engagement against State Sponsored Hackers," *Daily Mail*, 1 June 2011; http://www.dailymail.co.uk/news/article-1392746/Cyber-attacks-act-war-Pentagon-issue-new-rules-hackers.html.

31. Turney, *Rough Guide to the Future*, p. 247.

32. Nick Hopkins, "US and China Engage in Cyber War Games," *Guardian*, 16 April 2012; http://www.guardian.co.uk/technology/2012/apr/16/us-china-cyber-war-games; Ellen Nakashima, "US and Russia Seek Deal on Cybersecurity," *Guardian Weekly*, 4–10 May 2012, p. 7; David E. Sanger and Mark Landler, "U.S. and China Agree to Hold Regular Talks on Hacking," *New York Times*, 1 June 2013; http://www.nytimes.com/2013/06/02/world/asia/us-and-china-to-hold-talks-on-hacking.html?ref=global-home.

33. Raymond C. Kelly, *Warless Societies and the Origin of War* (Ann Arbor: University of Michigan Press, 2000), p. 2.

34. Azar Gat, *War in Human Civilization* (New York: Oxford University Press, 2006), p. 35.

35. Jean Guilaine and Jean Zammit, *The Origins of War: Violence in Prehistory*, trans. Melanie Hersey (Malden, MA: Blackwell, 2005), pp. 21–2, 24.

36. Lawrence H. Keeley, *War Before Civilization: The Myth of the Peaceful Savage* (New York: Oxford University Press, 1996), pp. 26, 175, 88.

37. See "The Irrelevance of Biology," in Keeley, *War Before Civilization*, pp. 157–9.

38. Arther Ferrill, *The Origins of War: From the Stone Age to Alexander the Great* (Boulder, CO: Westview Press, 1997), p. 15.

39. Ferrill, *Origins of War*, p. 13.

40. Ferrill, *Origins of War*, pp. 16, 17.

41. Frans de Waal, *The Age of Empathy: Nature's Lessons for a Kinder Society* (New York: Harmony Books, 2009), pp. 23–4. See also Robert M. Sapolsky, "A Natural History of Peace," *Foreign Affairs*, January/February 2006; available at: http://opim.wharton.upenn.edu/~sok/papers/s/sapolsky-foreignaffairs-2006.pdf.

42. Leslie E. Sponsel, "The Natural History of Peace: The Positive View of Human Nature and Its Potential," in *A Natural History of Peace*, ed. Thomas Gregor (Nashville: Vanderbilt University Press, 1996), p. 104.

43. Sponsel, "Natural History of Peace," p. 104.

44. Guilaine and Zammit, *Origins of War*, pp. x, ix.

45. Walter Goldschmidt, "Peacemaking and the Institutions of Peace in Tribal Societies," in *The Anthropology of Peace and Nonviolence*, ed. Leslie E. Sponsel and Thomas Gregor (Boulder, CO: Lynne Rienner, 1994), p. 111.

46. Kwame Anthony Appiah, *Cosmopolitanism: Ethics in a World of Strangers* (New York: W. W. Norton, 2006), p. 14.

47. Donald E. Brown, *Human Universals* (Philadelphia: Temple University Press, 1991), p. 154.

48. "Seville Statement on Violence," Seville, Spain, 16 May 1986; available at: http://portal.unesco.org/education/en/ev.php-URL_ID=3247&URL_DO=DO_TOPIC&URL_SECTION=201.html. This statement resulted from a conference on "The Brain and

Aggression" co-sponsored by the Department of Psychobiology, University of Seville, and UNESCO. It was later published in the October 1990 issue of *American Psychologist* and has been the subject of much critical discussion.

49. Evan Charney, "Behavior Genetics and Postgenomics," *Behavioral and Brain Sciences* 35/5 (September 2012), Abstract.

50. U.S. National Library of Medicine, Genetics Home Reference, "Somatic mosaicism"; http://ghr.nlm.nih.gov/glossary=somaticmosaicism.

51. Peter Kropotkin, *Mutual Aid: A Factor of Evolution* (New York: New York University Press, 1972).

52. Margaret Mead, "Warfare Is Only an Invention—Not a Necessity," *Asia* 40 (1940), pp. 415–21; available at: http://acme.highpoint.edu/~msetzler/IntlSec/IntlSecReads/MeadeWarCreated.pdf, p. 1.

53. This claim is supported by Kelly; see *Warless Societies and the Origin of War*, p. 43.

54. Mead, "Warfare Is Only an Invention" (Internet version), p. 2.

55. John Horgan, "Margaret Mead's War Theory Kicks Butt of Neo-Darwinian and Malthusian Models," *Scientific American*, 8 November 2010; available at: http://www.scientificamerican.com/blog/post.cfm?id=margaret-meads-war-theory-kicks-but-2010-11-08.

56. Winslow Myers, *Living Beyond War: A Citizen's Guide* (Maryknoll, NY: Orbis Books, 2009), pp. 52–3.

57. Kelly, *Warless Societies and the Origin of War*, p. 43.

58. Matthew Melko, *52 Peaceful Societies* (Oakville, Ontario: CPRI [Canadian Peace Research Institute] Press, 1973). pp. 1, 6.

59. Melko, *52 Peaceful Societies*, p. 9.

60. Bruce D. Bonta, *Peaceful Peoples: An Annotated Bibliography* (Metuchen, NJ: Scarecrow Press, 1993), p. 4 (emphasis in original).

61. Elise Boulding, *Cultures of Peace: The Hidden Side of History* (Syracuse: Syracuse University Press, 2000), p. 165.

62. Boulding, *Cultures of Peace*, pp. 92ff.

63. Douglas P. Fry, *Beyond War: The Human Potential for Peace* (New York: Oxford University Press, 2007), p. 6 (emphasis in original). See also Douglas P. Fry and Patrik Söderberg, "Lethal Aggression in Mobile Forager Bands and Implications for the Origins of War," *Science* 341, no. 6143, 19 July 2013, pp. 270-3.

64. Fry, *Beyond War*, p. 17.

65. Johan M. G. van der Dennen, *The Origin of War: The Evolution of a Male-Coalitional Reproductive Strategy* (Groningen: Origin Press, 1995), Appendices, pp. 595–674; available at: http://rint.rechten.rug.nl/rth/dennen/dennen6.htm.

66. Van der Dennen, *Origin of War*, pp. 539–40.

67. Van der Dennen, *Origin of War*, p. 589. This hypothesis would seem to receive support from Napoleon Chagnon's *Noble Savages: My Life among Two Dangerous Tribes—the Yanomamö and the Anthropologists* (New York: Simon & Schuster, 2013).

68. Van der Dennen, *Origin of War*, p. 594.

69. Keeley, *War Before Civilization*, p. 32.

70. Seyom Brown, *The Causes and Prevention of War* (New York: St. Martin's Press, 1987), pp. 13–14, 15.

71. Thomas Gregor and Clayton A. Robarchek, "Two Paths to Peace: Semai and Mehinaku Nonviolence," in *Natural History of Peace*, ed. Gregor, pp.159–88.
72. Gregor and Robarchek, "Two Paths to Peace," p. 160.
73. Gregor and Robarchek, "Two Paths to Peace," p. 164.
74. Gregor and Robarchek, "Two Paths to Peace," p. 164.
75. Yvonne Vissing and Quixada Moore-Vissing, "Warless Societies," in *The Oxford International Encyclopedia of Peace*, ed. Nigel Young (Oxford: Oxford University Press, 2010), e-reference edition; http://www.oxford-peace.com/entry?entry=t296.e754.
76. Gregor and Robarchek, "Two Paths to Peace," p. 162.
77. Gregor and Robarchek, "Two Paths to Peace," pp. 166–8.
78. Ervin Staub, "Basic Needs, Altruism, and Aggression," in *The Social Psychology of Good and Evil*, ed. Arthur G. Miller (New York: Guilford Press, 2004), pp. 72–3.
79. Vissing and Moore-Vissing, "Warless Societies."
80. Goldschmidt, "Peacemaking," p. 120.
81. Gregor and Robarchek, "Two Paths to Peace," p. 169.
82. Thomas E. Lovejoy, "Species Leave the Ark One by One," in *The Preservation of Species: The Value of Biological Diversity*, ed. Brian G. Norton (Princeton, NJ: Princeton University Press, 1986), p. 16.
83. Boulding, *Cultures of Peace*, p. 28.
84. Fry, *Beyond War*, p. 23.
85. Boulding, *Cultures of Peace*, p. 101.
86. Readers might like to know about these sources of good news (in the secular sense): *Yes!* magazine (www.yesmagazine.org); *DailyGood* (provides daily items of good news to subscribers: http://www.dailygood.org); *Good* magazine (http://www.good.is); *Avaaz Daily Briefing* (http://en.avaaz.org); Greater Good Science Center and magazine (http://greatergood.berkeley.edu); Charity Focus (http://www.charityfocus.org/new/about.php), an interesting website for positive change; HuffPost Good News (http://www.huffingtonpost.com/good-news); Care2 notifies members of monthly successes across a range of important causes (http://www.care2.com). See also Alfie Kohn, *The Brighter Side of Human Nature: Altruism and Empathy in Everyday Life* (New York: Basic Books, 1992).
87. Bruce M. Knauft, "The Human Evolution of Cooperative Interest," in *Natural History of Peace*, ed. Gregor, pp. 71, 73–4.
88. W. D. Hamilton, *Narrow Roads of Gene Land: The Collected Papers of W. D. Hamilton, Vol. 1: Evolution of Social Behaviour* (New York: W. H. Freeman, 1996), chap. 1; Robert Trivers, *Social Evolution* (Upper Saddle River, NJ: Benjamin-Cummings, 1985). My thanks to Brian Byrne for pointing out these findings to me.
89. Michael Tomasello, *Why We Cooperate* (Cambridge, MA: Boston Review/MIT Press, 2009), pp. 4–5.
90. Tomasello, *Why We Cooperate*, pp. 44, 53, 58. Tomasello comments that "from all of our studies, it seems clear that on the basis of just one or a few experiences in a collective activity with an adult, children readily conclude that this is how it is done, this is how 'we' do it" (p. 93).

91. Tomasello, *Why We Cooperate*, pp. 74–5, 85.
92. Tim Flannery, *Here on Earth: An Argument for Hope* (Melbourne: Text Publishing, 2010), p. 36.
93. Flannery, *Here on Earth*, p. 65.
94. Martin A. Nowak, "Why We Help," *Scientific American*, July 2012, p. 24. See also Martin A. Nowak, with Roger Highfield, *SuperCooperators: Altruism, Evolution, and Why We Need Each Other to Succeed* (New York: Free Press, 2012); Martin A. Nowak, "Why We Help," *Scientific American* 22/1 (Winter 2013), Special Collector's Edition on *What Makes Us Human*, pp. 92–7; Robert Wright, *Nonzero: The Logic of Human Destiny* (New York: Vintage Books, 2001).
95. Lee Smolin, *The Life of the Cosmos* (New York: Oxford University Press, 1997), as cited by John Gribbin, *In Search of the Multiverse* (London: Allen Lane, 2009), p. 190.
96. Peter Singer, ed., *Ethics* (New York: Oxford University Press, 1994), p. 44.
97. Singer, ed., *Ethics*, Part I; Frans de Waal, *Good Natured: The Origins of Right and Wrong in Humans and Other Animals* (Cambridge, MA: Harvard University Press, 1997), pp. 20–1.
98. Flannery, *Here on Earth*, p. 123.

3

Two Moral Arguments Against War

War, by its very nature, embodies the tyranny that it claims to address. . . .
The worst effect of any war . . . is that it destroys the ground of peace, erodes
its culture and wrecks its institutions, so preparing the way for new wars. . . .
For us to live together in any kind of safety or to meet the real needs of
human beings, like eliminating poverty or dealing with disease, the eradica-
tion of war is a prerequisite.

—Diana Francis, *Rethinking War and Peace* (2004)

3.1. WAR AND MORALITY

This chapter focuses on an explanation of the just war tradition as it has developed in the West, a critique of that mode of defending war, and a presentation of arguments against war from an ethical standpoint. Before we begin, however, it is worth noting that even warfare among tribal groups (including campaigns of revenge and retribution, inter-clan conflicts, and feuds) possesses readily recognizable moral aspects, making it possible to justify acts of armed hostility from their own cultural vantage point. Thus, as anthropologist Raymond Kelly points out, among hunter-gatherer and preindustrial agricultural societies, those who resort to warfare accept "lethal violence as *an instrument of the social group* and a legitimate means for the attainment of group objectives and interests." The legitimating conditions are that armed conflicts may be "collectively sanctioned by participants' community"; "morally justified in participants' viewpoint"; and that "participants [are] esteemed by others of their collectivity."[1]

A Spectrum of Attitudes toward Waging War

Modern Western attitudes toward war can be classified in various ways, but according to the most careful analyses, they may be arranged according to what we might call gradations of moral permissibility.[2] At one end of this scale, we find absolute pacifism, or the view that war is never permissible under any circumstances. Moving away from this end, a more moderate version of pacifism entails that war, although generally wrong, may be justified, at least in rare instances. When it is justified, certain principles must govern the manner in which it is prosecuted in order to uphold deeply entrenched ideals of humanity, mercy, and decency. Somewhat further along this line we encounter the just war view, namely, that there are "acceptable" or even "good" wars, which are the "last resort" in defending one's homeland and cultural values against aggression. This view presumes that a just war can only be waged by an "innocent victim" who is under attack.[3] Whether it may also be waged by an innocent victim who is manifestly about to be attacked (that is, whether preemptive or preventive war may be just) remains a matter of great contention among theorists.[4] Just intervention in aid of other innocent victims or to prevent large-scale atrocities has relatively recently been established as official United Nations doctrine—but such intervention is only to be implemented by a UN-approved force.[5]

The opposite end of the scale is anchored by the view that war is in itself a good thing, because of its unique power to bring out the best qualities in human beings, revitalize culture, clean out the weaklings of our species, and so on. Somewhat short of this Mussolini-like, Social Darwinist outlook, we would encounter the so-called "realist" position (often associated with nineteenth-century military strategist Carl von Clausewitz): that in a world in which people often behave irrationally and are subject to being blinded by emotion and naked self-interest, war—although inherently undesirable—must nevertheless remain an acceptable option in pursuit of a nation's policies and aims, and in any event, may be more or less inevitable.[6] Unlike the immediately preceding view, the realist stance does not eschew ethical restraints on the conduct (or waging) of war, even though it does largely put aside preventive moral checks against going to war, replacing them instead with pragmatic considerations. In other words, if it is seen to be necessary to resort to war in the national interest, then that is what must be done, reluctantly or otherwise. But the object of war is only to achieve some limited goal or else to neutralize an enemy by destroying its will and means to continue being politically troublesome and aggressive.

One can readily discern that both the "moderate pacifist" and "realist" views, dissimilar as they are, quickly confront questions about the justification

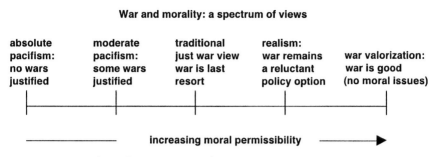

Figure 3.1 War and morality: a spectrum of views

of going to war and about what may and may not be done, once war has begun, to advance the goals of achieving supremacy and victory. It may be argued that "pro-war" postures of one kind or another stretch back to ancient history; but as Charles Guthrie and Michael Quinlan point out in their concise study of just war thinking, pacifism as much as realism has scriptural roots in Judaism, Christianity, and Islam, and probably took precedence over realism in the religious outlooks of the early Christian period.[7] Be this as it may, what we now know as the "just war tradition" has a history of a millennium and a half and, Guthrie and Quinlan attest, initially developed as part of a defensive response to invading armies sweeping across Europe from both West and East during the fifth to eighth centuries CE.[8] Aryeh Neier locates in "the rules of chivalry . . . antecedents of the laws of war of our era."[9] From our point of view here, the interesting thing about this tradition is that it springs from, and also reveals, moral tensions that verge on the self-contradictory. For this reason, as we shall see, just war thinking is ultimately unacceptable, leaving us with no rational alternative other than rejecting war altogether.

3.2. JUST WAR THINKING, AND SOME ISSUES

Because just war doctrine has been part of the background to waging war for a very long time, it has become for many an essential or default reference-point. The explanation for this is in part that would-be war-makers feel the need for a rationalization of their prowar stance and any decisions that flow from that stance. But we also must consider a general recognition (even on the part of most war-makers) that war represents a drastic failure and break-down of normality in human affairs, and an understanding that it exacts an extreme toll upon participants and their fellow citizens. Thus, a justification for going to war is perceived to be necessary, both for oneself (one's political group, country, alliance, and so on), and as an appeal to others who are likely to judge one's actions. When just war reasoning is applied, it is hoped that war will appear to be the "lesser of evils," and its total damage less than that of the alternatives—not only from the belligerent's standpoint, but also in the eyes of others. The positive judgment of others would, it is supposed, bestow objectivity and truth on the war-maker's position. Beyond this, we can note that both just war thinking and international laws of war affirm the need for civilization to continue after hostilities cease, and try to provide a framework in support of that goal. (More on this idea in a moment.)

Although past and present accounts of what constitutes a just war vary somewhat, certain core principles are invariably included. These divide into two groups, pertaining to *ius ad bellum* (the right to wage war) and *ius in bello* (right conduct during war).[10] Briefly, the principles are as follows.

Ius ad Bellum

- **Just cause:** Having right on one's side, or a morally compelling reason for going to war, such as response to aggression, to aid another nation that is being subjected to unprovoked attack, or to protect against violations of human rights. (Today, the reason, in order to qualify, would not only need to have the appearance of being morally compelling, but also be sanctioned by international law.)
- **Legitimate authority:** This term has customarily referred to the government or sovereign in charge at the time: a person or persons "having the right" to take military action on behalf of the state and its citizens or some other political entity. It is easy to see the nest of problems such a criterion faces in the contemporary world, where political corruption and collusion with vested interests is commonplace, and where various fragmentary and revolutionary movements—often lacking "legitimacy" by definition, at least initially—see their raison d'être as, for example, using armed force to combat oppression or to establish a religious state.
- **Last resort:** All other means to avert war have been tried and have failed, or are somehow blocked from realization. In accordance with this principle, President Obama has recently offered a just war defense of drone killings on foreign soil.[11] Political commentator Waleed Aly observes, in response to this defense, that "Sadly, we're in an era when civilian deaths are deemed an acceptable inevitability of war, rather than a reason to avoid it. . . . The central problem is drones permit a kind of no-risk, low-cost warfare. Indeed, they so radically and fundamentally alter the nature of war that they risk making war seem far less grave, and far easier to wage."[12]

- **Right intention:** Restoration and preservation of a peaceful state of affairs or remedying of wrong must be one's aim.
- **Proportionality:** The consequences of going to war must be more good than bad, both overall and in relation to alternative courses of action.
- **Probable success:** The odds favor the attainment of one's objectives by resorting to war, as outlined above.

Ius in Bello

- **Discrimination:** During warfare, noncombatants must not be deliberately targeted. Issues that immediately arise here are how to designate noncombatants and whether modern weapons technology (such as landmines and drones) and weapons of mass destruction (WMDs), terrorist activity, and using civilians as human shields make this principle obsolete. Most ancient warfare involved indiscriminate killing, brutality, and pillaging. The special tragedy of modern warfare is that the laws of war have not prevented it from falling into the same pattern. Indiscriminate use of large-scale weaponry and indiscriminate killing, more generally, have been features of armed conflict since World War I, and during World War II, they became deliberate strategic priorities for both ground assaults and attacks from the air.[13] In the new civil and guerrilla wars of our era, not only is very little attention paid to established norms of behavior, these are violated, intentionally and egregiously, in order to produce the maximum amount of disempowerment and terror among the populace.
- **Proportionality:** In the context of battle, cost-benefit calculations arise once more; the least harmful means (or least amount of violent force) that will achieve one's objectives must always dictate the choices made.

The Oddity of Having Laws to Govern War

One might be forgiven for thinking that there is something peculiar about the entire enterprise of devising moral principles for war (or even laws of war, for that matter). This is because what is being proposed is a set of rules intended to apply in a state of rule-collapse (or laws for a lawless domain). The very concept sounds absurd and self-negating. Indeed, we often think of war as a condition in which "anything goes." ("All's fair in love and war.") But on the other hand, as acknowledged earlier, the argument for having rules for war and laws of war is that wars come and go, but life must go on in spite of them; so it is best to retain at least a shred of decency and humanity in order to preserve some continuity of experience linking together the pre- and post-bellum human states within some framework of positive behavioral norms, however tattered by conflict it may have become. If there have to be wars, the argument goes, perhaps they can be prevented from reducing the participants to the lowest levels of depravity to which human beings can sink. Having laws of war is, so to speak, less bad than having none, for they represent and enshrine the idea that there are absolute limits on conduct against which we must not transgress. Furthermore, since, as Neier observes, "by far the largest number of severe human rights abuses take place in the context of armed conflict,"[14] we should do whatever we can to control and prevent these.

Now, what are the results of having such rules and laws in place? It must be said that the results have been mixed; but it might reasonably be claimed that they are better than if there had been no such regulations. However, like other counterfactual statements, this belief can be neither verified nor refuted. But then again, moral principles and laws have not prevented systematic abuse of human rights in non-war environments, either, so apparently being at war, while an extreme condition, cannot by itself explain unacceptable deviations from accustomed standards of decency and humanity. On a more positive note, Neier contends that, historically speaking, out of the humanitarian laws of war has developed the important body of international human rights law that exists today.[15]

Philosopher Nigel Dower places an interesting perspective on the oddity of the idea of rules for conducting wars ethically. According to his account, it derives from an internal tension generated by the discord between moral and pragmatic considerations relating to war.

> The fact is that war is dominated by the logic of the end, which is in conflict with the logic of the means. By this I mean that the prosecution of war *qua* war is dominated by an end or goal, that is, victory, and requires what is most effective to that end. By contrast, if the ethical conduct of war is shaped by the ethics of the means, then that suggests that there are certain ways of fighting which are acceptable and others which are not. The means has an independent moral character. It is not merely what is effective. The trouble is that the two clash.[16]

This helps explain why the whole enterprise of attempting to justify war in the first place, and to ethically rationalize the ways in which war operations are carried out, is bound to be riddled with inconsistency.

Martin Luther King, Jr. (clearly a very staunch pacifist) had a somewhat different outlook on the means-ends relationship under consideration, which focuses on the continuity between the two: "Destructive means cannot bring constructive ends because the means represent the ideal in the making and the end in progress. Immoral means cannot bring moral ends, for the ends are pre-existent in the means."[17] According to this view, no matter how righteous the ends we seek are thought to be, war cannot be a justified means of pursuing them. War claims many innocent victims and is always violent, and remains so, no matter how this violence is finessed by alleged justifications; and because of this, violence will infect and degrade our post-bellum condition. (On the legacy of violence, see the Introduction, section 3, "The Costs of War," and Chapter 4, section 4.2, "The Limitations of Violence.") There is also a more subtle point being driven home here. This is that anyone who wishes to practice peace needs to maintain consistency between words and actions. There is no point in publically advocating a moral stance using messages whose subtext contains threats of violence.

War and "Moral Exclusion"

Yet there is something far more worrying embedded in the reasoning that legitimizes wartime acts of killing (as well as of wounding, destroying, and various forms of wanton cruelty) than either Dower or King has pinpointed. A deeper concern is that just war notions rest on an attitude that psychologist Susan Opotow calls "moral exclusion." Moral exclusion "rationalizes and excuses harm inflicted on those outside the scope of justice. Excluding others from the scope of justice means viewing them as unworthy of fairness, resources, or sacrifice, and seeing them as expendable, undeserving, exploitable, or irrelevant."[18] In essence, it is as if they are expelled or cordoned off from the moral community (much as nonhuman animals have been, until quite recently). Just war theorists may retort that it is far from their intention to excommunicate certain groups from the human family or to deny to anyone his or her legitimate claim to moral consideration; in fact, quite the contrary. Yet as soon as human lives and welfare (even if "only" those of opposing soldiers) become capable of compromise in the name of expediency, it can be argued that moral exclusion has overshadowed our judgment.

In an interesting essay published in 1946—*Neither Victims Nor Executioners*—the Algerian-French existentialist philosopher and Nobel Prize author Albert Camus anticipated several of the points being argued here. He urges that war and the use of violence as an instrument of politics can only be abandoned if the frame of mind that legitimizes murder (including killing in combat and state-sanctioned capital punishment) is rejected. Individuals must take responsibility for governmental acts performed on their behalf, and put themselves in others' shoes: If we would wish not to be victims ourselves, then we should refuse to be executioners, either directly or by proxy. New ways of communicating and of solving human problems would then, of necessity, need to be found to replace the old ways. Some would accuse Camus of outright utopianism, but he has an interesting reply to offer:

> Let us suppose that certain individuals resolve that they will consistently oppose to power the force of example; to authority, exhortation; to insult, friendly reasoning; to trickery, simple honor. Let us suppose they refuse all the advantages of present-day society and accept only the duties and obligations which bind them to other men. Let us suppose they devote themselves to orienting education, the press and public opinion toward the principles outlined here. Then I say that such men would be acting not as Utopians but as honest realists. They would be preparing the future and at the same time knocking down a few of the walls which imprison us today. If realism be the art of taking into account both the present and the future, of gaining the most while sacrificing the least, then who can fail to see the positively dazzling realism of such behavior?[19]

Furthermore, Camus suggests that when such a "utopian" vision comes to shape the ways of the world, people will wonder that they ever saw things differently. As support for this claim, consider, for example, how antiquated and abnormal it is to believe nowadays, as people once took for granted, that women shouldn't vote; that there are "inferior races"; that being gay is evil; that children's education is only for the privileged; that workers have no rights; or that animal abuse is of no concern. Judgments about the success of Camus's particular thought-experiment will vary, but we will return to the topic of possibilities for a nonviolent future in Chapters 6 and 7, when we examine what it might mean to "build a culture of peace."

3.3. FURTHER CRITICAL REFLECTIONS ON THE JUST WAR CONCEPT

Difficulties in Applying the Principles

Next, a few general observations about just war theorizing are in order. These will be followed by some criticisms of specific principles. To begin with, it is commonly understood that the six *ius ad bellum* principles are individually necessary and only jointly sufficient to count as a justification for waging war. That is, *every one of the stipulated conditions must be satisfied* before going to war is permissible. The two *ius in bello* principles for the conduct of war are to be regarded in like manner. This obviously entails that the onus is always on the party contemplating war to undertake some very detailed calculations and explore exhaustively every option for preventing armed conflict. As a result, justification of war becomes potentially viable in only the most rare of circumstances. Second, while it is not a settled matter whether all eight principles are purely consequentialist in nature, most clearly are, possible exceptions being "just cause," "legitimate authority," and (maybe, at least in part) "last resort." This is significant because it means that reasoning about whether to go to war cannot be obfuscated merely by making questionable appeals to duty-based and nebulous abstractions (such as "the honor of the fatherland," "defense of our flag," or even "dying to protect what we stand for"). Instead, such reasoning must always rest upon a careful weighing of actions with regard to their probable and possible effects in the real world. Third, the whole apparatus of justification seems to work (at best) for an international community in which sovereign states are the only acknowledged moral agents, which by itself makes it of doubtful applicability to the world we actually live in. As one group of conflict-resolution scholars points out, "The dissolution of the Soviet Union brought to a close the long period in which a single international conflict dominated the international system. Instead, internal conflicts, ethnic conflicts, conflicts over secession and power struggles within countries became the norm in the 1990s. These reflected not so much struggles between competing centres of power . . . but the fragmentation and breakdown of state structures, economies and whole societies."[20] This trend continues today. Fourth, although well meaning, all of the principles invite flexibility of interpretation, some more than others. Fifth, and related to the previous point, appraisal of one's own cause, and of how well it fares under the various constraints imposed by the other seven principles, is based on self-evaluation, which is notoriously subjective and self-serving, even (or especially) in the face of criticism and when emotion takes over and the stakes are high.

Continuing along the lines of the last point, here are some specific problems. "Just cause" may look relatively uncontroversial and innocuous, but consider how easy it is to disguise—even from oneself—the real reasons for going to war (for instance, to secure a reliable supply of oil or to secure a geographical position of influence rather than just to overthrow a hated and hostile dictator). This quandary also infects "right intention." Furthermore, a just cause claim is often bolstered by the belief that "God is on our side"; and given that opponents, each with their own "just cause," make the same appeal, we must conclude that God is at war with himself and has chosen the victors of conflicts more or less inconsistently, and either haphazardly or arbitrarily, throughout history.

"Last resort" may look a good deal more easily determinable than it actually is. Diplomatic solutions and negotiations, compromise, tension-reduction
strategies, the freezing of assets and other economic sanctions, blockades, international isolation, and related measures are rich with promise and it takes
time to reap their benefits. Nonviolent resistance aimed at bringing about
change may sometimes work rapidly and sometimes more gradually. So, given
the uncertain and complicated relationship between means and ends, there
will always (or nearly always) be an issue over whether every course of action short of war has been tried and allowed time to achieve its objectives.
But the underlying and unspoken question percolating away in such situations may be: "How long are we prepared to wait?" or: "How patient are we
prepared to be?" and this is where the "last resort" issue merges with that of
"proportionality." There are no set answers in this area, but there are the challenges of how committed we are to peaceful ways of conflict resolution, and
of our degree of willpower to stay the course. If we are very committed, then
creative alternatives to war will always be available, and we will have faith that
they are difficult, if not impossible, to exhaust without getting a positive result.
(Imagine a world in which everyone agreed to outlaw war: There would then
be no alternative other than to find peaceful solutions to problems and so they
would inevitably have to be found. See "The Illegality of War," pages 129–30.)

With regard to the *ius ad bellum* criterion of "proportionality," the reader is
referred to the Introduction, section 3, "The Costs of War," which bears largely
on this issue.

Noncombatants at Risk

The *ius in bello* complications generated by the concepts of "discrimination"
and "proportionality" are quite serious and have become more so with today's
weapons. Leaving aside WMDs, which speak for themselves, and some of which
are already outlawed, newer generations of weapons and even "conventional"
weapons have become increasingly sophisticated, destructive, and hence dead-
lier, and so-called "smart" weapons (heat-seeking missiles, programmable rifle
ammunition, and GPS-guided, air-launched munitions, for example) do not
unerringly target only selected individuals. The same reservation applies to
the increasing use of lethal drone aircraft. (And extra-judicial assassinations
are morally and legally wrong to start with.) The historical trend toward intensive research, development, and industrial production of weaponry has had the
result that the potential for civilian casualties is greater than ever, both in actual combat and in the devastating legacy it leaves behind (ruined ecosystems,

uncharted landmines, depleted uranium, enriched uranium dumped at sea, unexploded cluster bombs, and so forth). World War II is deemed by most commentators to be the watershed event, in that the disregard for ordinary people's lives reached an apex when Nazi atrocities were matched in kind, if not in absolute number, by the Allies in their fire-bombing of major German and Japanese cities and their use of nuclear weapons.

The idea of noncombatant immunity from intentionally inflicted harm has a lengthy history, and whatever shreds of it still remain, these have now come under challenge, as noted earlier. Terrorists or insurgents may disguise themselves or co-opt ordinary civilians to do their deeds. Some belligerents hold that anyone who supports the enemy—from citizens working in the munitions industry, to others feeding the armed forces, to those on the streets cheering for victory or merely willing it silently in their hearts—is equally guilty and therefore constitutes a legitimate target. For terrorists, it is enough that their intended targets be citizens of some country that they accuse of killing or oppressing people they themselves claim to represent. But notwithstanding that some who do genuinely pose a direct threat are difficult to detect, and that the word "noncombatant" eludes easy definition and application, most thinkers about war and most average people agree that a line has to be drawn somewhere, in spite of the risks. This means that the benefit of the doubt about who counts as a noncombatant must always be given to civilians in any conflict.

In addition, the notion of proportionality seems to assume rational decision-making at all times, and, therefore, a restrained approach to war-making. Yet it is not hard to imagine that any nation or group which had access to WMDs would use them if it was desperate enough and had its back to the wall of defeat and decimation. This fact is one thing that made (and still makes) the presence of nuclear weapons in the world particularly frightening.

3.4. "LAST RESORT" AND THE CASE OF IRAN

How is it possible to tell whether all avenues to settling an international dispute nonviolently have really been exhausted? An answer to this question is something that requires to be carefully considered both by those who see war as a last resort *and* by those who say that war never is (or must never be) the last resort. Yet, although much has been learned about negotiation strategies, ways of compromising, mutual reduction of tensions, prisoner's dilemmas, and so on, no set formula is available to calculate the answer we seek. But what we do know—or should know—is that certain measures that have failed in the past are likely to fail again, that new thinking is required. (See Chapter 6, section 6.5, "Thinking Creatively about Alternatives.")

The current international standoff over Iran's alleged nuclear weapons development program is a case in point. This encounter is set against a background shaped by several factors: more than thirty years of hostile relations between Iran and the West (particularly the United States); the struggle to maintain a reliable supply of oil at a stable cost in order to meet increasing world demand; seemingly endless conflict between Israel and neighboring Muslim nations; Israel's possession of nuclear weapons and threat to destroy Iran's nuclear capability, if it eventuates; the widely held belief that possessing nuclear weapons is the key to commanding respect from other nations; the faltering global campaign to limit nuclear weapons proliferation in general (plus the hypocrisy of nuclear nations' dictating how nonnuclear nations must behave); and the continuing conflict between the UN and Iran over Iran's uranium-enrichment program and site inspection in that country. Nevertheless, we can also look at the encounter in its own right and zero in on a few relevant issues.

One of these is the escalation of rhetoric. Posturing and implied threats have a long history in international politics. The bluffing factor cannot be ruled out in any given case, but the general problem is that either side (or both) can become trapped by the momentum of verbal combat, which leaves little room to maneuver, out of fear of appearing "weak." As a seasoned journalist observes concerning the Iran crisis, "all sides risk becoming hostages to their own rhetoric."[21] A second factor revolves around the possibility of basic misreading of the situation by one side or both. Iran sees the United States as economically faltering and reeling from the failure of its wars in Iraq and Afghanistan, but also as possessing some thirty-five military bases in the Middle East.[22] The United States sees the regime in Iran as "evil," and as on the verge of collapse. (Some analysts argue that forcing Iranian regime change is the real American agenda, just as it was when the United States and the United Kingdom made Iran into a client state in 1953 by orchestrating a coup that overthrew the democratically elected Mosadegh government and installed the Shah.) But the more important issue is whether Iran actually *has* a nuclear weapons development program, which it has denied for many years. To go to war over this assumption, if wrong, would be to commit the same mistake that sparked the ill-fated invasion of Iraq in 2003. A third major issue is the tendency of rhetoric, direct and indirect threats, and threatening actions to produce results opposite to what was intended. For example, while the United States may be undergoing a difficult period, it has to a large extent defined itself in terms of worldwide military supremacy (see Chapter 7, section 7.4, "A Global Outlook"), and therefore—especially in an era in which control of governments everywhere is so fragile—it cannot be seen as backing down or vacillating in the face of Iran's threat to blockade the Strait of Hormuz. On the other hand, it has been observed, with reference to this situation, that "threats to the regime's hold on power will serve to accelerate Iran's nuclear program which they see as a deterrent to foreign intervention."[23] As usual, the ordinary people of Iran are those who suffer the most from sanctions and who would bear the burdens of war. Severe economic sanctions against Iran by the United States and the European Union may thus backfire and be counterproductive, just as UN-ordered sanctions have been (see further discussion of sanctions in Chapter 4, section 4.5). Fourth, and sadly typical of such confrontations, "heightened activity [on both sides] will increase the chances of an unplanned clash."[24] Some event could serve as a catalyst or "flashpoint" for mutually ruinous actions that would also have a severe impact on the Middle East and the world as a whole. If this were to happen, who would not then wish that some unexplored avenues toward a nonviolent solution to this crisis had been tried?

At the moment of writing, Iran has rejected unilateral talks with the United States, new multilateral talks in Kazakhstan have collapsed, and there are, as yet, no plans to resume these. Meanwhile, both houses of the US Congress have gone on record to declare that they do not authorize attacks on Iran.[25] Both the United States and Israel have warned repeatedly that time is running out for a nonviolent end to this crisis. And yet the election of a new president of Iran, Hassan Rouhani, who took office in August 2013, has sparked hopes of a more constructive dialogue with the US. Whatever peaceful resolution of the Iran situation might eventuate further down the road,[26] it should be evident that old habits, leading to the dangers outlined above, must be broken, and fresh approaches allowed to evolve. Included here, among "old habits" must be cyberattacks by the United States designed to cripple the computer systems that control Iran's nuclear enrichment facility at Natanz.[27] While some might be inclined to include this operation under the heading of activities that fall short of the last resort, it seems clearly to be the sort of provocation that could trigger a military response.

3.5. FIRST ANTIWAR ARGUMENT: THE FUNDAMENTAL PREMISE OF MORALITY

In this section and the next, two arguments are stated and examined that clinch the case against war. These moral arguments have been developed out of a line of thought formulated by Diana Francis in *Rethinking War and Peace*,[28] and they cut more deeply than the criticisms of just war thinking outlined so far. What has been established to this point is that the justification of war is an enterprise built upon shifting sands—hardly something to which we would wish to entrust our destiny as individuals, as groups, or as a species. Not only this, but most people now realize that they also have the fate of other species and of the planet itself to consider. This larger sphere of concern, however, has been almost entirely omitted from thinking about war, and certainly from discussions of "just war." (See also Chapter 7, section 7.2, "Respect for Other Animals and the Environment.")

The first antiwar argument can be stated succinctly as follows (where "**P**" stands for "premise," "**C**" for "conclusion," and the symbol "∴" for "therefore"). Many will recognize this argument, like the one to follow in the next section, as an example of deductive reasoning, of the type more technically known as a syllogism. We argue or make our points using syllogisms all the time. For instance: "When I help my neighbor do some yard work, then he owes me one. I helped him yesterday. So he owes me one (help in return) today." The structure of a syllogism is such that if the premises are true, and the conclusion flows logically (or validly) from them, then the argument is sound (or irrefutable). So if an argument of this kind is valid (structurally good), then the only way to refute it (show that it is unsound) is to question the truth of its premises. The first and second arguments will each be stated in abbreviated form, followed by a more detailed discussion.

Argument #1

P_1:   The fundamental premise of morality is unconditional "respect for the dignity and needs" of all human beings.

P_2:   War negates (that is, systematically denies and undermines) respect for the dignity and needs of human beings, and is inconsistent with it.

C_1:   ∴ War negates and is inconsistent with the fundamental premise of morality.

(First stage of the argument; C_1 is also the beginning premise for the second stage of the argument, which immediately follows; so C_1 becomes P_3.)

P_3:   War negates and is inconsistent with the fundamental premise of morality.

P_4:   "Morality is necessary to our well-being, as individuals and as a species."

C_2:   ∴ War negates and is inconsistent with a basic condition of our well-being, as individuals and as a species.

(The argument completed, with C_2 being its conclusion.)

A Closer Look at Argument #1

There are various ways to formulate what might be called "the fundamental premise of morality," but the one chosen for P_1 should be relatively uncontroversial. Most accounts of what it means to take a moral viewpoint on the world—or more specifically, on our actions in the world—adopt a universalizing principle such as that found in P_1. The word "universalizing" here signifies that all moral actions or rules must be consistent with the overarching principle stated. For example, the Golden Rule, the utilitarian maxim "Each to count for one and no one to count for more than one," and the Kantian imperative "Always treat others as ends-in-themselves, never merely as means to your own ends" all express the universalizing principle of morality in somewhat different ways. "Human dignity" may be understood in terms of the basic moral worth, autonomy, and independent value of people's lives, which command "respect," that is, an attitude of recognition, affirmation, and noninterference. The notion of having rights and of there being universal human rights is often used to capture these precepts. (See Chapter 7, section 7.1, "Respect for Differences and Human Rights.") "Needs" pretty much speak for themselves, inasmuch as there exist certain basic requirements of life, or minimum conditions, that everyone depends on having met in order to function at all, and to realize his or her potential. Food and shelter fall under this heading, as do certain "higher-order" needs such as friendship, love, freedom of expression, meaningful work, and personal fulfillment.

To clarify what it means to say that war "negates and is inconsistent with" respect for humans' dignity and needs (P_2), it is only necessary to point out what is well known to anyone who has thought seriously about the subject, namely, that in warfare, fighting forces are commanded and expected to commit acts that in everyday life would be condemned as immoral and punished as criminally culpable. Several authors have pointed this out, each in his or her own manner. For instance, it has been stated that "the right to live is not applied in times of war."[29] That highlights the issue in stark and simple terms. Other writers offer more detailed analyses. For example, Kent Shifferd notes that "In war time, people who in their normal lives would never hurt anyone support both the preparation for and the carrying out of massive violence. . . . Almost no one of these people [soldiers in combat] is evil, but they acquiesce to, and some of them perform, evil deeds."[30] This kind of transformation and the ways in which it damages human minds and devours human decency is vividly recorded in Philip Caputo's Vietnam account *A Rumor of War*.[31] To remain for a moment at the level of the impact of war on individuals, deliberately killing and maiming others and destroying their livelihood and families are the worst kinds of wrongdoing imaginable within commonplace moral and legal frameworks. (We may also recall that "Thou shalt not kill" is one of the unqualified Old Testament biblical Ten Commandments; and in the New Testament, "Love thy neighbor as thyself" is given as a supreme commandment, as well.[32]) Elaine Scarry argues that "in consenting to kill, he [the soldier] consents to perform (for the country) the act that would in peacetime expose his unpoliticalness and place him outside the moral space of the nation. . . . [H]e divests himself of civilization, decivilizes himself, reverses not just an 'idea' or 'belief' but a learned and deeply embodied set of physical impulses and gestures regarding his relation to any other person's body."[33] Scarry's insight is that, at a somatic, fleshly level, both killing and being killed in war tears apart the sociality that is materially part of people's identities, as it destroys their lives. The same could be said of maiming and being maimed in war. We know in the visceral core of our being that these acts are wrong, because this knowledge is not just cognitive: It is also ingrained and habituated into our comportment, our very sense of selfhood and of being human. (It may even be part of our evolutionary and biological heritage.) Yet killing and maiming are not only required by war, and are its essential and inescapable features; but they are also lauded and rewarded with honor by one's country—a troubling paradox. Some have argued as well that because humans (with the exception of sociopaths) have such strong inner constraints against killing their own kind, it takes carefully designed forms of conditioning to override them.[34] The famous—and true—story of the "Christmas Truce" in World War I, when enemies became friends for a brief while, reinforces this point. Although the Great War arguably represented more hazy "causes" to fight for than some later wars, it is still striking that commanders had to punish, threaten, and discipline soldiers in order to prevent them from fraternizing again with their foes.[35]

War therefore violates moral and legal norms at a fundamental level. "It is not a complete state of moral breakdown," just war theorists would hasten to insist, as we have already seen. But given the problems with just war doctrine discussed earlier and the fact that any universalized ethics is meant to embrace strangers as well as friends, it is not difficult to see that war is incompatible with morality. Strategies for waging war and the conduct of war in general (whether guided by particular strategies or not) lead to the entirely predictable outcomes mentioned above, and any historical example of war-making, even if rationalized by just war thinking, provides abundant evidence to illustrate the point.

A somewhat different standpoint on these issues is taken by Francis in the following passage:

> Wars are made up of acts of enmity rather than co-operation, of imposition rather than negotiation, of summary killing rather than due process, of destruction rather than

creation. Peace (positive peace), by my definition, is a state in which the culture of the people, the structures within which they live, the relationships between them, and the attitudes and behaviours which they display are characterised by mutual respect. If this is a fair description, trying to achieve peace by war is, to use a well-known metaphor, like trying to grow figs from thistles. . . . To put one's faith in war as a means of achieving a more ordered world is to ignore the fundamental lawlessness of having a world controlled by armed and economic might.[36]

Here, the emphasis is on war as a blunt and ill-conceived means to desired ends, in which it is a mistake to invest any credibility. But we do so—time and time again. In contrast, the premise of this book is that there are other (non-violent) means better suited to achieving our ends, which can be characterized both in general and in particular. What Francis means to stress is essentially that in keeping war open as an option, by allowing and promoting continuous war-preparations in our own and other countries, we have hitched our wagon to the wrong horse. That the war system is self-perpetuating, that it contains a momentum of its own which, if permitted, will hold any society hostage to its dictates, should be evident to anyone who contemplates the massive military budgets prevailing in the world today.

Now if the attempt to offer principles for justifying war fails (as already argued), then, as one author states, "War is morally wrong. We have a duty to refuse to participate in war." And this is so because "All human beings have a duty to refuse to participate in conduct that is morally wrong."[37] Turning our attention from morality to law (which is in large measure a reflection of moral precepts), let us shift our attention for a moment to international conventions of war prohibiting certain kinds of actions that are considered to be beyond the pale (such as the use of poison gas or the deliberate mistreatment of war prisoners). We can now see clearly that, by definition, since they are laws *of* and not *against* war, they are necessarily compatible with and therefore permit the killing, maiming, and massive destruction that are inseparable from warfare. Because of this, the existence of laws of war does not serve as a refutation of the moral case against war.

To sum up, then, since war negates and is inconsistent with respect for human dignity and needs, and since such respect is fundamental to morality, it follows that war negates and is inconsistent with the fundamental premise of morality (C_1/P_3).

Now consider whether morality is an essential condition of our well-being, as P_4 asserts. This would seem to be fairly self-evident to most individuals, and is supported by definitions such as the following: "Morality consists of the most basic and inviolable rules of a society."[38] "Morality is the stuff our social life is made of—even our personal life. . . ."[39] "The basis of morality is a belief that good and harm to particular people (or animals) is good or bad not just from their point of view, but from a more general point of view, which every thinking person can understand."[40] "The world is . . . actually, and not just potentially, a moral community, even if the sense of it is poorly developed in most people. We are global citizens even if we have not yet acquired our global souls."[41]

But then, if morality is essential to our common wellbeing, and war negates and is inconsistent with its fundamental premise, then war is also in conflict with our basic and common wellbeing (C_2).

3.6. SECOND ANTIWAR ARGUMENT: THE EXTENDED SPHERE OF OBLIGATION

The second antiwar argument moves from moral considerations relating to our own species to those governing our interactions with a broader range of beings.

Argument #2

P_5:   Human beings "exist in interdependence with all species and indeed all beings."

P_6:   Interdependent beings share a common fate.

C_3:   ∴ The fate of the human species and that of other species (and of the Earth itself) are interrelated.

(First stage of the argument; C_3 is also the beginning premise for the second stage of the argument, which immediately follows; so C_3 becomes P_7.)

P_7:   The fate of the human species and that of other species (and of the Earth itself) are interrelated.

P_8:   If we share a common fate with other beings (and the Earth itself), then in addition to moral obligations toward other humans, we also have moral obligations that extend to the nonhuman sphere.

P_9:   War negates and is inconsistent with the fundamental premise of morality.

(This was C_1 of the first antiwar argument in the previous section; so C_1 now becomes P_9.)

P_{10}:   If war negates and is inconsistent with the fundamental premise of morality, then it likewise negates and is inconsistent with any extension of morality to the nonhuman sphere that is derived from this fundamental premise.

C_4: ∴ War negates and is inconsistent with our moral obligations in general—whether to other human beings or to the nonhuman sphere.

(The argument completed, with C_4 being its conclusion.)

A Closer Look at Argument #2

All life on Earth exists in a complex web of interconnections. With many televised nature programs on offer, ecological knowledge sifting down through other popular media, discussions of species extinctions, debates over climate change, spectacular oil spills, educational features on cultures still living close to the land, ubiquitous rhetoric of "saving the planet," and so forth, very few people can remain unaware of this fact. And if various kinds of interdependence among species have been demonstrated (even if by no means fully understood), then it should be abundantly clear that living things share a common fate. This insight is usually expressed in terms of human impacts on the planet—for example, in Al Gore's widely viewed documentary film *An Inconvenient Truth* (2006), and in books with titles like *Silent Spring*; *The Fate of the Earth*; *On the Fate of the Earth: Peace on and with the Earth for All Its Children*; *The Revenge of Gaia: Earth's Climate Crisis and the Fate of Humanity*; *A New Green History of the World: The Environment and the Collapse of Great Civilizations*; *The World Is Blue: How Our Fate and the Ocean's Are One*; and *The Fate of Nature: Rediscovering Our Ability to Rescue the Earth*.[42] As well, works by scientists and scientifically knowledgeable creative writers—such as Edward O. Wilson's *The Future of Life*; Stephanie Kaza's *Mindfully Green: A Personal Guide to Whole Earth Thinking*; and Annie Dillard's *Pilgrim at Tinker Creek*[43]—help to underscore the message about connectedness. Interestingly, though, there is also the less-well-known reverse perspective that explains impacts of the natural world on human development, of which the following books provide a small sample: *Biophilia* (meaning "love of life"); *The Others: How Animals Made Us Human*; *Green Nature/Human Nature: The Meaning of Plants in Our Lives*; *The Companion Species Manifesto: Dogs, People, and Significant Otherness*; *Animal Lessons: How They Teach Us to Be Human*; *Fifty Plants That Changed the Course of History*; and *Fifty Animals That Changed the Course of History*.[44]

It is only a small step from affirming that forms of life on Earth are interdependent—and indeed dependent on their environments—to the insight that they share a common fate. We know, for example, that endangered animals are often in this state because of human behaviors that affect them; but we are also gaining an increased awareness that some human environmental impacts rebound to our own detriment. Rainforest destruction, for instance, not only contributes to the total amount of carbon dioxide in the atmosphere, but also destroys wildlife (and hence vital ecosystem integrity), as well as supplies of valuable resources for human life, such as plants that yield important pharmaceuticals, timber, nuts, and so on. Closer to home, turning high-quality farmland into concrete cities, mines, or sites for hydraulic fracturing to produce oil and gas wells at the very least closes out certain other options for human life, just as it transforms and disrupts the environment. Biologist Wilson points out simply that "biodiversity is our most valuable but least appreciated resource."[45] Scientist and social activist Vandana Shiva notes that "biodiversity is a people's resource... . [which] is fast becoming the primary site of conflict between worldviews based on diversity and nonviolence and those based on monocultures and violence."[46] We think little of these things as we continue to foul our own nest.

Since humans exist interdependently with other beings (and vice versa, as "inter" implies), and interdependent beings share a common fate, then the fate of all beings on Earth, and of the Earth itself, as a home for life, are interrelated (C_3/P_7).

Now P_8 posits that having a common fate with other beings (and with the Earth) entails an extension of our moral obligations to the nonhuman sphere. Why? Because (as we saw in "A Closer Look at Argument #1") morality concerns any being capable of experiencing good or harm "that every thinking person can understand." It is easy to accept that nonhuman animals fit in here. However, it may be argued that the Earth possesses this property, too—not as a conscious being in its own right, but as the condition (or really the set of conditions, the support system) without which no life is possible, and which therefore must be allowed to maintain its self-regulatory balances. Thus, we can extend moral obligations to the Earth for a variety of reasons: out of self-interest, from pragmatic concerns, because we care for the future of life, from an attitude of respect and awe, or owing to some combination of these and other considerations.

P_9 does not require further discussion, since it is merely carried forward from the first antiwar argument in the previous section (C_1). Concerning P_{10}, we may observe the following. Whatever the body of morality may be—a set of rules, a table of virtues, a formula for calculating ethical consequences of actions, or something else entirely—the assumption underlying the argument here is that morality is a consistent doctrine everyone can grasp and apply in her or his life. Therefore, any extension of morality to the nonhuman sphere,

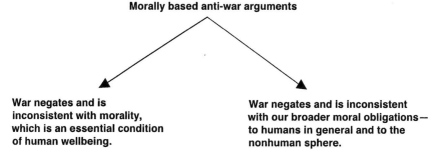

Figure 3.2 Morally based antiwar arguments

since it derives (in part at least) from considerations regarding the dignity and needs of all human beings, will be abrogated or undermined by anything that attacks the foundation it rests upon. Since war does have this demolishing effect, it follows that war is incompatible with the extension of morality to the nonhuman sphere, as already elaborated. (We will revisit the question of our relationship to animals and the environment in Chapter 7.)

Now, finally, we see that war negates moral obligations in both the usual and the extended sense (C_4). This sends us a very strong message that war is immoral and consequently wrong. If that is so, then no avenues are left for fine-tuning arguments justifying war, so we must abandon all such attempts as dead-ends.

3.7. EVALUATION OF THE ARGUMENTS AGAINST WAR

The two uncompromising arguments against war presented in this chapter will no doubt create some astonishment. For they purport to show that war is the most profound kind of wrongdoing, and as such, should never be fought. Many reasons may be offered for fighting wars, but it can no longer be claimed that it is ethically (or morally) right to wage certain kinds of wars, or some particular war. What are we to make of this startling result? More importantly, what difference do arguments such as these actually make? The short answer to these questions is that there are both theoretical and practical ways of moving beyond war as a means of settling human differences and animosities. "But arguments alone do not and cannot change the world," someone will protest. This is true, so far as it goes; however, the fact remains that neither does action alone change the world. Acting aimlessly and thoughtlessly is ineffectual; principled action is not. But then it follows that in order to effect meaningful and lasting change, people need to be guided by ideas. And ideas often come in the form of arguments, which clarify beliefs, sow the seeds of further ideas, indicate their relationship to action, and strengthen motivation leading to action, all of which *does* change things. The thinkers to whom we owe much of our social and cultural heritage have helped initiate change in the world through their many written and spoken words. Thus, the challenge before us is to see what can be done with ideas that have the potential to liberate us from slavish repetition of traditional, but failed ways of doing things.

Objections and Replies

It is also worth anticipating a pair of further possible objections here. First, one can imagine a devil's advocate—perhaps a political realist who believes that states are by their very nature competitive and power-driven entities, which interact according to purely self-serving, pragmatic principles—voicing a complaint of this sort: "These abstract arguments omit any meaningful context. We may not like war or going to war, but sometimes, unfortunately, it is the only way, or the most effective, time-efficient, and/or least costly way, all things considered, to check aggression or put a stop to an intolerable state of affairs."[47] This objection begs the question in two important respects, however. First, it assumes that general moral arguments cannot take precedence over situational ones, or prescribe principles we must not violate, no matter what. Second, it assumes a world model wherein war is ultimately unavoidable, alternatives to war are readily exhausted, and the costs of war can be known and calculated in advance (or at any rate controlled). That the present book proceeds from contrary assumptions will be well known by now. There *is* a moral framework in terms of which war can be judged (this much can be affirmed in common with just war theory); and there are *always* alternatives to war (including, but not limited to, surrender and nonviolent noncooperation), even if and when they happen not to be chosen. (Politicians, among others, frequently tell us: "I had no other choice," but, of course, we know in our hearts that this is wrong; *there is always a choice*, and a particular one has been made. An excuse is being sought by retreating into the supposed inevitability of events, including human choices.)

The second possible objection is that the broad ethical case against war developed in this chapter commits one to a very strong form of pacifism, which may entail some at least *prima facie* unacceptable consequences—for instance, the position that even military action aimed at protecting people against acute and systematic (often government-perpetrated) human rights violations cannot be justified. This is a particularly poignant issue in light of the 2005 UN document on the "responsibility to protect" (also known as R2P), which calls for international response, including, if necessary, the use of force, to "help protect populations from genocide, war crimes, ethnic cleansing and crimes against humanity."[48] Now one could reply that an international response of this kind does not really constitute an "act of war" as customarily understood, because (a) It is the UN that sanctions and conducts the operation; and (b) Such military action (which has a good probability of involving the use of lethal violence) is not pursued in the name of a particular political entity for a political objective (as is prohibited by the UN). Or so it is the case in theory anyway. Legal scholar Jules Lobel has argued that the responsibility to protect was envisioned as coming into play only when there are large-scale human consequences of the above sorts, and when these are causing serious follow-on effects in the international arena. (He also observes that so-called "humanitarian interventions" are often in fact highly politicized events.[49])

Should actions performed by the UN potentially involving the use of lethal armed force be exempt from moral judgment? Obviously not. What then? Should immoral actions be used to stop other (perhaps more gravely) immoral actions? The answer here too surely seems to be no. But is it any better for immoral actions, such as genocide, to be allowed to go on unchecked and unpunished when there is the means to stop them? Once again, it seems equally clear that the answer is no. We are thus caught in a dilemma that no one has satisfactorily resolved. Just war theorists may believe they can do so, but if the arguments against it stated earlier are correct, they are taking the wrong direction. Disappointingly, the Independent Commission on Intervention and State Sovereignty, in its 2001 Report, follows the customary just war doctrine to the letter in defining the conditions under which humanitarian intervention can legitimately take place.[50] And so the whole process of justification completes another revolution around the nucleus of the flawed ethical framework of just war theory.

Perhaps the only solution is this: (a) To recognize that the world is in a transitional state toward peace (not, therefore, one in which "anything goes," but an imperfect condition); (b) To rethink in every conceivable way the notion of "last resort," so that it is genuine and not self-serving; and (c) To make sure that UN humanitarian interventions are always markedly different in character from war. Item (c) does not just invite a verbal dispute over the use of the term "war." Rather, it is in keeping with proposals to establish a permanent UN Emergency Peace Service which, according to one suggestion, "must include a robust military composition; one capable of deterring belligerents, defending the mission, as well as civilians at risk. . . . While the proposed UN service would not be another 'force' for war-fighting, deployable military elements must have a capacity for modest enforcement to maintain security and the safety of people within its area of operations."[51] A pragmatic pacifist realizes that global peace and true world government (which the UN is not) take a great deal of time to evolve, and that moral ideals which can be importantly influential should not be abandoned just because events do not immediately conform to them.

There is a further sort of worry the two antiwar arguments generate. This concerns the justification of war as self-defense. We meet here a subject that has many aspects to it, and that has been treated at great length by others.[52] For the purposes of the present discussion, however, the main thing to note is that arguments upholding a nation's right to self-defense derive either from an analogy with an individual's right to self-defense or from a notion of citizens' collective right to self-defense. But an individual's right to engage in any act of lethal violence in the name of self-defense is normally limited in law by a "requirement of necessity," that is, "a requirement for threatened persons to retreat [from the given situation] if it is possible to avoid harm without resort to force by doing so."[53] This very strongly underlines the last resort criterion invoked by just war theorists, suggesting further that the number of cases dwindles dramatically in which a nation-state can justify its self-defensive actions that utilize lethal violence. Well, then, what about appealing to collective self-defense, as the summation of individual rights of this kind? Insofar as this derives from individuals' rights, the same problem unavoidably arises; but in any event, each party to a conflict can invoke an equal claim to collective self-defense once conflict looms or is engaged in, and quite apart from the merits of its own attempt to disclaim aggression or to claim that it is being aggressed upon.

These various considerations, however, probably will not help the staunch pacifist to escape from all criticism or secure a completely consistent position, because her or his stance is that the use of violence to resolve human disputes is *always* wrong (or wrong *in principle*). Still, there are degrees and kinds of wrongness, and, as suggested above, even an uncompromising opponent of war may hold that resort to minimal lethal force by the UN, in rare and extreme circumstances, with every effort made to adhere to ethical principles and legal restrictions, and with the ultimate purpose of bringing about a just peace, constitutes a notably lesser evil than what results when nations or groups resort to conventional warfare.[54]

One final issue to be considered is that there are those who may not be budged from holding a just war position, no matter what arguments are offered against it. The reference here is not merely to dogmatists with an entrenched opinion, but to people whose religious scripture incorporates just war ideas, for example, Muslims (see footnotes 7 and 32 to this chapter). The short answer to this problem—and one that should suffice if we are truly dedicated to seeking peace in the world—is to act in ways that give nobody cause to feel the need for invoking a "just" reason for making war. This, of course, is more difficult than it sounds, for it requires an entire overhaul and reorientation of the ways in which nations and other political entities interact with one another, and a genuine attempt to give others their due and to behave according to the fundamental principles of morality defended in this chapter, in a cosmopolitan spirit of partnership (see also Chapter 7, section 7.4, "A Global Outlook").

The Illegality of War

This chapter concludes by introducing the unexpected idea that war as such is (not just ought to be) *illegal*. This is, of course, different from saying that war is *immoral*. Traffic laws, building codes, and laws governing contracts set forth statutory obligations, not moral ones. And principles regarding good faith, promise-keeping, looking after one's friends, and being charitable, in and of themselves, prescribe moral but not legal obligations. (Legal and moral codes do coincide, however, when laws give extra force to moral values—for example, in relation to homicide, assault, theft of valuables, child pornography, and guarantees of justice and basic freedoms.) A recent book by David Swanson argues[55] that war *has* actually been declared illegal—by a now largely forgotten treaty known as the Kellogg-Briand Pact or the Pact of Paris (formally, the Treaty on the Renunciation of War) that arose from the aftermath of World War I and was initially signed in 1928 by fifteen nations, including all of the belligerents in the Great War, and eventually by sixty-five. Swanson points out that this pact was ratified almost unanimously by the US Senate, "and remains on the books (and on the US state department's website) to this day, as part of what Article VI of the US Constitution calls 'the supreme Law of the Land' "[55] (as are all treaties). The pact mandates that all disputes between nations, of whatever kind or origin, be settled by peaceful means, and prohibits resort to war "as an instrument of national policy." But there are several things it does *not* do: It neither outlaws military actions in self-defense, nor requires signatories to come to each other's aid in times of crisis, nor provides any mechanism for its own enforcement.[57]

We all know that the articles of this treaty (and those of the League of Nations) were trashed by subsequent wars. Yet might there be some significance and efficacy left to the idea that war is illegal and to the treaty in which this wonderful commitment is still enshrined? For, first of all, it means that acts of war are legally forbidden (delegitimized and renounced) at the international level, which overrides any unilateral approval of such acts by a signatory nation. Second, outlawing war has the consequence that war is not the norm, the way of the world that we must despairingly and painfully accept. Third, it adds considerable additional weight to the arguments against war examined in the Introduction, and reinforces the conclusion that war is immoral, presented in this chapter. Fourth, it provides an existing foundation on which international cooperation to end war can build.

But what of the fact that this treaty has been violated so many times (most egregiously in World War II), and that there are many more powerful nations and factions in the world today than there were in 1928, most of which are not signatories to this treaty, some of which are quite capable of waging war, and a few of which are even willing, if not eager, to do so? We also have to face the fact that for laws to be authoritative in regulating behavior, they need to be backed up by sanctions. In the absence of a UN or world government with enforcement measures at its disposal, laws against war seem rather hollow. And yet, as Swanson indicates, the forgotten and frequently contravened Treaty on the Renunciation of War was cited by both the Nuremberg and Tokyo Tribunals in support of trying various parties held responsible for instigating and participating in a war of aggression (World War II)—this kind of war now being defined (in part by this Treaty) as "the supreme international crime."[58] And this thinking has helped lead to the formation of today's International Court of Justice. Where we go from here will perhaps be an amazing journey toward international cooperation and joint jurisdiction.[59]

NOTES TO CHAPTER 3

1. Raymond C. Kelly, *Warless Societies and the Origin of War* (Ann Arbor: University of Michigan Press, 2000), p. 7 (emphasis in original).

2. Gradations of this sort are featured in the following books: Martin Ceadel, *Thinking about Peace and War* (Oxford: Oxford University Press, 1987); Nigel Dower, *The Ethics of War and Peace: Cosmopolitan and Other Perspectives* (Cambridge, UK: Polity Press, 2009); Duane Cady, *From Warism to Pacifism: A Moral Continuum*, 2nd ed. (Philadelphia: Temple University Press, 2010).

3. See, for example, Jeff McMahan, "The Moral Case against the Iraq War," September 2004; http://leiterreports.typepad.com/blog/2004/09/the_moral_case_.html.

4. See Brian Orend, "War," *Stanford Encyclopedia of Philosophy*, ed. Edward N. Zalta, Fall 2008 ed.; available at: http://plato.stanford.edu/cgi-bin/encyclopedia/archinfo. cgi?entry=war.

5. See Global Centre for the Responsibility to Protect, "Implementing the Responsibility to Protect—The 2009 General Assembly Debate: An Assessment," August 2009; http:// globalr2p.org/media/pdf/GCR2P_General_Assembly_Debate_Assessment.pdf.

6. It is important to note that this position is contrary to the principles on which the United Nations was founded, in particular, UN Charter, chap. I, art. 2.3 (all nations commit themselves to resolving disputes peacefully) and chap. VII, art. 51 (self-defense

is the only legitimate ground for unilateral military action, and then only until the Security Council can take over the situation).

7. Charles Guthrie and Michael Quinlan, *Just War—The Just War Tradition: Ethics in Modern Warfare* (London: Bloomsbury, 2007), pp. 2, 6, and appendix A. For specific discussions of just war within the frameworks of Judaism and Islam, see Michael Walzer, "War and Peace in the Jewish Tradition," in *War and Peace in an Age of Terrorism: A Reader*, ed. William M. Evan (Boston: Pearson Education/Allyn and Bacon, 2006), pp. 58–63; Sohail H. Hashmi, "Interpreting the Islamic Ethics of War and Peace," in *War and Peace in an Age of Terrorism*, ed. Evan, pp. 64–9.

8. Guthrie and Quinlan, *Just War*, p. 7.

9. Aryeh Neier, *The International Human Rights Movement: A History* (Princeton, NJ: Princeton University Press, 2012), p. 118.

10. There has also been discussion in recent times of a third dimension of the just war: *ius post bellum* (postwar justice), which we will not consider here. See, for example, Brian Orend, "Jus Post Bellum," *Journal of Social Philosophy*, no. 31 (2000), pp. 117–37; Gary J. Bass, "Jus Post Bellum," *Philosophy and Public Affairs*, no. 32 (2004), pp. 384–412; Mona Fixdal, *Just Peace: How Wars Should End* (New York: Palgrave Macmillan, 2012).

11. "Barack Obama Defends 'Just War' Using Drones," BBC News, 24 May 2013; http://www.bbc.co.uk/news/world-us-canada-22638533.

12. Waleed Aly, "When Making War Is So Easy, Obama's Doubts about Morality of Some Drone Strikes May Be Irrelevant," *Sydney Morning Herald*, 31 May 2013, p. 33.

13. James Sheehan, *The Monopoly of Violence: Why Europeans Hate Going to War* (London: Faber and Faber, 2008), pp. 84–7, 129–32.

14. Neier, *International Human Rights Movement*, p. 211.

15. Neier, *International Human Rights Movement*, chap. 5.

16. Dower, *Ethics of War and Peace*, p. 47 (emphasis in original). Cf. Diana Francis, *Rethinking War and Peace* (London: Pluto Press, 2004), p. 43.

17. Martin Luther King, Jr., *Strength to Love* (New York: Harper & Row, 1964), p. 116.

18. Susan Opotow, "Reconciliation in Times of Impunity: Challenges for Social Justice," *Social Justice Research*, no. 14 (2001), p. 156. See also Judith Butler's analysis of who counts as morally significant in times of war, in *Frames of War: When Is Life Grievable?* (London: Verso, 2009).

19. Albert Camus, *Neither Victims Nor Executioners*, trans. Dwight Macdonald (Philadelphia: New Society, 1986), pp. 50–1.

20. Oliver Ramsbotham, Tom Woodhouse, and Hugh Miall, *Contemporary Conflict Resolution: The Prevention, Management and Transformation of Deadly Conflicts*, 2nd ed. (Cambridge, UK: Polity Press, 2005), p. 4.

21. Paul McGeough, "Pressure on Tehran Ups the Stakes," News Review, *Sydney Morning Herald*, 14–15 January 2012, p. 13.

22. Saeed Kamali Dehghan, "Iran 'Ready to Fire' at US Bases," *Guardian Weekly*, 13–19 July 2012, p. 5.

23. McGeough, "Pressure on Tehran" (summarizing the views of Vali Nasr, Fletcher School of Law and Diplomacy, Tufts University).

24. "Iran: We'll Close Strait of Hormuz," *Guardian Weekly*, 13–19 January 2012, p. 2.

25. See Kate Gould, "Congress 'Un-Declares' War with Iran," Common Dreams, 23 May 2012; https://www.commondreams.org/view/2012/05/23; see also Senate Resolution S.RES.65.IS, 28 February 2013, sec. 2; http://thomas.loc.gov/cgi-bin/query/z?c113: S.RES.65.

26. For some interesting suggestions, see Bill Keller, "How About Not Bombing Iran?" *New York Times*, 22 January 2012; http://keller.blogs.nytimes.com/2012/01/22/how-about-not-bombing-iran/?ref=nuclearprogram; Kenneth N. Waltz, "Why Iran Should Get the Bomb: Nuclear Balancing Would Mean Stability," *Foreign Affairs*, no. 91 (July/August 2012), pp. 2–10.

27. David E. Sanger, "Obama Order Sped Up Wave of Cyberattacks against Iran," *New York Times*, 1 June 2012; http://www.nytimes.com/2012/06/01/world/middleeast/obama-ordered-wave-of-cyberattacks-against-iran.html?_r=1&ref=global-home.

28. Francis, *Rethinking War and Peace*, p. 3. (All quotations in the two arguments I present are taken from this page.)

29. Reported by Anwarul K. Chowdhury, Senior Special Advisor to the President of the UN General Assembly, "Time is Right for the Human Right to Peace," IDN-InDepth NewsViewpoint, 23 January 2012; http://www.other-news.info/2012/01/time-is-right-for-the-human-right-to-peace.

30. Kent D. Shifferd, *From War to Peace: A Guide to the Next Hundred Years* (Jefferson, NC: McFarland, 2011), pp. 5, 6.

31. Philip Caputo, *A Rumor of War* (New York: Holt, Rinehart and Winston, 1977).

32. Exodus 20:2–17; Mark 12:31 and Leviticus 19:18. The *Qu'ran*, on the other hand, seems to have just war ideas built into it; for example, Surah 22:39: "To those against whom war is made, permission is given (to fight), because they are wronged—and verily, Allāh is Most Powerful for their aid."

33. Elaine Scarry, *The Body in Pain: The Making and Unmaking of the World* (New York: Oxford University Press, 1985), p. 122. On the destruction of moral identity more generally—the process that makes not only war but also genocide possible—see Jonathan Glover, *Humanity: A Moral History of the Twentieth Century* (London: Jonathan Cape, 1999) and Zygmunt Bauman, *Modernity and the Holocaust* (Ithaca, NY: Cornell University Press, 2001).

34. For a good summary of opinion and research on this subject, see Killology Research Group, "Behavioral Psychology"; http://www.killology.com/art_beh_intro.htm. See also Albert Bandura, "Moral Disengagement in the Perpetration of Inhumanities," *Personality and Social Psychology Review,* no. 3 (1999), pp. 193–209.

35. The Christmas Truce of 1914 in Flanders, Belgium (near Ypres) is the subject of at least two films, as well as a historical study, several songs, and other depictions. For more information, see *Wikipedia*, "Christmas Truce"; http://en.wikipedia.org/wiki/Christmas_truce. I am grateful to Robin Fox for suggesting use of this example. As many as three unofficial truces (in 1915, 1916, and 1917) took place between Turkish and Australian troops at Gallipoli. (See Government of Australia, "Australian Troops Entertaining Themselves at the Front-line"; http://australia.gov.au/about-australia/australian-story/austn-troops-entertaining-themselves.)

36. Francis, *Rethinking War and Peace*, pp. 42–3.

37. Jim Martell, "Pacifism" (unpublished paper, used by permission), p. 1.

38. Robert C. Solomon, *Ethics: A Brief Introduction* (New York: McGraw-Hill, 1984), p. 6.

39. Nina Rosenstand, *The Moral of the Story: An Introduction to Questions of Ethics and Human Nature* (Mountain View, CA: Mayfield, 1994), p. 5.

40. Thomas Nagel, *What Does It All Mean? A Very Short Introduction to Philosophy* (New York: Oxford University Press, 1987), p. 67.

41. Nigel Dower, "World Poverty," in *A Companion to Ethics* ed. Peter Singer (Oxford: Blackwell, 1993), p. 280.

42. Rachel Carson, *Silent Spring*, 40th anniversary ed. (New York: Mariner Books/Houghton Mifflin, 2002); Jonathan Schell, *The Fate of the Earth* (New York: Alfred A. Knopf, 1982); Amy S. Kelly, ed., *On the Fate of the Earth: Peace on and with the Earth for All Its Children*, Proceedings of the Second Biennial Conference, 1984 (San Francisco: Earth Island Institute, 1985); James Lovelock, *The Revenge of Gaia: Earth's Climate Crisis and the Fate of Humanity* (New York: Basic Books, 2006); Clive Ponting, *A New Green History of the World: The Environment and the Collapse of Great Civilizations*, rev. updated ed. (New York: Penguin, 2007); Sylvia Earle, *The World Is Blue: How Our Fate and the Ocean's Are One* (Washington, DC: National Geographic Society, 2009); Charles Wohlforth, *The Fate of Nature: Rediscovering Our Ability to Rescue the Earth* (New York: Thomas Dunne Books/St. Martin's Press, 2010).

43. Edward O. Wilson, *The Future of Life* (New York: Vintage Books, 2003); Annie Dillard, *Pilgrim at Tinker Creek* (New York: Harper Perennial, 2007); Stephanie Kaza, *Mindfully Green: A Personal and Spiritual Guide to Whole Earth Thinking* (Boston: Shambhala, 2008).

44. Edward O. Wilson, *Biophilia* (Cambridge, MA: Harvard University Press, 1984); Charles A. Lewis, *Green Nature/Human Nature: The Meaning of Plants in Our Lives* (Urbana, IL: University of Illinois Press, 1996); Paul Shepard, *The Others: How Animals Made Us Human* (Washington, DC: Island Press/Shearwater Books, 1997); Donna J. Haraway, *The Companion Species Manifesto: Dogs, People, and Significant Otherness* (Chicago: Prickly Paradigm Press, 2003); Kelly Oliver, *Animal Lessons: How They Teach Us to Be Human* (New York: Columbia University Press, 2009); Bill Laws, *Fifty Plants That Changed the Course of History* (Richmond Hill, ON, Canada: Firefly Books, 2011); Eric Chaline, *Fifty Animals That Changed the Course of History* (Richmond Hill, ON, Canada: Firefly Books, 2011).

45. Edward O. Wilson, *The Diversity of Life* (New York: W.W. Norton, 1993), p. 281.

46. Vandana Shiva, *Biopiracy: The Plunder of Nature and Knowledge* (Boston: South End Press, 1997), pp. 66, 120.

47. This argument was framed for me by Tom Bristow (personal communication, 30 June 2012). I appreciate his input.

48. UN General Assembly Resolution A/RES/60/1, "2005 World Summit Outcome," 24 October 2005, sec. 139; http://daccess-dds-ny.un.org/doc/UNDOC/GEN/N05/487/60/PDF/N0548760.pdf?OpenElement.

49. Interview with Jules Lobel: "Does UN Charter Allow Libyan No-fly Zone?" (15 March 2011); http://therealnews.com/t2/index.php?option=com_content&task=view&id=31&Itemid=74&jumival=6408.

50. International Commission on Intervention and State Sovereignty (ICISS), *The Responsibility to Protect* (Ottawa: International Development Research Centre, 2001), chap. 4.

51. Ramsbotham, Woodhouse, and Miall, *Contemporary Conflict Resolution*, p. 157 (summarizing the views of H. P. Langille, *Bridging the Commitment-Capacity Gap: Existing Arrangements and Options for Enhancing UN Rapid Deployment Capabilities* [Wayne, NJ: Center for UN Reform Education, 2002]).

52. For example, David Rodin, *War and Self-Defense* (New York: Oxford University Press, 2002).

53. Rodin, *War and Self-Defense*, p. 127. So-called "stand-your-ground laws," enacted by thirty-one US states, appear to represent departures from this well-established practice.

54. In formulating this point, I am indebted to Dower, *Ethics of War and Peace*, p. 155.

55. David Swanson, *When the World Outlawed War* (Charlottesville, VA: davidswanson. org, 2011). See also Antony Adolf, *Peace: A World History* (Cambridge, UK: Polity Press, 2009), pp. 190–1; David Cortright, *Peace: A History of Movements and Ideas* (Cambridge, UK: Cambridge University Press, 2008), pp. 62–4.

56. Swanson, *When the World Outlawed War*, p. 6. Article VI reads: "This Constitution, and the Laws of the United States which shall be made in Pursuance thereof; and all Treaties made, or which shall be made, under the Authority of the United States, shall be the supreme Law of the Land; and the Judges in every State shall be bound thereby, any Thing in the Constitution or Laws of any State to the Contrary notwithstanding."

57. The full text of the Kellogg-Briand Pact can be found at: http://avalon.law.yale. edu/20th_century/kbpact.asp.

58. Swanson, *When the World Outlawed War*, p. 154.

Part II

A Window on Peace

4

Violence, Aggression, and Nonviolence

Nothing enduring can be built on violence.

—Mohandas K. Gandhi, *Young India*, 15 November 1928

Nonviolence seeks to "win" not by destroying or even by humiliating the adversary, but by convincing him that there is a higher and more certain common good than can be attained by bombs and blood.

—Thomas Merton (1915–68), French-born Catholic monk, mystic, author, and activist

4.1. VIOLENCE AND AGGRESSION

In order to discuss nonviolence meaningfully, it will be helpful to consider first what violence is. And further, a distinction must be made between violence and aggression. A common assumption is that violence is so ingrained in human nature, such a fundamental expression of it, that we will never be free of war. This belief was contested in previous chapters. An additional assumption that needs to be critically addressed is that aggression is just another expression of violence. As it turns out, the relationship between them is quite a bit more complicated.

Violence as the Norm?

Whether violence is on the decline in the world today, as some have argued (see Chapter 2, section 2.1, "A Future without War?"), one thing is for sure: We are daily assaulted by violent messages; reports about violent incidents; repulsive, scarring images of the effects of violent acts or of violence in the making; and entertainments featuring violence. On television, these messages are sand-wiched between advertisements for attractive and comforting consumer items we are supposed to "need." Even if violence were not the norm, some would argue that it is being normalized not just by the media, but also by militaristic values, environmental devastation, male sex-role stereotypes, products of pop culture, instantaneous reportage from every part of the Earth characteristic of the information age, and other influences. To say that "violence is being nor-malized" means that many are beginning to take it for granted as the obvious, and perhaps not even lamentable, response to political or social frustrations, insults, betrayals, forms of disempowerment, or aggressive behavior. As we've seen in the Introduction, violence is considered a positive attribute in times of war, and this value is embedded in societies of which war-preparedness is a central feature. Supposing (counterintuitively, many might say) that actual violence is declining in the world, it is still a prominent aspect—in reality and symbolically—of many cultures today. And violence is also a significant public health concern worldwide.[1]

The Nature of Violence

So what is violence? At first glance, it seems we could characterize it simply as the use of force to damage or inhibit the welfare of another person. We need to take a more careful look, however. Sociologist Peter Imbusch cau-tions that "Violence is one of the most elusive and most difficult concepts in the social sciences," and he adds that, as such, violence "should not be subject to hurried evaluation."[2] Anthropologist David Riches advises that "The social actions performed by people in 'other societies' and the collective representa-tions (mythology, aesthetics, etc.) of 'other cultures' may strike the English-speaking layperson as 'violent'—yet some of the essential meanings in the Anglo-Saxon idea may be missing from them altogether," though he also adds that "it may be a mistake to allow discussions of violence to be dictated by the presence or absence of particular terms in particular cultures."[3] With these caveats in mind, violence may be defined, within the context of the present discussion, as *force, coercion, or psychological manipulation of any kind, used in a harmful or destructive way against some being that has an interest in not being harmed or destroyed; or that is used reflexively by one who has abandoned this interest; or that is used against an object or entity some being has an interest in not seeing harmed or destroyed.* Violence may be directly intentional, as when a rape or other assault occurs; or it may be unleashed more mindlessly, as when a frenzied mob lynches a bystander suspected of belonging to a certain political group; or it may be unintentional and even nonaggressive, as when an epileptic in a seizure causes self-inflicted damage or when some kind of harm is a chance by-product of a person's violent behavior. Violence may be self-directed, too, as in suicide or acts of self-disfigurement or self-punishment. Furthermore, it may be, and often is, psychological rather than (or in addition to) being physical. Numerous varieties of manipulation, intimidation, undermining, bullying, and disempowerment are manifested globally. These actions occur overtly and covertly, and their victims may be either aware or unaware of the nature of the process affecting them. The purpose of psychological violence is usually one or more of the following: to hurt, control, render submissive, dehumanize, enslave, or kill someone. Politics professor John Keane prompts us to bear in mind as well that a human (one can say also nonhuman) victim of violence is viewed by the perpetrator of the violent act "not as a subject whose 'otherness' is recognised and respected, but rather as a mere object potentially worthy of bodily harm, or even annihilation."[4] Destruction of valued possessions or other property or entities that people care about or have some kind of investment in also falls within the scope of violence as we are considering it here.

Our definition of violence, then, is quite broad, and for that reason, it is also controversial, as such a definition is bound to be, and perhaps even should be. For one thing, it is capable of embracing beings other than humans as both the perpetrators and victims of violence, and, therefore, allows that violence can target not only people and their inanimate property, but also nonhuman living things, such as animals, trees, and ecosystems. Objects and other entities may be regarded as violently treated so long as some conscious being has a significant stake in the outcome. Some would argue that violence is always political (having to do with asserting, challenging, or reorienting power structures).[5] According to another type of view, violence is morally wrong in itself, though it is more commonly held that violence can sometimes be justified.[6] At the outer fringe of discussion, we find it argued, contrary to what is asserted here, that violence is undefinable.[7]

A few observations may be made in light of all these viewpoints. First, the meaning of the term "violence" we have adopted does not exclude the possibility that the use of violence might sometimes be morally justified (for example, in self-defense or—far removed from this—to make a statement or to bring about social or political change). But if the earlier discussion of the main principle of morality is correct (Chapter 3, section 3.5, "First Antiwar Argument"), then the onus of justification always falls on those who resort to violence.

Second, *justified* violence, if there is such, should be distinguished from *legitimate* violence. The latter signifies violence that is legally sanctioned and practiced by the state and other levels of government and by revolutionary regimes claiming legitimacy, or that is embedded in societal norms. But to say that violence is legitimated in any of these senses does not prove that it is justified. The reason is that all of these forms of violence may still be morally reprehensible and, as in the case of unjust laws, there must always remain an extralegal or critical-moral standpoint from which it is possible to make such judgments. (Otherwise, it will be the case that the law, or whatever society dictates, is always right by definition.) Justified violence (self-defense again, or the destruction of a torturer's equipment, for example) may be legitimate, but legitimated violence is less likely to be justified or even justifiable.

Third, violence generally concerns the exercise of power over others, in such a way that their freedom of action, security, and inviolability are limited or eliminated, or their lives are damaged to a significant extent, or ended. In this case, and to this extent, we have to accept that violence is political in nature. Gregg Barak, a criminologist and cultural studies specialist, argues that violence is a "social disease," and points out that "there is relatively little attention paid to the sources, origins, or causes of violence," because it is socially and politically easier to focus on violence as an aberrant interpersonal phenomenon rather than as an effect of structural and institutional factors.[8]

The Varieties of Violence

Many forms of violence are relatively obvious and pervasively present to our consciousness, such as violent crime and war. Others are more subtle or out of view, such as child pornography, neglect of the elderly, and animal cruelty. Institutional, structural, or systemic forms of violence are even less visible or invisible altogether—part of "the way things are done" in a given time and place. These forms flourish where domination, exploitation, or oppression of one or more groups by another frame their relationships. As mentioned above, these arrangements may express legitimated exercises of power, as, for example, in a racist or classist society, which may also exhibit sublimated and symbolic expressions of violence such as ethnic, sexist, or racist jokes; an intimidating police presence everywhere; mandatory identity cards, and so on. But violence may also be a means by which an overtly peaceful, even "decent" society enforces its rules—written or unwritten, but in any case internalized—determining how power is distributed and exercised within it and its sphere of influence. Almost everywhere, people are taught to accept certain instruments of legitimate violence, such as police, standing armies, and harsh penal codes, even if envisioned only as some sort of corrective measure or form of counterviolence designed to restore a hypothetical state of equilibrium when

Types of violence

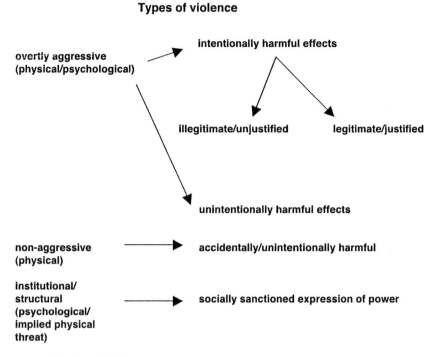

Figure 4.1 Types of violence

it gets disrupted. Such institutions exemplify the values that are supposedly upheld by a given society in general, or else are those of the powerful elements within that society. Yet these institutions are not merely subject to various forms of corruption, but also make it easier for other kinds of violence to slip by unnoticed and become well-established forms of abuse (what Aryeh Neier calls "official lawlessness"[9]). And, as we all witness, dominant power structures frequently turn to violence when existing hierarchies and related categories of social inclusion and exclusion are challenged. Many movements for social reform have run the gauntlet so described: trade union organizing, civil rights demonstrations, suffragist and feminist campaigns, and gay activism provide recognizable examples. These examples illustrate the point that while it is a commonplace and largely shared pretense that social orders exist to *prevent* violence, and that violence flares forth only as a passing note of discord, the truth is that violence often serves as an outlet for pent-up reactions to systemic, societal violence itself. As one anthropologist comments, "It is evident that when the term 'violence' is being used, attention should crucially be focused on *who* is labelling a given act as such and most especially their social position."[10]

Controlling Violence

Returning now to the fundamental meaning of "violence" with which we began, the question can be raised whether violence is controllable in human society. If this idea is interpreted to mean "Can violence be completely contained or eliminated?" the answer surely is "No." There have been theorists who dispute this conclusion. For example, Arthur Koestler, novelist and essayist, argued through the course of several books that the human tendency toward violence can only be controlled by genetic or chemical modification of the brain, aimed at reducing or eliminating this dimension of behavior.[11] Even if he were right, few would opt to go in this direction. In any case, many social scientists today contend that placing the accent simply on containment or elimination fails to get to the heart of the problem of violence. But if the issue about violence is reframed as one concerning whether levels of violence in any locale can be reduced—because alternatives to violence exist—there is likely to be much agreement. Imbusch notes that "Although human behavior has always had the option of violence, every society has also found means and ways of stemming violence and preventing it from becoming endemic, at least in the long term. . . . However intermittent this development may have been, people have learned to reflect on and adjust their behavior while withstanding aggressive impulses and the allure of violence—this is a core of their sociality."[12] Looking at the scientific evidence that has accumulated, Riches states that "social and cultural factors, together with ecological setting, are the chief factors influencing the type and frequency of violence in any social situation. . . ." Moreover, he adds, "in every instance, the relationship between social structure and violence is one of *influence* and *opportunity*; there is no suggestion that social structure *compels* violence—there are always alternative courses of action."[13]

Tim Jacoby, who specializes in politics and conflict analysis, agrees. He highlights "peer pressure, authority and modelling as examples of the way in which the violent behaviour of individuals may be conditioned through reinforcement and deterrence." An example of what he is talking about might be a mercenary who fights for pay. For him, it is all in a day's work to kill and maim. But isn't he a pawn in some larger game? Wouldn't he be peaceful if someone paid him to be? Jacoby also stresses the need "to understand the ways in which conditioning occurs collectively—in other words, the means through which group identities are created, consolidated and used as a basis for violent conflict."[14] Using Rwanda as an example, he argues further that "the way in which we learn to accept conflict and violence is difficult to separate from a general acceptance of inequality and injustice,"[15] and that the resolution of conflicts presupposes and depends, not on a general and apolitical theory of violence, but rather, on a detailed grasp of the specific contexts in which conflict occurs.[16] And as Seyom Brown, a specialist in peace, conflict, and coexistence studies, observes:

> The fact that some human societies exhibit markedly more violence than others, even when their material conditions are not basically different, strongly suggests that humans can be taught to be more or less violent or peaceful. . . . Explicitly or implicitly, groups (from families to gangs to nations) convey to their members what kind of conflictual or cooperative behavior is admired or disparaged; and such group norms can work to reinforce, channel, or deflect aggressive desires to dominate others or to strike out at those believed to be responsible for one's deprivations and frustrations.[17]

All of these analyses indicate that violence, while it may be a human tendency, need not predominate: *Humans are not "violent by nature."*

Taking a broader historical perspective reinforces this conclusion. Although humans still visit atrocities on one another with disturbing frequency, and continue to abuse animals wholesale, certain kinds of violence are (with very few exceptions) no longer either legitimated, justified, condoned, or tolerated as social practices. Sociologist Norbert Elias painstakingly documents and analyzes the changes in aggressive violence that have occurred over the course of human cultural development. His groundbreaking study *The Civilizing Process*, first published in 1939, demonstrates, for example, that in Western Europe, well into the sixteenth century and beyond, torture, mutilation, and other forms of cruelty (including cruelty to animals), provided great sources of entertainment not only for the powerful in society who could control the fate of the more vulnerable, but also for the multitudes, in public spectacles such as executions and various acts of punishment, degradation, and humiliation. Elias maintains that gradually, over time, the impulses toward violence have become negatively valued, with the result that "socially undesirable expressions of instinct and pleasure are threatened and punished with measures that generate and reinforce displeasure and anxiety."[18] This is a complex development, but the main point to grasp, as we've seen, is that *tendencies toward or away from aggression and violence are socially constructed.* Whether or not violence in general is on the decline, historically speaking, may be debated; however, the examples just given demonstrate that violent behavior is subject to social control and hence, is not the predominant factor in human nature.[19]

What Aggression Is, and How It Differs from Violence

Well, what, then, is the case with aggression? The word "aggression" comes from the Latin *aggressio*, meaning "go to," "set about (doing something)," "approach,"

"attack." Most commonly today, aggression is associated with the idea of an unprovoked attack. And in psychological theory from Freud onward, it is linked
to destructive behavior. Some anthropologists object, however, that when we
treat the phenomenon of aggression in this manner—as if it means the same
thing cross-culturally and at all times—we distort a "basically neutral term,"
through "simplistic and absolutist use,"[20] and they point out further that "aggression frequently lies in the eye of the beholder."[21] For instance, aggression
can equally well be understood as an act or display that conveys individual or
group self-assertion. In nonhuman animals, aggressive displays—such as puff-
ing up the body or fanning out an array of feathers, trumpeting, or growling—
are commonplace warnings to back off for fear of serious consequences. Now
while aggressive displays may be effective as threats alone, we all know that
sometimes actual violence will follow them. However, even if aggression may
be expressed violently or threaten violence, this does not automatically entail
that aggression and violence are the same thing. That they are not can be easily
shown with reference to everyday examples from the human sphere.

A tennis coach who advises a player to "Be more aggressive" does not mean
"Be more violent," but rather "Concentrate harder, put yourself forward more,
be active, strategic, energetic, assertive, relentless in pursuit of winning the
point," and so forth. An aggressive salesperson tries to coerce us into buying
something we may or may not need or want, but this behavior is not plausibly
described as either threatening or harmful. We can also speak of "the aggressive treatment of disease," which might be seen as violence toward pathogens,
but is meant to be beneficial, not harmful, to the diseased organism.[22] The New
Zealand All Blacks rugby team does its "haka" ceremonial display of aggression before the beginning of each game. Inspired by traditional Maori warrior
behavior, this is an impressive and daunting performance. It may have had the
original intent of threatening harm—or of deterring opponents from attacking.
But although rugby is an often brutal sport, it could hardly be claimed that the
aggressive haka display mounted by the All Blacks expresses in itself any intent
or goal to cause harm or injury. Someone with an "aggressive personality" does
not necessarily commit violent acts or even threaten us personally with violence
or harm, though we may dislike him or her for being pushy, obnoxious, domineering, inconsiderate of our feelings, and the like. There are those who are
good at handling aggressive personalities and are not threatened by them, while
others who are perhaps themselves less self-confident and self-assertive may
experience this type of aggression as intimidating and personally endangering.

It is clear, then, that how we define and understand aggression hinges on
much more than an arbitrary verbal dispute over whether we should label it
"violence" or not; nor is it even clear that behavioral science uniformly favors

the "attack" sense of aggression, as we shall see in a moment. Hence, one can only be surprised to encounter a statement by a learned scholar that "using the terms [violence and aggression] interchangeably does not seem to be problematic at all."[23]

Is Aggression Instinctive?

Several decades ago, animal scientist and Nobel Prize winner Konrad Lorenz's book *On Aggression* took the academic world by storm and greatly influenced popular thinking on the subject we are examining. According to Barak's assessment from today's standpoint, however, Lorenz's findings have long since been surpassed: "Lorenz . . . argued that animals and humans shared an instinct for aggressive behavior. He also argued that humans, unlike other species, lack developed mechanisms for the inhibition of aggression. Subsequent research and analysis repudiated both of these positions and basically put the 'killer ape' myth to rest. . . ."[24] Well, not entirely. As we've learned in the Introduction and Chapter 2, there are still plenty of theorists willing to buy into the idea that war is indelibly engrained in human nature. But it remains true that recent thinking about aggression is more divided than when Lorenz published his book. Although the evolutionary link between aggression and (often lethal) violence continues to be affirmed by some researchers, others see aggression either as not necessarily linked to violence, or simply as part of the human behavioral repertoire, on an equal footing, perhaps, with reciprocity, cooperation, bargaining, negotiation, empathy, altruism, and other, more constructive capacities. This latter view implies that aggression is not even *an* instinct, much less *the* basic instinct that defines our species. What does appear to be true, after the dust of the debate over Lorenz's claims clears away, is that in using violence against conspecifics (members of the same species), animals know when to stop; humans need to (and can) discipline and teach themselves to do so, but have thus far done a fairly poor job of it on the whole.

That aggression and aggressive violence are not uncontrollable, innate attributes was asserted by the authors of the Seville Statement on Violence (see Chapter 2, section 2.3, "Human universals"). But this has also has been independently demonstrated as well by highly respected scientists. Psychologist Loh Seng Tsai showed, for instance, that a domestic cat and a wild rat could be retrained to eat out of the same dish. In Tsai's view, "Such a discovery throws overboard the traditional dogma in psychology that in animal nature there is an ineradicable instinct of pugnacity which makes fighting or wars inevitable."[25] However remarkable this experiment is, it may strain credibility to claim that it proves there is no aggressive or violent instinct in animals and humans.

But note carefully what Tsai actually says he discovered: that there is no *ineradicable* instinct of the sort. And, we may add, if there is none in animals, then it cannot then be argued that humans, *just like animals* (or because of their evolutionary inheritance from animals) have an unalterable killer instinct.

Understood in this manner, Tsai's finding has received confirmation from several other quarters. Based on an exhaustive series of cross-species studies, Irenäus Eibl-Eibesfeldt, the founder of human ethology, concluded that there is no instinct to kill in humans.[26] And gathering the evidence yielded by many years of his own and others' research on aggression, anthropologist Ashley Montagu writes that:

> Many human societies cannot be characterized as aggressive. And there are many individuals in aggressive societies who are unaggressive and opposed to any form of aggressive behavior. Many societies that appear to be aggressive are, in fact, composed of individuals who for the most part are not usually aggressive. Most people in civilized societies get involved in wars not because they feel aggressive toward the socially defined "enemy," but because their leaders—who themselves are seldom motivated by aggressive feelings—consider it necessary to make war. Such considerations have nothing whatever to do with feelings, universals or instincts, but usually mainly with political constraints. . . . There are few societies in which some form of aggressive behavior, however slight, does not occur. . . . The variability and absence of stereotypy [in cross-cultural comparisons] suggest that violent behavior is largely learned. . . . Human beings can learn virtually anything. Among other things, they can learn to be virtually wholly unaggressive. . . .[27]

Barak elaborates the same theme, and confirms that not only are potentials for aggression and aggressive violence "largely learned," they are also routinely defused by internalized mechanisms of self-control: "Even in those societies which can be (or are) characterized as aggressive or violent, relatively few boys or men, and even fewer girls or women, actually kill or seriously wound anybody during the course of their lives. In social reality, no matter how angry or mad most people become even in the so-called violent societies, they have learned to control their 'aggressive natures'. This is not to deny that we are all born with the potential and capacity for learning both violence and nonviolence."[28]

Another challenging perspective on this issue is provided by primatologist Frans de Waal. As de Waal correctly remarks, "We are group animals to a terrifying degree. Since political leaders are masters at crowd psychology, history is replete with people following them en masse into insane ventures." But, he then observes, unexpectedly, that "When I look at a marching army, I don't necessarily see aggression in action. I see the herd instinct: thousands of men in lockstep, willing to obey superiors."[29] In a similar vein, Montagu remarks that "The 'fighting' man shoots at or drops his bombs on an 'enemy' he hardly ever sees, and from whom his emotional disengagement could scarcely be more remote. He is engaged in 'hostilities' in which there is no emotional enmity, and in 'aggressive' behavior in which there is no feeling of aggression. His behavior is not instinctively but state-directed toward the enemy."[30] This perspective supports the previously articulated view that aggression, violence, and violent expressions of aggression are potentials that are subject to being shaped and promoted (or discouraged) by social and cultural forces and other forms of conditioning.

These reports take us a very long way from the simplistic notion that the causes and conditions for aggression and violence are beyond our personal control, and beyond human control, more generally speaking. But again, if they are not beyond control, then it is up to us (individually and collectively) to inform ourselves more carefully about them and step forward to choose how we will deal with them.

An interesting reflection on the different meanings attributed to "aggression" is offered by Riches. He believes that human aggression is not just a more sophisticated replication of aggressive violence or displays in other species, which often carry the message to keep out of a certain territory, keep away from a source of food, a supply of females, and so forth. Some theorists, he notes, assert that "threats of violence obtain unconsciously (perhaps from natural selection), so that real violence never, in fact, happens." But Riches prefers the view "which sees threats of violence as a product of a distinctively human imagination. . . . [and] as an appropriate (and far from arbitrary) *symbol* of 'real' violence, based in the fact that people know that real violence can develop inexorably from quite mild acts of physical hurt."[31] As well as showing that human aggression is unique in its mode of expression, Riches's view seems to entail that the symbolism of aggression has to be learned from experience (in other words, that it is culturally transmitted). This theory makes a good deal of sense; but in the end, the import of both views is that aggressive displays or threats of violence may, in many cases, be deterrents to harm rather than either expressions of violence or preludes to it. It should be added that, understood in this way, the deterrent effect of aggression can be seen as self-directed as much as other-directed. That is, aggressive displays or threats often have the function in fact of *preventing* both a resort to violent behavior and its consequent impact.

Misleading Conceptions of Aggression

The above discussion casts doubt on the standard definition of aggression accepted by many in the social sciences. Social psychologist Susan Fiske, for example, defines aggression as "any behavior whose proximate intent is harm to another person."[32] Robert Baron and Deborah Richardson broaden this definition to include nonhuman animals. For them, aggression is "any form of behavior directed toward the goal of harming or injuring another living being who is motivated to avoid such treatment."[33] Peace psychologist Daniel Mayton simply states that "Intent to harm or injure is the central component of aggression."[34] Yet we have seen reason to believe that such definitions miss important aspects of aggression. First, as just noted, aggression may have (or may have come to possess) the purpose of *avoiding* violence or harm. Second, aggression, like any procedure or behavior functioning as a deterrent (such as a government's high tax on cigarettes or installing a security system to protect your house), is designed more to *prevent* certain acts than to harm anyone. It might be argued that a deterrent, in order to be credible, must be either a naked or thinly veiled threat of harm, the use of force, and so on. But it could equally be (and often is) just a bluff, which it is hoped will not be called. (This may be true, for example, of the behavior of some schoolyard bullies.) Plainly, in such cases, it cannot be said that the "proximate intent," "intent," or "goal" of the aggressive behavior is to harm or injure, since there is no such mental set. In other words, while aggression may often conform to these experts' definitions, there are many situations in which it does not, and therefore, the definitions appear to be both narrow and unnecessarily stipulative. Third, it follows from the cited definitions that defusing or neutralizing aggressive behavior is a matter of finding a way to thwart or escape from what is bound to be an imminent physical or psychological assault. But in view of the counterexamples offered earlier (sports behavior and aggressive personalities), we can see that dealing with aggression must be more complicated than this, and in fact, everyone alive—whether adept in nonviolence or not—has no doubt developed, or will develop, some stratagems for doing so. This includes preventing nonviolent forms of aggression from growing into violent forms. Fourth, aggressive behavior may only accidentally or incidentally cause harm or injury to (human or nonhuman) sentient beings or to valued objects. A young male driver roaring heedlessly down the road in a souped-up car above the speed limit is by any standard acting aggressively. While his behavior may be offensive and unsettling, no one would think to describe him as acting violently. He may not care whether he hurts someone, but he does not necessarily intend to cause any injury or harm, even if he ends up doing so. (In addition, not caring before the fact is quite different from not caring after the fact. If this driver killed or badly injured someone, that event could easily become a life-changing experience for him.)

We also need to reflect here on another major misconception about aggression: that it is caused by the hormone testosterone and expressed in proportion to the level of testosterone present in male individuals at a given time. To be sure, aggressive behavior is known to be associated with elevated levels of testosterone. But higher levels of testosterone do not predict more aggressive behavior in either individuals or groups.[35] This is because scientific research has not resolved some important issues:

- whether higher levels of testosterone cause more aggressive behavior;
- whether aggressive behavior produces higher levels of testosterone;
- whether other complex biological and social factors are most important in forming a predisposition toward aggressive behavior.

As we have seen earlier, there are societies in which aggressive violence is commonplace, and others in which it is virtually unknown. We have also learned that every society that has ever existed has of necessity needed to find ways of dealing with aggressive individuals and groups; and so, too, every individual living today (like those in the past) must acquire self-control in order to function in a socially responsible way. The many different patterns by which these challenges are resolved make it clear that there can be no single-factor diagnosis of the conditions that facilitate aggression and aggressive violence.

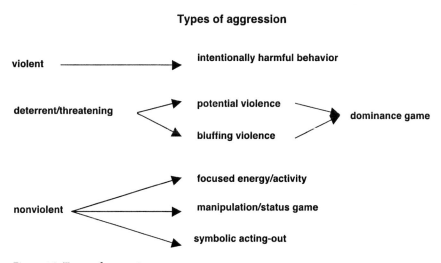

Figure 4.2 Types of aggression

The discussion in this section demonstrates, among other things, that *while most expressions of violence may reasonably be called aggression, aggression is not necessarily or always violent.* If some social scientists choose to single out aggressive, intentional violence for study, that is their prerogative, and the results may be valuable. But equating aggression with violence (and even goal-directed violence) is mistaken. Defining out of existence those forms of aggression that are not violent merely succeeds in giving a distorted picture of this class of behaviors, and causes us to miss some important insights.

Paul Chappell, a US army soldier turned peace advocate, makes the interesting suggestion that "The majority of aggression within our society results from *misplaced fear*, which occurs when we perceive a threat where no real threat exists. Insecure men are aggressive because deep down they are frightened all the time. Very secure men . . . do not feel a need to posture every time someone insults them. . . . Where a very insecure man is concerned, if you so much as look at him the wrong way he will feel the need to be aggressive toward you." Chappell believes that seriously insecure (and therefore aggression-prone) individuals are actually experiencing pain or suffering inside, which can stem from a number of sources, such as "frustration, loneliness, and hopelessness."[36] His insight evinces some of the contingent and conditioning factors of life-experience that can turn aggression into a violent and antisocial form of self-expression.

Psychologist Ervin Staub observes that violent acting out is related to the deprivation or denial of basic needs: "The need for long-term satisfaction is the need to feel and believe that things are good in one's life and that life is progressing in a desirable way (not necessarily in the moment, but overall) in the long run. . . . In general, in difficult times or at times of conflict, the more basic needs can be fulfilled by constructive means, without creating or intensifying enmity, the less likely that violence will develop."[37] Once again, the emphasis is on the sociocultural setting in which one's existence is played out. This approach to aggression and violence has a firm foundation in historical fact, as we have already established.

4.2. THE LIMITATIONS OF VIOLENCE

To say that violence does not always get its way is merely stating the obvious. Violence is motivated by the thought of a zero-sum outcome: someone gains, and someone else loses in more or less equal measure. But this is a deception. Violent action only offers the appearance of gain. The costs of war and its impact on all concerned were discussed in the Introduction, and some of these were seen to be quantifiable, and others not, though no less real and tragic for that. William Stafford, an American conscientious objector and writer, recorded in his daily journal the thought that "Every war has two losers." Reflecting in 1991 on the Gulf War, he wrote, "Listen to me; listen slow: In—this—war—again—humanity—lost."[38] Sometimes just a few well-chosen words make us turn around, take notice, and think in a way we have not before. Wars are not only costly in so many ways, but also have the effect of sowing the seeds for further violent hostilities, because they've either not settled the issues that started them in the first place, or have led to an unjust settlement, or have brutalized the participants beyond measure so that reconciliation becomes unlikely or next to impossible.

In the broader sense, many would argue, violence begets more violence. A nonviolent activist Catholic priest from Chile testifies that "Violence is the resort of the weak, who have no arguments and no moral authority. And violence can only create a state of affairs that needs to be sustained by violence."[39] At the group level or the personal level, acts of violence are likely to create deep psychological scars, as well as resentment, hatred, a drive for revenge, and related responses. And even those who like to think of themselves as nonviolent by nature may easily be mistaken about their own potential; with specific reference to retaliation, psychologist Steven Pinker notes that "Revenge is not confined to political and tribal hotheads but is an easily pushed button in everyone's brains."[40]

The negative impacts of violence linger, to affect, in many ways, not only the victims of violence, but also its perpetrators, including recipients of punitive counter-violence inside and outside of the world's prison systems. As one team of experts writes, "Violence to human beings hurts and harms body, mind, and spirit. Hurting/harming one of these usually affects the other two through psychosomatic transfers. This is an example of one of the most solid theorems in social science: violence breeds violence within and among actors, in space and over time."[41] Gerald Runkle, a political scientist, confirms these observations, noting that "Violence provokes greater violence and leads to general disorder in society. The agent too is directly harmed when he performs an act of violence: he is brutalized."[42] Similar conclusions were reached by the US attorney general's National Task Force on Children Exposed to Violence.[43] And political theorist Hannah Arendt, who studied violence, totalitarianism, and associated issues for many years, concludes that "The practice of violence, like all action, changes the world, but the most probable change is to a more violent world."[44]

Just as there is no simple, one-dimensional description of violence, so too there is no simple, one-dimensional explanation of it. However, it is known that many violent people have themselves been victims of physical or psychological violence (or both). Research suggests that "batterers 'learn' to use physical violence through exposure to violence in their families," but that "witnessing parental violence, as opposed to experiencing physical violence as a child," is more likely to be the precursor of future abusive behavior.[45] The perpetrator is therefore likely to be a disturbed individual, but is also equally likely to experience troubled relationships, social ostracism, encounters with the law, and possibly to have a criminal record. We have also seen (Introduction, "The Costs of War") some of the heavy, often unbearable weight that war experiences leave on the psyches of ex-soldiers. A recent report on this subject begins with the following headline: "One U.S. veteran attempts suicide every 80 minutes: Hidden tragedy of Afghanistan and Iraq wars."[46] Another study, by the University of Pennsylvania School of Medicine, summarizes the situation in this way: "An estimated 18 American military veterans take their own lives every day—thousands each year—and those numbers are steadily increasing."[47] So, the moral of this whole story would seem to be that if we want a society and a world in which there is less violence, the conditions causing violence are better understood, violence is more under personal and group control, and there are attractive and meaningful alternatives to violence as a means of self-expression and behavior modification in others, then we have to take steps toward bringing about these states of affairs.

In what follows, we will have a general look at nonviolence as a response to these personal and social needs. Chapters 6 and 7 will explore more particular issues relating to the creation of a culture of peace.

4.3. NONVIOLENCE: NARROWER AND BROADER VISIONS

Nonviolence is a topic that requires careful examination. When first encountering it, one might assume that nonviolence can be equated with passivity or weakness—which betrays a fundamental bias toward violence in our mental preoccupations. On the face of it, nonviolence is apparently the opposite of violence. But where does that get us? What exactly is "the opposite of violence"? Would we know it if we saw it right in front of us? If the argument pursued thus far in this book is on the right track, we do in fact have the opposite of violence in front of us and see it quite a lot of the time—in everyday acts of people (including ourselves) just getting along, helping each other out, being kind, coming to agreement, peacefully dealing with difficulties and disputes, and the like. But in the same way that violence is complex and often subtle, so too is nonviolence. To begin with, some proponents of nonviolence maintain that this word fails to do justice to what is being referenced, because the prefix "non-" merely indicates something that is unlike something else, but without revealing any of its own positive attributes. Similarly, to say that someone is an "atheist" only tells us that he or she does not believe in God (or is an anti-theist), but misses describing the alternative beliefs and principles (for example, ethical and humanitarian values) that such a person might follow instead.

Basic Nonviolence

A narrow view of nonviolence would focus on things like not fighting (physically or psychologically), obeying written and unwritten rules of various kinds, being open-minded and agreeable, letting annoying things roll off one's back, not bearing malice or grudges toward others, and being cooperative in the workplace, in the home, and elsewhere. These are commendable virtues to be sure, and are not to be denigrated. Nonviolence in this sense does not entail being a goody-goody, but rather something more like keeping friction-causing, fractious behavior under control and allowing the more generous side of one's personality to shine through. No fanfare or trumpets are called for, just a quiet, gentle, and supportive approach to interactions, a smile, an offer of a handshake, an invitation to mutual engagement, an assertion of our basic sociality and solidarity.

At the center of nonviolent thinking is the concept of *harm avoidance*. As it might be argued, "Do no harm" is perhaps the most basic moral precept (see Chapter 5, section 5.8, "Compassion: [ii] Action and Morality"). Even if one does not see oneself as acting from a moral principle or identify the above precept as the most basic, crucial to nonviolence is the avoidance of causing injury to others, and of being complicit in causing injury to them. These "others" may include only human beings; but they may also include nonhuman animals and entities that make up the environment, or the environment as a whole. A subsidiary belief is that doing harm produces bad consequences, whereas nonviolent behavior, through refusal to participate in wrongdoing, avoids creating bad consequences, and also produces good ones. Good and bad consequences may be felt by others, but in some outlooks, they may be experienced by oneself, too. The Buddhist doctrine of "karma" and the common expression "You'll reap what you sow" convey this concern for effects on oneself.

It may be argued that "Do no harm," being a negative principle, is too restrictive to convey the essence of morality (or of nonviolence). There is a lengthy tradition of couching moral guidelines in negative terms, but one argument against this approach is that such precepts tell us only half of the story; we want to know not just what we *ought not to do*, but equally, what we *ought to do*. Therefore (the argument continues), we need to recognize as well a principle like "Do good" or "Help others," which states a duty of benevolence toward those whom our behavior does or might affect.

Extended or Applied Nonviolence

The ideas stated thus far are the soil from which additional notions spring, such as peaceful protest against violence and injustice, being a public conscience by means of witnessing, conscientious objection to military service, and placing one's body literally on the line or one's personal safety and liberty at risk in order to prevent wrongdoing. (Socrates, notwithstanding his having been a soldier, declared that "To inflict wrong [or injustice] is worse than to suffer it,"[48] and many advocates of nonviolent resistance have courageously lived up to this principle.) As can readily be discerned, there is no clear boundary between dedication to doing right actions (or avoiding wrong ones) as an individual, and being motivated to affect a larger range of attitudes and behaviors, for example, those of bystanders, perpetrators of wrongdoing, or society as a whole. Nevertheless, there is a strong tradition of engaging in nonviolence as a tool for bringing about social and political change, which we will examine later in this chapter. In line with the explanation given above, it will become clear that "strategic nonviolence" springs from a vision of how things ought to be, or of how they could be better than they are, and hence is considerably more than a posture of negating the status quo with no alternative in mind.

As the example of Socrates might suggest, nonviolence cannot be equated with pacifism in any straightforward sense. Someone who is totally dedicated to nonviolence will no doubt be a pacifist; but a pacifist who accepts that there may (even if only very rarely) be just wars is not totally dedicated to nonviolence. Gandhi was as dedicated to nonviolence and as staunch a pacifist as anyone could be; and yet, as we shall see presently, he thought there might be occasions when violence would be permissible, although in saying so, he certainly did not mean to open the door to justifying war. Chapter 3 explained that there are absolute pacifists, who oppose any use of violence (even for self-defense), but also more qualified or conditional pacifists of various persuasions. The latter might oppose all wars without exception, but believe that violence may sometimes be the final appeal (for instance, when unavoidable for self-defense); or they might believe that there can be just wars or, at any rate, justifiable military operations (such as humanitarian rescues or interventions). So we see that even among those who are strongly dedicated to nonviolence, there are degrees of adherence to this ideal (exceptions to the rule), or different principles of conduct that are operative. Nonetheless, all advocates of nonviolence would stress that consistency of thought and action is a desirable goal that they strive to realize to the greatest extent in their own lives.

4.4. SELF-AFFIRMATION AND OTHER EVERYDAY
BENEFITS OF NONVIOLENCE

Nonviolence is not a recipe for solving all human problems. Nor, of course, is any other single kind of behavior, attitude, or policy. But nonviolence is a hugely significant and important factor in determining our quality of life, and it is therefore vital for societies everywhere to cultivate. Violence is pretty much one-dimensional in that, although it expresses itself in numerous ways, its intent is to cause harm and exert control. Violence scars and damages people physically and psychologically. It closes them down and creates hatred, which is self-imprisoning. Izzeldin Abuelaish is a Palestinian doctor who lost three beloved daughters in the most horrific circumstances during Israel's "Operation Cast Lead" (discussed in the Introduction, "The Costs of War"). Yet, remarkably, in spite of this tragedy, he has chosen to work for peace, forgiveness, and reconciliation in the Middle East. He says,

> I think the world is drowning in hate, and hate is destructive. It is a toxin that affects all aspects of life. It doesn't just affect the individual who carries it, it affects the community. If I hate, who is going to suffer? Myself. My children. My relatives. My community. I will be disconnected from the world. . . . Are we going to hate everyone who did something wrong to us? . . . I don't blame the soldier [whose tank shell demolished his home]. I don't want to blame . . . but if we want to blame, blame the system and start to correct the system. . . . No one is born violent. The violence is environmental. The violence is the symptom of a disease. Change the environment and there will never be violence. No one is born to hate.[49]

Nonviolence can be personally healing and remedial, as we see here. But beyond this idea, it builds people up and reveals opportunities for cooperation and trust, which in turn lead to unlimited numbers of possible productive outcomes. Psychologist Rachel MacNair, in a wide-ranging overview of peace research, offers the following contrast: "Once a violent solution is on the table, it precludes the development of alternatives. Violence as a problem-solving technique has the apparent advantage of being quick and efficient. One need only ignore the long-term aftermath and other negative impacts on society. Nonviolent alternatives must of necessity take more care, attention, resources, and time. They have obvious advantages in the long run, but the short-term consequence is more work."[50] Two points deserve emphasis here. One is that violence takes its toll, as we have seen, both in the case of war and in more general terms. As any concerned taxpayer and citizen knows, it also costs society a great deal of money and resources on an ongoing basis to cope with violent individuals and their actions—including the actions of political leaders who perpetrate violence. The other point is that simply getting along does take a lot of effort and ingenuity. Anyone in a committed relationship with friends, children, other relatives, life-partners, workmates, and so on understands (or should understand) this notion quite well. But it should also be recognized that trust, cooperation, friendship, nonviolence, and other forms of outreach involve making a choice and following it through day to day.[51]

Nonviolent ways of communicating and behaving express openness and receptivity toward others, and also represent an invitation to form bonds of mutual respect and affection. They invite others to be themselves and to flourish, but equally importantly, they have the same nourishing impact on oneself. Therefore, nonviolence is not only self-enriching but also energizing and self-affirming, because it encourages self-knowledge and creative yet controlled and thoughtful forms of self-expression. It follows too that nonviolence is not just an outlook that is intellectually constructed, but has emotional (and, as we shall see presently, spiritual) dimensions as well. Since we are highly social beings, with an enormous scope for self-realization, we need one another to encourage and facilitate our personal growth and maturity. The best state of affairs would be one in which, fundamental needs having been met, more complex (so-called self-actualization) needs can also be fulfilled for everyone. Nonviolence in our personal lives and in our institutions and societal structures is essential for the pursuit of this ideal. At the same time, however, we shouldn't whitewash human nature too much. Conflict is something we all need to deal with and is part of the everyday context as well (see Chapter 6, section 6.7, "Engaging with Conflict"). But nonviolence provides a pathway (or a set of pathways) for resolving or defusing conflict, and, indeed, nonviolence theory itself developed from thoughts concerning what to do about the problem of conflict, especially as manifested in power-struggles. Hence, nonviolence constitutes a holistic approach to living from which we can all learn valuable lessons.

4.5. STRATEGIC (OR TRANSFORMATIVE) NONVIOLENCE

An Overview of Nonviolence Theory and Practice

The sources of nonviolence theory and practice are many and are deeply rooted in different traditions. Philosophical origins of nonviolence can be identified in ancient Greek philosophy, as we saw in the previous section. There are several examples of nonviolent action in ancient Rome, as well. An incident occurred in the second century CE when the bakers of Ephesus engaged in what were essentially union meetings followed by a work slowdown, and then were ordered by the regional proconsul to cease and desist or be arrested and punished.[52] From the works of Livy (Titus Livius, 59 BCE-17 CE) we learn that Roman citizens used nonviolent tactics to exert pressure for change as early as 494 BCE.[53] Source ideas can also be found in venerated Eastern thought-systems that are many centuries old. For instance, in the *Tao Te Ching* of Lao Tzu (probably sixth century BCE), the foundational text of Daoism (Taoism), the following verses appear:

> Weapons are tools of evil, shunned and
> avoided by everything in nature.
> Because people of Tao follow nature,
> they want nothing to do with weapons.
>
> Unevolved people are eager to act out of strength,
> but a person of Tao values peace and quiet.
> This means that his enemies are his enemies
> second, his own brothers and sisters first. . . .
>
> Whoever delights in killing will not find
> success in this world.[54]

The Art of War, based upon Daoist principles and written by Sun Tzu more than 2,000 years ago, contains the following wisdom: "The general rule for use of the military is that it is better to keep a nation intact than to destroy it." Sun Tzu also states, "Therefore those who win every battle are not really skillful—those who render others' armies helpless without fighting are the best of all."[55] Whether the former maxim encapsulates a strategy of self-interest, and the latter, of subversion or deterrence, may be debated; but what both certainly disclose is a military thinker's attitude that less violent or nonviolent tactics are far preferable to battlefield slaughters and wholesale destruction.

Many religions, including Judaism, Christianity, Islam,[56] Hinduism, Sikhism, Jainism, Buddhism, Bahá'í, and Neopagan faiths (Wicca, Druidism, and others) have teachings about nonviolence and claim adherents who have been exemplars of nonviolence. The religious outlooks of the Society of Friends (Quakers), Unitarians, and Anabaptists (Amish, Mennonites, Hutterites, German Baptist Brethren), as well as of some less-well-known groups, have stood out historically as consistently advocating nonviolence in one form or another. Large numbers of preliterate societies have been built upon nonviolent rules and practices, as Chapter 2 demonstrates. Finally, leaders of movements for change and ordinary citizens by great numbers, whether philosophically or spiritually sophisticated or not, have, at various points in history, looked to nonviolent methods in order to assert their will and achieve successful results against entrenched power structures and intransigent rulers that had seemed to loom over them like immovable mountains. Thus, as peace scholar Brian Teixeira maintains, "Nonviolence is an evolving global phenomenon. It is not the product of one culture. It is based in a recognition of the interconnectedness of all life, and therefore an unwillingness to use harm to redress harm."[57]

It is important to recognize that nonviolent methods are used not only by individuals against governmental or institutional injustice, but also by states or groups of states against other states, with the intention of changing the target states' policies, behaviors, and even sometimes the regimes in power. These measures include trade and arms embargoes, freezing assets, recalling ambassadors, suspension of diplomatic relations, travel bans, and expulsion from sports federations. The UN mandates various kinds of economic and other kinds of sanctions as well: "The use of mandatory sanctions is intended to apply pressure on a State or entity to comply with the objectives set by the Security Council without resorting to the use of force. . . . The Council has resorted to mandatory sanctions as an enforcement tool when peace has been threatened and diplomatic efforts have failed."[58] Since 2004, the UN has imposed sanctions on the Democratic Republic of the Congo, Ivory Coast, Sudan, North Korea, Iran, and Mali, as well as the Taliban in Afghanistan and other groups and individuals. There is considerable room for disagreement, however, about whether some examples of these practices should properly be called nonviolent, for the reason that they may, and often do, cause a great deal of hardship and suffering among the ordinary population, which bears the brunt of their impact. Sanctions imposed on Iraq by the UN during the Gulf War lasted from 1990 to 2003, and are estimated to have cost the lives of 100,000 children, perhaps many more, owing to the embargoes on oil and other trade goods, which prevented essentials (such as safe drinking water) from being purchased and services from being maintained.[59] Sanctions put in place against Iran are hurting many whose place in the nation's economy is very remote from nuclear weapons research and production. Those suffering their "unintended consequences" include artists, university students, pharmaceutical manufacturers, and everyday consumers generally, hit by falling currency values.[60] Mindful of this problem, the UN established a working group to draw up criteria by which sanctions could be more carefully and precisely targeted,[61] but the evidence suggests that these criteria define what are still rather blunt tools for bringing about change. The political benefit of sanctions is also a matter of debate, with some commentators suggesting that they merely harden the resolve of target governments (such as North Korea's) to be more defiant in their ways.[62] In sum, sanctions have had mixed results, sometimes succeeding, other times not, which the historical record shows.

As a postscript to all this, it should be noted that interstate nonviolent measures are not all negative; they also include such things as "action in the form
of engagement—dialogue, regular diplomatic communications, and economic
incentives such as foreign aid and/or provisions of low-interest loans. . . ."[63]

Mayton, whose views were discussed earlier in this chapter, lists and analyses philosophical, anthropological, sociological, psychological, political, and
multidisciplinary views of nonviolence, with some theorists falling into more
than one of these categories.[64] In what follows, however, we will focus on two
strands of nonviolence theory: those promulgated by Gandhi and by American political scientist Gene Sharp. Nonviolence has an impressive history and
is also embedded in numerous societies. But as a systematic theory and pragmatic tool for creating change, it came to maturity in the twentieth century,
especially through the influence of Gandhi and Sharp.

Gandhi and the Foundations of Nonviolence

Most people associate the idea of principled, proactive nonviolent behavior
aimed at changing the status quo with Mohandas K. Gandhi, who began his
career as a lawyer and then transformed himself into a spiritual leader. As
such, he was instrumental in securing India's independence from the British
Empire in 1947, and he greatly inspired the civil rights activism of Martin Luther King, Jr. in the United States, and of many others elsewhere in the world.
(Gandhi was usually called "Mahatma," a title of honor and respect.) As the
work of Gandhi and King illustrates, nonviolence often involves extreme courage: Neither feared death, and both were killed for the beliefs they held and
acted upon.

While there is no doubt that Indian independence was historically the greatest achievement for nonviolent struggle, the roots of strategic nonviolence
extend considerably further back in time, as illustrated in previous sections
of this chapter. Gandhi realized that his own views and tactics were "experiments with truth,"[65] nourished by sources as diverse as Hinduism, Jainism, the
Christian pacifism of Russian novelist Leo Tolstoy, and the social activism of
American essayist Henry David Thoreau, who endorsed civil disobedience as
a duty of good citizenship.

Essential to an understanding of Gandhi's position are two concepts, *ahimsa*
and *satyagraha*. The first of these is grounded in ancient Hindu philosophy and
religion, but Gandhi gives it his own individual stamp: "*Ahimsa* means not to
hurt any living creature by thought, word or deed, even for the supposed benefit of that creature."[66] *Satyagraha* is a term he invented that translates roughly
as "soul-force" or "truth-force." The basic meaning of nonviolence, for Gandhi,
unfolds itself in knowledge of the truth plus the determination always to seek

the truth and to live peacefully in light of it. The concept of truth that Gandhi adopts is quite different from our normal one, which refers to a positive (but difficult to define) property of factual statements—their quality of expressing or designating what is the case, what is really so. For Gandhi, truth bears a closer resemblance to correct moral insight or intuition. While the truth, in both ordinary and Gandhian senses, is empowering in various ways, Gandhi's truth is meant to be spiritually (and sometimes politically) transformative and momentous.

His theory of *satyagraha* conveys the idea that nonviolence is proactive rather than reactive. He had unwavering confidence in our ability to grasp the truth, in his sense, and believed absolutely in its power and invincibility in the face of wrongdoing. As Jesse Richards observes, "Gandhi identified the ways people can resolve conflict: rational debate, violence, and moral appeal. . . . Gandhi felt that combining reason with a spiritual, moral appeal would work every time."[67] In practical terms, he understood that nothing can be accomplished by employing violence to take on an adversary that has all the means of violence at its disposal and does not hesitate to use them. Such an opponent is stronger and wins hands down at this level of conflict. Furthermore, counterviolence only reduces you to brutality and defines you and your message in the same image as that of your violent opponent. But there is another level of strength where different dynamics and rules apply, by means of which an independent moral stance can be derived and maintained, namely, that of nonviolent action. The point is to reconfigure conflict so that nonviolence becomes the source of superior power.

Gandhi took a very broad view of what counts as violence, and because of this, his vision of living peacefully includes not only avoiding violence of an obvious sort (the use of hurtful or coercive force), but also refraining from harming others by actions and words. As he applied the principle of *ahimsa* to political activities, the notion of *satyagraha* emerged, signifying the channeling of spiritual resolve into defiant but peaceful means of resistance to injustice. But *satyagraha* also entails not acting out of anger or a retaliatory frame of mind, and instead returning love for hate. It has a resolute purpose expressed by the claim that "it brings good both to the *satyagrahi* and his adversary."[68] What is this good? For Gandhi it is "truth, which is the very substance of the soul."[69] He held that there is a moral order in the universe and that if we are out of balance with it, we suffer accordingly. (See also Chapter 5, section 5.5, "From Inner Peace to Cosmic Peace.") This doctrine underlies his perception that nonviolent noncooperation (civil disobedience) is, paradoxically, at the same time a cooperative effort between agent and opponent. We will return to this idea shortly.

First, we need to consider more closely the concept of truth that is instrumental to Gandhi's outlook. According to Gandhi, ignorance, lying, deceit, and violence are alike in being corruptions of the human soul and essence. Lying and violence are intimately connected in his thinking, because they are harmful ways of treating others, as well as oneself. Treachery, the use of physical force, and domination are ultimately self-defeating since they are obstacles to truth, and fail to respect the moral personhood of the opponent; in addition, they do not generally resolve conflicts of interest, but rather infect the end toward which one struggles, and therefore, have the unhealthy consequence of leading to further acts of the same kind. As a result, violent behaviors cannot help us attain the goal of life, which is to "realize God who dwells within our hearts."[70] Only by following the path of truth can we achieve this goal, and if others deviate from it, we must help them find their way back. Gandhi firmly held that "a truthful man cannot long remain violent. He will perceive in the course of his search that he has no need to be violent and he will further discover that so long as there is the slightest trace of violence in him, he will fail to find the truth he is searching."[71]

This last statement voices the belief that in being violent, we divert our energy from, and thus betray, our own highest needs—for peace within ourselves and for self-knowledge and self-fulfillment. *Satyagraha*, as a form of nonviolent resistance to violence, aims "to open up the opponent's mind and heart so that rational discussion could take place in a climate of goodwill and critical self-reflection."[72] In this process, the practitioner of Gandhi's method shows respect for, and faith in, the humanity of his or her opponent, as well as hope for the possibility of finding a meeting place, eventually, in a dispassionate spirit of negotiation and on a level of equality. In respecting others, we affirm and consolidate ourselves as well.

Gandhi maintained that nonviolence emphasizes conversion rather than coercion.[73] The sense that change brought about by nonviolence aims at a win-win result is thus deeply embedded in this way of thinking. Half a world away from India, one can locate reverberations of Gandhi's approach in Brazilian education theorist Paulo Freire's highly influential book *Pedagogy of the Oppressed* (1968): "[S]ooner or later being less human leads the oppressed to struggle against those who made them so. In order for this struggle to have meaning, the oppressed must not, in seeking to regain their humanity, . . . become in turn oppressors of the oppressors, but rather restorers of the humanity of both."[74] We can conclude, in fact, that because nonviolence empowers both oneself and one's opponent, it is thus doubly liberating. And since the problem that gave rise to it in the first place is addressed, nonviolence represents a triple solution or threefold win.

The quest for truth, in Gandhi's view, does not culminate in political freedom, nor does it cease when this is secured. Indeed, it is a lifelong process.
Truth, peacefulness, and nonviolence must also govern our relationship with
nature as a whole: "God-realization means seeing Him in all beings. Or, in
other words, we should learn to become one with every creature. This can happen only when we voluntarily give up the use of physical force and when we
develop the nonviolence which lies dormant in our hearts."[75] A well-developed,
all-embracing nonviolence of this sort implies that nonhuman animals should
be treated with kindness and that vegetarianism is obligatory. Gandhi even
went so far as to affirm, in an often-quoted statement, that "the greatness of a
nation and its moral progress can be measured by the way in which its animals
are treated."[76] Since animals are by long tradition the lowest-placed occupants
of the moral ladder, or perhaps negligently not even placed on the first rung,
their status can be used to gauge the ethical and spiritual health of a society as
a whole. (See also Chapter 7, section 7.2, "Respect for Other Animals and the
Environment.")

Great psychological strength and consistency of thought and action are
required of those who would dedicate themselves to nonviolence, Gandhi
asserts. First, nonviolence must be identified with active engagement and self-
empowerment, not with weakness and passivity or quiescence. Persons showing the latter behaviors are easily co-opted and manipulated by the agents of
wrongdoing, since they do not challenge it directly. By contrast, nonviolent
resistance and lifestyle require intense self-assertion. While nonviolence is
always morally preferable to violence and is almost always the right course
of action, even when one has to suffer personally for its sake, there may be
exceptional circumstances in which violence may justifiably be used, although
it remains an evil recourse. In such a situation (for instance, defending a helpless stranger who is being mugged), "using physical force with courage is far
superior to cowardice."[77] Second, because life is itself a process not a result,
even though we will sometimes fall short of the ideal, nonviolence must always
be that which we strive to realize. Therefore, in practical terms, living nonviolently is not equivalent to being morally perfect—an unattainable goal—but
rather, to causing the least amount of harm possible.

As a practical strategy for political and social change, Gandhian nonviolence entails deliberately disobeying unjust laws and noncooperation with
injustice. Publically outlining issues and attempting to create dialogue with
the wielders of power, in the hope that they will engage in discussion and self-
reflection, is the first step. This action is premised on the love, respect, and
identification with the other described earlier, and also springs from a presumption of rationality as the underlying capacity that unites those of opposed
viewpoints. But where rational discourse is not possible, then nonviolence can

force the issue and help bring people to their senses, that is, to the realization that violent behavior is futile and self-destructive in the long run.

How these principles are put into practice is illustrated by Gandhi's famous Salt March. A bit of background to this event is necessary. In 1919, Indian protest against British colonization and governance culminated in a demonstration at which British troops opened fire on an unarmed crowd containing many women and children, killing (by different estimates) between 379 and 1,000, and wounding many hundreds. This is known as the Jallianwalah Bagh (or Amritsar) Massacre. A Non-Cooperation Movement emerged during the years 1920–22 as a reaction to this bloody event and the implementation of arbitrary search and seizure laws. The movement featured economic boycotts of British-made goods, commitment to purchasing locally produced handicrafts, workplace and public-service stoppages, picketing of liquor stores, and other tactics. (Alternative economic, social, and political activities and structures have become essential tools of nonviolent struggle.) The campaign "seriously challenged the economic and political power of the British,"[78] and is heralded as the beginning of the drive for Indian independence. But it was only in 1930, when Gandhi undertook the Salt March (or Salt *Satyagraha*), that large numbers of his fellow citizens were won over to nonviolence as a means of breaking down British colonial rule. This march posed a defiant challenge to the British monopoly on salt manufacturing and the associated taxes collected from it. Gandhi himself walked a great distance overland to the Arabian Sea north of Mumbai (Bombay), collecting large numbers of sympathizers along the way, making salt and talking about the campaign at several stops along the coast. At the salt works in Dharasana, hundreds were beaten by British soldiers, Gandhi was arrested, and worldwide publicity put the spotlight on their cause. There was no turning back, and the seeds were sown for eventual British withdrawal from a rebellious and increasingly ungovernable country.

Gandhi began the process of defining and maturing the philosophy and tactics of nonviolence and *satyagraha* as a young lawyer living for more than two decades in South Africa. During this period, he worked to improve the status of Indians, classified as inferiors under the harsh laws of apartheid. A wonderful anecdote from this time crystallizes much of his thinking and pragmatism that later energized the events already described. One has to first visualize the very slight Gandhi, properly dressed in a suit and tie, confronting a very powerful Boer military leader and administrator, General Jan Smuts. Biographer Eknath Easwaran reconstructs the conversation that took place as follows:

Gandhi . . . informing him quietly: "I've come to tell you that I am going to fight against your government."

Smuts must have thought he was hearing things. "You mean you have come here to tell me that?" he laughs. "Is there anything more you want to say?"

"Yes," says Gandhi. "I am going to win."

Smuts is astonished. "Well," he says at last, "and how are you going to do that?"

Gandhi smiles. "With your help."

Many years later Smuts admitted—not without humor—that this is exactly what Gandhi
   did. By his courage, by his determination, by his refusal to take unfair advantage, but
   especially by his endless capacity to "stick it out" without yielding and without retaliation, Gandhi managed at last to win the general's respect and friendship, and in 1914
   the laws most offensive to the Indians were repealed and basic civil rights voted into
   law.[79]

From this short sketch of Gandhi's ideas and methods in action, we learn that
nonviolence is much more than simply refraining from violence and from
causing harm, and therefore, too, it is much more than just "the opposite of
violence." Likewise, nonviolence is just as much taking a stand in favor of
something as it is refusing to do something else. Furthermore, it involves trying to see things from a conflicting viewpoint, where one's opponent is coming
from, as well as asserting one's own personal power in various communicative
and demonstrative ways.[80] All of this explains, to a large degree, why Gandhi
sought to recast nonviolence in his own novel manner.[81]

Gene Sharp and Contemporary Nonviolent Methods

Among the many theorists of nonviolent action to have been deeply influenced
by Gandhi is Gene Sharp, who has spent an entire academic career clarifying
and developing in detail the techniques by which this philosophy can be put into
effective practice. His massive three-part work *The Politics of Nonviolent Action*
(1973)[82] is the standard authority on this subject; his book *From Dictatorship to
Democracy* (1993),[83] translated into more than thirty languages, has been described as "the most influential book you've never heard of,"[84] and has stimulated
and guided protest movements in nations around the world, including Serbia,
Ukraine, Georgia, Kyrgyzstan, Belarus, Iran, Lithuania, Latvia, Estonia, Yemen,
and Egypt. The Albert Einstein Institute, which is dedicated to disseminating
nonviolent literature and promoting the techniques of strategic nonviolence,
reports unprecedented demand for Sharp's book *Waging Nonviolent Struggle* at
the present time.[85] An Institute newsletter testifies that "Recent events [includ-
ing the global Occupy movement] . . . have brought massive new attention to the
power of these ideas and their potential for bringing about important changes
in the world."[86] *The Politics of Nonviolent Action* lists literally hundreds of methods of nonviolent action, described by Sharp as "political jiu-jitsu at work."[87]
These fall under the headings of "nonviolent protest and persuasion," "social,
economic, and political noncooperation," and "nonviolent intervention."[88]

Sharp's general approach to nonviolence has two underlying premises. The first is that political power really belongs to the people, and therefore governments, as wielders of political power, remain so only by collective consent: "One can see people as dependent upon the good will, the decisions and the support of their government or of any other hierarchical system to which they belong. Or, conversely, one can see that government or system dependent on the people's good will, decisions and support. . . . Nonviolent action is based on the second of these views. . . ."[89] The next premise, following directly from the first, is that people have it within their power to withdraw the consent that invests power in the government (or other system), causing it to either change or collapse. Inasmuch as "political power is not intrinsic to the power-holder," it derives from "the obedience and cooperation of the subjects."[90] As Peter Ackerman and Jack Duvall put it, withdrawal of consent means the power structure in place "would have neither the cooperation it needed to govern nor the legitimacy to pretend to do so."[91] Consequently, disobedience and noncooperation, if systematically carried out, can upset the exercise of power and even shift it to the subjects, giving them "a new sense of self-respect, self-confidence, and a realization of the power people can wield in controlling their own lives through learning to use the nonviolent technique."[92] It is worth mentioning, in order to emphasize once again the long historical roots of nonviolent thinking, that Sharp cites as the earliest proponent of this theoretical view a sixteenth-century French writer, Étienne de la Boétie.[93]

Also central to Sharp's outlook is the perception that effective and successful nonviolent action has to involve a critical mass of opposition, comprising a collection of individuals committed to standing up to a regime's (often violent) countermeasures:

> If a ruler's power is to be controlled by withdrawing help and obedience, noncooperation and disobedience must be widespread and must be maintained in the face of repression aimed at forcing a resumption of submission. However, once there has been a major reduction of or an end to the subjects' fear, and once there is a willingness to suffer sanctions as the price of change, large-scale disobedience and noncooperation become possible. Such action then becomes politically significant. . . .[94]

Implied here is the steadfast adherence to nonviolence in spite of temptations and opportunities to resort to violence—a point also insisted upon by Gandhi, and by King during the American civil rights struggle of the 1950s and 1960s. For this reason, Sharp remarks that "Effective application of the technique of nonviolent struggle requires great care, much thought, skilled action, and strength."[95] In an interview at the beginning of 2012, Sharp asserts that when the opposition takes up arms, that is always the wrong way to go. He makes his case with specific reference to protests against the brutality of the Syrian government led by Bashar al-Assad. "Maintain nonviolence," he says. "Do not organise mutinying soldiers to use violence against the army. That is suicidal. That's what the government would want you to do. Don't play into their hands." (Syrian-American scholar, poet, and activist Mohja Kahf documents the fact that this uprising *was* a broadly based, grassroots, nonviolent movement for the first eleven months, before violent conflict took over.[96]) Further into the interview with Sharp comes the following exchange:

> So what would Sharp advise the people of the Syrian city of Homs to do when the tanks are rolling down the streets towards them? Like the famous man carrying a plastic bag in Tiananmen Square [during 1989 antigovernment demonstrations in Beijing, China], should they just stand there? Sharp's answer is yes.
>
> Regimes crumble when the military and police refuse to fire on the people. "They have to use mutinying soldiers to persuade the rest to mutiny," he said. The key moment comes when the army refuses to obey orders. The military will inevitably be better at violence than civilians, so taking up arms is a recipe for losing. Even winning isn't easy. "Bringing down a dictatorship is only Part 1," says Sharp. "Part 2 is constructing a new society, a democratic system."[97]

A critic or a cynic might challenge that "It's all very well for Sharp to prescribe a nonviolent strategy for Syria. He didn't have to put his body in front of the tanks." As this chapter is being written, a full-scale civil war rages in Syria. A cease-fire agreement is long since in tatters, government soldiers are showing no mercy or remorse over the slaughter and torture of their fellow citizens, poison gas has been used against civilians, rebel forces are accused of committing atrocities, outside forces are insinuating themselves into the conflict, and other nations are supplying armaments to both sides. Some of the most high-ranking army officers have defected to the opposition, and the prime minister has long-since fled the country. The international community is torn over the issue of how to bring peace to Syria. It is extremely difficult to give any definitive assessment of whether Sharp's views are right or wrong in this context. As they say, history will be the judge. But the example of the Philippines, where "Praying nuns, nursing mothers and old women in wheelchairs turned back bayonets and tanks"[98] may be recalled (see Chapter 1, section 1.5, "A Postscript on Nonviolence in History"). And as we have seen, many other examples demonstrate that nonviolence has its own unique effectiveness.

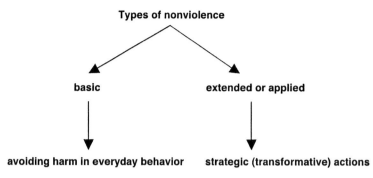

Figure 4.3 Types of nonviolence

4.6. CRITIQUES OF NONVIOLENCE AND ITS VINDICATION

Nonviolence has much to recommend it, in both everyday life and the political arena. But it possesses its own conceptual complexities that present difficulties—perhaps even contradictions. For instance, as Teixeira remarks, "It may be acceptable in certain situations to pressure or force someone to change his or her ways, whether they really want to or not, if it can be justified that this is not intended as harm but rather is in the best interests of everyone. Whether or not this constitutes a major inconsistency in nonviolence theory and practice—a significant conflict between means and ends—continues as an open question."[99] (Gandhi's definition of *ahimsa*, discussed in section 4.5, for example, may be thought to pose a difficulty of the same sort.) This issue does indeed evade easy resolution; but it must be added that it confronts every general moral theory as well, in one way or another. Most people would assume that taking a child for a painful medical procedure, the benefits of which she or he cannot comprehend, is nevertheless the right thing to do. And the same could be said of certain punitive measures aimed at changing the behavior of minors or adults who are stuck in self- and/or socially destructive patterns. Justifying coercion, however, is controversial and difficult to reconcile with any doctrine of freedom and personal responsibility, and it is probably best left to be worked through on a case-by-case basis. It is for reasons such as this that Runkle urges the following caution: "We should scrutinize nonviolent methods as closely as we do the violent ones. Violence may at least be open and direct, while nonviolence may be a deceitful mask for actions as productive of evil as violence itself."[100]

Strategic nonviolence is not unique in one respect. Like any method for bringing about major political, social, and economic change, it promises no guarantee of success. One charge made against nonviolence that we have encountered previously is that it cannot work (or could not have worked) against an opponent lacking in fundamental decency, conscience, compassion, a sense of justice, and so on, and accustomed to using brutality in order to get its way. But the nonviolent campaigns that ousted the Marcos regime in the Philippines and the rulers of Soviet satellite states during the 1980s show otherwise, as did the sporadic nonviolent activities conducted against the Nazis (see Chapter 1, section 1.5, "A Postscript on Nonviolence in History"). In any event, as David Cortright indicates,

> These criticisms reflect a common misunderstanding of how the nonviolent method works. Nonviolent action does indeed attempt to reach the heart of the oppressor, but its effectiveness does not depend upon an appeal to conscience. Rather, nonviolent resistance seeks to alter the political dynamics in a struggle by appealing to and winning sympathy from third parties and thereby undermining the power base of the oppressor. . . . It does not depend upon face-to-face persuasion or conversion of individual soldiers or political opponents. Its impact results from the pressure of effective mass action.[101]

Garnering support from large segments of the citizenry, the national and world media, and foreign governments, nonviolent actions can turn an oppressive state into an international pariah, which often brings about long-awaited reforms—and even much more sweeping changes.

There are also some who challenge the credibility of *any* claims to overall success on behalf of nonviolent tactics. Important revolutionary figures like Leon Trotsky, Mao Zedong (Mao Tse-tung), and Frantz Fanon are among these, having urged that truly radical change comes about only through violent means. During the US civil rights struggle of the 1960s, an African-American leader, H. Rap Brown (born Hubert Gerold Brown, and now Jamil Abdullah Al-Amin), famously opined that "Violence is as American as cherry pie." In a way, this approach is also captured by the sentiment that "violence is the only language that violent people understand." Certainly, numerous examples exist of this kind of revolutionary change occurring in history; but some of the stories of successful nonviolent transformation related in Chapter 1 and in the present chapter merit being labeled revolutionary as well.

A more serious version of the foregoing criticism surfaces in a discussion by political activist Peter Gelderloos. He writes,

> From India to Birmingham [Alabama], nonviolence has failed to sufficiently empower its practitioners, whereas the use of a diversity of tactics got results. Put simply, if a movement is not a threat, it cannot change a system that is based on centralized coercion and violence.

> Time and again, people struggling not for some token reform but for complete liberation—the reclamation of control over our own lives and the power to negotiate our own relationships with the people and the world around us—will find that nonviolence does not work, that we face a self-perpetuating power structure that is immune to appeals to conscience and strong enough to plow over the disobedient and uncooperative.[102]

To some extent, response to this broadside has already been provided above, and in earlier detailed descriptions of nonviolent campaigns and the theory of nonviolence. A few more points need to be made, however.

First, it is obvious that this controversy concerns different interpretations of history; but it also has the suspicious look of being about who "owns" history, whose version is definitive (see Chapter 1, section 1.2, "Constructing, Revising, and Controlling History"), which it would take another book to unravel and fully evaluate. Second, the stated criticism begs the question about how long it takes to bring about the most desired forms of social change. Brian Martin, an activist and nonviolence scholar, argues that "One of the greatest challenges for activists is to live in a society, fully aware of its shortcomings, while keeping alive the vision of a radical alternative, and maintaining enthusiasm for actions that may only seem to move the slightest distance towards that alternative. Reforms are more achievable than revolutionary transformation and offer concrete evidence that change is possible."[103] Do desired social changes need to evolve slowly, or can they really be speeded along by violent methods? Violence may be superficially attractive for a variety of reasons, but one should keep in mind the observation once made by American historian and social critic Theodore Roszak, that "People try non-violence for a week, and when it 'does not work' they go back to violence which hasn't worked for centuries."[104] In any case, it also needs to be asked what kind of results eventuate from the application of violent as opposed to nonviolent methods? Third, judging whether nonviolence successfully challenges and transforms state power in any given instance should not be contingent on judging every development that follows a particular campaign. Dictatorships in which the citizens have been conditioned to identify their nation with the persona of the glorious ruler, and states in which public institutions are nonexistent or in tatters due to years (if not decades) of neglect and corruption, are not magically uplifted into model democracies without a process that is long and arduous for all concerned. Fourth, there is much room for doubt about the long-lasting, transformative effectiveness of violence, as the aftermath of any war you choose to pick will illustrate (see Introduction, "War Myths," Myth #3); about the wisdom of violence as a means to challenge structures kept in place by those who have a near-monopoly on the tools of violence; and, more generally, about violence as a productive means of addressing human problems (see Chapter 4, section 4.2, "The Limitations of Violence").

The achievements of nonviolence in bringing about social or political change should be judged by the historical record, as Gelderloos correctly maintains. But it has to be added that a systematic international study will provide more credible evidence on this matter than an off-the-cuff generalization made from a limited standpoint. A broader study of this kind has in fact been conducted by Maria J. Stephan and Erica Chenoweth, who examine "the strategic effectiveness of violent and nonviolent campaigns in conflicts between nonstate and state actors using aggregate data on major nonviolent and violent resistance campaigns from 1900 to 2006." These authors consider a total of 323 uprisings, and report that "major nonviolent campaigns have achieved success 53 percent of the time compared with 26 percent for violent resistance campaigns."[105] Part of the explanation for the greater success of nonviolent campaigns is that they not only attract greater "loyalty shifts" among the population, and hence result in "mass mobilization," but also generate the degree of sympathy needed to stimulate timely international sanctions against repressive regimes.[106] While these findings do not end the critical discussion of nonviolence in action, they do clearly suggest that nonviolence is likely to be significantly more effective than violence in creating radical political transformation.

Yet another critique of nonviolence is that it is fostered by privileged white people and in fact amounts to a tactic for wittingly or unwittingly stalling and frustrating radical political and socioeconomic change—in other words, for preserving the status quo from which this class of individuals benefits the most. Therefore, from the standpoint of the oppressed, nonviolence merely plays into the hands of the oppressors. This argument is made by Gelderloos and others from within the American context, which is very volatile in an era of economic downturn, and especially since the beginning of the recent (and mostly nonviolent) Occupy movement. Any judgments about the prospects for change, and where they might most effectively be coming from, and leading to, would be hazardous. But from a global perspective, the above racial characterization is simply false. We have already seen that Gandhi (whose skin color itself refutes the claim) drew upon many sources, East and West, to shape his nonviolent outlook. Furthermore, nonviolent movements have united socioeconomic classes, ethnic groups, and races to bring about radical change in many places around the world. One way to reinforce this point is to take just a quick glance at the women who have been Nobel Peace Prize winners since 1990. In reverse chronological order, these are: 2011—Ellen

Johnson Sirleaf, Leymah Gbowee, and Tawakkol Karman (Liberia); 2004—Wangari Muta Maathi (Kenya); 2003—Shirin Ebadi (Iran); 1997—Jody Williams (USA); 1992—Rigoberta Menchú Tum (Guatemala); 1991—Aung San Suu Kyi (Myanmar/Burma). The most recent award (2011) is framed by the following "prize motivation" statement: "for their non-violent struggle for the safety of women and for women's rights to full participation in peace-building work."[107] Another affirmation of the global character of nonviolence is provided by the International Center on Nonviolent Conflict, which catalogues and tracks hundreds of historical as well as contemporary movements and campaigns.[108]

In the end, one can hear Gandhi's voice quietly, but persistently, asking, "Even if violence were the most efficient way to bring about radical change, would it be the most moral? People who are oppressed and brutalized seek redress; shall they become oppressors and brutalizers to make this happen? What would that do to the world around us and to the human soul within each of us?"

NOTES TO CHAPTER 4

1. United Nations, World Health Organization, "10 Facts about Violence Prevention," updated September 2011; http://www.who.int/features/factfiles/violence/en/index.html.

2. Peter Imbusch, "The Concept of Violence," tr. Tradukas, in *International Handbook of Violence Research*, ed. Wilhelm Heitmeyer and John Hagan (New York: Kluwer Academic, 2005), pp. 13, 35.

3. David Riches, "The Phenomenon of Violence," in *The Anthropology of Violence*, ed. David Riches (Oxford: Basil Blackwell, 1986), pp. 1, 23.

4. John Keane, *Violence and Democracy* (Cambridge, UK: Cambridge University Press, 2004), p. 36.

5. See Newton Garver, "What Violence Is," *The Nation*, 24 June 1968, pp. 817–22.

6. Gerald Runkle points out that making violence morally wrong by definition results in an unfortunate and absurd consequence: It erases two important debates by (a) abolishing the question whether violence can ever be justified; and (b) making pacifism and "nonviolentism" true by definition and the views of their critics self-contradictory. Runkle adds that because violence causes harm, it does call for justification; and he argues that "Justification for a violent act must rest upon the belief that it will produce a greater good or prevent a greater evil." An additional justifying criterion could be that a violent act, in the circumstances, is more timely and effective in achieving these ends. See Gerald Runkle, "Is Violence Always Wrong?" *Journal of Politics* 38 (1976), pp. 367–89 (esp. pp. 368, 378). See also Joseph S. Himes, *Conflict and Conflict Management* (Athens: University of Georgia Press, 1980), chaps. 1 and 5; Keith Burgess-Jackson, "Violence in Contemporary Analytic Philosophy," in *International Handbook of Violence Research*, ed. Heitmeyer and Hagan, pp. 992ff. It is worth noting as well that

if violence were wrong by definition, then the case against war would require no arguments at all (being self-evident), which is likewise an absurd conclusion.

7. See Robert Paul Wolff, "On Violence," *Journal of Philosophy* 66 (1969), pp. 601–16.
8. Gregg Barak, *Violence and Nonviolence: Pathways to Understanding* (Thousand Oaks, CA: Sage, 2003), pp. 9, 11.
9. Aryeh Neier, *The International Human Rights Movement: A History* (Princeton, NJ: Princeton University Press, 2012), p. 6.
10. Riches, "Phenomenon of Violence," p. 4 (emphasis in original).
11. See, for example, Arthur Koestler, *The Ghost in the Machine* (London: Hutchinson, 1967); Arthur Koestler, *Janus: A Summing Up* (New York: Random House, 1978).
12. Imbusch, "Concept of Violence," p. 35.
13. Riches, "Phenomenon of Violence," pp. 23, 25 (emphasis in original).
14. Tim Jacoby, *Understanding Conflict and Violence: Theoretical and Interdisciplinary Approaches* (London: Routledge, 2008), p. 86.
15. Jacoby, *Understanding Conflict and Violence*, p. 102.
16. Jacoby, *Understanding Conflict and Violence*, pp. 189–91.
17. Seyom Brown, *The Causes and Prevention of War* (New York: St. Martin's Press, 1987), p. 15.
18. Norbert Elias, *The Civilizing Process*, 2 vols., trans. Edmund Jephcott (Oxford: Basil Blackwell, 1978, 1982), vol. I, p. 204. My thanks to John Scott for bringing this work to my attention.
19. I owe this point to Brian Byrne (personal communication, 30 July 2012).
20. Roy Willis, "The 'Peace Puzzle' in Ufipa," in *Societies at Peace: Anthropological Perspectives*, ed. Signe Howell and Roy Willis (London: Routledge, 1989), p. 143.
21. Paul Heelas, "Identifying Peaceful Societies," in *Societies at Peace*, ed. Howell and Willis, p. 239.
22. I owe this example to Mary E. Clark, "Aggressivity and Violence: An Alternative Theory of Human Nature"; available at: http://www.gmu.edu/programs/icar/pcs/clark.htm#N_3_.
23. Daniel M. Mayton II, *Nonviolence and Peace Psychology: Intrapersonal, Interpersonal, Societal, and World Peace* (Dordrecht: Springer, 2009), p. 4.
24. Barak, *Violence and Nonviolence*, p. 212.
25. Loh Seng Tsai, "Peace and Cooperation among Natural Enemies: Educating a Rat-killing Cat to Cooperate with a Hooded Rat," *Acta Psychologia Taiwanica* 3 (1963): 4.
26. Irenäus Eibl-Eibesfeldt, *Biology of Peace and War: Men, Animals, and Aggression* (New York: Viking Press, 1979).
27. Ashley Montagu, "Introduction," in *Learning Non-Aggression: The Experience of Non-Literate Societies*, ed. Ashley Montagu (New York: Oxford University Press, 1978), pp. 3–4, 5, 6.
28. Barak, *Violence and Nonviolence*, p. 213.
29. Frans de Waal, *The Age of Empathy: Nature's Lessons for a Kinder Society* (New York: Harmony Books, 2009), p. 22.

30. Ashley Montagu, *The Nature of Human Aggression* (New York: Oxford University Press, 1976), p. 272.

31. Riches, "Phenomenon of Violence," pp. 21–2 (emphasis in original).

32. Susan T. Fiske, *Social Beings: A Core Motives Approach to Social Psychology* (New York: Wiley, 2004), p. 363. The same definition is given by Craig A. Anderson and Brad J. Bushman in "Human Aggression," *Annual Review of Psychology* 53 (2002), p. 28.

33. Robert A. Baron and Deborah R. Richardson, *Human Aggression* (New York: Plenum Press, 1994), p. 7.

34. Mayton, *Nonviolence and Peace Psychology*, p. 2.

35. See Robert Sapolsky, "Testosterone Rules," *Discover*, March 1997; available at: http://discovermagazine.com/1997/mar/testosteronerule1077#.UXB5IXBC9UQ; J. Bland, *About Gender: Testosterone and Aggression—Crimes of Violence*, 2002; available at: http://www.gender.org.uk/about/06encrn/63faggrs.htm; Christopher Mims, "Strange but True: Testosterone Does Not Cause Violence," *Scientific American*, 5 July 2007; available at: http://www.scientificamerican.com/article.cfm?id=strange-but-true-testosterone-alone-doesnt-cause-violence.

36. Paul K. Chappell, *The End of War: How Waging Peace Can Save Humanity, Our Planet and Our Future* (Westport, CT: Easton Studio Press, 2010), pp. 28, 33 (emphasis in original).

37. Ervin Staub, "Basic Needs, Altruism, and Aggression," in *The Social Psychology of Good and Evil*, ed. Arthur G. Miller (New York: Guilford Press, 2004), pp. 58, 64.

38. William Stafford, *Every War Has Two Losers: William Stafford on Peace and War*, ed. Kim Stafford (Minneapolis: Milkweed Editions, 2003), pp. 34, 135.

39. Unidentified Chilean Catholic priest in "A Force More Powerful: Chile—Defeat of a Dictator," film by Steve York (Washington, DC: WETA, 2000).

40. Steven Pinker, *The Better Angels of Our Nature: Why Violence Has Declined* (New York: Viking/Penguin, 2011), p. 530.

41. Johan Galtung, Yakin Ertürk, and Chrissie Steenkamp, "Violence," *Oxford International Encyclopedia of Peace*, ed. Nigel Young (Oxford: Oxford University Press, 2010), e-reference edition; http://www.oxford-peace.com/entry?entry=t296.e747-s1.

42. Runkle, "Is Violence Always Wrong?" p. 372.

43. See Robert J. Listenbee, Jr., Joe Torre et al., *Report of the Attorney General's National Task Force on Children Exposed to Violence* (Washington, DC: U.S. Department of Justice, Office of the Attorney General), 12 December 2012.

44. Hannah Arendt, *On Violence* (San Diego: Harvest Books, 1970), p. 80.

45. Eric T. Gortner, Jackie K. Gollan, and Neil S. Jacobson, "Psychological Aspects of Perpetrators of Domestic Violence and Their Relationships with the Victims," in *The Psychiatric Clinics of North America*, ed. Maurizio Fava, vol. 20, no. 2: *Anger, Aggression, and Violence* (Philadelphia: W. B. Saunders, June 1997), p. 345.

46. *Daily Mail* Reporter (UK), Mail Online, "One U.S. Veteran Attempts Suicide Every 80 Minutes: Hidden Tragedy of Afghanistan and Iraq Wars," 3 November 2011; http://www.dailymail.co.uk/news/article-2057061/One-U-S-veteran-attempts-suicide-80-minutes-Hidden-tragedy-Afghanistan-Iraq-wars.html.

47. Penn Medicine News Release: "A War Inside: Saving Veterans from Suicide," 28 June 2011; http://www.uphs.upenn.edu/news/News_Releases/2011/06/veterans.

48. Plato, *Gorgias*, 475c, in *Plato: Socratic Dialogues*, trans. and ed. W. D. Woodhead (Edinburgh: Thomas Nelson and Sons, 1953), p. 228.

49. Izzeldin Abuelaish, quoted in David Leser, "Healing Heart," *Good Weekend* magazine, *Sydney Morning Herald*, 14 May 2011, pp. 20, 21.

50. Rachel M. MacNair, *The Psychology of Peace: An Introduction*, 2nd ed. (Santa Barbara, CA: Praeger, 2012), p. 108.

51. Charles E. Collyer, "There's More to Nonviolence Than I Thought," in Charles E. Collyer and Ira G. Zepp, Jr., *Nonviolence: Origins and Outcomes*, 2nd ed. (Victoria, BC, Canada: Trafford, 2006), p. 158.

52. Gene Sharp, *The Politics of Nonviolent Action* (Boston: Extending Horizons Books, 1973), p. 540.

53. Sharp, *Politics of Nonviolent Action*, pp. 75–6, 102 n. 5.

54. Lao Tzu, *Tao Te Ching*, trans. Brian Browne Walker (New York: St. Martin's Press, 1995), sec. 31.

55. Sun Tzu, *The Art of War*, trans. Thomas Cleary (Boston: Shambhala, 1988), pt. 3, pp. 66, 67.

56. See, for example, Hadji Haidar Hamid, "The Qur'anic Principle of Peace," *Journal of Shi'a Islamic Studies* 2 (2009), pp. 159–80.

57. Brian Teixeira, "Nonviolence Theory and Practice," in *Encyclopedia of Violence, Peace, and Conflict*, ed. Lester R. Kurtz and Jennifer Turpin (San Diego: Academic Press, 1999), vol. 2, p. 564.

58. United Nations Security Council Sanctions Committees, "Security Council Sanctions Committees: An Overview"; http://www.un.org/sc/committees.

59. "Sanctions against Iraq," *Wikipedia*, rev. 23 January 2012; http://en.wikipedia.org/wiki/Sanctions_against_Iraq#Effects_on_the_Iraqi_people_during_sanctions.

60. Tehran Bureau correspondent, in partnership with *The Guardian*, "Optimism in Short Supply on Streets of Tehran as Sanctions Grind Iran Down," *The Guardian*, 13 January 2013; http://www.guardian.co.uk/world/2013/jan/13/western-sanctions-hitting-iranians; Sune Engel Rasmussen, "Iranian Artists Hit by Sanctions," *The Guardian*, 22 January 2013; http://www.guardian.co.uk/world/2013/jan/22/iran-art-scene-sanctions.

61. United Nations Security Council, "Report of the Informal Working Group of the Security Council on General Issues of Sanctions," S/2006/997, 22 December 2006.

62. See, for example, Simon Jenkins, "North Korea or Iran—Sanctions Won't Work," *Guardian Weekly*, 22–28 February 2013, p. 18.

63. Dursun Peksen, "Why Sanctions Won't Work," *Foreign Policy*, 3 March 2009; http://experts.foreignpolicy.com/posts/2009/03/03/why_sanctions_wont_work.

64. Mayton, *Nonviolence and Peace Psychology*, chap. 3.

65. Mohandas Karamchand Gandhi, *An Autobiography: The Story of My Experiments with Truth*, trans. Mahadev Desai (Boston: Beacon Press, 1957).

66. Mohandas Karamchand Gandhi, "*Ahimsa* or Love," in *The Moral and Political Writings of Mahatma Gandhi, Vol. 2: Truth and Non-Violence*, ed. Raghavan Iyer, (Oxford: Clarendon Press, 1986), p. 577.

67. Jesse Richards, *The Secret Peace: Exposing the Positive Trend of World Events* (New York: Book & Ladder Press, 2010), p. 171.
68. Mohandas Karamchand Gandhi, "Soul-force and *Tapasya*," in *Moral and Political Writings*, ed. Iyer, vol. 3, *Non-Violent Resistance and Social Transformation*, p. 46.
69. Gandhi, "Soul-force and *Tapasya*," p. 45.
70. Mohandas Karamchand Gandhi, "Non-violence of the Strong and of the Weak," in *Moral and Political Writings*, ed. Iyer, vol. 2, p. 405.
71. Mohandas Karamchand Gandhi, "After-effects of War," in *Moral and Political Writings*, ed. Iyer, vol. 2, p. 460.
72. Bhikhu Parekh, *Gandhi* (Oxford: Oxford University Press, 1997), p. 54.
73. Daniel Ritter, "A Two-dimensional Theory of Nonviolence," 12 August 2005; http://www.allacademic.com/meta/p21970_index.html.
74. Paulo Freire, *Pedagogy of the Oppressed*, trans. Myra Bergman Ramos (New York: Continuum, 1989), p. 28. Translated into many languages, over one million copies of this book have been sold worldwide.
75. Gandhi, "Non-violence of the Strong and of the Weak," p. 406.
76. Mohandas Karamchand Gandhi, cited by Steven Rosen, *Diet for Transcendence: Vegetarianism and the World Religions* (Badger, CA: Torchlight, 1997), p. 121.
77. Gandhi, "Non-violence of the Strong and of the Weak," p. 405.
78. "The Non-cooperation Movement 1920–22," *India Unlimited*, 6 May 2011; http://www.india-intro.com/history/history-of-india/572-the-non-cooperation-movement-1920–22.html.
79. Eknath Easwaran, *Gandhi, the Man: How One Man Changed Himself to Change the World*, 4th ed. (Tomales, CA: Nilgiri Press, 2011), pp. 63–5.
80. See Pat Patfoort, *An Introduction to Nonviolence: A Conceptual Framework* (Nyack, NY: Fellowship of Reconciliation, 1987).
81. Richards, *Secret Peace*, p. 170.
82. See above, note 52.
83. Gene Sharp, *From Dictatorship to Democracy: A Conceptual Framework for Liberation*, 4th US ed. (East Boston, MA: The Albert Einstein Institution, 2010); available online at http://www.aeinstein.org/organizations/org/FDTD.pdf.
84. John MacBeath Watkins, "Prof. Gene Sharp and Nonviolent Action: The Most Influential Book You've Never Heard of," 24 February 2011, Booksellers versus Bestsellers; http://booksellersvsbestsellers.blogspot.com.au/2011/02/prof-gene-sharp-and-nonviolent-action.html.
85. Gene Sharp, *Waging Nonviolent Struggle: 20th Century Practice and 21st Century Potential* (Manchester, NH: Extending Horizons Books, 2005).
86. The Albert Einstein Institution, "Breakthrough: An Update on the Work of The Albert Einstein Institution" (East Boston, MA: The Albert Einstein Institution, n.d.).
87. Sharp, *Politics of Nonviolent Action*, p. 107.
88. Sharp, *Politics of Nonviolent Action*, p. 2.
89. Sharp, *Politics of Nonviolent Action*, p. 8.
90. Sharp, *Politics of Nonviolent Action*, pp. 11, 12.

91. Peter Ackerman and Jack Duvall, *A Force More Powerful: A Century of Nonviolent Conflict* (New York: Palgrave, 2000), p. 225.
92. Sharp, *Politics of Nonviolent Action*, p. 807.
93. Sharp, *Politics of Nonviolent Action*, p. 34.
94. Sharp, *Politics of Nonviolent Action*, p. 32.
95. Sharp, *Waging Nonviolent Struggle*, p. 469.
96. Mohja Kahf, *Then and Now: The Syrian Revolution to Date: A Young Nonviolent Resistance and the Ensuing Armed Struggle*, 28 February 2013, vol. 1.1, a special report from Friends for a Nonviolent World, St. Paul, MN; available at: http://www.fnvw.org/vertical/Sites/%7B8182BD6D-7C3B-4C35-B7F8-F4FD486C7CBD%7D/uploads/Syria_Special_Report-web.pdf.
97. "Gene Sharp—A Frail Man with Powerful Ideas," interview by Lindsey Hilsum, Channel 4 News (UK), 31 January 2012; http://blogs.channel4.com/world-news-blog/gene-sharp-a-frail-man-with-powerful-ideas/20024.
98. Ronald J. Sider, *Non-Violence: The Invincible Weapon?* (Dallas: Word Publishing, 1989), p. 55.
99. Teixeira, "Nonviolence Theory and Practice," pp. 564–5.
100. Runkle, "Is Violence Always Wrong?" p. 384.
101. David Cortright, *Peace: A History of Movements and Ideas* (Cambridge: Cambridge University Press, 2008), p. 227. See also Srdja Popovic, Andrej Milivojevic, and Slobodan Djinovic, *Nonviolent Struggle: 50 Crucial Points—A Strategic Approach to Everyday Tactics* (Belgrade: Centre for Applied NonViolent Action and Strategies [CANVAS], 2006); available at: http://www.canvasopedia.org/legacy/files/various/Nonviolent_Struggle-50CP.pdf.
102. Peter Gelderloos, "Arms and the Movement: Pacifism Equals Pacified to This Activist," *Utne Reader*, May-June 2007, p. 45. See also Peter Gelderloos, *How Nonviolence Protects the State* (Boston: South End Press, 2007); Peter Gelderloos, *The Failure of Nonviolence: From the Arab Spring to Occupy* (Seattle: Left Bank Books, 2013).
103. Brian Martin, *Nonviolence Versus Capitalism* (London: War Resisters' International, 2001), p. 185.
104. Theodore Roszak, quoted in Petra K. Kelly, *Thinking Green! Essays on Environmentalism, Feminism, and Nonviolence* (Berkeley, CA: Parallax Press, 1994).
105. Maria J. Stephan and Erica Chenoweth, "Why Civil Resistance Works: The Strategic Logic of Nonviolent Conflict," *International Security* 33 (2008), p. 8; available at: http://belfercenter.ksg.harvard.edu/files/IS3301_pp007–044_Stephan_Chenoweth.pdf. See also Erica Chenoweth and Maria J. Stephan, *Why Civil Resistance Works: The Strategic Logic of Nonviolent Conflict* (New York: Columbia University Press, 2011).
106. Stephan and Chenoweth, "Why Civil Resistance Works," p. 42.
107. "Nobel Prize Awarded Women," Nobelprize.org; http://www.nobelprize.org/nobel_prizes/lists/women.html.
108. International Center on Nonviolent Conflict, "Movements and Campaigns"; http://www.nonviolent-conflict.org/index.php/movements-and-campaigns/movements-and-campaigns-summaries.

5

The Meaning(s) of Peace

Peace comes from within. Do not seek it without.

—Siddhārtha Gautama (the Buddha)

But why . . . do we still think of peace as the resolution of war, not as the way to prevent war?

—Anne Deveson, writer, documentary filmmaker, social activist, and
Officer of the Order of Australia, *Waging Peace: Reflections on
Peace and War from an Unconventional Woman* (2013)

*Peace . . . is the struggle to solve concrete problems in ways that enable us to
agree to work together in the future.*

—J. Gray Cox, *The Ways of Peace: A Philosophy of
Peace as Action* (1986)

5.1. APPROACHES TO PEACE

Once upon a time, there was a radio quiz show called *The 64 Dollar Question*. As new technology, monetary inflation, and get-rich-quick schemes shaped the decades that followed, a popular TV program was born: *The 64,000 Dollar Question*. Today, quiz shows regularly feature monster prizes of up to one million dollars. What if the big prize question were: "What is peace?" The answer would have to be priceless.

Much has been written in response to this question, but at a certain level, it is not even clear how one ought to begin to address it, or whether any universally meaningful answer could be arrived at, even in principle. Leaving aside ideologies and politics (as much as possible) and trying to get to the heart of the matter, consider:

> What does peace mean to a warlord in Afghanistan?
> To a person who has never known peace or lives in a situation of oppression?
> To an ordinary man or woman in the armed services of any country?
> To his or her commanding officers?
> To a pacifist?
> To a political realist?
> To a believer in any particular religion?
> To an atheist?
> To a combat veteran?
> To a parent who has lost a child to war or random street violence in a major city?
> To a child who has lost a parent to war or has been orphaned by war?
> To a child whose life-situation is more or less normal?
> To a person whose life is dedicated to helping others?
> To a victim of violence in a remote civil war?
> To a peace volunteer on assignment?
> To someone who has a firm commitment to sustainability and animal rights?
> To someone who is selfish and self-centered?
> To a victim of domestic violence?
> To the CEO of a major corporation?
> To an individual, anywhere, who is struggling just to get by?
> To an ordinary middle-class person, anywhere?
> To a young person hoping to find his or her way in the globalized world of today?
> To a severely disabled person?

Would it be an elusive dream to some; a practical objective for a few; to others, a grim joke; to others still, the object of cynicism and disbelief? There are as many answers as there are questions—many perspectives on peace. Still, we can identify what might be recurring themes or some essentials to which everyone can relate. As background to the discussion that follows, the list of "Home Truths" at the end of the Introduction should be borne in mind.

Negative Peace

Analyzing the concept of peace usually begins with the distinction between negative and positive peace. "Negative peace" refers to the *absence* of something, namely, war, other kinds of armed conflict, large-scale injurious violence (such as ethnic cleansing, persecution of minorities, civil unrest, rioting, or high levels of street crime), and threatening hostilities of various sorts. (This kind of characterization has been classified as "definition by exclusion,"[1] that is, explaining something by what it is *not*.) Peace, viewed in its negative dimension, is a condition without which life cannot run as normal.

But anyone who asserted that peace is (and must be) more than this—namely, a *presence* of something—would be on the right track. For one thing, nonwar is compatible with global weapons proliferation, arms races, Cold War–type nuclear deterrence stalemates and mutual assured destruction (MAD) strategies, repression regimes, and structural violence (classism, racism, poverty, and so on). Furthermore, defining peace only negatively brings about the same problem we encountered in Chapter 4 when discussing nonviolence (section 4.3, "Nonviolence: Narrower and Broader Visions"): Peace would then be reduced to nonwar, a lack of something, an other-than-something-else (as nonviolence is the antithesis of violence), with no defining qualities of its own that could be listed, considered, or evaluated. In addition, the examination of historical narratives in Chapter 1 and of human beings' peaceful potential in Chapter 2 invite us to try thinking of peace as our normal condition and war as our aberrant condition, rather than the reverse. It has also been argued that any negative definitions of peace could be "reframed to [express] more positively defined views of peace. For example, 'peace as the absence of war and physical violence' could be positively recast as 'creating nonviolent, sustainable ways to resolve conflicts within society and the world without resorting to violence or warfare.'"[2] While this may seem to be an obvious point, it has not succeeded in preventing definitions of peace from languishing in the negative zone of meaning for many generations. Nor has it deterred some peace advocates from framing their activities as "waging peace"—a concept that makes the meaning of peace parasitic on the language of war, and invites us to think about working for peace as akin to armed conflict. A final point here is that *enforced* peace is very different from *evolved* peace. As the rest of this chapter shows, peace is a process, and like any process, unfolds according to its own inner principles.

As we saw in the Introduction ("The Obstacle of War"), a reversal of perspectives is necessary to appreciate what peace genuinely is. By this is meant that *we must make peace the foundational concept by which we understand ourselves*, while accordingly, violence and war become derivative or second-order concepts. Much of the argument of previous chapters turns on this reversal. Nevertheless, it is probably good to preserve the distinction between negative and positive peace for two reasons: First, because peace is an *alternative* to a given condition, it is worth knowing what state we desire to move away from in contrast to that we wish to move toward, and these positions are almost certain to be thought of quite differently; second, because peace typically *develops in stages (or incrementally)*, it needs to be underlined that cessation or reduction of violence and other harmful activities must precede the fuller evolution of substantive processes that transform and stabilize relationships between humans, and (ideally) between humans and the rest of nature.

Positive Peace

What happens if we take up the challenge to shift our perspective and define peace in positive terms? By channeling our thoughts in a new direction, it would force us to be creative in an important way. We considered above that peace might mean many things to differently situated individuals, but also that common threads connect these outlooks. The term "positive peace" indicates that *peace—whether it is conceived of as a state, a condition, or a process—has attributes of its own that can be identified and affirmed*. This view, which has a distinguished history, was formally stated three-and-a-half centuries ago by the philosopher Baruch Spinoza, in response to the political theory of Thomas Hobbes. Spinoza beautifully expresses the point as follows: "For peace is not mere absence of war, but is a virtue that springs from force of character. . . . Peace . . . consists . . . in a union or agreement of minds."[3]

According to the evidence presented in Chapter 2 and the arguments developed from it, not only are there cultures which have learned to control and manage internal and external conflict, but also everyday interactions among people everywhere, at varying times and places, which are for the most part peaceful, that is, harmonious, cooperative, and mutually supportive. To make this claim is not to idealize human life, but merely to point to what normally goes unnoticed and unremarked upon. These characteristics are the lubricant (or the elixir, depending on your viewpoint) that enables social relations—and indeed society itself—to thrive. Examples range from ordinary niceties, such as courtesy and respect, sharing ideas, news, and friendship in general, to promises, acts of trust, collegiality, contract-making, empathy, helping out mates or strangers in trouble, being a good citizen, and exhibiting altruistic behavior (see Chapter 2, section 2.6, "Peace in Everyday Life"). No one would be so naïve as to think that these kinds of everyday interactions alone constitute peace; however, they do provide some benchmarks for thinking about peace in a larger sense. So, for instance, a society (or a world) in which such examples predominated would be closer to peace than where we are at present.

As it may be clear by now, peace is part actuality and part ideal. The actuality of peace is manifested in the sorts of examples just given. Peace as an ideal is disclosed by the longings that people have and by their ability to imagine a better life for themselves and their children, others they care about, and the groups to which they belong. What do people long for? Countless volumes of nonfiction and fiction have addressed this question throughout the ages. But some obvious things are: having their basic needs met, a desirable quality of life (including health and welfare, meaningful and rewarding employment, personal contentment, and self-fulfillment), friendship and love, security, and fair treatment by others. (See the Introduction, "Home Truths.") It does not take too much thought to understand that many people (perhaps including oneself) fall short of realizing one or more of these essentials, and that in circumstances of severe shortage, deprivation, or turmoil and political instability, these essentials can become merely elusive dreams.

Three conclusions can be drawn from these reflections. The first is that peace does depend on external (and to some extent material) conditions, at least up to a point. These include nonwar and a state of affairs that is conducive to actualizing what we long for. Second, peace concerns what we as individuals choose to do or fail to do with the opportunities available to us. Third, peace is not static, but rather, is an ongoing event (or series of events) through time. Norwegian sociologist, mathematician, and peace and conflict specialist Johan Galtung, whose theoretical work has greatly enriched our understanding of negative and positive peace (among many other topics), argues that negative peace is *"the absence of violence of all kinds"*—by which he means to include every form of "direct violence" (verbal or physical harm to the body, mind, or spirit), "structural violence" (harm embedded in and instantiated by routine or mandated ways of doing things), and "cultural violence" (attitudes and values that encourage or tolerate harm).[4] He also states that "By positive peace we mean a cooperative system beyond 'passive peaceful coexistence', one that can bring forth positively synergistic fruits of the harmony."[5] These ideas, like others developed thus far, suggest that there is much more fertile content to the concept of peace, which we need to explore.

5.2. PEACE AS A STATE OF WELL-BEING, AS A GOAL, AND AS A PROCESS

You come outside on a beautiful, sunny day, when all is quiet except for some birds chirping, without any cares that weigh you down, and with some purposeful activity that guides you (even if it is only to take a nice walk by the lake, read the newspaper in the backyard hammock, or have morning coffee with a friend). This is easily recognized as being in a peaceful time and space. In fact, a sense of well-being like this may seem to represent a kind of paradigm of peace. No doubt so; but within the larger sphere of life, which *does* involve all the cares and concerns and political realities we share, this is only a sheltered micro-cosm, a slice of peace that is relatively isolated from the pressures and stresses of events, jobs, debts, conflicts, crises, and so on. But peace is neither a momentary nor a lingering state of leisure, calmness, or euphoria; it is more complex and multi-dimensional. a lingering state of leisure, calmness, or euphoria; it is more complex and multidimensional. Still, well-being is an important anchor of peace, as we shall see.

We can find an expression of this sense of peace in the Old Testament. As one commentary on the Bible states, "The Hebrew word for 'peace' [*shalom*] has a very broad meaning. It really means 'wholeness' and describes fullness of life in every respect. It can refer to bodily health, or a long life which ends in a natural death. It is also used to describe safety, and harmony for the individual and for the community. Peace is the most precious of all gifts, and it comes from God himself."[6] The New Testament echoes this view, inasmuch as the figure of Christ represents the bringer of peace and fellowship, and the gateway to heaven.

There are traditions according to which peace is modeled as a goal, a final destination of some kind. "Rest in peace," an expression often carved into grave-stones, illustrates this notion in a fairly crude way, as does the biblical image of a distant time when "The wolf also shall dwell with the lamb,"[7] the messiah will (re) appear, or paradise will be gained. Other traditions teach that peace is a process. This message is the import of the remark that "There is no way to peace, peace is the way";[8] and the entire concept of "peacebuilding" is predicated on the need to create peace through dedicated and unceasingly progressive activity of a certain focused type. Fortunately, we do not have to choose between these alternatives, because it seems we have learned already that peace is not only something to be pursued but also the pursuit itself—that *peace is both a goal and a process*.

To say that peace is a goal entails that it is an end-state, a final point to be reached. Or does it? That would be the usual interpretation; but one can just as well think of a goal as akin to an ideal, that is, as something we aim to attain and toward which we consider it highly worthwhile to direct our effort, yet which we know will likely never be fully realized and hence will always persist as "to-be-attained." In spite of the fact that "idealists" are often dismissed as being out of touch with reality, having ideals is neither a waste of time nor a misguided, woolly-headed delusion. Far from it. We cannot live without them. And they can be powerful motivators: recall Martin Luther King, Jr.'s famous 1963 "I have a dream" speech, for example.[9] Paradoxically, to say that peace will forever elude us is not inconsistent with being able to say that we are now living in peace. To be "living in peace" would mean, first, that negative peace prevails, and beyond that, that the things people long for (outlined above) are realized to a significant extent. But because human life, looked at overall, is a dynamic series of events, an unfolding drama, so too "peace," or any other label describing this series of events, denotes a process at work, a project that evolves, has to meet and overcome many obstacles, and must perfect itself over time. Thus, those who have proclaimed history to be "at an end," or who have thought of successful revolution as leading to a static condition of finished business, do an injustice to human energy and ingenuity, which create ever-new vistas of desire as well as novel responses to them.

If we think of peace as embodying an agenda such as making "progress toward a freer and more just world,"[10] then anybody can see that there is a very long way to go in order to reach this goal, and that any end-state, if there is one, is so remote as to be merely hypothetical in character. Inasmuch as human activities proceed by trial and error, such progress is also highly unlikely to be linear in any event, and, human nature being what it is, there is bound to be backsliding and a requirement for redoubled effort along the way. Further-more, so far as one can tell, conflict will always remain a part of human com-munities, and building constructive, nonviolent solutions to it will be a very large project in itself. (See Chapter 6, section 6.7, "Engaging with Conflict.") In sum, peace is determined as a process by both the impediments to it that must be faced and overcome, and by the fruitful developments through which it becomes defined, understood, and established as durable.

5.3. THE RELATIONSHIP BETWEEN NONVIOLENCE AND PEACE

Peace, as we have seen, is first a situation in which large-scale violence is absent and lower-level violence is minimized, contained, and defused. Nigel Dower helpfully suggests that peace, in contrast to war and violence, is "a condition in which there are not the seeds of future conflicts."[11] One could say, then, that peace is characterized by the absence of violence and the prev-alence of nonviolence. Nonviolence, we have learned, is not just the absence of something, but is instead the presence of committed activism in search of improving the conditions of human life. Therefore, a conceptual paral-lel unites peace and nonviolence, suggesting that they have an intimate con-nection. It is neither sufficient nor accurate, however, to say that they are the same thing. Living nonviolently requires striving to minimize harmful behavior in oneself and others. Nonviolence has its own inner guiding prin-ciples, but it also involves strategies for bringing about peace. Peace, for its part, embraces many means to the end of harmonious coexistence besides nonviolence. It follows that *there can be nonviolence without peace, but not peace without nonviolence prevailing.* Another way of putting this point is to say that nonviolence is a necessary, but not a sufficient condition for peace to be realized.

5.4. INNER PEACE AND OUTER PEACE

There has been a lengthy debate among peace theorists over the issue whether peace should be thought of primarily as an internal (or intrapsychic) state or as an external state of one's sociopolitical environment. To a certain extent, this is a clash over who can offer the best stipulative definition of peace; but at a deeper level, it concerns the order of priority to be assigned to internal and external conditions of peace. The position taken here is that this is a false dichotomy: Both factors are necessary and mutually dependent.[12] Although people's hearts and minds must be in the right place for there to be genuine and lasting peace, being in a condition of having at least relative peace in their surroundings is essential for the cultivation of peaceful selves. Stated differently, peace is both an individual project and a shared project, something we must pursue in common. As one peace scholar observes, "When we think peace, we act out peace, thereby reducing the fears of others,"[13] and, it could be added, we thereby invite and welcome reciprocal acting out in kind from others.[14] This applies at the level of individual behavior, but it is equally true at the group and international levels. As the world becomes more globalized and connected through politics, trade, communications, and regulations, we also become more interdependent and our fates become mutually entangled. Only the very narrow-sighted today could believe in unilateral guarantees of security and material well-being.

The Subjective Viewpoint on Peace

But there is another sense in which debating whether peace is an internal or external state may prevent a larger kind of understanding. This is because peace should be viewed from both subjective and objective points of view. Subjectively, peace originates and emanates from within the self; objectively, it concerns the material conditions of existence, negative peace (as already described), plus a range of social and political understandings, arrangements, and goods. The idea that peace is an inner state or process of the self is well expressed by the slogan "Peace begins with me." This maxim appears in numerous contexts, ranging from refrigerator magnets and clichés of self-help manuals to the more profound insights of spiritual teachings. Nobel Peace Prize laureate Aung San Suu Kyi, who has for decades led the struggle against oppression in Myanmar (Burma) at enormous personal risk, states that "I think of peace as inner calm and serenity. If you're haunted by any kind of fears, then certainly you cannot say you're at peace, even if your surroundings are peaceful. So, peace is . . . freedom from fear."[15] We can broaden the central notion that peace stems from a calm and balanced mind (or soul), in order to illuminate peace as derived from self-knowledge and self-discipline, together with a kind of cleansing of oneself in relation to negative feelings and destructive impulses. As it is often said, putting one's own house in order must precede trying to help others. Individuals who have acquired inner peace may be called "enlightened" in some traditions, but most persons who have moved in this direction will only be somewhere along the difficult and demanding path to self-awareness and compassion.

Self-awareness or self-knowledge is a very ancient precept of morality and of wisdom in the art of living. It has sources in both Eastern and Western traditions of religion and philosophy, and has sometimes been regarded as a human being's highest achievement. Linda Groff and Paul Smoker contend that all religions originate with a figure who has had a mystical or revelatory experience of union with the divine principle of the universe, which, by all accounts, provides a profound sense of inner peace. However, inner peace does not presuppose or require such an experience, but rather what these authors describe as an openness to "development of an inner life of the spirit," in which we "discover and encounter the deeper aspects of our being."[16] This insight is confirmed by the fact that the principle of self-knowledge has roots in many secular writings, and that "Know thyself" is one of the oldest adages, with examples dating from ancient Egypt, Greece, India, and China.[17]

While to make this one's vocation is a daunting task, the basic idea is not difficult to grasp: that we should cultivate the ability to identify and be self-critical about our values, motivations, emotions, beliefs, desires, and fears, so that they do not control us subconsciously or distort our relationships. Closely connected is the capacity to face with equanimity the many challenges of living. The general implication embedded in this approach is that to the extent that an individual gains mastery of her- or himself, such a person will be liberated from negative modes of being, including animosities and destructive tendencies. On the plus side, he or she will gain in self-confidence, as well as openness and generosity toward others. This in turn will lead to the realization that we are all alike, all striving to be ourselves and to lead our lives in the best way possible, and that reducing harmful interactions and increasing cooperative interactions between us are key facilitating factors in each person's quest for happiness and satisfaction in measuring up to life's tasks. As an interesting aside, one US surgeon general defines mental health as "a state of successful performance of mental function, resulting in productive activities, fulfilling relationships with other people, and the ability to adapt to change and cope with adversity."[18] By this standard of psychological well-being, those who engage in violent interactions with others—whether in civil society or on the battlefield—do not measure up very well.

The upshot of looking at peace from the subjective standpoint is to acknowl-edge that peace, as a state of affairs in which people live and work together in mutually supportive and cooperative ways, is a product of what emanates from each of us—our state of mind, the signals we give out, and the behaviors we engage in. In this way, peace depends upon each of us as individuals. This conclusion will be important when we consider ways to bring about peace in the next two chapters.

The Objective Viewpoint on Peace

On the other side, there are external conditions of peace, which some would say are, if not all that matters, at least the bedrock of and catalyst for peace in any sense of the word. Earlier the material conditions of life and the state of negative peace were described, which sums up much of what is meant here. The following remark by a Thai peace activist captures the external perspective on peace pretty well: "Realistically speaking, you cannot expect the hungry and the oppressed whose basic human rights are violated to sit still while in-tellectuals and technocrats debate the vagaries of peace. Peace to these people means being free to attain their potential in life, to raise a family, find a place in their community, and to be able to have control of at least the most crucial aspects of their destiny."[19] As we can see here, both subjective and objective considerations are at play, but overall, the emphasis is on rectifying wrongs—on crucial conditions of life that are often taken out of people's control by those who seek to aggrandize themselves through dominating others. In addition, external factors promoting peace also include institutions of various kinds, from equitable economic and legal systems to international organizations such as the UN and established regimes of international law and treaty observance.

Another attempt to highlight and clarify the positive and more specific ob-jective conditions of peace is embodied in the following definition:

Peace: A political condition that ensures justice and social stability through formal and informal institutions, practices, and norms. Several conditions must be met for peace to be reached and maintained:

- balance of political power among the various groups within a society, region, or, most ambitiously, the world
- legitimacy for decision makers and implementers of decisions in the eyes of their respective group, as well as those of external parties, duly supported through transparency and accountability
- recognized and valued interdependent relationships among groups fostering long-term cooperation during periods of agreement, disagreement, normality, and crisis

- reliable and trusted institutions for resolving conflicts
- sense of equality and respect, in sentiment and in practice, within and without groups and in accordance with international standards
- mutual understanding of rights, interests, intents, and flexibility despite incompatibilities.[20]

As in many formulations of this kind, strong emphasis is placed on a structured system of participation that is shaped by justice, equitable power sharing, trust, responsibility, accountability, recognition of the interdependence, moral status, and political enfranchisement of others, mutual respect for their otherness, and procedures for resolving conflicts.

One final point to note is that improving people's conditions of life does not entail trying to make everyone's situation equal in every way, even if that were possible. It means, instead, aiming as a society and as a global community at what is normally termed "equality of opportunity." There is a great deal packed into this concept, which is itself the subject of controversy and many learned studies. Probably inequalities of natural advantage (such as degrees of talent, skills, and intelligence), privileges of various kinds, and rewards can never be eliminated or neutralized; nor it clear that it would even be desirable to do so. What is called for, however, is a social and political system, created by people acting in the common interest, that is capable of giving everyone "a fair go." The hungry and oppressed, mentioned in the preceding paragraph, are certainly not interested in waiting for scholars to settle what counts as equality, equality of opportunity, or social justice. They would be grateful for just some small movement in a direction more favorable to realization of their interests and satisfaction of their urgent needs.

Interaction between Subjective and Objective Viewpoints

The subjective and objective viewpoints on peace are intertwined, of course, as we've seen. For most people, how they feel about their situation depends primarily on how they interpret the facts about it; and the actual conditions of their existence, as far as these can be described accurately, greatly influence their state of mind. For example, one study shows that in "post-conflict" Sierra Leone, "most women did not consider themselves to be living in peace.... [because of] 'high rates of poverty and violence against women, including domestic violence, mental abuse and abandonment.'"[21] This explains why Galtung (as quoted earlier) insists that negative peace entails "*the absence of violence of all kinds.*" What these women are experiencing is that important objective criteria of negative peace have not yet been met for them, even if those criteria have been for men; hence, for women, the subjective state of positive peace remains elusive.

5.5. FROM INNER PEACE TO COSMIC PEACE

Inner peace has meant many things to different people. Some thinkers have argued that it entails withdrawal from the world, while others see it as not only compatible with, but even as a prerequisite for, involvement in the affairs of the world. For many, peace is found in the spiritual sanctuary of prayer or communion with what is holy. Religions now extinct, as well as those of today, have charted this path. Others regard inner peace as produced by the quieting of the mind, the silencing of its daily busyness. Practices of meditation and yoga, and the Buddhist quest for enlightenment, exemplify this latter approach. All of these methods of attaining inner peace seem to suggest that it is something that occurs away and apart from the routines and exigencies of daily living, and certain points of view or interpretations of existence reinforce such a claim.

Peaceful Being in the World

But inner (or intrapersonal) peace, however defined and by whatever method gained, has also, and perhaps more commonly, been understood in connection with full engagement *in* the world. The Greco-Roman Epicureans dedicated themselves to the cultivation of *ataraxia*, "a lucid state, characterized by freedom from worry or any other preoccupation. For the Epicureans, *ataraxia* was synonymous with the only true happiness possible for a person. It signifies the state of robust tranquility that derives from eschewing faith in an afterlife, not fearing the gods because they are distant and unconcerned with us, avoiding politics and vexatious people, surrounding oneself with trustworthy and affectionate friends and, most importantly, being an affectionate, virtuous person, worthy of trust."[22] This sounds like the paradigm of a self-oriented quest for peace—peace as an escape to the world within. Yet the later development of Epicureanism produced individuals of influence who opposed war and mediated conflicts.[23]

Stoics sought to develop the resolve to live in accord with nature, accept one's fate with indifference, and bear suffering as a task to be dealt with courageously and with an independent mind. Epictetus famously stated that even a slave in chains could be free by internally affirming his or her spirit and the meaning of life in the face of adversity. But, even so, he emphasized that there are bonds between us all, and ways we turn out that have not been chosen by us, which some must bear with the wisdom to see beyond such limitations.[24] Marcus Aurelius, on the other hand, projected a more socially conscious notion of self-development: "Say to yourself in the early morning: I shall meet today ungrateful, violent, treacherous, envious, uncharitable men. All of these things have come upon them through ignorance of real good and ill. . . . I can neither be harmed by any of them, for no man will involve me in wrong, nor can I be angry with my kinsman or hate him; for we have come into the world to work together. . . . "[25] We find surfacing here the Socratic idea that no one does wrong willingly, but only out of ignorance. A new perspective also emerges—that the self can be made immune to harm from without and that the purpose of life is to seek to realize a common good.

In the tradition of Buddhism, similar precepts are evident. There are Buddhist monks and nuns dedicated to enlightenment alone; there is also a very strong and prominent form of Buddhism that seeks involvement with the world. The Dalai Lama writes that "Through inner peace, genuine world peace can be achieved. In this the importance of individual responsibility is quite clear; an atmosphere of peace must first be created within ourselves, then gradually expanded to include our families, our communities, and ultimately the whole planet."[26] According to this more activist or transformative strand of Buddhism, inner peace is followed by an outward movement that embraces and influences an ever-larger sphere of relationships. Inner peace is not just a route to the end of interpersonal peace and ultimately world peace, but may even be said to exist for the sake of these things. We need to take responsibility not just for ourselves, but also for all those around us. Vietnamese Zen master Thich Nhat Hanh expresses such a viewpoint even more strongly: "The peace we seek cannot be our personal possession. We need to find an inner peace which makes it possible for us to become one with those who suffer, and to do something to help our brothers and sisters, which is to say, ourselves. . . . This peace is not a barricade which separates you from the world. On the contrary, this kind of peace brings you into the world and empowers you to undertake whatever you want to do to try to help."[27] (See also the discussion of compassion later in this chapter.)

But why should we want to help? What motivates us in this way? Without going into great detail concerning the philosophy of Buddhism, two of its primary teachings deserve mention here. The first is the doctrine of "dependent origination." This is the view that all things exist in causal and other reciprocal connections with one another, with the circle (or sphere) of dependency radiating outward (and inward), as far as you wish to track it. Taking this idea seriously means that all humans (as well as humans and nonhuman animals, humans and their environment) are related and therefore, too, that all suffering is (or should be) of concern to every being that is capable of experiencing and thinking about it. The second teaching regards "letting go." According to this precept, an essential step toward self-control, and being able to move beyond one's narrow ego concerns to reach out to the world, is "moderating excessive attachment to material possessions, to emotions, or to the status quo in our lives."[28] These are all considered to be related to desire in some way or other, and to be the causes of suffering. Thus, letting go of anger (as most people can attest to from personal experience) is liberating and enables a movement forward, past some particular hang-up, or makes it possible to reconnect with a friend or loved one who has been the object of the angry feelings.

The notion that understanding peace translates into mapping an expanding sphere of effects is also developed in traditional African cultures. South-African Nobel Peace Prize recipient and Anglican bishop Desmond Tutu writes that a concept widely shared by African language groups is togetherness:

> We belong in a bundle of life. We say, "a person is a person through other people" (in Xhosa *Ubuntu ungamntu ngabanye abantu* and in Zulu *Umuntu ngumuntu ngabanye*). I am human because I belong, I participate, I share. A person with *ubuntu* is open and available to others, affirming of others, does not feel threatened that others are able and good; for he or she has a proper self-assurance that comes with knowing that he or she belongs in a greater whole and is diminished when others are humiliated or diminished, when others are tortured or oppressed, or treated as if they were less than who they are.[29]

The sense of community and interdependence as sources of identity and empowerment is the most striking feature of this worldview.[30] And it suggests that peace must be a function of both the experience of self and that of belonging: the two are inseparable. Because African cultures also presuppose "a fundamental unity between theory and practice and between knower and known,"[31] peace in oneself is dependent upon both thought and action. Furthermore, inner peace and the behavior that flows from it depend on the health of the larger whole of which the individual is part, just as the reverse also holds true.

The Wider Domain of Peace

A closer look at traditional African cultures reveals a commonly held outlook—a metaphysics or cosmology—which teaches that "all of life is . . . an integrated whole. Nature, living things, humans, the ancestors, and a supreme being or beings all share in one world, a world to which all of them equally belong."[32] Within such an integrated perspective, peace is understood as the norm, the state in which things are functioning as they should be, and in which humans are venerating life through appropriate words and deeds.

Similarly, in the lore of many North American First Peoples, there can be found a "vision of the oneness and holiness of all things. Each part of Creation is endowed with equality and wholeness, wisdom, love, and beauty, along with life."[33] Violent conflict, disharmony and dissent within one's group, and warfare, within this context, are ruptures of the natural order and offend against it, while peace is its restoration. More basically, peace is what the "vision of oneness and holiness" points to, and mandates. Peace results from being in touch with this fundamental standpoint and therefore builds outward to become, among other things, a state of harmony with the universe as a whole. In this sense, the "universe" is not some remote realm of materiality and events that is totally beyond comprehension, but is, more accurately, the larger compass of reality of which humans and all other living things are interconnected, functioning, influential parts. Someone who has this kind of attunement with the whole, and, as it were, "lives in it," will be assured of calm and balance within her- or himself. But this attunement is a two-way street, as well.

In the words of Black Elk, an Oglala Lakota Indian,

> The first peace, which is the most important, is that which comes within the souls of men when they realize their relationship, their oneness, with the universe and all its Powers, and when they realize that at the center of the universe dwells *Wakan-Tanka* [the Great or Holy Mystery], and that this center is really everywhere, it is within each of us. This is the real Peace, and the others are but reflections of this. The second peace is that which is between two individuals, and the third is that which is made between two nations. But above all you should understand that there can never be peace between nations until there is first known that true peace which, as I have often said, is within the souls of men.[34]

Here we have the idea that inner peace leads to and creates instances of outer peace, which are impossible without it. Yet inner peace is defined in terms of connection with the full totality of which one is a part. Inner and outer are inseparable correlates. As one peace scholar observes, "This approach to peace recognizes different dimensions and levels of consciousness. . . . [and] the importance of inner peace as an essential condition for creating a more peaceful world. In this view, all aspects of outer peace, including one's perceptions and experiences of the world, reflect one's inner state of consciousness and must therefore be based on inner peace."[35] In this larger or enriched sense, then, we return again to the idea that "Peace begins with me."

Cosmologies of the type considered here also may include recognition of conflict, war, and destruction as elemental principles in the workings of the universe. Such a perspective is evident, for example, in the Hindu scripture the *Bhagavad Gita*, where Lord Krishna appears in the guise of the "destroyer of worlds."[36] These portrayals spring, in part, from a recognition that disruptions of social life do occur from time to time, and that human misdeeds may incur reprisals from the gods or spirits that rule over things, or call for acts of restitution of some kind in the interest of universal justice and balance. Nothing here entails, however, that peace should yield its place as the desired norm. For example, in Akan [West African] traditional ethics, "What is . . . good will be that which promotes human interests and is conducive to harmonizing the conflicts that inevitably arise among them. Human behavior is right or good not because it conforms to a set of rules, but because it builds up instead of tearing down."[37] Thus, peace can be identified, within this kind of worldview, as not only good in itself, but also as good by virtue of its healing power and contribution to the common weal.

5.6. PEACE AS A PRESCRIPTIVE CONCEPT AND A VISION

Apart from all that has been said about peace above, and all of the properties ascribed to it thus far, peace is also about how we wish the world to be, or how it might be if certain preferred modes of action were followed and encouraged to prevail over other, more harmful types of action. More specifically, what is meant by calling peace a "prescriptive concept" is that it reflects a perception that humanity ought to commit itself, as a matter of principle, both to abandoning some kinds of behavior and to cultivating others in their place. Such a notion designates how things *should be*, and how our conduct is responsible for the state of affairs we experience—whether we are talking only about relationships between humans, or humans' relationship with the larger sphere of existence that they inhabit. Hence, prescriptions for peace are ethical or moral directives and should be understood and acted upon accordingly. Peace is not just something that would be nice to have, all things being equal; instead, we have a serious duty or obligation to pursue peace, and to be peaceful within ourselves and in our conduct toward others. This notion is important to acknowledge, because it brings home the idea that peace is much more than incidental icing on the cake of life; wanting to realize peace is not merely positing an aspirational value, it is also acknowledging an imperative that calls for us to help create a better world.

Another significant outcome of the discussion thus far is that there are many visions of peace. In saying so, we are not inviting ourselves to choose from a grab bag of competing notions, as if it were a matter of indifference which one we fastened on to. The point, rather, is that peace is an organic concept—one that grows as we consider it in greater detail, and in which the different facets of meaning are intimately interconnected. This way of comprehending peace will help avoid the charge of relativism that might be expressed by statements like: "Oh, it really doesn't matter which idea of peace you choose; each is as good as any other" and: "One person's peace is another person's war." Why

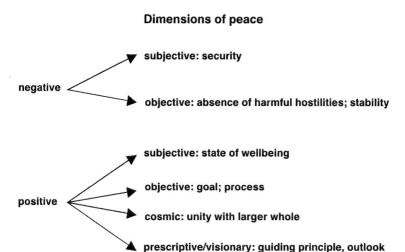

Dimensions of peace

subjective: security

negative

objective: absence of harmful hostilities; stability

subjective: state of wellbeing

objective: goal; process

positive

cosmic: unity with larger whole

prescriptive/visionary: guiding principle, outlook

Figure 5.1 Dimensions of peace

such generalizations must be rejected is that what we have been talking about are not incompatible but rather complementary visions of peace. Even if an individual does not share in a cosmic outlook of some kind, or perhaps lacks one altogether (if that is possible), there is still common ground with such a view, in that it also speaks to the need for harmony in both the inner and outer conditions of human life.

H. B. Danesh, who is a psychiatrist, peace educator, and member of the Baháʼí faith, writes that "peace is a psychosocial and political, as well as a moral and spiritual condition, requiring a conscious effort, a universal outlook, and an integrated and unifying approach."[38] This very perceptive formula captures quite well the point of view advanced in this chapter, and indeed throughout this book. Without acknowledging and giving due emphasis to all of these dimensions of the subject of peace, we would be left with a pale substitute for what it is we seek.

5.7. COMPASSION: (I) WHAT IT IS, AND IS NOT

Chapter 2 showed that we need to dig beneath the surface if we wish to identify the human potential for nonviolent ways of living, and hence, of peace. The purpose of doing so is in part to celebrate the most worthy kinds of humanity residing within us; but more importantly, it is to acquire a deeper appreciation of the personal resources that are available for creating a more peaceful world. Looking at ways in which humans cooperatively interact with one another on a daily basis provides a good deal of insight into our peaceful capabilities. Another path that leads in the same direction is to investigate compassion, which is a unique capacity that holds much promise for helping to build peace. First, we will look at what compassion is—what defines it and distinguishes it from anything else to which it might be compared. Then we will examine the relationship between compassion and peace and evaluate the role compassion can play in realizing a peaceful and nonviolent world order.

Some Attributes of Compassion

Compassion, to most people, is a highly admirable human trait. (And perhaps it belongs to some nonhuman animals as well.[39]) Compassionate people are universally seen as kind, generous, helpful, understanding, and accepting. Furthermore, they give of themselves, not out of weakness, but from a position of inner strength. Compassion may be thought of as a virtue in the Aristotelian sense. This means two things: that it is a disposition we ought to have; and that in order to have it, we need to act compassionately on a regular basis. Compassionate behavior, in other words, is a positive habit we either have naturally or are taught, and a way of doing things that we must practice in order to reinforce it in ourselves. "Yet however valuable compassion may be, surely it plays only a very small part in life—even in peaceful living?" one may ask. This is a shortsighted view. It is unfortunate that relatively few studies of peace single out compassion for special attention, although, arguably, many do illustrate compassionate attitudes and conduct on the part of peacemakers and ordinary individuals alike, in times of crisis and even as they quietly go about their daily affairs. The point here is that when we seek to understand compassion, we need to think beyond the boundaries that confine us to dwell too much on rare, iconic, high-profile public figures like Mohandas Gandhi, Martin Luther King, Jr., Florence Nightingale, or Jane Addams. Not that these examples are unimportant, but we need to look for what lies closer at hand—for a tendency that resides innately within each of us.

A Definition of Compassion

The root meaning of "compassion" is "suffering with." This signifies something more than sympathy, empathy, kindness, or pity, and something less than taking on another's burden as one's own. Sympathy is the ability to be affected by, and resonate with, another's feelings. Empathy involves a more complex understanding that embraces another's situation, feelings, and motives. Kindness

is a sort of warmth coupled with generosity, wherein we reach out, at least temporarily, from our egocentric concerns to be considerate and give something
to others for their own sake, with no guarantee of reward or reciprocation.[40]
Pity is a more passive form of sympathy, including sorrow or regret over another's misfortune. Of these other states, none necessarily calls for any action
on our part, except for kindness. Compassion is different even from kindness,
however, being well defined as: "*Deep awareness of the suffering of another coupled with the wish to relieve it.*"[41] While compassion motivates acts of kindness,
the co-suffering element of compassion suggests an additional ingredient, not
captured by the notion of kindness, one which we will come to presently.

Now to say that compassion is something *less* than taking on another's burdens as one's own means that, rather than just being infected and weighed
down by another's sad feelings or plight, and rather than merely understanding and being weakened by sorrow or regret, *compassion entails a resoluteness
and an active will to change things, to make a difference.* "When that feeling
arises," according to the Dalai Lama, "no matter if your own situation is difficult or easy, your mental attitude is, 'I'm okay.'" He observes that the change
of focus from self to other gives one "mental peace" and freedom from anxiety,
fear, anger, and insecurity, which feed off of self-absorption. The compassionate individual, then, does not take on board or "own" the other's suffering, but
she or he both identifies with the sufferer and yet maintains a pragmatic distance from the other person's suffering, which enables her or him to consider:
"What can I do to help?"[42]

As we see here, to speak of compassion presupposes a relationship between
two or more different (sentient) beings, both of whom are moral agents in
their own right. A proper understanding of compassion, then, rules out the
idea of "compassion toward oneself" that some authors favor. What they are
trying to get at is better framed as taking an attitude of acceptance, patience,
or kindness concerning oneself.

5.8. COMPASSION: (II) ACTION, AND MORALITY

Compassion is the source of caring acts of kindness or benevolence, as noted
above, namely, those behaviors that surpass the limits of ego and begin to relate us to the world as an arena of concerns greater than our own, as a place
where we can and want to make a difference. This is because the compassionate mind-state opens us up to truly appreciating others as persons with needs,
desires, and interests like our own. It follows that the sort of non-egocentricity
that characterizes compassion is not to be equated in any simplistic way with
self-sacrifice. The compassionate individual may well engage in unselfish,

supererogatory, or self-sacrificing acts; but these should not be supposed to originate in an attitude of disregard or neglect for one's own safety or personal welfare, or lack of self-love, considering others only and never oneself, and so on. Compassionate behavior may sometimes require putting some of one's own needs, desires, and interests on hold, at least temporarily, and there are of course models of compassionate conduct who do so nearly all of the time, such as the exemplary individuals mentioned earlier. But in the more interesting sense, compassion signifies being able to stand in someone else's shoes, see the world from her or his perspective, understand how others feel and why, regard the good of others as of the same value and importance as one's own, plus having the drive to help realize this good, even in the face of adversity.

Ethics of Compassion

It will not be any surprise, then, to hear that compassion is sometimes regarded as the foundation of morality. Great thinkers who've espoused this position include the Buddha and German philosopher Arthur Schopenhauer. The Buddha taught that compassion is not only present within each of us, but is also the appropriate response to suffering that we encounter in the world at large, in one another, and in sentient beings generally, of whatever species. And, according to Schopenhauer, the only morally praiseworthy behavior—the sole action that possesses "genuine moral worth"—is that which springs from compassion. Compassion, for him, is what kindles "fellow feeling" and gives rise to sympathy, mercy, forgiveness, altruism, and "loving-kindness."[43]

The creed of compassion embraces two guidelines: (1) "Do no harm" (known as the harm principle or the principle of nonmaleficence), which we encountered in Chapter 4, section 4.3 ("Nonviolence: Narrower and Broader Visions"); and (2) "Whenever possible, do good" (the principle of benevolence or beneficence). Naturally, what seems at first quite simple gets complicated when we start to analyze it more closely. We can ask, for example, what is harmful and what is good, and whether these notions are relative to time, place, and individual situations; whether we can conceivably avoid causing harm altogether or only seek at best to minimize doing so; whether there are degrees of compassion, and, if so, when each is appropriately shown; and whether all obligations can be generated and explained by appeal to compassion and its derivative principles. Although we can no doubt refine our concepts to address such issues,[44] there will still remain the daunting and more important question of how to produce compassionate individuals. Perhaps "produce" is not the right word here, for the idea of compassion as the source of morality is predicated on the assumption that everyone has within her- or himself the capacity to show compassion and, given the right circumstances, to lead a compassionate existence. So, what we really need to put in place are the conditions that bring forth and maximize this human potential, especially in children, that release it most fully and effectively, because (as previously observed) it is axiomatic that compassionate individuals will want and tend to act compassionately.

As one can quickly grasp, this issue is crucial to promoting peace and containing violence in the world at large. Peace scholar and organizer Kent Shifferd reflects that "What makes humans reluctant to kill each other is both a strong sense of empathy and a rational calculation of prudence. The former is the more important of the two. Empathy is that ability to feel another's pain and suffering as if it were your own. You know what grief, fear, sorrow they are going through, and you know you would not want to go through that yourself. You feel compassion for them and would not want to be the cause of inhumane deeds that put them in that way."[45] Here, a clear connection between empathy and compassion is established, as well as the notion that compassion has a harm-avoidance element built into it, in addition to the wanting-to-help ingredient featured in the general definition given earlier. Would having more compassionate individuals create a more compassionate society? This result is not guaranteed, since any whole is more than the sum of its parts. But the probability is great that people who think about their fellow human beings (and other sentient beings on the planet) in more positive ways would want to act differently, with more constructive, mutually beneficial ends in view, than do many at present. That said, however, the issue of how to make compassion shine forth in the human personality is best left to psychologists, educators, and social theorists.[46] (This topic will be revisited in Chapter 7, section 7.3, "Education for Peace.")

5.9. COMPASSION: (III) SEEING THINGS WHOLE

What remains to be considered is the role of compassion in the quest for peace. So far, we have established that compassion is a powerful force that allows and even compels us to extend moral concern and engagement beyond ourselves, but also that it does not imply self-denial or total immersion in the life of the other. Instead, compassion hinges on the realization that we are all in the same boat and share a common existential situation to this extent: that humans (and nonhumans as well) are vulnerable and, at a very basic level, quest after security and an environment in which to flourish biologically and pursue some form of fulfillment. *We are ourselves therefore as much in need of compassionate treatment from others as they are from us.*

As the next chapter will explain in more detail, peace both requires an absence of ongoing violent hostilities and conflicts, and entails finding some state of equilibrium that enables each to attain the goals listed in the previous paragraph. Harking back to the original meaning of compassion, peace scholar Michael Nagler suggests that "when we suffer with others we grow, and when we close our hearts against them we die within."[47] Galtung proposes that compassion assists one "to assess better the consequences of one's own action. . . . [and] foster a sense of responsibility, for oneself, and for others."[48] Meanwhile, peace historian David Cortright observes that "Compassion for the stranger is the litmus test of ethical conduct in all great religions. So is the capacity to forgive, to repent and overcome past transgressions. The key to conflict prevention is extending the moral boundaries of one's community and expressing compassion toward others."[49] Finally, the Dalai Lama says, "Peace is actually, I believe, an expression of compassion, a sense of caring." Compassion helps us to become "fully engaged" in trying to solve human problems "without adding any harm to the situation."[50] Thus, compassion nurtures inner strength and a spirit of patience, generosity, and openness (and, if necessary, forgiveness) toward others. It stands against the image (addressed in Chapter 2) of humans as "naturally" and predominantly aggressive, violent, cruel, selfish, greedy, competitive, and exploitative. And it helps us envision a society that is caring, less conflict-ridden, and more accepting of others in their otherness. Compassion, then, is one of the key components of a peaceful mind-set that enables us to place ourselves within a larger picture of human life and concerns, and to involve ourselves actively in trying to make the world a better place.

This section ends with a brief anecdote. While working out some thoughts on compassion, a scholar stopped by a copy shop and began chatting with the woman who worked there. He told her he was on his way to a conference where he would be speaking on the relationship between compassion and peace. She immediately replied, "They sound like the same thing to me." The scholar could not help thinking that maybe she had gotten to the heart of the matter, stating a profound truth in this remarkably succinct fashion.[51]

5.10. THE WILL TO PEACE

Philosophically minded psychologists and psychologically minded philosophers have sometimes called attention to the unique spiritual strengths of human beings by appealing to the concept of will. Thus, for instance, William James spoke of "the will to believe"; Schopenhauer, of "the will to live" (or "the will to life"); Friedrich Nietzsche, of "the will to power"; and Viktor Frankl, of "the will to meaning."[52] We do not need to dispute any of these postulates, for humans have many special qualities that often manifest themselves in challenging circumstances. "The will to peace" is another of these, and may even be, as some believe, an aspect of the will to live, otherwise known as "the survival instinct."

The point here is not to add just another catchy phrase to discussions about human nature, but rather, to recognize that peace is virtually universally desired and also correctly understood as a condition of survival. At a certain level, to say that peace is universally desired is a no-brainer. Perhaps there was a time past when this was not so obvious; when the warrior ethos dominated and peace was seen as an inferior state, while war was valued both as the necessary principle of turmoil that rejuvenates the world and as the fulfillment of humanity.[53] But today average people do understand that war and violence mean the destruction of everything they care about, whereas peace is required in order for these things to flourish. They understand further that living with one another is a challenge that must be met, and that it can be met either by freezing relationships in a mold of hostility, or by learning to get along, even when this is hard work. They understand too the need for give-and-take in human affairs. John Paul Lederach, a leading authority on peacebuilding and reconciliation, observes that "In the real world, the element that historically assures extinction is unidirectionality and tunnel vision, a single-mindedness of process and response in pursuit of a purpose. Survival requires adaptation to constantly changing environments, finding ways to move sideways while maintaining clarity of purpose."[54] We do know these things, even though the worse side of our nature often gets the better of us.

Nagler states that "peace is the deepest drive in our human being."[55] In the course of defending this claim (which can be seen as a version of the will to peace theory), he notes that some kind of vision of peace beyond war motivates even those who engage in violent armed conflicts. Evidence in favor of Nagler's assertion can be extracted from the lengthy just war tradition and the more recent international laws of war, discussed in Chapter 3; for these presuppose a very strong desire for the continuity of humanity and for peaceful dealings after war, like the ones that existed at some point before it.

Further Support for Affirming the Will to Peace

Inspirational words and teachings about peace abound in the history of humankind, and frequently appear in religious scriptures, as well as in works by philosophers, spiritual leaders, political thinkers, psychologists, and peace-minded scientists. Because they have been so influential over time, we must assume that they reflect more than merely personal opinions and perspectives and, on the contrary, reflect the widely shared values that peaceful living represents.

But if the question being asked were, "What direct empirical evidence is there for the existence of a will to peace?" we might come up empty-handed. Attempts to discover any experiments to prove that there is such a thing are unlikely to bear fruit or even to be pursued by today's social scientists. There is, however, a great abundance of social-scientific research on peaceful personalities, conflict resolution, mediation, and negotiation strategies, nonviolent living, and related topics. Perhaps it might be illuminating to regard this research as *presupposing* rather than establishing a will to peace. The fact that this empirical work is widely applied today in conflict situations around the world supports the conclusion that there is a perceived need and demand for ways to realize peace. In Chapter 2, section 2.7 ("Cooperation and Coevolution"), we examined recent studies of cooperation that show evidence of this tendency even in preverbal infants. Although cooperation is also a feature of war-making (see Chapter 1, "War Myths," Myth #6), what is different about the experiments done with infants is that they reveal not only that cooperation is built into us (rather than just selfishness and aggression), but also *caring* cooperation (helping people in distress). This strongly points to at least one innate behavioral trait of human beings that shapes a peaceful outlook.

The Peaceful Personality

The conclusion we have reached is that the will to peace is not scientifically demonstrable, but rather, is a more-than-reasonable hypothesis for explaining some of our most basic attributes, attachments, and life choices. More than any of the other "wills" mentioned at the beginning of this section (which are also experimentally "unproven"), the concept of a will to peace certainly encourages research into ways of bringing about stable and sustainable peace in the world. Accepting such a hypothesis may also help generate a deeper commitment to trying out new methods of conflict resolution and peacebuilding. For even assuming an underlying desire for peace among humans, this does not entail that we all know how to go about realizing it in our own lives and beyond.

A step in the direction of better understanding of the possibilities for actualizing peace—and just one of many—is the empirical study of the "peaceful personality." Although this subject of study is still in its early days, tentative models of what constitutes a peaceful person (including agreeableness, anger control, empathy, forgiveness, cooperativeness, trust, good communication skills, and so on) have been conceptually constructed and to a certain extent validated by attitude and value choice tests and correlation with observations of behavior.[56] These have an unmistakable relevance to education for peace, which we will consider in Chapter 7, and also implications for the connection between inner and outer peace, as described earlier.

Another stream of inquiry aimed at understanding the peaceful personality is conducted by laypersons who have involved themselves for many years in peace movements of one sort or another, and have learned important lessons by sensitive observation of the world around them, from which they have formed certain intuitions along similar lines to what social scientists are propounding. For example, Winslow Myers, an artist, teacher, and antiwar activist, suggests to each of us the idea that "I can transform my own role in perpetuating ill will and war" by adopting three "core personal practices":

- I will resolve conflict. I will not use violence.
- I will maintain an attitude of goodwill. I will not preoccupy myself with an enemy.
- I will work together with others to build a world beyond war.[57]

Another example is provided by Colman McCarthy, a veteran *Washington Post* columnist, who developed a set of principles for cultivating self-awareness as well as communication and peacemaking skills while teaching peace in a variety of school and prison settings. "As a classroom teacher," says McCarthy, "my experience-based belief is that unless we teach our children peace someone else will teach them violence."[58] In addition to being a powerful statement about education, this comment is also a tribute to the potential for peace residing within everyone.

To conclude these reflections on the subject of the will to peace, consider for a moment a view that truly comes from out of left field. According to a little-known psychologist,

> Naturally, the common people don't want war; neither in Russia nor in England nor in America, nor for that matter in Germany. That is understood. But, after all, it is the *leaders* of the country who determine the policy and it is always a simple matter to drag the people along, whether it is a democracy or a fascist dictatorship or a Parliament or a Communist dictatorship. . . . [V]oice or no voice, the people can always be brought to the bidding of the leaders. That is easy. All you have to do is tell them they are being attacked and denounce the pacifists for lack of patriotism and exposing the country to danger. It works the same way in any country.[59]

The source of these remarks is a postwar interview with Hermann Goering, Hitler's supreme military commander, deputy, designated successor—and a mass killer. There is much food for thought in these acute observations, but, for our purposes, what is of interest is the recognition that people basically do not want war, and, of course, there is also the plausible claim that they get it anyway because their leaders manipulate them so as to override their natural predisposition to be peaceful. This testimony is no doubt given by a discredited, morally bankrupt, and despicable individual; yet it could be argued that if even such a person as this postulates the will to peace, then there must surely be something to the notion.

5.11. PEACE AS A WAY OF LIFE

We have examined what peace means beyond negative conditions (absence of war and violence) and found that, when looked at positively, it can include a component of self-awareness, inward calm, and balance; one of outward stability, security, and social harmony; and, lastly, one of what might be called a sense of belongingness or connection to the world at large, or, perhaps, even to the cosmos as a whole. These are not alternatives but rather complementary aspects of peace. Whether each is present in any given individual's outlook is a matter of inquiry to determine. Peace is both a goal and a process of reaching that end. Viewed in this manner, peace is a function of both thought and action, in one's own private sphere and also collectively, and requires deep commitment and patience to develop. Such an understanding shows that *peace is a way of life*.

What does it mean to call something "a way of life?" Essentially this expression suggests *an orientation toward existence that is guided by a principle or set of principles, together with corresponding values, which determine self-expression through thought and action.* Our way of life is how we consolidate our stance in the world and what it signifies in human terms. And it makes a statement to which others can respond in one fashion or another. A peaceful way of life will be such as to incorporate nonviolence toward oneself and others, and will be guided by cooperation, mutual respect, creative problem-solving, negotiation of differences, and caring concern or compassion. In a down-to-earth way, we can appreciate that peace has a profound, many-sided social aspect. A young researcher, helping to build peace through field work in East Timor (Timor-Leste) reports that "Even a very basic community project—building a well—can be more about social engagement than it is about being able to tick off a box that says 'job done'. It reveals who we are and how we express our identity."[60] Most of us are able to relate to this insight through our own experience of collaborative projects, even if our lives are generally governed by routine. Some of the activities that reach the greatest level of satisfaction are of this type, where the processes of consolidating oneself and of helping others come harmoniously together.

NOTES TO CHAPTER 5

1. Anatol Rapoport, "Peace, Definitions and Concepts of," in *Encyclopedia of Violence, Peace, and Conflict*, ed. Lester R. Kurtz and Jennifer Turpin (San Diego: Academic Press, 1999), vol. 2, p. 669.

2. Linda Groff, "Evolving Views of Peace," *Oxford International Encyclopedia of Peace*, ed. Nigel Young (Oxford: Oxford University Press, 2010); online edition available at: http://www.oxford-peace.com/entry?entry=t296.e241-s2.

3. Baruch Spinoza, *Benedict de Spinoza's Political Treatise*, trans. A. H. Gosset, ed. R. H. M. Elwes (London: G. Bell & Son, 1883), chap. 5, sec. 4 and chap. 6, sec. 4. (Spinoza's *Tractatus Politicus* was first published in 1670.)

4. Johan Galtung, *Peace by Peaceful Means: Peace and Conflict, Development and Civilization* (Oslo: PRIO International Peace Research Institute/London: SAGE, 1996), p. 31 (emphasis in original).

5. Galtung, *Peace by Peaceful Means*, p. 61.

6. *The Lion Encyclopedia of the Bible*, new rev. ed. (Oxford: Lion, 1986), p. 154.

7. Isaiah 11:6.

8. This quotation is usually credited to Dutch-American Rev. A. J. Muste, but it is also attributed to Gandhi.

9. Martin Luther King, Jr., "I Have a Dream" speech, 28 August 1963. Video excerpts of King's famous speech can be found on the Internet, but for copyright reasons no full-length video of it can be posted at present.

10. David Cortright, *Peace: A History of Movements and Ideas* (Cambridge, UK: Cambridge University Press, 2008), p. 7.

11. Nigel Dower, *World Ethics: The New Agenda*, 2nd ed. (Edinburgh: Edinburgh University Press, 2007), pp. 209–10.

12. Linda Groff and Paul Smoker make the same claim by means of the following summary argument: a) If one focuses only on outer peace and creating social justice in the world, but not on inner peace, then people's unresolved inner conflicts can be projected out onto the world, creating scapegoating, prejudices, and conflicts, therefore making it difficult to create social justice and peace in the world (the ostensible goal). b) If one focuses only on inner peace, then social injustices and structural violence in the world, which are not addressed by society and people, will tend to make it difficult for most people to transcend their outer conditions of life, thus making it difficult for them to attain inner peace (the ostensible goal). c) Clearly there is a dynamic and synergistic relationship between inner and outer peace: by focusing on both aspects of peace, each aspect of peace—i.e., inner or outer—increases the probability that more people will also be able to attain the other aspect of peace (Linda Groff and Paul Smoker,

"Spirituality, Religion, Culture, and Peace: Exploring the Foundations for Inner-Outer Peace in the Twenty-first Century," *International Journal of Peace Studies* 1 [1996]; available at: http://www.gmu.edu/programs/icar/ijps/vol1_1/smoker.html).

13. Kent D. Shifferd, *From War to Peace: A Guide to the Next Hundred Years* (Jefferson, NC: McFarland, 2011), p. 108.

14. It might be argued, though, that there is an important difference between what peace is and what it entails. These ideas are confused, for example, by Scott A. Hunt when he says (speaking of Gandhi and Einstein), "They both saw peace as a deeply moral obligation that required faith, vision, and courage" (Scott A. Hunt, *The Future of Peace: On the Front Lines with the World's Great Peacemakers* [New York: HarperOne, 2004], p. 8). The correct way of stating this is that the moral obligation we have to seek peace in the world derives from an understanding of what peace is, or might be.

15. Aung San Suu Kyi, quoted by Hunt, *Future of Peace*, p. 34.

16. Groff and Smoker, "Spirituality, Religion, Culture, and Peace."

17. See examples at http://thyselfknow.com.

18. U.S. Department of Health and Human Services, *Mental Health: A Report of the Surgeon General* (Rockville, MD: U.S. Department of Health and Human Services, Substance Abuse and Mental Health Services Administration, Center for Mental Health Services, National Institutes of Health, National Institute of Mental Health, 1999), p. 4; available at: http://profiles.nlm.nih.gov/ps/retrieve/ResourceMetadata/NNBBHS.

19. Sulak Sivaraksa, "Buddhism and a Culture of Peace," in *Buddhist Peacework: Creating Cultures of Peace*, ed. David W. Chappell (Boston: Wisdom, 1999), p. 45.

20. Christopher E. Miller (ed. Mary E. King), *A Glossary of Terms and Concepts in Peace and Conflict Studies*, 2nd ed. (Addis Ababa: University for Peace, Africa Program, 2005), pp. 55–6; available at: http://www.upeace.org/pdf/glossaryv2.pdf.

21. Julian Borger, "Women Are Creating Harmony, but Only Men Broker Peace Deals," *Guardian Weekly*, 28 September–4 October 2012, p. 3.

22. "Ataraxia," *Wikipedia*; http://en.wikipedia.org/wiki/Ataraxia.

23. Anthony Adolf, *Peace: A World History* (Cambridge, UK: Polity Press, 2009), p. 51.

24. This account of Epictetus's thought is based on Victor Daniels, "Psychology in Greek Thought," paper presented at the Western Psychological Association Conference, Seattle, 26 April 1997; available at: http://www.sonoma.edu/users/d/daniels/Greeks.html.

25. Marcus Aurelius, *Meditations*, bk. I, pt. 1.

26. The Dalai Lama (Bsatn-'dzin-rgya-mtsho, Dalai Lama XIV), quoted by Kenneth Kraft, "Introduction," in *Inner Peace, World Peace: Essays on Buddhism and Nonviolence*, ed. Kenneth Kraft (Albany: State University of New York Press, 1992), p. 2.

27. Thich Nhat Hanh, *The Sun My Heart* (Berkeley, CA: Parallax Press, 1988), pp. 127–8.

28. Mike George, *Discover Inner Peace: A Guide to Spiritual Well-Being* (San Francisco: Chronicle Books, 2000), p. 66.

29. Desmond Tutu, *No Future without Forgiveness* (London: Rider, 1999), pp. 34–5.

30. For further discussion, see Susan T. Fiske, *Social Beings: A Core Motives Approach to Social Psychology*, 2nd ed. (New York: Wiley, 2010).

31. Helen Buss Mitchell, *Roots of Wisdom*, 4th ed. (Belmont, CA: Wadsworth Thomson Learning, 2005), p. 250.
32. Mitchell, *Roots of Wisdom*, p. 94.
33. Mitchell, *Roots of Wisdom*, pp. 93–4.
34. Black Elk, *The Sacred Pipe: Black Elk's Account of the Seven Rites of the Oglala Sioux*, recorded and ed. Joseph Epes Brown (Norman: University of Oklahoma Press, 1989), p. 115.
35. Groff, "Evolving Views of Peace."
36. "Time I am, destroyer of worlds," *Bhagavad Gita* 11.32.
37. Mitchell, *Roots of Wisdom*, p. 450.
38. H. B. Danesh, "Education for Peace: The Pedagogy of Civilization," in *Addressing Ethnic Conflict Through Peace Education: International Perspectives*, ed. Zvi Bekerman and Claire McGlynn (New York: Palgrave Macmillan, 2007); cited by Sara Clarke-Habibi, "Transforming Worldviews: The Case of Education for Peace in Bosnia and Herzegovina," *Journal of Transformative Education* 3 (2005), p.38; available at: http://efpinternational.org/dev/wp-content/uploads/2011/11/education_for_peace_case_study.pdf.
39. See Dacher Keltner, Jason Marsh, and Jeremy Adam Smith, eds., *The Compassionate Instinct: The Science of Human Goodness* (New York: W. W. Norton, 2010), pt. 1.
40. For more on this interesting and rich concept, see Adam Phillips and Barbara Taylor, *On Kindness* (New York: Farrar, Straus and Giroux, 2009).
41. *American Heritage Dictionary*, 4th online ed., 2000 (emphasis added) (http://education.yahoo.com/reference/dictionary/?s=compassion). See also the Charter for Compassion (http://charterforcompassion.org/the-charter/#charter-for-compassion).
42. The Dalai Lama (Bsatn-'dzin-rgya-mtsho, Dalai Lama XIV), cited by Hunt in *Future of Peace*, p. 84.
43. Arthur Schopenhauer, *On the Basis of Morality* (1840), secs. 13, 14, 16.
44. See, for example, Martin Rowe, ed., *The Way of Compassion* (New York: Stealth Technologies, 1999); Damien Keown, *Buddhist Ethics: A Very Short Introduction* (Oxford: Oxford University Press, 2005); Christina Feldman, *Compassion: Listening to the Cries of the World* (Berkeley, CA: Rodmell Press, 2005); Richard Reilly, *Ethics of Compassion: Bridging Ethical Theory and Religious Moral Discourse*, (Lanham, MD: Lexington Books, 2008).
45. Shifferd, *From War to Peace*, p. 41.
46. Education for compassion is the objective of a number of organizations, examples of which are provided by the Institute for Humane Education (http://humaneeducation.org/sections/view/what_is_humane_education) and World Animal Net (http://www.worldanimal.net/resources/humane-education-resources).
47. Michael Nagler, *The Search for a Nonviolent Future: A Promise of Peace for Ourselves, Our Families, and Our World* (Novato, CA: New World Library, 2004), p. 260.
48. Galtung, *Peace by Peaceful Means*, p. 110.
49. Cortright, *Peace*, p. 184.
50. The Dalai Lama, cited by Hunt, *Future of Peace*, pp. 70–1.

51. This exchange took place in Washington, DC during 2009. The scholar is the author of *Understanding Peace: A Comprehensive Introduction*, and the copy shop employee is Ms. Mary Vincent.

52. William James, *The Will to Believe: And Other Essays in Popular Philosophy* (Charleston, SC: Nabu Press, 2010) (many other editions available); Arthur Schopenhauer, "On the Affirmation and Denial of the Will-to-Live," in *The World as Will and Representation*, trans. E. F. J. Payne (New York: Dover, 1958), vol. 2, pp. 568–72 (also available in editions of selected writings by Schopenhauer); Friedrich Nietzsche, *The Will to Power*, trans. Walter Kaufmann (New York: Vintage Books, 1968) (discussions of the will to power occur in many of Nietzsche's other books as well); Viktor E. Frankl, *Man's Search for Meaning* (Boston: Beacon Press, 2006) (other editions available).

53. I owe this point to Brian Byrne (personal communication, 30 July 2012).

54. John Paul Lederach, *The Moral Imagination: The Art and Soul of Building Peace* (Oxford: Oxford University Press, 2005), p. 119.

55. Nagler, *Search for a Nonviolent Future*, pp. 253–4.

56. See Daniel M. Mayton II, *Nonviolence and Peace Psychology: Intrapersonal, Interpersonal, Societal, and World Peace* (Dordrecht: Springer, 2009), ch. 4.

57. Winslow Myers, *Living Beyond War: A Citizen's Guide* (Maryknoll, NY: Orbis Books, 2009), p. 11.

58. Colman McCarthy, *I'd Rather Teach Peace* (Maryknoll, NY: Orbis Books, 2002), p. xvii.

59. Hermann Goering, quoted in G. M. Gilbert, *Nuremberg Diary* (New York: Farrar, Straus, 1947), pp. 278–9 (emphasis in original).

60. Richard Jones, "Living Arts: Developing Creativity Programs in Post-conflict Timor-Leste," talk delivered to School of Humanities Research Seminar, University of New England, Armidale, NSW, Australia, 16 March 2012.

6

Building a Culture of Peace (1): Fundamentals

Your worst enemy cannot harm you as much as your own thoughts, unguarded. But once mastered, no one can help you as much, not even your father or your mother.

—Siddhārtha Gautama (the Buddha)

If we desire peace, we must prepare for peace. The most important thing is to build a culture of peace.

—Anwarul K. Chowdhury, Bangladeshi diplomat,
specializing in issues of development, peace,
and the rights of women and children

Establishing lasting peace is the work of education; all politics can do is keep us out of war.

—Maria Montessori (1870–1952), Italian physician, educator,
and creator of the Montessori teaching method

6.1. FIRST THOUGHTS

We have looked at peace in its own right, as well as the wider sphere of peace, and found that peace is—or should be—of universal concern. But let us ask again, "*Why* should it be?" If we take a somewhat different perspective, we can put the matter this way: There is a self "in itself," which we experience in our more introspective and private moments; but beyond this, the self is a product of relations to the things, places, and people around us. (The last ingredient

207

may not apply for a small number who are hermits, ascetics, or mentally disturbed in certain ways.) It follows that having these relations in balance will instrumentally affect our own stability and prospects for long-term welfare and happiness. Is this a selfish reason for wanting peace? Not really; rather, it reflects a realization that who we are and how we fare in the world is contingent on many factors besides our own egos, ambitions, and deeds; and that self-fulfillment goes hand in hand with promoting the welfare of others. Self-interest is a good thing, and it is not selfishness when intertwined with others' interests.

We have learned in previous chapters that peace, when pursued by nonviolent methods, takes time to evolve—plenty of time. But it is also important to comprehend that many things can and do contribute to building peace, and, in connection with this awareness, that peace comes from many levels of human society and endeavor; Lisa Schirch demonstrates this idea in *The Little Book of Strategic Peacebuilding*, which covers such topics as values and relational skills for peacebuilding, and transforming relationships.[1] It was explained in Chapter 5 that peace is a way of life and a dynamic process. This point is also advanced by Abigail Disney, filmmaker and philanthropist, who draws from her extensive experience the observation that "we need to think of peace as a verb. Peace as something you are *actively* making all the time. . . . So, for me, peace looks like *work*. It looks like the work of our lives. . . . It's a positive, describable state that we can make a conscious effort to build toward, and that needs to be the work of our lives."[2]

Where Does the Impetus for Peace Begin?

It is commonplace to ask whether peace originates from the bottom or the top of the political spectrum, that is, whether it springs from everyday behaviors and grassroots activism, on the one hand, or from powerful leadership and inspiration at the helm of the state, for example. But the fact of the matter is that both are true, in reality and ideally. Peace trickles up, and it trickles down. Not only this, but peace also arises from many strata in between, because it develops from many different sources, wherever they happen to be situated within the power spectrum. No part of society has to wait for any other to act in order to be able to pursue peace itself. And this is a really good phenomenon, since it means that moves toward peace at various levels of human organization can stimulate and interact with each other, producing positive synergistic results (creative transformations). The abolition of legalized slavery and child labor in most countries is such an occurrence, as is the founding of the UN and the liberation of women, where and to the extent that it has happened.

We should take note, too, that because the kind of culture that nourishes peace (to be described below and in the next chapter) emerges slowly, developments typically take place by steps or stages, which need to be appreciated in their own right. Peace scholar Helen Ware and her colleagues observe that "From one perspective it is true that real peace will not be achieved until justice is attained and structural violence ceases. But from the perspective of the poorest individuals and the poorest countries, they might rather be poor in an atmosphere of calm than poor and subject to ravaging bands of government troops or rebels ready and willing to kill, rape and maim them or take their children as soldiers."[3] In mathematics, subtracting a negative number from another negative number yields a sum that is an overall positive gain over the number with which one started. So, too, even negative peace creates a gain, as compared to people's prior condition of deprivation, suffering, oppression, and despair—a state of affairs that is "less bad" and therefore better than before, even if not yet fully good.

6.2. OBSTACLES TO PEACE—AND REASONS FOR HOPE

Homo sapiens is a peculiar species. We perform the greatest acts of compassion and self-sacrifice in relation to our own kind, but we also commit against one another the most degrading and brutal atrocities imaginable. We produce the most sublime creative works and also the trashiest and flimsiest of artifacts. Many of us value, respect, and venerate nature, but many of us—including some of the foregoing group—also treat the environment like an inexhaustible storehouse, and, at the same time, as a refuse dump. We fancy ourselves to be rational beings supreme, yet we often behave irrationally, and even our vaunted rationality, when serving extreme self-interest and shortsighted goals, may be directed toward irrational choices. In many ways, we are a species divided against itself, and, as a result, we have made a world that is divided against itself. The discovery and realization of peace must start from within this zone of contradiction.

Exploring the Zone of Contradiction

On the plane of war and peace, one author states rather starkly that "everyone wants peace but supports war."[4] Is this so? As with most big questions, there is no simple answer. Armed multinational coalitions violently remove certain hated dictators, while others are left alone to carry on coercing, impoverishing, and tormenting their own people. Civil wars and ethnic conflicts grind on, as does the killing, while the world watches, or, as is often the case, looks the other way. The international arms trade continues to grow. Yet although most countries have armies, a few have no standing military forces at all. One small country (Bhutan) even attempts to measure its progress not merely by its Gross Domestic Product but by reference to a "Gross National Happiness Index."[5] Meantime, the knowledge and resources already exist to end human misery and create a world for the betterment of all, but these remain for the most part in the arena of untapped potential.

What, then, is holding peace back? Some would say the answer is to be found in the age-old problems of good versus evil, greed and selfishness. These are here to stay, they would argue, and we have to accept that this is how the fabric of the universe (or at least of *our* universe) is constituted. Well, in a sense, this is right. Unless we are totally lost in untethered optimism, we do have to accept that humans are flawed and that an ideal world will ever elude us. What we do not have to accept, however, is any story that condemns us to self-destruction, or to a weary negativism that judges ideals not worth working toward. We do have it within us to make a difference, to choose how we want to be, as individuals and as collectivities, and to decide what kind of world we will bring into being. *The future always begins now.*

Roadblocks

From the standpoint of peace, there are numerous barriers to progress, a few of which will be identified. But we must move beyond these—just as it was argued in the Introduction that we must get past the myths of war—if we want to gain as clear a view as we can of the possibility for nonviolent and peaceful co-existence with one another and with the planet as a whole. And, while it is important in the short term to be realistic about what can be accomplished on the road to peace, it is equally vital not to be dragged down into pessimism, gloom, and cynicism about the size of the task that is before us, for these are self-reinforcing attitudes that can only be debilitating through negative feedback.

The purpose of this section is not to offer a depressing litany of impediments to peace, but rather to provide a shared awareness of the kinds of issues needing resolution, and a sense of their magnitude. The first and probably most serious of these—because its ripple effects set all the others in motion—is the war/violence mentality. The Introduction and subsequent chapters have devoted a good deal of attention to this subject, but we need to revisit it briefly here. Kent Shifferd gives a detailed analysis of "the war system," in both its international and intra-national dimensions. By his reckoning, in the absence of an international system to truly delegitimize war and enforce commitments to peace, it is no surprise that national sovereignty and self-interest prevail; and when these are fueled by an excessively dim view of human nature, constant planning for the worst-case scenario, and cultures that in many ways promote violence, the result is war-preparedness just waiting to be kindled into armed confrontation. This set of dynamics also closes down other options for dealing with conflicts of interest.[6] Moreover, as Shifferd notes, "in a war system, peace gets narrowly conceived of as security and security gets defined as a military problem. Of course, this perpetuates the entire system. It runs on the basis of self-fulfilling prophecy. That is one of the reasons it looks so inevitable. . . . [N]ational security planners and operatives are always looking for and preparing for the next war and they see it everywhere."[7] There is a fair amount of accuracy in these observations—enough to make them thoroughly unsettling. At the same time, we have to be careful to avoid exaggeration. Military establishments are not necessarily monoliths, comprising people who all think the same way; and one can be sure that their meticulous planning and expertise also often take into account scenarios such as small-scale operations, humanitarian interventions, engineering projects, and assistance in natural disaster zones. And while it would be foolish to underrate the influence of embedded cultural norms that promote war (which remains a formidable problem), the normal state of the greatest number of people is peaceful coexistence, as already explained in Chapter 2.

The Arms Trade

The global arms trade—both legal and illegal—is a very worrying factor in promoting violent solutions to human problems.[8] According to a report by the Stockholm International Peace Research Institute, "The volume of international transfers of major conventional weapons was 17 per cent higher in the period 2008–12 than in 2003–2007. . . . The five biggest suppliers in 2008–12 were the USA, Russia, Germany, France and China. . . . The five biggest recipients were India, China, Pakistan, South Korea and Singapore."[9] Some statistics revealing global weapons expenditures have been summarized in the Introduction (section 3, "The Costs of War"). In addition, there is a very significant black market trade in small arms and light weapons, ammunition, parts, and so forth. According to one source, "The journey of small arms begins from the legal circuit and eventually falls into illegal clutches. There are multiple ways through which the legally originated arms get diverted to illegal spheres. Shipping through dangerous routes, stockpile mismanagement, loots, corruption among officials, warzone seizures are a few of them."[10] The good news is that under the auspices of the United Nations, negotiations on an international Arms Trade Treaty have achieved success. This idea originated in the early twentieth century, and a draft convention was produced in 1925 by the ill-fated League of Nations, but failed to be enacted. More recently, serious and intensive talks have been proceeding since 2006, with the United States throwing its considerable weight behind the initiative in 2009, under the then-new Obama administration. In early April 2013, this treaty—the first of its kind ever adopted in world history—was approved by 154 nations, with a few notable abstentions and negative votes. The Arms Trade Treaty is by no means an agreement to ban such commerce altogether, but rather is meant to "create a universal binding instrument setting out international standards of transparency and control for the import, export and transfer of conventional weapons."[11] The intent of the treaty is to help prevent warlords, dictators, and other human rights abusers from unaccountably obtaining military hardware behind the scenes, but, unfortunately, not to reduce global weapons arsenals.

Nuclear Weapons

Massively built up during the Cold War, nuclear weapons have since been dramatically reduced in number; but they still represent a global menace, especially with the failure of the Nuclear Non-Proliferation Treaty (1970) to achieve its main objective. While this treaty has 189 signatories, including five nations that possess nuclear weapons plus Iran, others that have, or probably have, them are not parties to the agreement (India, Pakistan, North Korea, Israel). The carrot-and-stick approach of this treaty was that nuclear have-nots would agree to abandon the quest for weapons in exchange for nuclear haves' relinquishing them. Obviously, this has not happened. But again, there is hope in President Obama's initiative to abolish nuclear weapons, begun in 2009.[12] Meanwhile, a new START arms control treaty between the United States and Russia has been ratified by the US Senate and went into effect in 2011. This requires both sides to reduce "strategic nuclear armaments to no more than 1,550 deployed warheads; 800 deployed and non-deployed intercontinental ballistic missile (ICBM) launchers, submarine-launched ballistic missile (SLBM) launchers, and heavy bombers equipped for nuclear armaments; and to have reduced their deployed ICBMs, SLBMs, and heavy bombers equipped for nuclear armaments to no more than 700."[13] There still remains the need for an agreement to withdraw and deactivate approximately 2,400 "tactical" nuclear weapons—generally agreed to be strategically useless—that remain stationed in Russia and Western Europe.[14]

One must keep in mind, as John Horgan comments, that "people don't kill simply because they have the means to do so, and if they want to kill each other, they will find a way."[15] Nevertheless, while true, what this perspective misses is that it is more tempting to translate anger into violent attack and easier to kill when there are weapons ready to hand or standing by on hair-trigger alert for launching. This is why control of armaments—and of small arms—is so important to us all.

The American Quest for Global Supremacy

In terms of military issues, mention should be made here as well of two guiding ideas that are helping to shape the military posture of the United States: "full spectrum dominance" and "prompt global strike." Briefly, the first of these identifies "the ability of U.S. forces, operating alone or with allies, to defeat any adversary and control any situation across the range of military operations."[16] The second expression refers to the policy of developing "a new class of weapons capable of reaching any corner of the earth from the United States in under an hour and with such accuracy and force that they would greatly diminish America's reliance on its nuclear arsenal."[17] A glance around the world right now reveals that full spectrum dominance is not proceeding too well, but its intent seems clearly imperialistic in the grandest sense. With respect to the prompt global strike strategy, it is laudable that the United States, as we saw above, envisions a future without reliance on nuclear weapons. But one cannot take much joy in the prospect of the weapons that may replace nuclear weapons, such as drones, now being deployed and refined for many kinds of information gathering and for extrajudicial killings, plus war robots and cyberwarfare programs (see also Chapter 2, section 2.1, "A Future without War?"); nor is the attitude toward war encouraged by these technologies at all realistic, according to some.[18] These strategies apparently enact a plan to control the world and fashion it according to the American image of how things ought to be. It remains to be seen, however, whether this domination approach bears fruit, or passes instead into the realm of fantasy, along with Ronald Reagan's "Star Wars" anti-missile defense project. Americans are rapidly learning the bitter lesson that the costs of empire are enormous, and that the world is changing too rapidly for any single country to play the role of universal policeman.

Terrorism

Another range of issues concerns terrorism and various forms of subversion. It is pretty clear by now that a purely violent anti-terrorism strategy is not going to work (violence begets more of the same), nor is terrorism simply going to disappear on its own, as long as it is perceived by its agents to be an effective means to their ends. Interestingly, a comprehensive global study by the Rand Corporation covering the period 1968–2006 reveals that "most [terrorist] groups ended because of operations by local police or intelligence agencies or because they negotiated a settlement with their governments. Military force was rarely the primary reason a terrorist group ended, and few groups within this time frame achieved victory."[19] What is needed, therefore, is some radical rethinking of world political behavior, as well as of the causes of simmering hatreds and resentments and how to constructively keep them from spinning out of control and defuse them. It requires nations that are not only powerful but also characterized by self-honesty and rational/emotional self-control to take responsibility for the harmful as well as the helpful conduct they engage in, and which is part of their historical record. This rethinking must counter their own tendencies to overreact and resort to military might, so they can address, by means of more constructive interventions, what is at bottom a set of human problems of living.

Terrorists choose to die for a cause rather than to live; but they were not born terrorists. Many studies have shown that young, unemployed, uneducated men who have little opportunity for achievement or self-development are prime candidates for indoctrination and recruitment into criminal or terrorist activity. This is an obvious problem to target with monetary and other resources for maximum universal benefit. Countering terrorism therefore entails "the putting together of a broadly-based program . . . inside the breeding grounds of terrorists" aimed at "the fulfillment of ontological needs."[20] Oliver Ramsbotham, Tom Woodhouse, and Hugh Miall also point out that a comprehensive "policy framework for addressing terrorism" would include the element of persuasion, namely, a "strategy to convince political groups and their constituencies that non-terror tactics are better" for getting the results they seek: "In innumerable postcolonial transitions, designated terrorists have transformed themselves into government officials, if not heads of state. . . ." They observe, too, that "the response to terrorism is one part of a response to a much larger set of global issues, which have to do not only with violence but also with human rights, opportunities for livelihood and free expression, and the life-chances of ordinary people."[21] None of these ideas fosters an attitude of being "soft on terrorism," but rather using sensible judgment, the best psychological and humanitarian insights available to us, and long-range planning in place of knee-jerk employment of bankrupt doctrines that center on problem-solving through domination.

It is an assumption made here, and commonly asserted, that governments are generally unwilling to confront the basic causes of terrorism or admit that they have played a role in its genesis, but also that they actually have constructive options—other than warfare—for containing and de-escalating the violence. The Dalai Lama argues, for instance, that "Nonviolence can contain terrorism in the long run. . . . Retaliatory military action may bring some immediate satisfaction, but it will not ultimately root out the underlying problem of terrorism. Far-sighted measures need to be taken. Force is not the long-term answer to this complicated problem."[22] Even the proponents of violence and advocates of a "war on terror" confirm that there is no "quick fix" available here. Nor are nonviolent strategies capable of yielding an overnight solution.

Senthil Ram and Ralph Summy suggest that there are three ways to "model" terrorism: as military action akin to revolutionary warfare; as criminal behavior; and as a response to "a history of deep-rooted humiliation and conflicts." According to the third option, which they support, "Its prevention is possible only through economic and social development in the repressed and repressing societies that breed terrorists. . . . This approach requires large scale financial commitment from a coalition of developed countries."[23] The process envisioned here obviously is a slow and evolving one, and hence, interim security measures to thwart terrorist attacks, close down terrorist operations, and capture and put on trial those responsible for acts of atrocity will be needed as well, for some time to come. A case in point is Indonesia, the world's most populous Muslim nation, whose policy is to do a careful job of foiling terrorist plots while also acting to moderate extremist tendencies with the cooperation of community organizations.[24]

In the end, a general move toward nonviolent solutions to terrorism will require national governments to exercise restraint and proceed only in line with international law and the principles of morality (which would rule out measures such as imprisonment without charges, "rendition" to secret places of incarceration, torture, targeted assassinations, and other items in the repertoire of violent response). Following the path of wrongdoing is counterproductive in that it encourages further violent response and makes real solutions more elusive.

All of the diagnostic claims and remedial measures outlined above are only part of the story in relation to terrorism, however. Equally important is the entire arena of international relations and diplomacy. Bringing about stable and lasting peace in troubled regions like the Middle East, Pakistan-Afghanistan, and central Africa should have clear priority for international conflict resolution efforts. More sensible and humane ways of resettling immigrants and refugees would also be a key element in addressing terrorism. Indeed, these two issues go hand-in-hand, inasmuch as many refugees are fleeing from highly dangerous conflict zones. Strict control of the arms trade, abolition of nuclear weapons, and general disarmament are additional avenues to reducing international tensions and removing both material and ideological support for terrorist activities, and these efforts must be supported by democratization and enhanced respect for human rights. Improving the living conditions in countries where terrorists are operating and from which refugees are fleeing would of course create the biggest positive gains.

Not too distantly related to terrorism are acts of subversion, whereby agents of one or more governments overthrow or assassinate foreign leaders, carry out extrajudicial killings and torture on foreign soil, and hire operatives to advance the interests of powerful nations and large corporations in ways that are both marginally legal (or illegal) and immoral. In relation to the matter raised last, a great deal of interest and controversy surrounded the publication of books like James Henry's *The Blood Bankers*, John Perkins' *Confessions of an Economic Hit Man*, and Richard Peet's *Unholy Trinity*.[25] The argument of these books is that a massive behind-the-scenes world economy exists, dedicated to promoting and perpetuating debt in developing nations, using foreign aid as a tool primarily for the enrichment of large corporations and banks, the advancement of political domination, money laundering, tax evasion, and so forth. These sorts of exposés are relevant to discussion of the prospects for world peace because they help explain (and give voice to) animosities that now exist toward economically advanced nations, and which fan the flames of terrorism and inspire vengeance toward Western countries and their citizens.

Economic Instability and Inequality

The global economy has suffered severe setbacks over the past few years, affecting nearly everyone. As one observer states, this crisis "first erupted in the banking system . . . and has since wreaked havoc on public finances, jobs, services and living standards throughout the western world. . . . [T]he Eurozone breakdown is also the product of a generation of EU treaty-enforced privatization, market deregulation and corporate liberalisation that paved the way for the crisis across Europe, including in Britain."[26] Most of us are mere onlookers at this spectacle, and many are hurting badly from this colossal failure of our major institutions. What everyone needs is not to have their opportunities undermined by scarcity or other material impediments. Currently, and for many reasons, this condition is not being met for a large number of people worldwide.

Finally, the growth of the world's population, projected to reach about 9.6 billion by mid-century, is bound to aggravate many problems that stand in the way of peace: the disparity between rich and poor,[27] food shortages, water shortages, competition for these and various other resources, housing issues, refugee and human-rights issues, environmental devastation, and climate change. The best outcome that can reasonably be anticipated in relation to all of these challenges is that population levels will stabilize and international agreements and forms of aid will keep pace with demographic realities in some measure.

A spin-off effect of these global problems is the increase in "home-grown" acts of terrorism, including domestic ideologically inspired and religiously motivated mass murders now plaguing various nations. This form of violent disruption, with its own complexities, is not easily remedied by any simple measures, and threatens to become worse over time until it becomes more thoroughly understood and its root causes addressed.

Taking Charge and Finding Solutions

Large-scale problems and trends such as those just reviewed make people feel depressed, disempowered, and hopeless. After all, what can one individual do to stop or reverse some of the most formative global events? Quite a bit, as it turns out, so take heart. To begin with, every vote, every presence at a public demonstration, every letter to an elected representative, every petition signed, every letter to an editor, every online posting, every monetary donation to a worthwhile cause counts for something and can make a difference. "Passion for peace," Stuart Rees says, "presupposes that almost anyone can make a contribution towards a long-term goal and experience a small victory in a short-term cause."[28] The big proviso here, of course, is that discouragement and fatalistic negativity must be kept at bay. This much is perhaps obvious by now; but what is less so is that the past few decades have seen a surge in the growth of nongovernmental organizations (NGOs), peace research groups, peace studies programs at universities, and peace action groups with which one can ally oneself. A few prominent examples of peace-promoting NGOs are: Citizens for Global Solutions, Metta Center for Nonviolence, Canadian Voice of Women for Peace, Search for Common Ground, Project Ploughshares, Common Dreams, War Resisters League, Friends Committee on National Legislation, Physicians for Social Responsibility, Veterans for Peace, PeaceEarth, US Peace Memorial, and Avaaz.org. According to one source, there are 400 peace studies programs worldwide.[29] Another source lists 172 conflict and peace studies graduate programs in the US alone.[30] There are also a number of educational and research institutes devoted completely to training in peace issues and conflict resolution. The University of Peace, based in Costa Rica, was established by the United Nations in 1980. Many other related centers could be mentioned, such as the National Peace Academy in Vermont, US; the Pearson Peacekeeping Centre based in Ottawa, Canada; the Peace Research Institute Oslo; the Stockholm International Peace Research Institute; the Institute for Peace Research and Security Policy at the University of Hamburg; the Centre for Conflict Resolution at the University of Bradford, UK; the Toda Institute for Global Peace and Policy Research in Tokyo, and the West Africa Network for Peacebuilding based in Accra, Ghana. Focusing on the last of these for a moment as an example of what is going on in this area, WANEP has networks in fifteen African countries, a partnership with the Economic Community of West African States and with other peace-building organizations. In addition to education and training, its other endeavors include fostering preventive measures in crisis situations, such as helping maintain peace and procedure in Liberian elections, and establishing dialogue and reconciliation in conflict zones, like the Ivory Coast (both in 2011).[31]

An inventory, compiled by the author, of peace organizations and training programs in Washington, DC and area alone netted thirty-eight listings. One of these, the United States Institute of Peace, was actually founded in 1984 by the US Congress, and originally funded by it. (The bill was signed into law by President Ronald Reagan.) The Institute has recently opened new headquarters on the National Mall near the Lincoln Memorial, at a spot where George Washington reportedly envisioned that a "proper peace establishment" should be built. Although the House of Representatives voted in 2011 to terminate all federal funding for the USIP, this was restored in 2012.[32]

The Bigger Picture

These rich and diverse activities demonstrate that there is considerable worldwide interest in promoting ideas about peace and in trying to do something to make peace a reality locally, regionally, and globally. We cannot (nor should we) dictate to other countries and societies what they ought to do in the interest of peace, or how they ought to solve their own problems. But we can do what is best for ourselves: become a peaceful society; improve our skills of persuasion and negotiation in order to reach common understanding and cooperative relationships with a wider group of nations. By doing these things, we can offer a model for the rest of the world to learn from. To the extent that we are "part of the problem" as others perceive it, we can clean our own house so that this ceases to be the case—so that we become a helping hand rather than a force whose motives are always under suspicion, or whose actions inspire apprehension and reactive belligerence. Elise Boulding correctly observes that "One of the greatest dangers of our time is despair, and feelings of helplessness in the face of macro-level social forces."[33] But the vital human response to this predicament is to rebel against it and take it on in spite of the odds. A crucial step in this process is to analyze the parts of the problem and scale them down to manageable targets for action. This insight is expressed in the well-known saying "Think globally, act locally." Yet we need to do more than this: We need to think both globally *and* locally, act locally, and do whatever we can to promote constructive global solutions that are beyond our own limited means to put into effect. The remainder of the chapter will try to capture this spirit as it examines ways of building peace.

6.3. WHAT IS A CULTURE OF PEACE?

Perhaps it will come as a surprise to many that the United Nations sponsored an "International Decade for a Culture of Peace and Non-violence for the Children of the World" in the years 2001–10.[34] This project was the culmination and consolidation of much work and complex debate among member nations that began in 1995. In 1999, a "Declaration and Programme of Action on a Culture of Peace" was adopted by the General Assembly. Seventy-five million people across the world signed a manifesto in 2000 "promising to work for a culture of peace in their daily lives." In the official UN document, "Eight programme areas for a culture of peace [were] identified" as focal points for action: "*Culture of Peace through Education; Sustainable Economic and Social Development; Respect for all Human Rights; Equality between Women and Men; Democratic Participation; Understanding, Tolerance and Solidarity; Participatory Communication and Free Flow of Information and Knowledge;* and *International Peace and Security.*" These indices describe what would be necessary to bring about a culture of peace and, in effect, what the framework of such a culture would look like. It would have an educational system designed to promote peace; embed certain specified values; enhance the economic improvement of people's lives; respect environmental limits; and be dedicated to disarmament processes. While there are other, more far-reaching and inclusive definitions of a culture of peace,[35] and a somewhat different range of its many aspects will be considered in the following sections of this chapter, the UN's approach should be accepted as a working statement of principles and objectives, considering its wide international endorsement. In general, it would seem clear that a culture of peace is one in which individual human beings have the freedom and opportunity to achieve a fulfilling existence for themselves, and to live in harmony with one another and with their natural

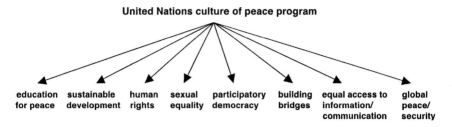

Figure 6.1 United Nations culture of peace program

surroundings. This entails their basic needs being met, so that they can go on to achieve self-realization. Robert Burrowes points out that that the expression of needs is shaped by one's society and is therefore not the same everywhere; but he characterizes as "cooperative security" that condition in which human needs are satisfied for all in a sustainable way.[36]

And how is the world responding to the program of action outlined by the UN? According to a 2010 *Report on the Decade for a Culture of Peace* compiled by a group of global volunteers from civil society,

> The global movement for a culture of peace is advancing. . . . This is the conclusion of most organizations from around the world. . . . It is documented by over 5,000 pages of information, both text and photographs, submitted before 15 May 2010 by 1,054 organizations from over 100 countries. . . . This information is the tip of an even larger iceberg, as indicated by the many partnerships listed by participating organizations. They number in the many thousands, corresponding to the call for partnerships for a culture of peace in the Programme of Action on a Culture of Peace.[37]

As might be expected, the two primary limitations on progress noted by respondents from all parts of the world are: lack of funding to promote peace and media inattention. This strongly underlines the points made previously in this book about the need to put resources into peace work rather than war work, shift away from the sensationalism about violence and the negativism that skew today's media perceptions of what is most newsworthy or of greatest entertainment value, and move toward advances of real positive and enduring significance.

To illustrate, a group of scientists, asserting the premise that "*seeing* [the world] differently results in *acting* differently," demonstrates in a recent paper "the possibility that severe personal and social dysfunctions, which have defied solution for decades, can sometimes be relieved by interventions [for example, therapies or reward systems] that require just a handful of hours. . . ." Arguing for "a science of intentional change centered on evolution [that] can be applied to any real-world behavioral or cultural issue," they provide case studies where "conditions that favored the selection of behaviors or cultural practices that were desired by individuals and communities," rather than forced upon them, were effective instruments of change.[38] This nascent approach unifies the ideas presented in Chapters 2 and 4, respectively, that having and maintaining a culture of peace requires the cultivation of peaceful values, and that the expression or inhibition of violent and aggressive behaviors is to a large measure culturally determined. It follows that if a more peaceful world is what we want, then there are scientifically grounded methods for helping to bring it about. Peaceful societies, such as those discussed in Chapter 2, have ingeniously worked out and implemented these principles themselves, by trial and error and by design.

6.4. WOMEN AND PEACE

As we saw in the previous section, respect for human rights and sexual equality are keystones of peace. These ideas very clearly place women at the focal point of discussion. Women have always been in the forefront of antiwar and peace movements, and have written some of the best books and essays about peace. Not all women are actively opposed to war, however, or would identify themselves as pacifists. And there are some women for whom equality in the workplace means being able to assume frontline combat roles in wartime, alongside men. Nor are all women feminists. Nevertheless, in recent decades, feminist scholarship across many disciplines has significantly altered the way in which topics such as peace are thought about. Three features of this transformation merit special mention.

First, feminists (and others who are concerned with developing a more comprehensive, global outlook on human affairs) have shown—what is arguably obvious and need not be proved—that situations affecting the interests of women as human beings (including peace) are not merely "women's issues" but ones that have an impact on everyone, and therefore ought to concern everyone. This broadening of concern applies not just to peace, but also to reproductive choices, access to adequate childcare, equality in the workplace, and a range of other matters. The reason it is obvious that these issues are of universal importance is, to begin with, that if we really believe in equality, then opportunities have to be maximized: Everyone should have fair access to the best things that life can offer, regardless of gender and other basic differences, and conditions of access need to be assured. On a more pragmatic level, if the lives of women, who constitute half of humanity, are impoverished and endangered, then the quality of life for everyone is bound to suffer. Therefore, when women gain control over their own lives, personal safety and security, a better standard of living, and significant influence in social and political decision-making, everyone benefits. (See also Chapter 7, section 7.3, "Education for Peace").

Second, feminist analyses have demonstrated the interconnection between different kinds of oppression, domination, and exploitation—for example, those of women, visible minorities, the poor and disadvantaged, nonhuman animals, and the environment generally. This territory has also been explored by Marxists, social ecologists, Green theorists, and the environmental justice movement, some representatives of which are feminists and some not. But what is unique to feminists is the argument that many forms of discrimination derive from and are supported by distinctions of gender. That is, the interconnections between these forms of discrimination are shaped by a hierarchical mindset in which not just anthropocentric (human-centered) but also androcentric (male-centered) values prevail; these values are instrumental to the construction of a certain outlook on the world and determine the character of relationships between the beings that exist in the world. The outlook in question has commonly been designated as "patriarchal," meaning that human social arrangements and our relationship with nature are structured to promote and ensure male supremacy. A more nuanced view of patriarchy suggests that it is "the institutionalized system of male dominance in which (1) all women are subordinated *and* (2) a small elite of men further subordinate other men and appropriate for themselves a vastly disproportionate share of power and wealth."[39] The implication of this definition is that within such a social structure, men are considered (by men, of course, since they for the most part control the dominant discourse about the world and events happening in it) to be more real, valuable, perfect (or at least perfectible), and deserving of power than women or any nonhumans ever could be. One can readily see how a perspective of this kind generates sexism, speciesism, warism, and other forms of the self-aggrandizing quest for supremacy. However, we live in a fluid world, a world that is in flux, and many old ideas are giving way under the challenge to patriarchal thinking that feminism represents. Patriarchal norms have been deconstructed by careful conceptual, empirical, and other modes of analysis, with the result that voices previously silenced can now be heard, and values that traditionally went uncontested are now being undermined and rendered obsolete. This dynamic, among other things, opens up the opportunity for women to explore new identities and achieve social and political affirmation and influence, and for peace to be reexamined as a way of life that is desirable for a whole variety of reasons, and is therefore worthy of our dedication.

Third, feminist writing has forced people to confront and give more urgent attention to specific problems such as rape, relationship violence, genital mutilation, access to birth control and safe abortion, and lack of basic freedoms for women in numerous societies. While such issues are far from being resolved, they are on the national and international agenda as items that now need to be seriously discussed and practically addressed in an ongoing manner.[40]

Feminism has historically underlined the fact that war has particularly devastating effects on women, as primary homemakers, mothers, and caregivers— in short, as those who are responsible for the continuation of society. It has also highlighted the violence in warfare that is directed against noncombatant women (and children). In more recent times, feminist thinkers have sought to "demonstrate the continuity between male violence toward women in the home or in the streets, and war. . . . Feminists argued that both were expressions of the same mentality of patriarchy."[41] And a good deal of energy has subsequently gone into seeking ways to empower women and to construct outlooks that promote nonviolent solutions to human problems rather than violent ones. A representative manifesto of this campaign states that "Feminism fundamentally rejects the power principle of domination and subjugation. . . . [and] must question social structures based on this principle at every level, from the competition of men and women in personal relationships to the competition of the nations of the globe. . . . We seek an alternative . . . principle of empowerment in community rather than power over and disabling of others. Such enabling in community is based on a recognition of . . . fundamental interconnectedness. . . . Nobody wins unless all win."[42] If the force of this perspective is felt, then it is vital for male as well as female sex roles to change, as indeed they have been doing. Equally vital is the reduction of violence in personal and social contexts (see Chapter 4). A culture of peace depends on these things.

6.5. THINKING CREATIVELY ABOUT ALTERNATIVES

A Rapidly Changing World

Everyone understands from his or her own experience, as well as from a variety of external sources, that we live in a time of rapid change. Even the rate of change is accelerating, as can be discerned from the example of information technology alone. A study released in 2011 by the International Data Corporation states that "The world's information is doubling every two years. . . . By 2020 the world will generate 50 times the amount of information [compared to 2010] and 75 times the number of 'information containers' [files]."[43]

This alone suggests that all over the world, people (as well as governments and other institutions) have a huge task ahead of them to cope with all this change and derive benefits from it. A group of specialists in conflict resolution looks even further into our shared predicament, observing that "All over the world, societies are facing stresses from population growth, structural change in the world economy, migration into cities, environmental degradation and rapid social change. Societies with institutions, rules or norms for managing conflict and well-established traditions of governance are generally better able to accommodate peacefully to change; those with weaker governance, fragile social bonds and little consensus on values are more likely to buckle."[44] What all of this shows is that a great deal of innovative thinking is urgently required about how to handle these transformative changes safely and most advantageously; also needed are international cooperation and mutual sharing of many different kinds of possible solutions and amelioration efforts. This involves a willingness on the part of politicians to become cooperative and sharing, to move beyond posturing, scare-mongering, and intransigence in order to serve the broader interests they were elected to serve. Chaotic, events, such as widespread social upheavals and consequent disruption of people's individual lives, without moderation, sow the seeds for violent backlashes and broader forms of armed conflict.

Addressing Human Needs

Many human needs call for international attention so that crisis situations can be mitigated or averted. To begin with, there is the priority matter of limited access to the basic necessities of life, such as food, clean water, and shelter. The UN Millennium Development Goals program (see Chapter 2, section 2.1, "A Future without War?") has been a catalyst for improvements in these and other problem areas, and will continue to serve this function. But, in addition, there are people's aspirational goals (some would call them rights) for a decent quality of life and standard of living. These are in fact defined as rights in the UN's foundational document, the Universal Declaration of Human Rights (Articles 22–28).[45] (See Chapter 7, section 7.1, "Respect for Differences and Human Rights.") As increasingly global and globally aware citizens, we must take seriously the prescriptions for conduct framed by the UDHR, as well as the philanthropic duties they obviously devolve on us, both individually and collectively.

Humans are all in the same boat together, and mutually dependent, within a global economy, for their material wealth, which in turn funds public services and all other amenities that enhance life. The age is past when certain nations could simply exploit other ones for their own benefit without compunction, and ever-fewer less-developed countries are willing to tolerate being short-changed in this way and dictated to politically. In a similar manner, people who belong to traditionally exploited classes or groups are also demanding their rights and opportunities for fulfillment. Levels of economic inequality are growing within many nations, even as overall global inequality is gradually de-creasing, and there is no clear consensus among experts on how (or whether) to address income disparity and ease the plight of the poor.[46] Commitment to the belief that poverty can be abolished, and that everyone has a legitimate claim to health and welfare, is a powerful motivator for seeking change. There-fore, solutions clearly must be found if inequality is to be prevented from be-coming a permanent structural feature of societies, and general trends toward a better, more peaceful world are to succeed in being established.

It can be argued that there is an inverse correlation between betterment of the human condition and global military expenditures. And, if that is so, then a worthwhile objective is to not only reduce these expenditures significantly, but also to eliminate the conditions that result in the perceived need to possess huge arsenals of armaments. The Introduction (section 3, "The Costs of War") considered the dependency of some modern industrial economies on milita-rization and the sacrifices to social welfare that this entails. And above in this chapter (section 6.2, "Obstacles to Peace—and Reasons for Hope"), we looked at the international arms trade. The trends marked out in these discussions may suggest to those with vested interests and impartial observers alike that there is no other way to conduct our business and keep our industries profitable. But if world peace is ever to happen, then one must be found. Economies that thrive on weapons production and export sales cannot truly function in the interest of world peace, and furthermore, "Armaments production deprives the economy of resources and diverts these to fabricate tools of destruction,"[47] as we have already seen. In addition, as a recent study shows, "military spending is a weak job engine compared to other investments."[48] For these reasons, it is contrary to the welfare of citizens and of the global community that a significant amount of industry should remain indefinitely locked into the same patterns of military resource consumption, research, manufacturing, and distribution.

Arms Conversion

One interesting idea that has been around for several decades—a mod-ern variation of "beating swords into plowshares and spears into pruning hooks"[49]—concerns the conversion of military production and research to civilian endeavors (often called *economic conversion* or *arms conversion*). The central notion is easy to grasp, even though the problems needing to be solved along the way are formidable. Military contractors would change to providing goods for the consumer market or some other specialized form of output. Workers would retrain to qualify for participation in the new industrial initiatives. Those who have studied the matter point out that to avoid "causing social and economic dislocation requires a planned process of transferring resources from military to civilian purposes."[50] Such changeovers would ideally fill economic niches where the need is greatest, and where attractive opportunities exist for innovation and investment. Of course, part of the planning process would feature government initiatives and partnerships to help create these opportunities. Some exemplary areas of interest might be: health care technology, housing, renewable energy, workplace modernization and safety improvements, and infrastructure improvements (including school rebuilding, overhaul of highways and bridges, mass urban and high-speed intercity transit systems, water recycling, and waste management).[51]

Could this miracle really take place? In 1970, Seymour Melman, an early theorist of conversion, commented that:

> The problem of conversion from military to civilian work is fundamentally different now from the problem that existed after World War II. At that time, the issue was reconversion; the firms could and did go back to doing the work they had been involved in before the war. They could literally draw the old sets of blueprints and tools from the shelf and go to work on the old products. At the present time, the bulk of military production is concentrated in industries, firms, or plants that have been specialized for this work, and frequently have no prior history of civilian work.[52]

The degree to which this description applies today is open to debate. After the Vietnam War, when US military expenditures were scaled down, arms producers responded by "diversifying," that is, buying into (or buying up) nonmilitary companies; but it has been claimed that this is not in itself a step toward conversion and arguably offers fewer benefits for society as a whole.[53] Another kind of diversification involves producing both civilian and military goods of a particular type (for instance, both armored personnel carriers and cars and trucks) as some corporations do today. However, for conversion to become a truly attractive alternative requires the existence of incentives for companies to depart from the status quo and make a genuine transition to manufacturing for the consumer market. "With such a strategy in place, reversing the arms buildup becomes a social and economic opportunity, not a penalty," writes Michael Renner, a senior researcher with the Worldwatch In-stitute.[54] As things currently stand, there is little to entice firms into deviating from military production, which has top governmental priority, conveys po-litical power to producers, and is highly profitable. Although some countries (notably Japan and Germany, for historic reasons) have made successful con-versions, in the United States and United Kingdom, the few companies that have experimented with conversion on their own have met with unhappy results.[55] In some other arms-producing economies, for example, those of France, Israel, Saudi Arabia, and North Korea—each for different reasons—the idea of conversion would be a nonstarter under present circumstances.

But grassroots pressure to examine economic conversion realistically and openly from a twenty-first-century perspective might yet come from a coali-tion of peace groups, church groups, labor alliances, and NGOs. Many people around the world were disappointed when the so-called "peace dividend"—reduction in military expenditures following the end of the Cold War—failed to translate into an ongoing disarmament and economic renewal process. But now, in an era in which military budgets in some countries (notably the United States) are being cut back of necessity, a combination of interests could conceivably open up a fresh dialogue about conversion. And it is important to note that, although we have been considering economic conversion as a creative alternative to conventional thinking, it clearly would have to be an es-sential ingredient of a large-scale world peace system, as previously noted. The Bonn International Center for Conversion supports this viewpoint by stress-ing that "the attainment of the MDGs [Millennium Development Goals, dis-cussed above in this section and in Chapter 2, section 2.1, "A Future without War?"] will certainly be influenced by, if not actually depend on, progress in strengthening security, particularly through conflict prevention and conflict resolution. . . . [C]onversion-related policies have a key supportive role to play in this historic endeavor. . . ."[56]

Closely related to the idea of conversion is that of a "Global Demilitariza-tion Fund." First proposed by Costa-Rican president and Nobel Prize winner Oscar Arias Sánchez in the 1990s, and as refined by Renner, the suggestion is that this fund would comprise three initiatives: a "restitution account" to help impoverished nations recover from the effects of war; a "transformation account" to assist in disarmament and economic conversion; and a "peace-building account" to foster conflict management, fair elections, and other di-mensions of stabilization. The long-term financial health of such a fund would eventually become a matter for the UN to ensure by building contributions into the regular cost of membership.[57]

Other Innovative Approaches to Promoting Peace

Another interesting and promising kind of "conversion"—one that is actually occurring worldwide—is the creation of new economies. The field of activity known as "microfinance," developed by 2006 Nobel Peace Prize winner Mohammad Yunus, has received wide exposure in the media. This is the lending of small amounts of money to people with low-incomes who do not qualify for normal banking services, in order that they can invest in a new business initiative. The International Finance Corporation, a branch of the World Bank, has made 130 million loans of this type, and other organizations (NGOs) also have programs of this type, to which anyone can contribute support.[58] In the United States, an "alternative economy" is rapidly growing in the wake of big bank failures and the "Occupy" movement. "The broad goal is democratized ownership of the economy," with community development and ecological sustainability being on the agenda as well, according to economics professor Gar Alperovitz. "Thousands of real world projects—from solar-powered businesses to worker-owned cooperatives and state-owned banks—are underway across the country."[59] Meanwhile, in the EU, schemes that utilize "social money or alternative currency" are expanding in several countries in response to financial austerity and high unemployment. Bearing resemblance to systems of bartering, these schemes feature credits that can be exchanged instead of cash for goods and services.[60] "Bitcoin" digital currency is a growing economic force in a number of countries around the world.[61] It is too early to tell what size of impact these new economies will have, but it can be argued that any shift toward greater participatory democracy and sustainability of livelihood represents a welfare gain for average people and therefore constitutes a contribution to peace.

In a different sort of initiative begun in 1999, filmmaker Jeremy Gilley defied odds by persuading world leaders, including former UN Secretary General Kofi Annan, UK Minister of State for Foreign Affairs John Battle, and UN High Commissioner for Human Rights Mary Robinson, to help change the UN's annual and movable day of peace observance (established in 1981) to a fixed date. This goal was achieved in 2001, when a unanimously adopted General Assembly resolution set the International Day of Peace as 21 September. In an energetic global campaign, assisted and popularized by eminent figures such as actors Angelina Jolie and Jude Law, and singer Annie Lennox, Gilley's movement Peace One Day then succeeded in getting many governments, organizations, and even combatant factions in the world's most dangerous wars to set targets for this special day—a ceasefire, a repatriation, allowing supplies and medical aid to reach the needy, vaccination of children against polio, as well as peaceful cooperative activities of many other sorts. Peace One Day now has some important international corporate sponsors and runs continuously updated online blogs and reports to describe current initiatives and forthcoming events.[62]

Mention must also be made of proposals that address specific political issues where the balance between war and peace is precarious. An example comes from *Peace First: A New Model to End* War, by Uri Savir.[63] Savir is a significant figure in contemporary peace negotiation and conflict resolution, having been Israel's chief representative during meetings that generated the Oslo Accords in the 1990s. He has also founded the Peres Center for Peace and the Glocal Forum ("global" + "local"), which speaks to his ongoing commitment to peace. Savir's belief is that peace comes first, then democracy, rather than the reverse. (Peace plants the seeds of openness, tolerance, and pluralism—essentials for the flourishing of democracy.) In line with this view, his strategy—part common sense, part lessons gleaned from experience—is to build peace from the bottom up as much as (or more than) from the top down. As Savir notes, humans' desire to survive "must be translated into the most basic right, to live and let live,"[64] and many concrete actions can be seen to flow from this premise. He also holds that "Too often, peacemakers treat security as a means to achieve peace, but it should be the other way around."[65] (Compare the "Home Truths" in section 5 of the Introduction to this book.) Savir's conception of peacebuilding after conflict embraces economic stimulus projects, the promotion of tourism, projects in technology and the arts, and youth activities such as sports. There are many opportunities here for cross-border and inter-group cooperation and interaction, and for international funding and NGO involvement. He also holds that creative diplomacy is the process of bringing about win-win scenarios. These are just a few of the positive attributes of Savir's approach; but a truly eye- (and mind-) opening idea of his is to create a joint-administrative solution to the problem of Jerusalem—one that makes it the capital of both Israel and Palestine, and also includes a UN declaration of the city as "the world capital of peace."[66] While this may seem to some an absurd and utopian scheme, Savir says it has already received "encouraging reactions" from both Israeli and Palestinian leaders. A related proposal envisions the Golan Heights as "a special demilitarized zone for eco- and health tourism," to be overseen by a new international organization, the "Mediterranean Partnership for Peace."[67]

Currently, Israel is busy completing its own version of the Great Wall of China, isolating itself from surrounding hostile lands by an impenetrable barrier,[68] and supplementing this with an overhead shield of missiles that calculate the path of incoming rockets and destroy them mid-air.[69] Conflict between Israel and the Palestinians has never seemed more intractable. Iran seems in the eyes of many to be on the verge of obtaining nuclear armaments. (See Chapter 3, section 3.4, "'Last Resort' and the Case of Iran.") Most of the remaining states of the Middle East are engulfed in political chaos of one degree or another. This scenario makes Savir's plan look very remote indeed. And yet his is exactly the kind of creative breakthrough thinking the world needs. *Peace of some sort must come one day. That is the constant hope; but it is also the lesson of history.* Good sense and the realization that endless hostile conflict is a huge drain on valuable resources eventually win out over petty hatreds and vendetta mentalities. When this point comes (and assuming a nuclear holocaust can be avoided), a fund of fresh insights for establishing a lasting peace will be crucial.

All of these national and international peace initiatives could be advanced by the formation in all countries of federal Departments or Ministries of Peace, with cabinet status. After World War II, a number of nations changed their Departments of War into the more euphemistic Departments of Defense, but globally, the idea of Departments of Peace has thus far gained very little traction, politically speaking. Costa Rica, Nepal, and the Solomon Islands, however, each have one; and there are active campaigns to promote the idea in the United States, Canada, the United Kingdom, Australia, Israel, Denmark, Ghana, Japan, and many other nations.[70] A bill to establish a Department of Peacebuilding came before the US House of Representatives in 2013.[71] Costa Rica, which is in the vanguard of the world peace movement, hosted a Global Alliance Summit for Ministries and Departments of Peace in 2009, which was attended by representatives from thirty-five countries.

Other innovative ideas help shape activities at the local and grassroots level, but in a different way. A quite novel project of this kind is the campaign known as "Peace Happens," first begun in 2011 in the US city of Charleston, South Carolina. A city-based branch of Peace One Day (described above) called for efforts to "do something for peace" during a "peace week" in September (again centering on the UN-declared International Day of Peace). In a locale where the American Civil War started and that is not known for promoting peace or for countercultural initiatives, more than eighty groups nonetheless participated. A large-scale effort was undertaken to raise awareness, with the focal question being: "Who are you in relationship to this planet, what are you good at, and how can you use those gifts to give back to the whole of life?" Peace signs appeared in busy locations; jazz musicians played peace songs; schoolchildren planted peace poles; peace films were featured in one cinema; entire schools tried to integrate tolerance and cooperation into their teaching and learning experiences across the disciplines; businesses participated in symbolic ways. A campaign organizer, Reba Parker, sums up the event this way: "Can actions of real peace become the new norm, the thing to do, the default position, and hence a part of our everyday lives? . . . With a reimagining and re-messaging that draws attention and awareness, action and change are soon to follow."[72] Many other initiatives of a similar kind are presented by Margaret Wheatley and Deborah Frieze in their book *Walk Out Walk On: A Learning Journey into Communities Daring to Live the Future Now.*[73]

In October 2012, seventy US cities (and many elsewhere in the world) observed "Keep Space for Peace Week," a collection of local events and actions aimed at putting a stop to the advancing militarization of outer space.[74]

Another interesting grassroots civic campaign is the Mayors for Peace movement, which now boasts more than 5,000 members in 153 countries and regions. This organization aims at consciousness-raising about peace issues and solving local problems with the aid of shared helpful information.[75] This is the largest and fastest-growing local government linkage in the world.

What we see here are examples of mobilization for peace. It is clear that people are willing and eager to join in on such a process of exploring what peace might mean. Just as obvious is the fact that ventures of this sort can only continue to be energized and to flourish if there are some tangible benefits to reward the effort put in. These would include things like expanding alliances with campaigns in different cities, election of peace candidates to various levels of government, widespread publicity, local government subsidies, and permanent changes to the curriculum and pedagogical methods in local schools. But this challenge notwithstanding, we can see that promoting peace, thinking about peace as the norm, and doing something to establish it as such, are matters where the imagination is free to creatively discover and nourish a limitless range of initiatives and opportunities. We may say, then (paraphrasing a famous remark about politics[76]) that peace is the art of the possible. And indeed, if peace is possible, it must be one of the possibilities that comprise the "art" of politics. Most importantly, perhaps, this slogan implies that *concern for peace must be forward-directed*; for the future is the domain of imaginative possibility.

These peace-promoting activities would be enormously advanced by encouragement from politicians at higher levels of government and by other leaders. If anything like the amount of attention that is lavished on war activities and ceremonial observances were devoted to the work of peace and its celebration, the sky would be the limit in terms of what average citizens, working together, could achieve. Walter Russell Mead pronounces on "the embarrassing lack of a detectable connection between the work of peace activists and actual peace."[77] But, as we have seen, there are innumerable avenues to peace that make (and can make) an incremental contribution to overall peace. These need encouragement and support in order to be able to flourish enough to influence the larger picture, and such creative inputs will also grow and have a greater impact as they receive positive feedback and reinforcement from power structures that are open to transformation, or else are forced to transform themselves. It is difficult, in any case, to see where else change is likely to begin.

6.6. EVERYDAY PEACEFUL CONDUCT
AND ALTERNATIVES TO VIOLENCE

Violence is all-too-often seen as the means of settling conflicts and/or of exerting power and control over others (as noted in Chapter 4). There are some people who do not seem to understand any other way of settling disputes, or else are particularly prone to choosing violence for this purpose, as well as to satisfy the need for self-affirmation and recognition. But in order to instantiate a culture of peace within a given society, different approaches have to be cultivated as well as different personality-formations. This problem must be tackled at all levels: domestic violence against women, children, and men; bullying and harassment in schools and the workplace; cyberbullying; street violence; structural or institutionalized violence of all kinds; and so forth. Even the language we use—which often relies on war metaphors and allusions to killing—needs careful scrutiny here (see Introduction, section 1, "The Obstacle of War."). The performance of the state and of its leaders, as well as of prominent figures who are role models and image-makers are cultural linchpins that profoundly influence people from the top down. But equally important—or even more so—are the everyday behaviors of ordinary individuals, who shape society from the bottom up.

A good deal has already been said on this topic in Chapter 2 (section 2.6, "Peace in Everyday Life"). But it is worth expanding upon here. We discovered in Chapter 5 that peace is a multidimensional concept, which reflects not only the many organizational strata of human life where it plays a significant part, but also the fact that nonviolence and peace evolve throughout the range of our beliefs and self-expressive behaviors. The slogans "Peace begins with me" and "Peace begins at home" have very concrete meanings. Implicated here are how we speak to one another, resolve minor and more serious problems between ourselves, respond to others who are either different from us, in need, or unkind or thoughtless toward us; how we act in the schoolyard, in line at the supermarket, in corporate boardrooms, on the subway, when stuck in crowded urban traffic or cut off on the highway; and how we relate as friends, lovers, parents, co-workers, family members, acquaintances, strangers, and in the rest of our roles. Much attention has been devoted just to the issue of the choice and power of words and how they can shape either a violent or a nonviolent outlook, thwart or encourage self-confidence, serve as a form of intimidation or a defense against it, create or challenge sexual stereotypes, and the like.[78] In the same gentle, graceful manner with which he crafts the characters of his *No. 1 Ladies' Detective Agency* novels, Alexander McCall Smith states, "I think that manners and civility and the small transactions of life are the building blocks of the greater picture."[79] Sensibilities such as these need to be universally cultivated. But most importantly, a thoughtful and sensitive approach to others and a vigilant yet tolerant approach to oneself will enable greater mutual respect and personal accomplishment.

It is equally important, when considering everyday interactions between people to speak to the issue of alternatives to violence. As noted in the Introduction (section 2, "War Myths"), William James heralded the need for a "moral equivalent to war" a century ago. Psychologists who study the conditions of peace generally agree that there is such a need, by whatever label one chooses to call it. But how this need can best be satisfied is a matter of ongoing investigation. A crucial point, though, is that activities many commonly suppose to be safer outlets for violent aggression (such as certain spectator sports or hunting) really are not safer, properly speaking. As anthropologist Ashley Montagu states, "the popular 'letting off steam' conception of human aggression . . . has no counterpart in the nervous system of any known organism. . . . The evidence we have overwhelmingly shows that the [overt] expression [of aggressiveness] contributes not to its reduction but to its reinforcement."[80] To elaborate, there are alternative ways of venting emotion-driven violent aggression other than war, but (perhaps contrary to expectation, and disappointingly) they fall short of contributing to peacefulness in society. Conflict resolution specialist Mary E. Clark summarizes the essence of what research has shown in relation to this topic as follows:

> Violent body-contact sports, such as boxing and football, although not a form of communication in themselves (i.e. the rivals are not communicating anger or disappointment or fear or resentment of one another as exists in true aggression), are modeling, in play, such aggressive acts. They, too, despite all the touting of sportsmanship, are teaching that violent aggression, if carried out by rules, is acceptable. It leads to a kind of moral absurdity embodied in the rules of war. This caveat about the symbolic meaning gleaned from certain violent sports can also be applied to those video games and fantasy television dramas that employ physical violence as [the] solution to human conflict.[81]

The moral absurdity of rules of war was discussed extensively in Chapter 3. But here we see that violent sports (one can include rugby, ice hockey, professional wrestling, cage fighting, and more), as well as other forms of popular entertainment (including sanitized and more overt simulations of homicide), can send out strong messages of approval for violent action. Anthropologist Walter Goldschmidt proposes an interestingly different set of options: "Institutions of peace can . . . redirect these aggressive impulses into more amicable kinds of ego-gratifying actions. To do so, they require not only the existence of material goods that serve as social markers, as symbols of value, but also the ennoblement of other human attributes—empathy, generosity, restraint of impulses, and the like—all of which are in the repertoire of human behavior." On the international level, he recommends "a competition that evoke[s] the highest values in our respective cultures, far more noble than human aggressiveness."[82] This is what Freud might have called the "sublimation" or channeling (redirecting) of aggressiveness into more creative and constructive endeavors, instead of just displacing them into socially condoned forms of violence that are surrogates for war.

Closely related to the devotion to aggressive activities is the contemporary focus on "extreme" sports and other pastimes with which we are all presumed to be fascinated. It has become a cliché of our time, probably imported from the drug culture, that very high up on the list of what people seek in life is the "adrenalin rush" allegedly found in everything from jogging to bungee jumping to . . . yes, war. This bizarre construction of human psychology perhaps contains some truth, but in a distorted, escapist fashion that relegates human peak experiences to some fantasyland realm, often dangerous in reality.

Another "adrenaline rush" activity, on offer in ever bigger and better forms, is violent video games. While there has been much discussion pro and con, with some pundits claiming that these are harmless avenues for venting aggression and violent impulses, research by René Weber and his colleagues leaves considerable room for skepticism on this score: "Our results indicate that virtual violence in video game playing results in those neural patterns that are considered characteristic for aggressive cognition and behavior."[83] While this result does not prove that video and computer game violence causes real-life violence, it does suggest that it may be a contributing factor.

Concerning media violence, peace psychologist Rachel MacNair reports that "More than a thousand studies say that violence in the media is connected to aggressive behavior in some children. All overviews of the studies find positive correlations. . . . [W]e have now reached the standard of proof that there is not a reasonable doubt about this."[84] Clearly, some keys to de-escalating everyday violence and creating a culture of peace are: sensible and meaningful control of firearms; efficient, ethical, and well-informed law enforcement; countering violence-approval; making alternative pastimes and uses of the media more attractive; and encouraging a different evolution of the entertainment industry, which can be expected to respond very directly to what consumers opt to spend their money on. In a perceptive study of visual material depicting human suffering, writer, filmmaker, and activist Susan Sontag classifies many media images as "part of the normality of a culture in which shock has become a leading stimulus of consumption and source of value."[85] Perhaps a different kind of "cultural normality" could be encouraged to evolve. And perhaps this is just as much a call to promote the development of different sorts of *personalities*, so that more healthy alternatives will actually be sought (see Chapter 7, section 7.3, "Education for Peace").

Some authors maintain in addition that classic nonviolent activities and campaigns do actually offer many goals, processes, and outcomes equivalent in satisfaction to those of war. Nonviolent resistance (for example to injustice), Richard Gregg contends, is "much more dramatic and interesting and alluring" than James's suggestion for a universal conscription of youth into various types of labor as an "army against *Nature*" (these would include civil engineering, resource-gathering, building, and so on).[86] Whether or not one agrees with Gregg's assessment, it seems plain that forms of behavior providing attractive alternatives to those that promote a culture of violence are sorely needed. Once again, a careful and deep rethinking of what we are all about and what behaviors can and do provide rewards calls out to be made. This is particularly important in an age of uncertainty and loss of traditional values.

6.7. ENGAGING WITH CONFLICT

A Universal Phenomenon?

The first thing to affirm about conflict is that it exists everywhere, at all times and places: between and within nations, societies, and groups, between and within individuals. Even so, it does not follow that human relationships and subjective mental states are never free from conflict. Harmonious interactions and inner contentment are commonplace, as we have already seen in previous chapters. To affirm that conflict is universal in human societies simply means that none lacks examples of it, and all have a need to deal with it. But some people also appear to believe that nothing interesting is happening unless there is active conflict going on. Given the theory of peace advanced in this book, and the peaceful endeavors we have examined, however, we would have to say that this is a false perception, which should therefore yield to a more accurate one. Arguably, basing institutions and procedures (in education, business, politics, the legal system, and elsewhere) on competition and adversarial relations is bound to maximize the level of conflict within a society. Yet even where this is not the case, conflicts arise from other, more basic sources.

Many scholars endorse the universality-of-conflict view. Elise Boulding comments, for example, that "The differences in wants, needs, perceptions, and aspirations among individuals and among groups, stemming from individual uniqueness, require a constant process of conflict management in daily life at every level. . . . What keeps this unceasing process of conflict from degenerating into the war of each against all is the equally ubiquitous need of humans for one another, for the social bonding and nurturance without which no society could function."[87] Ware and her colleagues observe that "Taken as an opportunity, conflict can create new openings or solutions not previously considered. Most importantly, finding ways to resolve differences between people can strengthen and deepen the relationship."[88] The Dalai Lama, focusing on the self, asserts that "One learns to welcome conflict in order to strengthen self-restraint, as well as to clarify and deepen conviction."[89] And as Friedrich Nietzsche famously and simply declared, "Whatever does not kill me makes me stronger."[90] Oliver Ramsbotham, Tom Woodhouse, and Hugh Miall take a similar approach to Boulding's, characterizing conflict as "an expression of the heterogeneity of interests, values and beliefs that arise as new formations generated by social change come up against inherited constraints. But the way we deal with conflict is a matter of habit and choice. It is possible to change habitual responses and exercise intelligent choices."[91] They add elsewhere that "Both democracy and the market economy are inherently conflictual processes."[92] While these institutions might be only "less bad than all the rest" (to extend Winston Churchill's appraisal of democracy), they appear to be increasingly ensconced worldwide and are therefore becoming established as the dominant realities of human life.

Although *the consensus here is that conflict is omnipresent among humans,* the insights of these scholars yield quite a different perspective from the Hobbesian/realist view that universal conflict can only be checked by a superior force that keeps all parties in awe and under control. The interpretive viewpoint put forward by Boulding and by Ramsbotham, Woodhouse, and Miall is more in line with the observations on human psychology endorsed in previous chapters of this book, and will be adopted here.

Not everyone subscribes to the thesis that conflict is an inescapable feature of human life, however. In a very thoughtful and sensitive article, Sara Clarke-Habibi, of the International Education for Peace Institute, offers the following challenge:

> The assumption that conflict constitutes an inherent feature of the human reality represents a *conflict-oriented worldview.* . . . Most of the peoples of the world live with conflict-oriented worldviews . . . [which are] so firmly positioned as the norm in our societies that they pass undetected. . . . The result is a perpetuation of cultures of conflict in which

people feel themselves to be conflicted, engage in conflicts at home and at work, prepare themselves and their children for future conflicts, and recount their past conflicts in cultural and historical narratives.[93]

This minority perspective deserves to be taken very seriously and explored further. But while it is entirely laudable and worthwhile to attempt to change worldviews in this manner, so that conflict is not the default perspective on life, it nevertheless remains true that everyday competitions and clashes are in the nature of being human, and they therefore need to be understood and moderated. They are, as Boulding observes, part of the dialectic of "individual uniqueness," on the one hand, and "social bonding," on the other. And as Ramsbotham, Woodhouse, and Miall affirm, "intelligent choices" are the answer to conflict—which would no doubt be aided by the kind of transformational training that Clarke-Habibi advocates. Bryan Teixeira sums up the matter quite well when he writes, "Since interpersonal contact at its simplest as well as its more complex levels will always involve differing perceptions of reality, conflict is unavoidable. What nonviolence places before us is the challenge of addressing conflict humanely. Peace is then not the absence of conflict—which would be an impossibility—but rather a context in which conflict is addressed with as much respect [for the other] as possible."[94]

Transforming Conflict

Efforts to manage ordinary conflict and to resolve open (unmanaged) large-scale hostilities are predicated on (a) the desire of some to help others (as well as themselves) avoid the destructive consequences of violence and war; and (b) the inner desire of those who are in conflict to see an end to it, and their capacity to grasp the benefits of peaceful problem-solving. Another factor should also be included here: (c) that humans have a very strong sense of justice (or fair treatment), even if it is not always well thought-out or articulated. Because of this, every human relationship or social arrangement features some kind of balancing of interests and needs, and although these are often skewed in favor of one party or another when self-interest gets in the way, the ethical evolution of our species is largely concerned with coming to acknowledge and affirm the legitimacy of competing quality-of-life claims. This trend is illustrated by, among other things, "the growing use of mediation in civil matters like divorce and neighborhood disputes, and the involvement of patient advocates in health matters."[95]

Viewing conflict as part of life means not only that it is (almost certainly) here to stay, but also that conflict can energize innovations in social arrangements we are all part of, and create changes in our personal outlooks as well. Hence, it is helpful to acknowledge, as philosopher Bernard Williams does, that "Disagreement does not necessarily have to be overcome. It may remain an important and constitutive feature of our relations to others. . . ."[96] And as Nobel Prize economist Amartya Sen points out, people can agree to opt for certain common goods and the institutions that will provide them without being in agreement about other social choices, or indeed in the absence of agreement about how best to bring about a just society.[97]

What about conflict that threatens to get out of control and cause real and perhaps lasting damage to people and their vital interests? The ideal form of response here must be to defuse the situation so that heightened emotions and escalations of negative rhetoric and harmful actions and reactions can be contained, in order to allow for constructive solutions to be found, preferably of the win-win variety. In everyday life, we mostly muddle through to outcomes of this type, and, if we are sensitive to where others are coming from, are accommodating, maintain goodwill, and are lucky, things tend to work out, at least over the long haul. We can all recognize that when matters get out of control between ourselves, it is time to step back, take a deep breath, perhaps apologize, start over, and try to find a better direction in which to express our differences, map out common ground to offset divisive influences, hammer out a compromise, and let go of issues that are getting in the way of cooperation, collegiality, friendship, or intimacy. Or if all else fails, we simply have to avoid persons and situations we really cannot deal with. These observations are equally true in relation to the ones we care most about as in the workplace or the community at large. And while it is a genuine achievement to transcend or remove sources of conflict once and for all, we also have to face the fact that conflicts can be ongoing or periodically flare up again, especially when deeply held values and convictions or strong vested interests are (or seem to be) at stake. Numerous organizations—such as the Alternatives to Violence Project, which has programs in more than fifty countries[98]—have utilized insights such as these to develop strategies for nonviolently transforming conflict in prisons, schools, and other settings.

Many of the same principles apply on the larger scale of human life, where groups of people acting together produce synergies that result in greater and more dangerous types of conflict. Ramsbotham, Woodhouse, and Miall define this kind of conflict as "the pursuit of incompatible goals by different groups,"[99] and go on to suggest that "the aim of conflict resolution is to transform actually or potentially violent conflict into peaceful (non-violent) processes of social and political change. This is an unending task as new forms and sources of conflict [inevitably] arise."[100] According to Ware and her colleagues, "Civil conflict generally results from a deep level of emotional frustration. . . . Almost invariably the conflict is [really] about scarce resources and who should get access to them, not about 'age-old' ethnic divides."[101] This is not to deny that group identity is often invoked as an excuse for relationships of friction or exclusion. The allocation (or withholding) of resources is often determined, during the course of conflict, by ethnic membership. As is well known from many international examples, racism (and other forms of prejudice) tend to flourish in severe economic times.

The process of conflict resolution is enormously complex, and there are numerous theoretical approaches and myriad techniques and projects for conducting this vital work.[102] Just getting hostile parties to come together in order to negotiate their grievances and differences is often a major accomplishment, especially in "asymmetric conflicts" where one side has a power advantage over the other. Basically either common interests or the grounds for addressing competing interests must be discovered and clearly defined, and the intransigence generated by entrenched, adversarial positions must be overcome. *Eventually, we must talk to our enemies, find another way to deal with one another, and learn to coexist.* How far can we go with this? Much attention is paid in the field of conflict studies to strategies for transforming conflict from something that is unmanageable into a reframed mode of opposition that reveals the real underlying issues, is forward looking, and therefore has at least a hope of facilitating settlement by means of mutual understanding, bargaining, and ultimately compromises that prove durable. A key to this is "for participants to learn how to reinterpret the conflict as a shared problem,"[103] which they can "own" and then work together to solve, realizing that there is more to be gained from peaceful settlement than from continuing hostilities.[104] Dubbed by one team of researchers "cooperative conflict resolution," this method of proceeding "emphasizes active coworking by parties in conflict; they attempt to develop creative solutions that each can affirm and support."[105]

John Paul Lederach is a sociologist, conflict studies specialist, and experienced international mediation trainer and peace-builder, who has spent many years developing and refining the transformational approach. He cautions that because conflicts are part of life, "resolving" or "managing" them is not always possible. And because conflicts often provide the dynamics for producing constructive change, it is not always desirable to resolve or manage them either. The transformative outlook must be shared by both the mediators of and the parties to the conflict. *To look at a conflict transformatively entails seeing what is at stake in the immediate sense, but also appreciating the larger interpersonal, social-structural, and cultural context from which it unfolds, as well as refocusing on positive goals that can be developed out of the conflict in question.* "The primary task of conflict transformation is not to find quick solutions to immediate problems, but rather to generate creative platforms that can simultaneously address surface issues and change underlying social structures and relationship patterns," writes Lederach.[106] This complex process is also guided by the aims of replacing violence by nonviolence and dialogue, disempowerment by empowerment, and increased mutual respect and justice as features of the resulting outcomes and ongoing relationships.

Sociologist Joseph Himes suggests that "a strategy for conflict resolution . . . includes five functionally linked operations," which may occur simultaneously or successively: "preliminary contacts and arrangements"; "cease-fire" (or ending hostilities, of whatever kind); "resolution-communication" (which involves "generat[ing] substantial areas of agreement and joint action"); "exchange and sharing" (realizing commonly-held values, such as "justice, freedom, security, or dignity," or bargaining over "territory, natural resources, status, or other values that are presumed to be limited"); and finally, "formalization of agreements."[107] This is an extremely fruitful way of looking at the process of conflict resolution, because it foregrounds the essential elements of cooperation, confidence building, and compromise. Working together—whether learning how to get along in everyday life or to remedy the effects of conflict—is perhaps the very best way to overcome suspicions and insecurities, and to turn former enemies into partners and even friends. Greater involvement of women in key negotiating and peacemaking roles is now recognized as an area in need of urgent development, inasmuch as women's viewpoints and interests need greater representation, and women often have special skills and sensibilities they can bring to these processes.[108]

Experts in dealing with large-scale conflict, such as civil wars in various parts of the world, agree that while outsiders can often make a useful contribution to bringing about nonviolent solutions, foreign military intervention typically leads to more deadly conflicts.[109] *But it is highly important to help mobilize and support local peacemakers and peacemaking traditions, which are resources that exist everywhere.* In this process, though, it is equally vital for outsiders to refrain from trying to impose their own culturally specific values, because these are likely to be poorly received and ineffectual in creating a lasting solution.[110] This illustrates a principle that applies to all levels of disagreement and conflict in human life: that *respect for others' viewpoints, however challenging it may be to summon up, is a prerequisite of peacefully surmounting the differences that divide us and learning to negotiate positive ways of coexisting.*

NOTES TO CHAPTER 6

1. Lisa Schirch, *The Little Book of Strategic Peacebuilding* (Intercourse, PA: Good Books, 2004).

2. Abigail Disney, interview by Sofia Stefanovic, *Dumbo Feather: Conversations with Extraordinary People* 32 (Third Quarter 2012), p. 37 (emphases in original).

3. Helen Ware, ed., et al., *The No-Nonsense Guide to Conflict and Peace* (Oxford: New Internationalist, 2006), p. 84.

4. Kent D. Shifferd, *From War to Peace: A Guide to the Next Hundred Years* (Jefferson, NC: McFarland, 2011). p. 9.

5. See "Gross National Happiness"; http://www.grossnationalhappiness.com/articles.

6. Shifferd, *From War to Peace*, chap. 3.

7. Shifferd, *From War to Peace*, p. 58.

8. For a full discussion of the problem and what might be done about it, see Michael Renner, *Small Arms, Big Impact: The Next Challenge of Disarmament*, Worldwatch Paper 137 (Washington, DC: Worldwatch Institute, 1997).

9. Paul Holtom, Mark Bromley, Pieter D. Wezeman, and Siemon T. Wezeman, Stockholm International Peace Research Institute, "Trends in International Arms Transfers, 2012," SIPRI Fact Sheet March 2013; http://books.sipri.org/product_info?c_product_id=455.

10. Aditi Malhotra, "The Illicit Trade of Small Arms," Geopoliticalmonitor.com, 19 January 2011; http://www.geopoliticalmonitor.com/the-illicit-trade-of-small-arms-4273.

11. Mara Hermann, "UN's Arms Treaty Will Not Infringe on Domestic Rights," *The Interdependent*, 18 August 2011; http://theinterdependent.com/110818/uns-arms-treaty-will-not-infringe-on-domestic-rights.

12. "Obama Prague Speech on Nuclear Weapons: FULL TEXT," *Huffington Post*, 5 April 2009; http://www.huffingtonpost.com/2009/04/05/obama-prague-speech-on-nu_n_183219.html.

13. Defense Treaty Inspection Readiness Program, "New Strategic Arms Reduction Treaty (New START) (NST) and Predecessors"; http://dtirp.dtra.mil/TIC/synopses/start.aspx.

14. Benjamin Loehrke, "A Nuke by Any Other Name," *Bulletin of the Atomic Scientists* 17 (May 2012); http://www.thebulletin.org/web-edition/op-eds/nuke-any-other-name.

15. John Horgan, *The End of War* (San Francisco: McSweeney's Books, 2012), p. 119.

16. See Jim Garamone, "Joint Vision 2020 Emphasizes Full-spectrum Dominance," 2 June 2000; http://www.defense.gov/news/newsarticle.aspx?id=45289. See also F. W. Engdahl, *Full Spectrum Dominance: Totalitarian Democracy in the New World Order* (Wiesbaden: edition.engdahl, 2009).

17. David E. Sanger and Thom Shanker, "U.S. Faces Choice on New Weapons for Fast Strikes," *New York Times*, 22 April 2010; http://www.nytimes.com/2010/04/23/world/europe/23strike.html.

18. Rory Carroll, "US Raises a New Drone Generation," *Guardian Weekly*, 10–16 August 2012, pp. 1–2; Lev Grossman, "Drone Home," *Time*, 11 February 2013, pp. 14–21; Craig Whitlock, "U.S. Shifts Drones to New Frontiers," *Washington Post*, 21 July 2013, pp. A1, A6; H.R. McMaster, "The Pipe Dream of Easy War," *New York Times*, Sunday Review section, 21 July 2013, p. 9.

19. See Seth G. Jones and Martin C. Libicki, *How Terrorist Groups End: Implications for Countering al Qa'ida*, Rand Corporation Research Brief, 2008; available at: http://www.rand.org/content/dam/rand/pubs/research_briefs/2008/RAND_RB9351.pdf.

20. Senthil Ram, "Understanding the Indirect Strategy of Terrorism: Insights from Nonviolent Action Research," in *Nonviolence: An Alternative for Defeating Global Terror(ism)*, ed. Senthil Ram and Ralph Summy (New York: Nova Science, 2008), p. 88.

21. Oliver Ramsbotham, Tom Woodhouse, and Hugh Miall, *Contemporary Conflict Resolution: The Prevention, Management and Transformation of Deadly Conflicts*, 2nd ed. (Cambridge, UK: Polity Press, 2008), pp. 256, 261, 263.

22. The Dalai Lama (Bsatn-'dzin-rgya-mtsho, Dalai Lama XIV), "Foreword," in *Nonviolence: An Alternative for Defeating Global Terror(ism)*, ed. Ram and Summy, p. ix.

23. Senthil Ram and Ralph Summy, "Nonviolent Counter to Global Terror(ism) and Paradigms of Counter-terrorism," in *Nonviolence: An Alternative to Defeating Global Terror(ism)*, ed. Ram and Summy, pp. 7, 8, 9.

24. Andrew Higgins, "Keeping the Peace," *Guardian Weekly*, 7–13 September 2012, p. 30; Aymeric Jamir, "Indonesia's Radical Terror Threat Lurks in the Shadows a Decade on from Bali," *Guardian Weekly*, 23–29 November 2012, p. 9.

25. James Henry, *The Blood Bankers: Tales from the Global Underground Economy* (New York: Basic Books, 2005); John Perkins, *Confessions of an Economic Hit Man* (Berrett-Koehler, 2004); Richard Peet, *Unholy Trinity: The IMF, World Bank and WTO*, 2nd ed. (London: Zed Books, 2009).

26. Seumas Milne, "We Must Ditch Failed Economic Model," *Guardian Weekly*, 1–7 June 2012, p. 20.

27. See "The Cost of Inequality: How Wealth and Income Extremes Hurt Us All," Oxfam Media Briefing, 18 January 2013; http://www.oxfam.org/sites/www.oxfam.org/files/cost-of-inequality-oxfam-mb180113.pdf.

28. Stuart Rees, *Passion for Peace: Exercising Power Creatively* (Sydney: University of New South Wales Press, 2003), p. 39.

29. Kroc Institute for International Peace Studies, University of Notre Dame; http://kroc.nd.edu/about-us/what-peace-studies.

30. GradSchools.com, "Conflict & Peace Studies Graduate Programs"; http://www.gradschools.com/search-programs/conflict-peace-studies.

31. See http://www.wanep.org/wanep.

32. See Wesley Kanne Clark, "Why Did Congress Cut Funds for Peace in a Time of War?" *Christian Science Monitor*, 21 March 2011; http://www.csmonitor.com/Commentary/Opinion/2011/0321/Why-did-Congress-cut-funds-for-peace-in-a-time-of-war; Alliance for Peacebuilding, "Funding for Peacebuilding"; http://www.allianceforpeacebuilding.org/?work_pbfunding; Wikipedia, "United States Institute of Peace; http://en.wikipedia.org/wiki/United_States_Institute_of_Peace.

33. Elise Boulding, "Women's Movements for Social Change: Social Feminism and Equity Feminism," address to the International Sociological Association's Symposium on "Old and New Forms of Solidarity and Identity," Bielefeld, Germany, July 1994; available at: http://www.wilpfinternational.org/publications/1994eliseboulding.htm.

34. The account that follows and the quotations within it are taken from Decade for a Culture of Peace Youth Team, *Report on the Decade for a Culture of Peace: Final Civil Society Report on the United Nations International Decade for a Culture of Peace and Non-violence for the Children of the World (2001–2010)*; http://decade-culture-of-peace. org/2010_civil_society_report.pdf (emphases in original).

35. See, for example, the definition of "peacefulness" given by Bonta, quoted in Chapter 2, section 2.4, "The Existence of Peaceful Societies," and summarized in Figure 2.1. See also Elise Boulding, *Cultures of Peace: The Hidden Side of History* (Syracuse: Syracuse University Press, 2000); Joseph de Rivera, ed., *Handbook on Building Cultures of Peace* (New York: Springer, 2009); Daisaku Ikeda, *For the Sake of Peace: Seven Paths to Global Harmony—A Buddhist Perspective* (Santa Monica, CA: Middleway Press, 2001); Patrick U. Petit, ed., *Shaping the Culture of Peace in a Multicultural World* (New Brunswick, NJ: Transaction, 2011); Glenn H. Stassen, ed., *Just Peacemaking: The New Paradigm for the Ethics of Peace and War*, new ed. (Cleveland: Pilgrim Press, 2008).

36. Robert J. Burrowes, *The Strategy of Nonviolent Defense: A Gandhian Approach* (Albany: State University of New York Press, 1996), pp. 55, 149.

37. Decade for a Culture of Peace Youth Team, *Report on the Decade for a Culture of Peace*, Executive Summary, p. 4; available at: http://decade-culture-of-peace.org/2010_civil_ society_report.pdf.

38. David Sloan Wilson et al., "Evolving the Future: Toward a Science of Intentional Change," *Behavioral and Brain Sciences* 36 (2013), in press (emphasis in original).

39. Bonnie Kreps, *Authentic Passion: Loving without Losing Your Self* (Wellesley, MA: Roundtable Press, 1990), p. 14 (emphasis in original).

40. For example, as this was being written, the group of G8 nations signed an agreement to end rape and sexual violence in wartime. See "G8 Inks Historic Agreement against Rape in War Zones," *Indian Express*, 11 April 3013; http://www.indianexpress.com/news/g8-inks-historic-agreement-against-rape-in-war-zones/1101054. See also "UN, DRC Agree to Stop Rape," news24, 2 April 2013; http://www.news24.com/Africa/News/UN-DRC-agree-to-stop-rape-20130402. This describes an agreement between the UN and the Democratic Republic of Congo to tackle the problem of rape in the Eastern Congo war zone.

41. Rosemary Radford Ruether, "Feminism and Peace," *Christian Century*, August 31–September 7, 1983, pp. 771–6; available at: http://www.religion-online.org/showarticle. asp?title=1685.

42. Ruether, "Feminism and Peace."

43. International Data Corporation (IDC), "Digital Universe Study 2011: Extracting Value from Chaos"; http://www.emc.com/leadership/programs/digital-universe.htm.

44. Ramsbotham, Woodhouse, and Miall, *Contemporary Conflict Resolution*, pp. 7–8.

45. United Nations, *Universal Declaration of Human Rights*; http://www.un.org/en/ documents/udhr.

46. "The Rich and the Rest: What to Do (and Not to Do) about Inequality," *The Economist*, 20 January 2011; available at: http://www.economist.com/node/17959590.

47. Michel Rogalski and Carlos Yakubovich, "Strategies for Conversion of Armaments Industries," *Peace Works for People*, ACFOA Development Dossier No. 10 (Canberra:

Australian Council for Overseas Aid, September 1982), p. 12. (Originally published in *Development: Seeds of Change*, [Journal of the Society for International Development, Rome], 1982/1.)

48. Phys.org, "New Analysis of Government Data Shows That Military Spending Is a Weak Job Engine Compared to Other Investments," 1 December 2011; http://phys.org/news/2011-12-analysis-military-weak-job-investments.html.

49. Isaiah 2:4.

50. Michael Renner, *Swords into Plowshares: Converting to a Peace Economy*, Worldwatch Paper 96 (Washington, DC: Worldwatch Institute, June 1990), p. 5.

51. For some valuable discussion of conversion strategies, see Ann Markusen and Joel Yudken, *Dismantling the Cold War Economy* (New York: Basic Books, 1992), chap. 9.

52. Seymour Melman, *The Defense Economy: Conversion of Industries and Occupations to Civilian Needs* (New York: Prager, 1970), p. 7.

53. On the debate over defense industry specialization, see Maryellen R. Kelley and Todd A. Watkins, "The Myth of the Specialized Military Contractor," *Technology* Review 98 (1995), pp. 52-8; available at: http://www.lehigh.edu/˜taw4/TR.html; on the argument against diversification as the answer, see Renner, *Swords into Plowshares*, pp. 8–9.

54. Renner, *Swords into Plowshares*, p. 9.

55. Renner, *Swords into Plowshares*, pp. 10–11; Todd Sandler and Keith Hartley, *The Economics of Defense* (Cambridge, UK: Cambridge University Press, 1995), pp. 286-7.

56. Bonn International Center for Conversion, *Conversion Survey 2005: Global Disarmament, Demilitarization and Demobilization* (Baden-Baden: Nomos, 2005), pp. 13–14, 21. See also Russell Faure-Brac, *Transition To Peace: A Defense Engineer's Search For An Alternative To War* (Bloomington, IN: iUniverse, 2012), chap. 5.

57. Michael Renner, *Budgeting for Disarmament: The Costs of War and Peace*, Worldwatch Paper 122 (Washington, DC: Worldwatch Institute, November 1994), pp. 52–3.

58. See http://www1.ifc.org/wps/wcm/connect/corp_ext_content/ifc_external_corporate_site/home. For organizations that welcome public investment, see: http://www.kiva.org and http://www.grameenfoundation.org/take-action.

59. Gar Alperovitz, "The Rise of the New Economy Movement," Common Dreams, 22 May 2012; https://www.commondreams.org/view/2012/05/22–2. My appreciation to Robin Fox for pointing out this reference. See also David Korten, *Agenda for a New Economy: From Phantom Wealth to Real Wealth*, 2nd ed. (San Francisco: Berrett-Koehler, 2010).

60. Ariana Eunjung Cha, "Spain's Crisis Spawns Euro-free Economy," *Guardian Weekly*, 7–13 September 2012, p. 17.

61. See "Bitcoin or Bit-con? Meet the Crypto-currency That's Taking over the Internet," *The Journal*, 23 April 2013; http://www.thejournal.ie/bitcoin-explainer-irish-users-862707-Apr2013.

62. Peace One Day (http://peaceoneday.org).

63. Uri Savir, *Peace First: A New Model to End War* (San Francisco: Berrett-Koehler, 2008).

64. Savir, *Peace First*, pp. 4–5.

65. Savir, *Peace First*, p. 77.

66. Savir, *Peace First*, pp. 191–2. The joint-capital idea is also explored by Cecelia Albin in "Negotiating Intractable Conflicts: On the Future of Jerusalem," *Cooperation and Conflict* 32 (1997), pp. 29–77.
67. Savir, *Peace First*, pp. 193–9.
68. Jillian Kestler-D'Amours, "Israeli Wall Isolates Palestinian Communities," *Al Jazeera*, 1 January 2013; http://www.aljazeera.com/indepth/features/2012/12/20121225825178 322.html.
69. Harriet Sherwood, "Israel Races to Fortify Its Frontiers," *Guardian Weekly*, 6–12 April 2012, pp. 1–2; "U.S., Israel Map out Joint Missile Plan," UPI.com, 29 June 2012; http://www.upi.com/Business_News/Security-Industry/2012/06/29/US-Israel-map-out-joint-missile-plan/UPI-13551340987053/?spt=hs&or=si.
70. Global Alliance for Ministries and Infrastructures for Peace; http://www.mfp-dop.org/campaigns/directory.
71. "U.S. House Bill Number HR-808 to Establish a Department of Peace." See The Peace Alliance, "About the U.S. Department of Peacebuilding"; http://www.thepeacealliance.org/issues-advocacy/department-of-peace/index.html.
72. This account, and the quotations within it, are taken from Reba Parker, "What If Peace Were Popular?" *Peace Chronicle* (newsletter of the Peace and Justice Studies Association), Winter 2012, pp. 8–9. Details of ongoing activities can be found at: www.bepeaceful.org or http://cp1d.org.
73. Margaret Wheatley and Deborah Frieze, *Walk Out Walk On: A Learning Journey into Communities Daring to Live the Future Now* (San Francisco: Berrett-Koehler, 2011).
74. See http://www.space4peace.org/index.htm.
75. Mayors for Peace; http://www.mayorsforpeace.org/english/index.html.
76. "Politics is the art of the possible." The saying is usually attributed to Otto von Bismarck (1815–98), but there is apparently no definitive evidence to back up this claim about its origin.
77. Walter Russell Mead, "Peace Myth," *Australian Financial Review*, 14 December 2012, p. 1.
78. See, for example, Mary Zournazi, *Keywords to War: Reviving Language in an Age of Terror* (Carlton North, VIC, Australia: Scribe, 2007); Marshall B. Rosenberg, *Nonviolent Communication: A Language of Life* (Encinitas, CA: PuddleDancer Press, 2003); Christina Schäffner and Anita Wenden, eds., *Language and Peace* (Aldershot, Hants, UK: Dartmouth, 1995).
79. Alexander McCall Smith, quoted in Susan Chenery, "Uncommon Courtesy," Spectrum, *Sydney Morning Herald*, 24–25 September 2011, p. 10.
80. Ashley Montagu, "Introduction," in Ashley Montagu, ed., *Learning Non-Aggression: The Experience of Non-Literate Societies* (New York: Oxford University Press, 1978), pp. 8–9.
81. Mary E. Clark, "Aggressivity and Violence: An Alternative Theory of Human Nature"; available at: http://www.gmu.edu/programs/icar/pcs/clark.htm#N_3_.
82. Walter Goldschmidt, "Peacemaking and the Institutions of Peace in Tribal Societies," in *The Anthropology of Peace and Nonviolence*, ed. Leslie E. Sponsel and Thomas Gregor (Boulder, CO: Lynne Rienner, 1994), pp. 127, 128.

83. René Weber, Ute Ritterfeld, and Klaus Mathiak, "Does Playing Violent Video Games Induce Aggression? Empirical Evidence of a Functional Magnetic Resonance Imaging Study," *Media Psychology* 8 (2006), p. 51; available at: http://bscw-app1.let.ethz.ch/pub/bscw.cgi/d5907585/WeberRitterfeldMathiak-Does%20Playing%20Violent%20Video%20Games%20Indu.pdf.

84. Rachel M. MacNair, *The Psychology of Peace: An Introduction*, 2nd ed. (Santa Barbara, CA: Praeger, 2012), pp. 211–2.

85. Susan Sontag, *Regarding the Pain of Others* (New York: Farrar, Straus and Giroux, 2003), p. 23.

86. Richard B. Gregg, *The Psychology and Strategy of Gandhi's Nonviolent Resistance* (New York: Garland, 1972), p. 100; William James, "The Moral Equivalent of War" (1910), in *William James: Writings 1902–1910*, ed. Bruce Kuklick (New York: Library of America, 1987), p. 1291 (emphasis in original).

87. Boulding, *Cultures of Peace*, p. 89.

88. Ware, ed., et al., *No-Nonsense Guide to Conflict and Peace*, p. 26.

89. The Dalai Lama (Bsatn-'dzin-rgya-mtsho, Dalai Lama XIV), *Harvard Divinity Bulletin* 29/1 (2000), p. 19; cited by Ira G. Zepp, Jr., "Agape and Ahimsa in Practice," in Charles E. Collyer and Ira G. Zepp, Jr., *Nonviolence: Origins and Outcomes*, 2nd ed. (Victoria, BC, Canada: Trafford, 2006), p. 93

90. Friedrich Nietzsche, *Ecce Homo: How One Becomes What One Is*, trans. Walter Kaufmann (New York: Vintage Books, 1989), "Why I Am So Wise," sec. 2; see also Friedrich Nietzsche, *Twilight of the Idols*, in *Twilight of the Idols, or How to Philosophize with a Hammer/The Anti-Christ*, trans. R. J. Hollingdale (London: Penguin Books, 1990), "Maxims and Morals," sec. 8.

91. Ramsbotham, Woodhouse, and Miall, *Contemporary Conflict Resolution*, p. 13.

92. Ramsbotham, Woodhouse, and Miall, *Contemporary Conflict Resolution*, p. 195.

93. Sara Clarke-Habibi, "Transforming Worldviews: The Case of Education for Peace in Bosnia and Herzegovina," *Journal of Transformative Education* 3 (2005), pp. 33–56; H. B. Danesh and Sara Clarke-Habibi, *Education for Peace Curriculum Manual: A Conceptual and Practical Guide* (Vancouver: EFP-International Press, 2007).

94. Brian Teixeira, "Nonviolence Theory and Practice," in *Encyclopedia of Violence, Peace and Conflict*, ed. Lester R. Kurtz and Jennifer Turpin (San Diego: Academic Press, 1999), vol. 2, p. 558.

95. Robin Fox (personal communication, 15 July 2012).

96. Bernard Williams, *Ethics and the Limits of Philosophy* (London: Fontana Press/Collins, 1985), p. 133.

97. Amartya Sen, *The Idea of Justice* (London: Penguin, 2010), pp. 399–400.

98. Alternatives to Violence Project (http://avpinternational.org).

99. Ramsbotham, Woodhouse, and Miall, *Contemporary Conflict Resolution*, p. 27.

100. Ramsbotham, Woodhouse, and Miall, *Contemporary Conflict Resolution*, p. 30.

101. Ware, ed., et al., *No Nonsense Guide to Conflict and Peace*, p. 49.

102. For a list of current UN peacekeeping activities, see United Nations, "Peacekeeping Fact Sheet"; http://www.un.org/en/peacekeeping/resources/statistics/factsheet.shtml.

103. Ramsbotham, Woodhouse, and Miall, *Contemporary Conflict Resolution*, p. 290.

104. For an in-depth look at strategies of this type, a classic work is: Roger Fisher, William L. Ury, and Bruce Patton, *Getting to Yes: Negotiating Agreement Without Giving In*, 2nd ed. (New York: Penguin, 1991).

105. Steven Brion-Meisels et al., "Use Cooperative Conflict Resolution," in *Just Peacemaking*, ed. Stassen, p. 71.

106. John Paul Lederach, "Conflict Transformation," *Beyond Intractability*, ed. Guy Burgess and Heidi Burgess, Conflict Information Consortium, University of Colorado, Boulder, October 2003; available at: http://www.beyondintractability.org/bi-essay/transformation.

107. Joseph S. Himes, *Conflict and Conflict Management* (Athens: University of Georgia Press, 1980), pp. 242, 248, 251.

108. Julian Borger, "Women are Creating Harmony, but Only Men Broker Peace Deals," *Guardian Weekly*, 28 September–4 October 2012, p. 3.

109. Human Security Report Project, *Human Security Report 2012: Sexual Violence, Education, and War—Beyond the Mainstream Narrative*. Vancouver, BC, Canada: Human Security Research Group/Human Security Press, 2012. http://hsrgroup.org/human-security-reports/2012/text.aspx.

110. Ramsbotham, Woodhouse, and Miall, *Contemporary Conflict Resolution*, pp. 217–21; Ware, ed., et al., *No-Nonsense Guide to Conflict and Peace*, p. 16.

Building a Culture of Peace (2): The Way Forward

All thinking about peace must now be global.

> —Kent D. Shifferd, *From War to Peace: A Guide*
> *to the Next Hundred Years* (2011)

Peace is development in the broadest sense of the term.

> —Edward Azar (1938–91), Lebanese professor of government
> and politics, *The Management of Protracted Social*
> *Conflict: Theory and Cases* (1990)

The greatest gift we can give to our children is to raise them in a culture of peace.

> —Louise Diamond, American peace scholar, expert in organizational
> transformation and systems dynamics, founder of The Peace
> Company, and author of *The Peace Book: 108 Simple*
> *Ways to Make a Peaceful World* (2001)

7.1. RESPECT FOR DIFFERENCES AND HUMAN RIGHTS

Getting to Know One Another

Chapter 5 explored the subject of compassion in detail. Compassion, understood as a deep connection with, and grasp of, what others feel, of their plight, whatever it might be, and of the need to assist them, is not only a basis for respecting others, but also emerges out of that same respect. But it seems that respect, for some people, is not always that easy to summon up. *One of the biggest barriers to respect (and peace) is xenophobia*—literally, the fear of what is foreign or strange—but more broadly, suspicion, dislike, and antagonism toward those who are perceived as very different from oneself and one's identity group; as threatening to what this group stands for; as unintelligible in their behavior; and so on. A mixture of a lack of understanding, misunderstanding, and fear is at work here, and it readily feeds into stereotyping, name-calling, blame games, and hostilities of various sorts. How do we get from xenophobia to mutual acceptance, friendship, cooperation, trust, and perhaps even compassion?

Much is known and has been written on the subject concerning constructive ways to make this transition.[1] But some scientists caution that heredity determines, to a substantial degree, whether an individual is endowed with the character traits associated with peacefulness (see Chapter 5, section 5.10, "The Will to Peace").[2] The same is found to be the case with regard to ways in which she or he interprets ambiguous situations (for instance, whether being bumped into by another person is considered merely as an accident or as an act of aggression).[3] These results do pose a challenge to ideas about how attitudes might be changed to foster peaceful coexistence and mutual understanding. But the problem is not insurmountable. One obvious ingredient of the answer is familiarity, or learning about different cultures, ethnicities, religions, value-systems, customs, languages, and political structures through exposure to them. Author and peace activist Fran Peavey suggests the simple rule that "When you're wondering about a group of people who are different from you, find someone from that group and ask them to teach you."[4] *Person-to-person contacts have traditionally provided the best avenue toward overcoming xenophobia, but reading, participating in communal activities, and specific training are also well tested routes.* In a recent book, David Cannadine argues that history shows how basic differences in identity among humans have been successfully negotiated in an ongoing way, and that commonalities have proved more significant in shaping events over the long haul than the accidental qualities of culture that separate us, even though the opposite point of view is fed to us regularly by various sources.[5]

Some interesting recent research suggests that prejudice can be decreased and tolerance increased by cognitive exercises that encourage "counter-stereotypic thinking."[6] Compassion enters in at the level of trying to see what the world looks like from the other's point of view, and appreciating her or his issues in confronting life. Often, this kind of effort culminates in the formation of some kind of positive bond, but at least *we learn that people are in many respects just like us, with the same joys, frustrations, concerns, and basic desires and ambitions; we discover in a very concrete fashion our common humanity.* It is heartening to know that numerous organizations are dedicated to the pursuit of mutual understanding across religious and ethnic boundaries, a few of which are listed here: Seeds of Peace, A Simple Peace, Peace Camp Canada, Middle East Peace Camp for Children, Creativity for Peace, The Dialogue Project, Interfaith Encounters Association, Seeking Common Ground, Hands of Peace, and The Compassionate Listening Project.

Of course, we need to have the desire to pursue these routes to greater understanding and tolerance, but where this does not exist, education (see below, section 7.3, "Education for Peace") and other opportunities and serendipitous encounters can have a decisive impact. To speak of breaking down the barriers between people and getting to know them as they really are is not meant to deny or downplay our differences, which are, after all, part of the spice of life. *In a peaceful world, however, difference (or otherness) would be accepted and affirmed—perhaps even celebrated.*[7]

One approach to nurturing respect takes its inspiration from an insight provided by the school of philosophy known as phenomenology.[8] This is that humans are socially constituted; that language, emotions, learning of all kinds, and even selfhood result from immersion in the world and interactions with others from the moment of birth onward. Taking this a bit further, as noted in Chapter 6 (section 6.1, "First Thoughts"), the self is a relational entity, a function of choices one makes in response to the experiences of people, places, and events that fill one's life. Thus, we do not need to *become* connected with others; what we need to learn is how to appreciate and utilize the connectedness that *already exists* for working together in a mode of mutual understanding. James Ferrell, of the Arbinger Institute—an organization that offers training in leadership, problem-solving, and conflict resolution—develops these ideas as follows:

> [C]onnection, properly understood, is not something that happens *between* people but rather something that happens *within* people. How does this affect our everyday lives? Acts of cooperation (or lack of cooperation) that we witness among people are but a manifestation of the level of collaboration we are feeling within. This means that attempts to improve outward collaboration that do not start by changing the nature of our inward connections with others fail to have lasting and significant impact. If two groups of people are seeing each other as objects, for example, you won't be able to bring about meaningful collaboration until you first help them to see the people in the other group as people like themselves. When we see others in this way, we feel the desire and obligation to consider others' desires and needs when deciding how we ourselves might act. . . . Outward collaboration is what happens when we begin to think and feel in a collaborative way.[9]

History professor Steven Hahn emphasizes that a new reality emerges through such a meeting of minds, noting that "when different groups meet one another on more level planes, slowly get to know and trust one another, and define objectives that are mutually beneficial and achievable, they learn to think of themselves as part of something larger—and they actually become something larger."[10] What these insights entail is that we already possess, for the most part, the basic equipment for building relationships of understanding and co-operative endeavor, even though these may remain buried out of sight, unrecognized, and in need of cultivation. One good way to become connected with the larger picture of humanity, in a positive sense, is to start with information, such as that provided by the website explore.org, which champions "the selfless acts of others" that often go unnoticed by the world.

Understanding and Affirming Human Rights

This brings us to the vast, widely discussed, and often vexing subject of human rights. There are those who contend that the concept of rights is a Western invention that sits poorly within the value-system of traditional non-Western societies, which feature obligations grounded in considerations of kinship, clan membership, rites of passage, religious views about relations between the sexes, shaming, "saving face," "family honor," and so forth. But as pointed out earlier in this book, rights have become—via the Universal Declaration of Human Rights (or UDHR, adopted by the UN General Assembly in 1948)—the *de facto* basis for international morality and the reference point for assessing social and political well-being and progress worldwide. Human-rights historian Aryeh Neier reinforces this claim when he urges that "The extent to which the [human rights] movement has matured in [diverse] regions, and the degree to which it is focused on matters that are universally recognized as core human rights concerns seem to refute the argument that human rights is a Western construct of limited application in other parts of the world."[11] (See also Chapter 4, section 4.6, "Critiques of Nonviolence and Its Vindication.") Italian international relations specialist Fulvio Attinà explains this evolving awareness as follows: "In principle, the international law of human rights has the effect of socializing all states in the value and practice of human rights. It provides a reference point for domestic legal systems and promotes the adoption of human rights ideas into the cultures of all states."[12] One of the original drafters of the UDHR adds, furthermore, that international human rights law asserts "the inalienable right to live free from want and oppression and to fully develop one's personality."[13]

These are readily recognized as essential conditions for both inner and outer peace, as discussed in Chapter 5.

As a corollary of the above, rights-discourse is arguably now well established as the *lingua franca* for dialogue and debate about the treatment of groups and individuals that take place within several major arenas: diplomacy, conflict-intervention, humanitarian aid, and well-being and violence monitoring. "Indeed," the UN states, "the UDHR has inspired more than 80 international human rights treaties and declarations, a great number of regional human rights conventions, domestic human rights bills, and constitutional provisions, which together constitute a comprehensive legally binding system for the promotion and protection of human rights."[14] It should be noted, too, that the committee charged with drafting the original UDHR was composed of representatives from Australia, Belgium, Byelorussian Soviet Socialist Republic, Chile, China, Egypt, France, India, Iran, Lebanon, Panama, Philippines, the United Kingdom, the United States, USSR, Uruguay, and Yugoslavia. The document was then approved by the UN General Assembly by a vote of 48–0, with eight abstentions.[15]

The global human rights regime now comprises two additional documents that have the status of treaties: the International Covenant on Civil and Political Rights (ICCPR) and the International Covenant on Economic, Social, and Cultural Rights (ICESCR). These are supplemented by a number of further international and regional agreements and customary international law that, together with the aforementioned treaties, form the basic legal framework under which nations operate (or at any rate are committed to operate) in today's world.[16] The UN's vision of a culture of peace (discussed in Chapter 6, section 6.3, "What Is a Culture of Peace?") rests upon this broader foundation of human rights.

In December 2011, the UN General Assembly adopted a supplementary document, the Declaration on Human Rights Education and Training, which establishes everyone's "right to know about rights," that is, to be informed about what human rights are and how to exercise them. States or other governmental authorities are assigned the principal responsibility of providing their people with access to this information on an equal basis.[17] We have to be aware, however, that treaties, declarations, and conventions are only as good as the will to carry them out, since the UN does not have the capacity or authority to be an enforcer agency. It has been reported recently, for example, that with respect to the environment, "many countries sign agreements at international conferences like Rio [de Janeiro] with great fanfare, but then quietly fail to ratify them or pass them into domestic law."[18] Nor are these agreements always observed in fact. It scarcely needs to be said that from a global perspective, the record on applying human rights law is likewise far from perfect.

The basic idea of rights, in the context under discussion, is that as autonomous agents, all people deserve to be treated with dignity, respect, and justice. They should be immune from unreasonable intrusions into their moral space. As philosopher Andrew Fagan puts it, "Human rights are certain moral guarantees . . . [and] are said to be possessed equally, by everyone."[19] If rights, in the most general sense, are furthermore considered "advantageous positions conferred on the possessor" by some act or condition,[20] then human rights should be thought of as "conferred" just by the fact of being a member of the species *Homo sapiens*. Why so? The short answer is that *human rights express a recognition, at a fundamental level, that each person is an independent, self-directing being of equal moral and legal status, with interests and needs that are subject to harm by the unwanted and/or forcible actions and interventions of others.* Attinà makes a related point when he suggests that "It is . . . the capacity of humans to suffer because of hardships and physical and moral injuries which makes human rights a good which every person must enjoy."[21] Because of this universalizing feature that makes human rights what the philosophical tradition classifies as "natural rights," they "can be used as an independent standard in terms of which to criticize the laws and policies of governments and other organizations."[22] Rights talk has not been without its detractors even among Western thinkers through the ages, but when all is said and done, it remains as good a way as any of recognizing and validating humans' moral status and of setting up a normative barrier against violating (or obstructing) the mode of being that allows us to become unique and fulfilled individuals.

When we look more closely at the spectrum of human rights that have been posited as universal, it becomes evident that these are claimed against the state, and increasingly, against *any* state. They are also claimed against any and all other individuals, acting separately or together. However, some rights (the so-called "social and economic rights") represent claims for benevolent actions to be performed by the state. The Universal Declaration of Human Rights specifies a large variety of rights, and some of these describe liberties, others express entitlements, and still others are legal rights. Examples of the first are: rights to life, liberty, and security, not to be tortured, freedom of movement and residence, freedom of thought, opinion, and expression, freedom of assembly. The second group comprises: rights to an adequate standard of living, to education, to marry and raise a family, to social security, to rest and leisure, and to have intellectual or creative work protected. In the third class are found: the right to equality before the law, to presumption of innocence, to seek remedy for rights violations, to a fair, public, and impartial hearing of criminal charges.

All of these categories involve claims of status (being recognized as a person), and/or to be treated in a certain way (being free to do something), and/or for others to refrain from certain kinds of treatment (being free from interference or cruelty). When the "human rights record" of particular countries becomes a matter of international concern, or is seen as cause for outside intervention, all three of these claims are usually at stake in one respect or another, though generally violation of the first type of rights is the most pressing issue. In recent times, there has also been discussion of a universal "right to peace." The latest major developments in this regard are the 2010 Santiago Declaration on the Human Right to Peace and the establishment of the Open-ended Inter-governmental Working Group on the Draft United Nations Declaration on the Right to Peace, which held its first meeting in Geneva in February 2013.[23] While such a right may be difficult to define and unlikely to be implemented in the near future, it would serve as a connection between many of the other rights set out in the UDHR.

The concept of rights has a complex and interesting history, which we needn't go into here, but it is significant to note that every organized society has basic rules according to which its members may or may not do certain things, and that grant special powers, privileges, or entitlements to some members by virtue of their position within the group.[24] It may also be suggested that the concept of fair treatment (which we now call "justice") is as old as these practices, and even that humans have a feel for fairness that has become second-nature (as we saw earlier in Chapter 6, section 6.7, "Engaging with Conflict"). This goes together with the sense that unfair treatment requires some kind of (hopefully nonviolent) redress to restore a balance that existed before the disruption took place. Modern ideas of rights violation plug into these more or less intuitive perceptions rather directly, although they often go beyond them when basic personhood is under attack. Then, the response is one of outrage and anger. The point of having public (and internationally endorsed) statements of universal human rights—apart from stipulating norms of decent and just treatment, and of nonviolation of our common humanity—is to lay down conditions for acceptable social and political order and for appropriate concern and necessary action by the world community when agreed-upon minimum standards fail to be met. International conflict intervention, in circumstances where there is a crisis of human rights violation, is intended to handle the matter on a level of engagement that is beyond partisan retaliation, retribution, revenge, vendetta, or civil war. And such intervention is generally held to be justified when governments are unable or unwilling to protect rights, or else are themselves egregious rights violators.

We saw earlier that human rights may be considered as "guarantees" of a certain basic form of decent treatment, and also that they are universally possessed. Fagan notes that "A conventional corollary of this claim is that everyone has a duty to protect and promote the human rights of everyone else."[25] Yet it is evident that, while everyone has an obligation to respect and promote human rights, only governments and international organizations have it within their power to guarantee, protect, and enforce the observance of these rights. So what can we, as individuals, actually do to promote human rights? The answer is limited only by the time and energy one has available, but a little money in the form of donations helps, too. Nongovernmental organizations like Anti-Slavery International (the world's oldest international human rights group, founded in 1839), Amnesty International, Human Rights Watch, Global Witness, the Carter Center, Peace Brigades International, the Coalition Against Trafficking in Women, Madre, Children's Rights International, Witness, Human Rights First, Pax Christi International, and many, many more are in need of encouragement, support, and volunteers.[26] Most of these organizations have an international focus, as will be evident from their names; and through their monitoring activities, they make great contributions to the process of securing compliance of nations with international human-rights law.[27] However, we should never forget that, like charity, rights protection begins at home, and this means that there are many challenges we need to attend to in our own backyards. Alleviating problems of poverty, homelessness, racism, and the treatment of refugees, native peoples, women, and children are some things we can begin with, where the actions of average citizens can make a difference. The suggestion being made here is not that these are alternatives to involvement with international issues, but that we should avoid merely pointing the finger elsewhere and also realize, once again, that *peacebuilding starts wherever we are situated.*

What needs to be universally recognized and accepted is that *everyone deserves to have her or his rights recognized and respected at all times, and doing so is in everyone's best interest, both morally and practically speaking.* In their controversial but much-praised book *The Spirit Level*, public-health researchers Richard Wilkinson and Kate Pickett have demonstrated that "More equal societies work better for everyone." This conclusion is based on an analysis of eleven parameters: physical heath, mental health, drug abuse, education, imprisonment, obesity, social mobility, trust and community life, violence, teenage pregnancies, and child well-being.[28] We see here what is often (though not always) the case: that the morally correct choices also yield benefits in terms of pragmatic concerns, such as maximizing overall personal and social well-being.

7.2. RESPECT FOR OTHER ANIMALS AND THE ENVIRONMENT

The view that human ethics is evolving has been around for some time—at least as long as the idea of the evolution of the human species itself. The development of our ethical or moral sensibility (in particular, empathy and compassion) and related concepts (rights, obligations, and so on) is best expressed by the spatial image of an expanding sphere of concern, from localized, parochial preoccupations with self, family, tribe, and religious or ethnic group, on to nation, region or alliance, world, and then beyond. What is this "beyond"? In some distant future, it may include the rest of the solar system, beings, if any, that inhabit other planets, and the larger cosmos. But, in another sense, it signifies Earth's own animals and plants, species (known and unknown), and ecosystems, as well as the totality of nature (the biosphere). *A broader conception of the moral community by now has become a firmly established part of contemporary thought*, and this important shift has had accompanying effects on human behavior in terms of a greater sense of responsibility for protecting and enhancing life on Earth.[29]

Obligations to Members of Other Species

Animals enter the picture by virtue of a human sense of kinship and empathy with members of other species, and a significant amount of attention has also been paid in our era to the conditions that determine moral status or claims to moral consideration. Several different theoretical approaches argue for the extension of ethics to nonhuman animals. One view of this sort features an emphasis on "sentience" (or the capacity to experience pleasure, pain, and suffering). Another focuses on recognition of animals' value as independent life-forms, and hence, as objects of respect and bearers of rights. (Human rights, while they may confer special moral status, in no way cancel out the possibility of animal rights coexisting with them. Animals do not need to have *all* of the same rights as humans, in order to have *any*.) A third view highlights respect or reverence for life and compassion. Rapidly growing knowledge about the biological, cognitive, emotional, and behavioral similarities between humans and other animals also carries weight among ethicists, as does the awareness that a purely anthropocentric outlook on the natural world has now revealed itself to be as outmoded and counterproductive as the geocentric perspective was for advanced thinkers of the Renaissance.[30]

These are some of the philosophical grounds for extending ethics to non-humans. But if we look at things from a more emotion-guided perspective, assisted by reason, we arrive at the same result. Many, perhaps even most, of us currently enjoy or have grown up in the companionship of domesticated animals and have derived pleasure and personal enrichment from the experience. Through exposure to captive animals in zoos, nature parks, aquariums, as well as to animals roaming free in wilderness areas, we learn much about other creatures as well as about ourselves. Animals play a large part, in all sorts of ways, in the life of the imagination, in cultural myths, in the arts, and in scientific studies throughout the ages. They have nourished us, clothed us, protected us, entertained us, helped define who we are today; and at some future time, we may have the humility to acknowledge the debt of gratitude, generosity, compassion, and justice we owe to them. (See Chapter 3, section 3.6, "Second Antiwar Argument: The Extended Sphere of Obligation.") Many humans understand what it means to care for and about animals. But this understanding has not prevented our species from ruthless exploitation and extinction of nonhumans, which still continues and in some places and in certain respects is getting worse. Truly caring about animals, owning up to our moral obligations to them, and realizing our own capacity to evolve as ethical beings entail learning to cohabit the planet with them nonviolently and with respect for them as beings whose lives are of inherent value. But this also requires abandoning at least the most deplorable practices of animal violation we depend upon day in and day out, such as factory farming, transporting and slaughtering of live animals under very inhumane conditions, habitat destruction, and invasive research and product testing, while seriously addressing the complex general problem of animal cruelty (see "Education for Peace," section 7.3 below).

Obligations to the Biosphere as a Whole

The environment has come to be appreciated by thoughtful individuals as a realm of inherent value, which does not exist merely to fulfill human needs and wants.[31] This is evident, for instance, in a growing preoccupation with the impact of human behavior on land and sea wilderness areas, species diversity, rain forests, and water supplies. Preservation (the need to protect ecosystems for their own sake) sits alongside conservation (more carefully planned human use) as imperatives for the present and future. Notions like stewardship, natural heritage, and caretaking of the planet in the interests of those who will follow us no longer seem to be quaint relics of nearly forgotten indigenous peoples or of merely scriptural visions of paradise, but have risen to challenge mainstream ideas of human dominion over and subduing of nature. A slow change of consciousness is beginning to make it possible to admit that nature is more than just a collection of resource instrumentalities. (See Chapter 3, section 3.6, "Second Antiwar Argument: The Extended Sphere of Obligation.") At the same time, many people are coming to realize that responsible management of our home planet must be based on sustainable principles, because all of life and the conditions that support it are interconnected in very complex ways that are under severe pressure everywhere. We are using up resources (or "natural capital"), laying waste to ecosystems, and creating global warming, and by doing so, are severing our own lifelines and placing a viable future in question. Among other things, sustainability requires finding alternative energy sources, limiting global population, and moving toward a vegetarian diet, which is far less wasteful of resources and less environmentally polluting. Vegetarianism is also a meeting point of concern for the biosphere and for animals, inasmuch as providing for the world's insatiable demand for meat hinges on a food economy of untold suffering and massive killing of beings whose lives have intrinsic value.[32]

Will Tuttle argues, in *The World Peace Diet*, that there is a strong connection between the food we choose to eat, violence, and peace. While many might dismiss such a claim out of hand as far-fetched, it is not so easy to negate Tuttle's proposition that war and other forms of human violence "will not stop until we stop the *underlying* violence, the remorseless violence we commit against animals for food. We teach this behavior and this insensitivity to all our children. . . . [F]orcing our children to eat animal foods wounds them deeply. It requires them to disconnect from the food on their plates, from their feelings, from animals and nature. . . ."[33] One could reinforce this set of observations, which serve as a kind of wake-up call, with others about the routine cruelty toward animals practiced in the intensive livestock industry, transport and slaughtering, dairy production, scientific and military research, product testing, hunting and poaching, commercial fishing, zoos and circuses, the fur industry, feral animal control, and everyday neglect and abuse of pets and other animals. Violence prepares the way for more violence, we have learned (see Chapter 4, section 4.2, "The Limitations of Violence"). So, similarly, dominating and exploiting animals prepares the way for dominating and exploiting the natural world as a whole; and these practices continuously replicate and reinforce the mentality of control that places humans first and everything else in a subservient position.

7.3. EDUCATION FOR PEACE

Contrasting Theories and Practical Methods

Education is unquestionably the greatest tool for change, whether we are speaking of formal learning, self-education, life experience, or other kinds of education and training. Out of the field of peace studies, there has arisen a discipline of peace education or education for peace. Some of the ideas found therein are fresh, but others are part of a more enlightened agenda for education that has been around for quite some time. Examples of the latter include the need for young people to learn about the dynamics of successful relationships, parenting skills, and exposure to other cultures and different religions. Also worthy of mention is the approach known as "cosmic education," developed by Maria Montessori and her son Mario Montessori after World War II. The underlying philosophy here is that children should understand where they fit in the universe, and that this process will show them that in their own quest for personal identity, the same principles obtain as for everyone else in the world. As one Montessori guidebook states, "Although humans have made remarkable progress throughout history, they are simply changing the way they meet the universal, constant needs of all humans throughout time and space." Fully appreciating this insight is intended to teach children "the unity of humanity."[34]

Newer pedagogical frameworks comprise education in compassion, negotiating skills and conflict resolution, critical studies of war and peace, plus other approaches and solutions to problems.[35] In a recent book, education professor Nel Noddings maintains that "All educators must become keenly aware of their responsibility to promote moral awareness and a commitment to peace." She suggests in addition that a higher purpose of education is to foster "a way of life that pursues understanding and an attitude of openness to new ideas and knowledge." Noddings posits further that "This is perhaps our greatest task in peace education—teaching people to listen to one another and maintain the lines of communication."[36] These are vital qualities that teaching and the learning experience should incorporate.

But a more radical view of education also has a valid claim on our attention. This was stated four decades ago by Neil Postman and Charles Weingartner, who argue that "education has as its purpose the development of . . . an actively inquiring, flexible, creative, innovative, tolerant, liberal personality who can face uncertainty and ambiguity without disorientation, who can formulate new meanings to meet changes in the environment which threaten individual and mutual survival. . . . The purpose [of education] is to help all students develop built-in shockproof crap detectors as basic equipment in their survival kits."[37] The notion of a "crap detector" (borrowed from Ernest Hemingway) signifies the ability to sift through nonsense, disinformation, and fallacious appeals. This has obvious application in critically examining the seductive language of advertising and political rhetoric, but it is equally important for the subject of peace, for example, in deconstructing the mythology of war and patriotism (as discussed in the Introduction, section 2, "War Myths"). It may be thought that this more radical approach is just pie in the sky, but interestingly, the San Francisco Board of Education voted unanimously to adopt Joel Andreas' *Addicted to War: Why the U.S. Can't Kick Militarism*, a cartoon anti-war book, as a supplementary history text, and it is widely accepted as a free-of-charge donation by many other school districts across the United States.[38] Noddings laments that educational reforms in the interest of peace are often thwarted: "The very things that stand in the way of their implementation also support the continuation of war."[39] One cannot disagree with this assessment; yet the example just described shows that other tendencies also exist within at least some schools.

It may be that the optimal educational approach for promoting change lies somewhere in between the openness-encouraging outlook of Noddings and the more confrontational view of Postman and Weingartner—if only because that would be more likely to receive the kind of widespread endorsement needed for implementation. Attention has also been directed to classroom settings and special configurations for learning. Elliot Aronson, for example, describes a "jigsaw classroom," in which students are organized into "diverse, six-person learning groups." He reports that "Because students benefit from *each* student's performance in a cooperative task, they are prone to appreciate that performance by making encouraging statements to one another. This encouragement reinforces good performance, which in turn tends to raise the self-esteem of the person doing the reciting. The jigsaw method also requires people to participate more actively when they are required to recite and when they raise questions as active listeners."[40] Meanwhile, a team of researchers led by Douglas Fuchs has developed a technique called "peer assisted learning," and demonstrated its success in improving reading skills at various levels of schooling. Higher- and lower-achieving students are paired and trained in how to interact in reciprocal fashion, sometimes being tutor, sometimes tutee, and given assigned tasks to work through. A system of rewards promotes improved performance by both partners, according to measurable standards.[41] A win-win outcome emerges from the two classroom innovations discussed above, because they de-emphasize competitiveness in favor of collaborative learning. The introduction of group meditation activities into classrooms is another innovation, but this time, one that is sweeping North American elementary schools while catching on more slowly elsewhere. This addition to the curriculum has been shown to lower aggression, increase emotional self-control, and assist learning in various ways.[42]

Education in compassion also appears to have a good deal of merit as a contribution to personal development. A promising approach, known as *humane education*, succeeds in bringing compassion down to a very concrete level. According to one definition, "The aim of Humane Education is to create a culture of empathy and caring by stimulating the moral development of individuals to form a compassionate, responsible and just society. It is a means of introducing children to the reactions and emotions of animals, as well as linking this to an understanding of environmental issues and ecosystems."[43] Another statement of principles explains that "Humane education programs teach students how to be responsible citizens. From caring for their families' animal companions to taking action to prevent animal suffering, students learn to be compassionate toward all living beings." Among the "reasons for promoting humane education" included in this view are these: "It helps *prevent violence* and helps students apply the *concepts of respect and kindness* toward animals in their own lives. It helps students understand current and *past social justice movements*. It empowers students to realize that they can *make a positive difference* in their communities and the world around them."[44] Twelve US states now have laws mandating humane education in public schools.[45] Humane education is also offered outside the school setting, for example by People and Animal Learning, a Milwaukee-area program in which at-risk youths are involved in socializing shelter dogs to become good adoptive pets. "The children gain an increased sense of self-worth, develop compassion, and learn the importance of success through positive means," says the organization in charge of this program.[46] This kind of project capitalizes on the well-established psychological insight that rewards and reinforcements promote learning and behavior change much better in general than do punishments and deprivations.

Some factual considerations underpin the humane education perspective. First, empirical evidence now indicates a link between abuse of animals and domestic and other forms of violence against humans: "[C]hildren who are cruel to animals are at higher risk of growing up into violent adults, and adults who are cruel to animals are at higher risk of committing domestic violence, child abuse, and elder abuse."[47] Even though no clear causality has been established between animal abuse and antisocial behaviors, and existing studies have certain limitations, these findings are disturbing and call for a carefully considered response. Second, there is also evidence that animal abuse is used by violent individuals as a way of controlling family members and forcing them into acts performed against their will.[48] Third, although more studies of the effectiveness of humane education are needed, there are solid grounds for believing that early interventions of various kinds can help reduce the frequency of abusive behavior in children, with positive follow-on effects as they become more responsible adults.[49] Experiencing empathy and compassion toward animals reinforces these same attitudes toward humans.[50] Ideally, children should also be taught not to compartmentalize pet animals off from animals used for food, hunting, experimentation, and other human purposes—as if pets, but not other animals, deserve compassion, caring, and respect. Humane education by itself will not stop domestic violence, but it might at least help guide young people who are still in their formative years away from violence and toward a more positive orientation to living things.

We have seen that humane education is a focused educational program that promotes compassion, which is a contribution to peace as viewed from a wider perspective. Sociologist and Holocaust survivor Samuel Oliner, summarizing relevant research, reports that "Pedagogical approaches in class that express the positive consequences of caring increase the likelihood that those students will discover their own compassionate natures. Acting in a caring and altruistic manner encourages even more caring and altruistic behavior in the future, which also includes empathy for others and willingness to forgive." He adds, without qualification, that "It is the responsibility of all involved in education to participate in the dissemination of kindness and concern for others," and this is meant to include not only teachers but also parents and anyone else who serves as a role model for young people.[51] Oliner's conclusion is endorsed here because it embodies the belief that *peace begins within the smallest and most modest influences of life, in which we all take part in one way or another.*

Masculinity and Violence

A related theme that is currently receiving considerable attention is the education and socialization of boys. Given the disproportionate amount of violence attributable to males, not only in wartime but also in everyday life, this is a reasonable preoccupation. Certainly, we must admit that if we want a less violent or nonviolent society, then the rearing and education of boys must be scrutinized and new directions taken. This issue cannot be addressed, however, in isolation from considerations about patterns of consumption, role modeling, the value attached to macho and violent behavior in society at large, and the stereotyping of women in contrast to men. If there is any area of peacebuilding where common sense and fresh ideas are called for, surely this must top the list.

A few cautions are in order at the outset. Although men are not inclined to talk about what being male means to them, a little personal experience with focus groups where they do discuss this shows that there is a huge range of ways in which individual men understand and construct their masculinity. Such a realization shatters many entrenched ideas and opinions. This sort of anecdotal evidence is backed up by more scientific approaches. While some scholars use the concept of "hegemonic" (or dominant) masculinity in their work, others question it. A case in point is sociologist and criminologist James W. Messerschmidt, who argues that "Hegemonic masculinity influences, but does not determine, masculine behavior—the cultural ideals of hegemonic masculinity do not correspond to the actual identities of most men. Thus, masculinity . . . reflects unique circumstances and relationships. . . . In this way, men construct varieties of masculinities through specific practices as they simultaneously reproduce, and sometimes change, social structures."[52] If you doubt this standpoint, ask yourself how many men you know, or have ever heard of, actually fit (or aspire to fit) the mold of Sylvester Stallone, Chuck Norris, Randy ("Macho Man") Savage, or Mike Tyson—and whether you'd even want them to. Although "male violence itself is not particularly rare," say a criminologist and a sociologist, "most men are not violent."[53] So the key question is: *Why* are some men violent and others not? Both sides of this question are equally important to investigate. No generalized answer will be attempted here; but it is worth mentioning that these same authors suggest one potent formula that can lead young men to go off the rails: "They are not only failures in school and unable to find a job, but also people of color who face institutional racism on a daily basis."[54] When options are shut down and human rights abused, it is not surprising to find an antisocial backlash in the making.

Education professor R. W. Connell proposes that the objective of creating a less violent and more peaceful society will be well served by "develop[ing] gender practices for men . . . that move towards equality, nonviolence, and mutual respect between people of different genders, sexualities, ethnicities and generations," and that new links need to be forged between behavior and virtues customarily associated with masculinity, such as "courage, steadfastness, ambition."[55] This is a laudable and vital kind of initiative, which should be seen as a liberating of minds and possibilities for more healthy types of relationships rather than as a form of indoctrination. (Some, of course, may see *all* education as indoctrination, in which case this is a better sort than the kind that produces domineering macho bullies.)

Nonviolence Education Projects

A commonly expressed view is that it is up to younger generations to make large-scale changes in the world happen. This cannot be the whole story, since young people do not exercise dominant political power in any society. *Everyone needs to play a part in creating a different future, and everyone is capable of changing*. As Gabriel Moran points out, "educating toward a nonviolent life begins at birth and continues as long as a person lives."[56] Even so, it is nevertheless true that if children and young adults are to think differently, schools must educate them differently too, as the preceding discussion indicates. Yet here a dilemma enters the picture. Following Karl Marx, let us call this the problem of "Who will educate the educators?"[57] In order for new ideas and methods to enter an educational system, there has to be a critical mass of influential and aware people who are in tune with these, and capable of implementing and conveying them. However, the hypothesis we started with was that it is (at least substantially) the young who will be able to change the world, but older generations who have the power to do so (or not) at present. So where are the teachers going to come from to inspire, challenge, and enlighten the young? More specifically, who will initiate educational reforms from within an inertia-bound system that does not reward peaceful behaviors, and a society that is structured to foster and reward nonpeaceful behaviors? Fortunately, institutions and societies are diverse, and, in some ways, internally contradictory, which means that there are forces within them that promote constructive change through slow and patient effort, and that also seize those moments when the time is ripe for transformation.

An example of this process comes from a high school in one of Chicago's most violent neighborhoods. There, a coalition of teachers, students, and administrators took action to introduce the Kingian Nonviolence training method into the school. The goal was to prevent violence by means of creating a peace culture. Students as a whole are rewarded in various ways for consecutive days without fighting. Most importantly, "The students took ownership of their community and began keeping the peace themselves." When fights do occur, restorative justice is implemented instead of punishment; those who have engaged in violence have to work out with a jury of their peers some act of restitution that all parties agree to and that will also benefit the school. Some attempts have even been made to extend peace activities into the community beyond the school. As one measure of the success of this program, "With the savings made from not having metal detectors and security guards, the school created a new program called Phoenix Rising, which sends students to various summer leadership, wilderness, and academic programs around the country."[58]

As this book was going to press, another was released (with an accompanying video) that provides an additional impressive example of teaching peace within an unexpected setting: *World Peace and Other 4th Grade Achievements*, by John Hunter. Hunter creatively taps into the game culture of today's young people in order to teach peaceful cooperation and problem-solving. According to the advance publicity for this book, over a period of eight weeks, "The children learn to collaborate and communicate with each other as they work to resolve the Game's conflicts. They learn how to compromise while accommodating different perspectives and interests. Most importantly, the students discover that they share a deep and abiding interest in taking care of each other."[59]

Other ways of empirically gauging success can also be applied in order to assess training in nonviolence. Daniel Mayton summarizes these in *Nonviolence and Peace Psychology*: "There are several sound measures of nonviolence that are appropriate for use with various age groups as outcome measures in interventions designed to reduce violence and/or to increase nonviolent dispositions and behaviors."[60] This supports the conclusion that *teaching peace, in addition to being theoretically and practically well-grounded, has become a scientifically respectable approach.* In short, it is feasible and therefore ought to compel public attention and commitment.

Advancing Girls and Women

Another frontier of reform, with international implications for peace, is the education of females. As one comprehensive study reports, "A growing number of organizations and governments recognize that focusing on women and girls is the most effective way to fight global poverty and extremism." The primary reason why this is so is that "Evidence suggests that women with more control over resources will spend more money on basic living needs (e.g., food and health) and education."[61] They will also tend to limit family size. Greater levels of education lead to expanded opportunities for women in various fields, including politics, and thereby also to greater equality. Quite a number of observers of the present scene express the fact that women—as half of humanity—possess vast and largely unacknowledged and underutilized resources for ameliorating serious problems that the world faces. (See also Chapter 6, section 6.4, "Women and Peace," and section 6.7, "Engaging with Conflict.") Another large study, conducted by political scientist Valerie Hudson and her associates, concludes that "the very best predictor of a state's peacefulness is not its level of wealth, its level of democracy, or its ethno-religious identity; the best predictor of a state's peacefulness is how well its women are treated. What's more, democracies with higher levels of violence against women are as insecure and unstable as nondemocracies."[62] If any further proof were needed that improving the situation of women carries a huge payoff for everyone, this is it. Such improvement is vital because women deserve it, and it is therefore the right thing to do for them; but even self-interest on the part of men and policy-makers in general should demand the same action. Treating females better at all stages of life does not by itself bring about world peace, but it is clear that the quality of women's lives is an indicator of other important dynamics within a body politic that also point to this as the right thing to do. *When people's basic needs are met and their aspirations encouraged, equal opportunity and security (at the individual as well as higher levels of organization) can develop as well.*

Final Reflections

Without in any way minimizing the special contributions at every age level that education can make to peace, we must also realize that education cannot solve all problems. Schools are routinely asked and expected to step in to do things that should be done elsewhere in society, and especially by parents actively rearing their children. Humane education is often introduced under the rubric of "character education." But surely, children's character should be formed at home, first and foremost. And it is, in one manner or another. As education professor Kieran Egan states, "What children know best when they come to school are love, hate, joy, fear, good, and bad. That is, they know best the most profound human emotions and the bases of morality."[63] A lot depends on how this preschool learning takes shape and what perspectives on relationships are encouraged or modeled. Children raised in environments of domestic abuse can hardly blossom into caring, compassionate adults merely because of a few after-the-fact lessons in values they encounter in a "learning module" at school. *To develop young people into peaceful adults who behave nonviolently is a holistic process in which many influences inevitably play a part.*

7.4. A GLOBAL OUTLOOK

It has been argued, by numerous authors and in various ways, that *seeking peace in the present age must be a global effort*. Most of our actions will be local, but they can and often do have much wider applications and results. International relations specialist Kimberly Hutchings observes that "At the level of everyday life, from eating habits to religious beliefs, in a globalized world strangeness and strangers are no longer at a distance; they are living in the neighbourhood. And social, economic and political activities that originate locally have intended and unintended global implications."[64] Because of this unprecedented degree of interconnectedness and mutual impact, the ethical dimensions of our relationships with one another are more prominent than ever before.

On Being Agents of Change

Unless we are super rich or at the helm of a particular state, there is very little any of us, as individuals, can do to directly effect change anywhere else in the world—to bring about democratic governments, stop human rights abuses, give the poor a better life, end civil wars, curtail the arms trade, eliminate disease, prevent environmental devastation, and so on. *But what we can do is change ourselves and our own society and political process.* And we should never underestimate the fact that by doing so, we set an example and send out a message of peace and conciliation that can have a strong and ongoing indirect influence on others. Metaphorically, we extend a hand of good will, welcome, and trust. Not only this, but we can also make our own country a more agreeable place to live in at the same time. *If we change ourselves and how we act toward others, then we have the possibility of changing others* by the very fact that they now have to respond in turn to a different reality. This kind of effect is no insignificant matter in a troubled relationship or a troubled world.

Where do we start trying to change things? An obvious place is by joining campaigns and using our votes to reduce international tensions that are caused by militarization. The United States has by far the largest armaments budget and the most extensive arms export trade, as we saw in the Introduction. It also has an established military presence in 150 countries, by its own reckoning.[65] The misguided vision known as "American exceptionalism" (its being a unique model of what is best among nations), and the self-awarded role of policing the world in the name of freedom and protecting "American interests," are mostly to blame for this adventurism. American investment capital has traditionally thrived in this world "made safe for freedom." For better or worse, the United States at present holds the keys that can unlock the doorway to world peace. The Obama administration wants to pursue the goal of eliminating nuclear weapons. But to make any advance, the United States has to take a holistic and integrated approach to reducing tensions and weaponry in the world—one that addresses the problems caused by its unrestrained use of drones,[66] the global spread of its own military bases, publicized strategies for American domination, and other policies that create animosity, fear, suspicion, outrage, mistrust, and insecurity.

It must be mentioned that at the same time all of this militarization is going on, the United States has also undertaken some initiatives that work in the opposite direction, and may hold promise for the future. Three are of special interest here. The first is the Complex Crisis Fund, set up in 2010. This is "an account appropriated by Congress that provides much-needed, unprogrammed money for the State Department and United States Agency for International

Development (USAID) 'to prevent and respond to emerging or unforeseen crises'. The CCF has been used to help mitigate violence in critical places like Kenya, Sri Lanka, Kyrgyzstan, Côte D'Ivoire, Tunisia and Yemen."[67] The second is the US State Department Bureau of Conflict and Stabilization Operations, set up by then Secretary of State Hillary Clinton in 2011. This government department focuses on "conflict prevention, crisis response and stabilization, aiming to address the underlying causes of destabilizing violence."[68] The third is the Atrocities Prevention Board, championed by President Obama's human rights adviser Samantha Power and created by a presidential directive in 2012. A White House release states that *"Preventing mass atrocities and genocide is a core national security interest and a core moral responsibility of the United States,"* and that "President Obama has made the prevention of atrocities a key focus of this Administration's foreign policy." The purpose of this innovative approach is to develop a range of nonmilitary and military responses for intervention where atrocities are actual or perceived as imminent.[69] Programs like these of course are subject to congressional funding, and the will of lawmakers is notoriously fickle. They also depend on which party is in power at a given time. And last, while they do disclose the better, more generous spirit of America, they illustrate, too, the contradictory (or dialectical) character of international politics, in which war and peace initiatives sit side by side within a nation's range of prerogatives and priorities.

The problem of militarism, of course, is not owned by the United States alone. According to Dutch political scientist and peace researcher Wilbert van der Zeijden, "Foreign military bases are found in more than 100 countries and territories. The US currently maintains a world-wide network of some 1000 military bases and installations. In addition, other NATO countries, such as France and the UK, have a further 200 such military locations within the network of global military control."[70] When British Prime Minister David Cameron made his first visit to Libya, newly liberated from Muammar Gadaffi's iron rule, he had representatives of six arms manufacturers in tow. However, in the final analysis, American militarism is most worrying. A recently reported development, for example, is that "The US military is expanding its secret intelligence operations across Africa, establishing a network of small air bases to spy on terrorist hideouts from the fringes of the Sahara to jungle terrain along the equator. . . ."[71] These policies generate resentment, unrest, and strong anti-Western attitudes, and worrisome but in some ways understandable forms of backlash. In the words of a former senior Iraqi army officer, "Colonialism may be dead, but many commentators think that a neocolonial system exists, in which rich and powerful nations still seek to dominate and control poorer and weaker (but often resource-rich) nations by means of free trade agreements, the International Monetary Fund, the World Bank, cultural influence, and armed intervention, when considered necessary and 'just'."[72]

But perhaps we should look at the matter more realistically, some might say. "After all, isn't the world a dangerous place that is in need of security arrangements and policing, if only to ensure that terrorism and war don't break out everywhere? Don't these arrangements themselves result from adopting a global outlook?" Apart from the response (given throughout this book) that *nonviolent policies and actions are much more likely to yield peace than measures based on violence or threats,* there are specific ways in which war preparations not only help provoke conflict, but also create unnecessary damage to societies even in peacetime. For example, as van der Zeijden continues, "Bases cause social and environmental problems at a local level. Communities living around the bases often experience high levels of rapes committed by foreign soldiers, violent crimes, loss of land or livelihood, and pollution and health hazards caused by the testing of conventional or non-conventional weapons. In many countries the agreement that permitted the base stipulates that foreign soldiers who perpetrate crimes cannot be held accountable, since they are granted immunity."[73] Does it need to be demonstrated that this dangerous and human-rights-violating scenario must be relegated to the trash-bin of history? Does it need to be proven that countries' "national interests" are now interdependent, and more likely to thrive and evolve over the long term in a world of equals?

If you want to get involved in advancing a more peaceful global outlook and introducing a greater level of sanity into national defense, all you need to do is look up "peace organizations" on the Internet and go from there. There are also effective routes such as helping organize festivals that promote peaceful ideas, supporting peace candidates—if and when you can find them—or being one yourself, and doing whatever else you can to affect the political process, change minds, and help develop a culture of peace at any level of human activity (including your own).[74]

Cosmopolitanism

Taking a closer look at what a global perspective entails, some useful concepts emerge from the literature on the subject. The first of these is *cosmopolitanism*. Nigel Dower defines this as "the claim that all human beings are in some sense 'citizens of the world'," and relates it, among other things, to an "affirmation of our common humanity" and of a "world ethics."[75] (See "Global Ethics," below.) Another approach, taken by Kwame Anthony Appiah, maintains that cosmopolitanism embraces two notions: "One is the idea that we have obligations to others, obligations that stretch beyond those to whom we are related by the ties of kith and kind, or even the more formal ties of a shared citizenship. The other is that we take seriously the value not just of human life but of particular human lives, which means taking an interest in the practices and beliefs that lend them significance." Appiah sees this not as a settled formula for how we should act in the world, but as a "challenge" to be creative in the ways in which we reach out to strangers.[76] Soran Reader argues that "The core cosmopolitan intuition is that human beings have a moral worth as such, which is unaffected by all properties except those for which they are responsible. This intuition brings with it a universal human right to decent treatment, and a universal duty to treat [others] decently." He further urges that this double (or reciprocal) obligation is compatible with every theory about the grounds of morality.[77] (See Chapter 3, section 3.5, "First Antiwar Argument: The Fundamental Premise of Morality.") We can discern that in all of these views, cosmopolitanism carries with it duties to people who are in need, or just in need of being treated decently, whoever and wherever they may be. (We will come back to this point in a moment.) Notice, too, that Appiah includes in his description the responsibility to learn about different ways of life and the cultures that nurture them, which is a time-honored procedure for overcoming ethnocentrism and xenophobia and encouraging respect for diversity, a point that was discussed earlier in this chapter. A cosmopolitan person will also be an internationalist, to the extent that he or she supports and strives to promote state-generated, organizational, or networking initiatives aimed at enhancing mutual understanding and peaceful relationships across the world community.

Pacificism

The second concept that may help shape at least some individuals' global outlook is known as *pacificism (pacific-ism)*. This is the position that war can be eliminated and that, as world citizens, we all have an obligation to promote and work toward this end.[78] "Pacifism," in contrast, a more commonly recognized view, is that war and violent means of settling disputes are inherently wrong and should in general or in principle be opposed. It seems to be understood that pacifists would also feel committed to work for the positive goal of encouraging nonviolent ways of living and resolving disputes, not merely for the negative goal of resisting and abolishing war. Whereas the pacifist, then, will almost certainly be a pacificist, the reverse does not necessarily hold true; for a pacificist usually accepts the necessity of maintaining armed forces and their possible use in the short term to prevent aggression.

Nevertheless, pacificism holds the key to realizing the dream of pacifists of all persuasions, as discussed in Chapter 3. This is because pacificism represents a motivation and an undertaking to end war, which brings activities serving this purpose to the front and center of human affairs. In a practical sense, pacifists could not ask for more.

Global Ethics

An expansive view of the world as a rapidly integrating community depends, some maintain, on the adoption of a specifically *global ethics*. The reason for this is that cooperative and concerted international action is urgently required in order to address problems that have either come more vividly to general awareness (for example, world hunger, civil wars, water shortages), or are exacerbated by policies of various nations (for example, environmental degradation, nuclear weapons proliferation, terrorism), or are products of the dynamics of economic interdependence (for example, exploitative labor, the narcotics trade, collapse of world fisheries). A shared approach, endorsed by all relevant parties, seems to be the only basis for such action. As Rodrigue Tremblay comments, "humanity has no other choice than to adopt the most civilized rules of private and collective behavior that can best guarantee its chances of survival."[79] Thus, there is a pragmatic reason for adopting a global ethics.

But "collective prudence" is not by itself a sufficient foundation for such a code.[80] An ethics also entails obligations (to do the right thing and avoid the wrong thing) that we have in view of certain beliefs we hold. "Most people have a world ethic of some kind," Dower contends, "even if it is poorly articulated, rarely thought about and largely implicit. . . . It may merely be the natural expression of their ordinary ethical beliefs in certain contexts."[81] (The relatively recently developed notion of "crimes against humanity," for instance, could be seen as the outcome of a shared world ethic.) Some suggestions concerning the need for a more explicit global approach to ethics have already been made in earlier sections of this chapter dealing with respect for human rights, other animals, and the environment. The notion was presented there that we are witnessing the cultural evolution of a more sophisticated view: *an expanding sphere of obligation that encompasses the world at large (and even things beyond it)*. And earlier in the present section, the ethically significant concepts of cosmopolitanism and pacificism were introduced.

The idea of a global ethics, for most advocates, turns on the belief that *there are at least some values and principles of conduct that everyone shares*, even if these are overlain by dissimilar religious and spiritual, cultural, philosophical, and other notions. One account of the essence of morality goes like this: "Morality serves two universal human needs. It regulates conflicts of interest between people, and it regulates conflicts of interest within the individual born of different desires and drives that cannot all be satisfied at the same time. Ways of dealing with these two kinds of conflict develop in anything recognizable as human society."[82] This is a useful way of looking at ethics (or morality) because it emphasizes the universal element but refrains from insisting that everyone must accept a single uniform code, allowing for some variation across cultures and belief-systems. Most ethical scholars recognize, for example, that *certain things would be considered wrong in all societies*, so we would therefore expect to find in the belief-systems of any culture such precepts as "prohibitions against killing the innocent, stealing, breaking of promises, and lying,"[83] or "the torture of persons at whim,"[84] although there might be significant differences surrounding things like "rules regarding sexual mores and regulations of property."[85]

We could add to the above definition of morality (or ethics) that it also serves the universal need for groups to find ways of coexisting with other groups and to understand and carry out their reciprocal obligations. This idea may be considered as implicit in the idea of "regulating conflicts of interest between people," but on its own, one might reasonably conclude that this refers only to relationships between individuals. Adding groups into the mix enables global ethics to gain a foothold in our thinking.

Hutchings' overview of the global ethics field reveals that the following concerns stand out in the literature: "peace and war; aid, trade and development; and the environment," as well as "humanitarian intervention and issues of economic justice." She argues, however, that "issues that have traditionally been counted as part of 'private morality', the morality surrounding reproduction, sexuality and family life," should also be counted, inasmuch as they are "aspect[s] of the globalized condition."[86] Obviously, much in this assessment invites agreement, but equally, there is considerable room for disagreement. Whether sexual life, for example, is part of the "globalized condition," and what exactly this might mean, are possible areas of extreme contention. It is important to note in addition that (as we saw earlier in relation to human rights) some ethical or moral issues, or certain aspects of them, are appropriately viewed as things individuals can affect just by acting on their beliefs, whereas others must be addressed by groups, organizations, governments, alliances, and so forth. But individuals can support and influence collective policies and behaviors, too; so in discussing global ethics, we are not talking about completely independent levels of analysis, values, principles, and actions.

The problems of coordinating individual and collective ethical outlooks are underlined by Hutchings as follows:

> even if one is confident of one's ethical position in the abstract, that confidence is hard to translate to a consistent set of behaviours in our personal lives, let alone to the behaviours of collective actors such as states, international organizations or international charities. . . . In the peculiarly complex and hierarchically structured world in which we live, acting rightly may sometimes involve putting one's moral convictions on one side or rethinking them in the light of not living in the best of all possible worlds. . . . In this respect, . . . we also need to cultivate in ourselves capacities for responsibility, sympathy, generosity, kindness and humility as qualities that will enable us to live well with others and work to recognize shared values where they exist, and to recognize when and how it may or may not be possible to construct them when they do not.[87]

There is a rich vein of wisdom in these remarks, suggesting, as they do, that nurturing certain virtues in ourselves may be as significant for participation in the affairs of the world as is any theoretical ethical stance. They are also virtues that strengthen the bonds of our own civil societies. Moreover, there is a strong down-to-earth message here, in that "doing the right thing"—whether as individuals or collectivities—will often require compromise. We tend to think, when engaging with moral issues, that compromise is necessarily a bad thing, because it entails abandoning what you believe in for reasons of expediency. This can indeed be worrisome; but the point being made by Hutchings is of a different order: *There has to be some give-and-take among those whose values resist reconciliation; no one has the right or authority to dictate a "correct" ethical world-view.* We can notice, too, a resonance between the list of virtues she validates and the discussion of compassion as an important key to peace offered in Chapter 5. There is no easy route to agreement on value-laden issues that separate individuals or groups. But encountering one another across cultural space in a spirit of good will and openness, and with the ability to see another point of view, or at least to negotiate seriously, goes a long way toward settlement of even the most difficult disputes. Any sort of self-sustaining world peace would depend upon such factors.

World Governance

A fourth useful concept for orienting oneself toward a global vision is *world governance*. Globalization, in the economic sense, everyone acknowledges to be, in one form or another, the wave of the future. But as the many activities of the United Nations to improve the quality of life indicate, there is much more that remains to be globalized, for the benefit of all. From a common-sense standpoint, as one author puts it, "goods, money, people, ideas, and pollution are traveling around the world with unprecedented speed and scale."[88] And as Michael Renner, a disarmament expert, observes, "there is growing recognition that security in an interdependent world requires cooperation, not confrontation, and that social equality, economic vitality, and environmental stability are more important to a country's fortunes than martial qualities."[89]

The main idea behind global governance is that a world federation of some kind is the appropriate level of organization (for cooperation, administration, legislation, and enforcement) to deal with overarching international issues and problems. While the UN is, in many ways, a very successful experiment in international cooperation, it is in reality a federation of sovereign states and not a world government by anyone's definition. Much of the work of peace can be and is conducted by a large number of peaceful alliances (notably the European Union, African Union, Association of Caribbean States, Commonwealth of Independent States, Association of Southeast Asian Nations, Shanghai Cooperation Organization, and Union of South American Nations), as well as by nongovernmental organizations of almost infinite variety, many of which are specifically devoted to peace and conflict resolution, international development, human rights, and other constructive causes. Attinà convincingly argues that although the level of cooperation among states is far from what it could be, the image of international politics as purely anarchic and driven by self-interest is outmoded. In fact, he claims, even in the absence of full-fledged international government, global politics today, to be understood properly, must be seen as the result of an unprecedented degree of regulation and rule-following behavior. This approach yields a picture of the world "as if it were a unit whose actors—formerly just states but now also international organizations and other non-state actors—have created a public arena and constituted a political system whose institutions have a global range, and which evolve along a trajectory of long-term change."[90]

But still greater cooperative efforts are demanded by the nature of the major issues that confront humanity. As Thomas Weber argues,

It is now clear that the problems besetting the world cannot be solved within the boundaries of nation states. Poverty, hunger, overpopulation, scarcity of resources, pollution, and injustice, the consequences of nuclear accidents, and rises in sea level caused by global warming do not respect national borders. Given the possible consequences of nuclear war and environmental destruction, perhaps the only hope for human survival, even in the short term, is to move to full-scale forms of world governance. This may be especially so given that war, one of the main dangers to our existence, is a product of the nation state.[91]

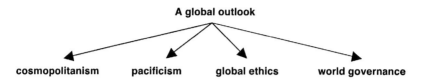

Figure 7.1 A global outlook

What kind of international government this should be is a highly controversial matter, both because few countries are keen on divesting themselves of their most substantial sovereign powers and because any such arrangement would have to include checks against this grand federation's morphing into a repressive super-state. Going beyond Attinà's viewpoint, Weber continues, with the intriguing speculation that "While we may not be moving rapidly toward a world government we are, perhaps without even noticing it, moving incrementally toward a form of world governance or global polity that does not require us to take any active steps"; and, he adds, an entity of this type "that includes civil society and nonstate actors has been gradually emerging through multiple forms of globalization."

Clearly, though, as Weber indicates, inequality and injustice have to be high up on the agenda of world governance, which might make the idea appear even more remotely placed over the horizon than would other considerations. For any such move toward political union to occur, economic globalization will have to evolve into a fairer distribution of wealth, opportunity, and resource allocation as well. Exploitative labor and investment will have to be monitored and eliminated. But the payoff is enormous: In a world of greater equality of means, there would be less of a perceived need for armaments, foreign bases, and overt and covert power plays and various forms of treachery.

7.5. EVALUATING WHERE WE ARE AND WHERE WE ARE HEADING

This book has highlighted many trends and tendencies, some of which point toward continuing violence and war, others of which demonstrate that nonviolent and cooperative patterns of behavior are already extending and developing our moral compass. Constructive forms of collaboration may evolve further, hopefully, changing the course of human events in positive but barely foreseeable ways, as the future eclipses the present and the past. This journey we share remains a long and difficult one. If social and moral progress are painfully slow, consider how much slower global progress toward peace must be.

Amartya Sen notes that "The world is certainly divisive, but it is diversely divisive, and the partitioning of the global population into distinct 'nations' or 'peoples' is not the only line of division."[92] This is disquieting, perhaps, because it calls attention to religious, ethnic, professional, economic-class, organizational-membership, and other identities that separate people across borders and on different continents. But it is simultaneously encouraging, because there are ties connecting people that may in the end prove stronger than the political geographies that set them in opposition to one another, historically as well as today. And in a world of highly mobile individuals—vacation travelers, Olympian and other athletes, diplomats and negotiators, conference attendees, international students, journalists, consultants, investors, foreign workers, immigrants, refugees—no one should underestimate the transformative power of these ties.

Measuring Progress toward Peace

Is the world getting any closer to peace? If you look at the daily headlines, the conflict statistics, and the seemingly overwhelming global problems that beset humanity, it is hard not to be somewhat cynical and fatalistic about our capacity to rise above war and violence. But if you concentrate instead on things like progress toward realizing the UN's Millennium Development Goals, successful conflict-resolution and peacebuilding efforts, international collaboration of various sorts, and levels of violence today compared with the past, a brighter picture emerges. Other items of promise shine forth as well. The *Global Directory of Peace Studies and Conflict Resolution Programs* is a "fully searchable data-base [that] profiles over 450 undergraduate, Master's, and Doctoral programs, centers, and institutes in over 40 countries and 40 U.S. states."[93] Compiled by the Peace and Justice Studies Association and the International Peace Research Association Foundation, this details the huge amount of effort, thought, and commitment that is going into training people in peace-promoting outlooks and peace-making skills. Also of note is the *Global Nonviolent Action Database*, a project of Swarthmore College in Pennsylvania, which, at latest count, contains 870 case studies from over 190 countries in an interactive format. The database reportedly attracts 300–500 visits daily, representing 177 countries to date.[94]

Is there any objective measure of peacefulness that can assist in the drawing of conclusions about where we are at and what needs to be done? Actually, yes. Again, projects like Millennium Development provide part of the answer. But also worthy of mention here are the Global Peace Index and the United States

Peace Index—both compiled annually by the nonprofit Institute for Economics and Peace, with offices in Sydney, Australia, New York, and Washington, DC, and promoted by the affiliated organization Vision for Humanity—and the Happy Planet Index.[95] The purpose of the Global Peace Index is explained as follows:

> The GPI ranks independent countries by their "absence of violence" using metrics that combine both internal and external factors. . . . The Index is composed of 23 indicators, ranging from a nation's level of military expenditure to its relations with neighbouring countries and the level of respect for human rights. . . . [and it] has been tested against a range of potential "drivers" or determinants of peace—including levels of democracy and transparency, education and national wellbeing. The team has used the latest available figures from a wide range of respected sources. . . . The project's ambition is to go beyond a crude measure of wars—and systematically explore the texture of peace. The hope is that it will provide a quantitative measure of peacefulness, comparable over time, that will provide a greater understanding of the mechanisms that nurture and sustain peace. This, in turn will provide a new platform for further study and discussion, which will hopefully inspire and influence world leaders and governments to further action.[96]

This sort of monitoring yields a set of consistent, empirically based criteria by means of which countries can evaluate their own level of peacefulness and be evaluated accordingly by the world community. While no one would claim that such measurements are flawless, they do offer a viable approach to assessing progress toward (or movement away from) peace in a meaningful sense. Shining the spotlight on places where peace is a priority, and where it is not, cannot help but attract international attention and occasion positive or negative judgments that may have a local as well as global impact.

The United States Peace Index "provides a comprehensive analysis of peacefulness at the state and city levels, as well as an analysis of the costs associated with violence and the socio-economic measures associated with peace. The USPI measures peacefulness according to five indicators: the number of homicides, number of violent crimes, the incarceration rate, number of police employees and the availability of small arms." In addition to ranking the fifty states according to peacefulness, some sixty-one major cities are also ranked at present. Perhaps unexpectedly, according to this index "the U.S. is more peaceful now than at any other time over the last twenty years."[97]

The Global Militarization Index displays military budgets by nations, but "also defines the level of militarization of a country by the relation of military expenditure to its gross domestic product (GDP) or other areas in society, such as health care."[98] The Human Development Index correlates life expectancy, education, and income for all UN member nations.[99] The Happy Planet Index, a relative newcomer, attempts to gauge the relationship between life satisfaction, life expectancy, and environmental impact for each nation and to rank their "sustainable wellbeing" scores.[100]

While it might initially be tempting for politicians and reactionary individuals and organizations of one kind or another to dismiss such sampling and monitoring techniques as inaccurate, poorly constructed, or ideologically motivated, they will find it increasingly difficult to deny the facts presented, and the social pressures for change in response to these that are likely to mount as time goes by. We can hope that day is already beginning to dawn.

7.6. CONCLUSION

We know that war and violence are counterproductive attempts to control what goes on in the world. *In the end, cooperation and coexistence are the only solutions to hostile conflict and the sole guarantees of mutual benefit.* Since the methods of violence are failures in the end, we surely have nothing to lose by turning to peace. But the project before humanity is to build not just cultures of peace here and there, but *a global culture and system of peace*—a world order that respects and affirms interdependence, but also difference and diversity. That will be the greatest accomplishment of all, and more importantly, one from which everyone—without exception—will benefit, and to which everyone without exception can contribute.

Sometimes it seems that everyone is living in a delusion. There are those who think they can dominate the world by force of arms, terrorism, sabotage, espionage, or a combination of these. There are those who think the world and humankind are doomed. And there are those who think that peace is possible. The conditions of peace, however, are not a mystery—or at any rate no more than a "mystery in broad daylight" (to borrow Jean-Paul Sartre's excellent expression).[101] What remains a mystery, however, is how to motivate people to make it happen on a global scale. A prominent expert in foreign affairs cautions that "the work of promoting social change is hard and unforgiving. It is much easier to fail than to succeed, and success is likely to be modest. Humanity does not agree on the best way forward; there are passionate disagreements about the kind of world we want to build and the best way to build it."[102] Everyone who has ever done community work or been involved in activism of any kind already knows this. But we have examined many ways in which peace exists or is evolving, can be promoted, and can thrive on the local and regional levels. Peace truly is a global issue, with economic integration, modern weaponry and alliances, national, religious, and ethnic ambitions, swelling populations, poverty and inequality, overarching impacts on the environment, massively irresponsible banking, and other factors being what they are. It has been said that "the more things change, the more they stay the same." But the human will to survive and flourish has been tested many times, and there is still much more to be learned about it. The question is whether the will to survive can be refocused in intelligent, unselfish, and compassionate ways in response to the multidimensional crises that the world faces today. Codevelopment, compromise, reciprocity, and care for all future beings—human and nonhuman—must become governing principles. For this transformation to occur, humans are going to have to show qualities of restraint, cooperation, generosity, honesty, openness, responsibility, respect, trust, and good will as never before. *These qualities do not have to be invented; they already exist.* They will need to come to the fore, however, and guide the choices we make and whatever we do, individually and collectively. *Peace does not require of us that we be perfect, but rather, that we discover and affirm the better side of our nature.* That would truly be the ultimate triumph of human intelligence.

NOTES TO CHAPTER 7

1. See, for example, Ina Corinne Brown, *Understanding Other Cultures* (Englewood Cliffs, NJ: Prentice-Hall, 1963); Patty Lane, *A Beginner's Guide to Crossing Cultures: Making Friends in a Multicultural World* (Downers Grove, IL: IVP Books, 2002).

2. See, for example, K. L. Jang, W. J. Livesley, and P. A. Vernon, "Heritability of the Big Five Personality Dimensions and Their Facets: A Twin Study," *Journal of Personality* 64 (1996), 577–91; available at: http://onlinelibrary.wiley.com/doi/10.1111/jopy.1996.64. issue-3/issuetoc. I am grateful to Brian Byrne for pointing out this research to me.

3. See, for example, Lusia Stopa and David M. Clark, "Social Phobia and Interpretation of Social Events," *Behaviour Research and Therapy* 38 (2000), pp. 273–83; available at: http://www.sciencedirect.com/science/article/pii/S0005796799000431; Edith Chen, Karen A. Matthews, and Fan Zhou, "Interpretations of Ambiguous Social Situations and Cardiovascular Responses in Adolescents," *Annals of Behavioral Medicine* 34 (2007), pp. 26–36; available at: http://www.springerlink.com/content/1528630683412521. I am grateful to Brian Byrne for pointing out this research to me.

4. Fran Peavey with Myra Levy and Charles Varon, *Heart Politics* (Philadelphia: New Society, 1986), p. 9.

5. David Cannadine, *The Undivided Past: Humanity beyond Our Differences* (New York: Alfred A. Knopf, 2013). See also J. Robert Du Bois, *Powerful Peace: A Navy SEAL's Lessons on Peace from a Lifetime at War* (New York: Morgan James, 2013).

6. Milica Vasiljevic and Richard Crisp, "Tolerance by Surprise: Evidence for a Generalized Reduction in Prejudice and Increased Egalitarianism through Novel Category Combination," *PLOS ONE* 6 March 2013; available at: http://www.plosone.org/article/info%3Adoi%2F10.1371%2Fjournal.pone.0057106.

7. For additional insights, see Ryszard Kapuscinski, *The Other* (London: Verso, 2008); DeWight R. Middleton, *The Challenge of Human Diversity: Mirrors, Bridges, and Chasms*, 3rd ed. (Waveland Press, 2011).

8. For a brief introduction to phenomenology, see Michael Allen Fox, *The Remarkable Existentialists* (Amherst, NY: Humanity Books, 2009), chap. 5.

9. James Ferrell, "How Modern Philosophy Is Killing You," 21 February 2012 (emphases in original); http://www.arbinger.com/2012/02/21/how-modern-philosophy-is-killing-you-2. See also The Arbinger Institute, *The Anatomy of Peace: Resolving the Heart of Conflict* (San Francisco: Berrett-Koehler, 2006); Lorenzo Kamel and Daniela Huber, "The De-threatenization of the Other: An Israeli and a Palestinian Case of Understanding the Other's Suffering," *Peace & Change: A Journal of Peace Research* 37 (2012), pp. 366–88.

10. Steven Hahn, "Political Racism in the Age of Obama," *New York Times*, 10 November 2012; http://www.nytimes.com/2012/11/11/opinion/sunday/political-racism-in-the-age-of-obama.html?_r=0.

11. Aryeh Neier, *The International Human Rights Movement: A History* (Princeton, NJ: Princeton University Press, 2012), p. 6.

12. Fulvio Attinà, *The Global Political System*, trans. Antoinette Groom, with A. J. R. Groom (New York: Palgrave Macmillan, 2011), p. 156.

13. Hernán Santa Cruz, quoted in United Nations, "The Universal Declaration of Human Rights: History of the Document"; http://www.un.org/en/documents/udhr/history.shtml.

14. United Nations, "The Universal Declaration of Human Rights: The Foundation of International Human Rights Law"; http://www.un.org/en/documents/udhr/hr_law.shtml.

15. See Johannes Morsink, *The Universal Declaration of Human Rights: Origins, Drafting, and Intent* (Philadelphia: University of Pennsylvania Press, 1999).

16. Neier, *International Human Rights Movement*, p. 108.

17. United Nations General Assembly, "United Nations Declaration on Human Rights Education and Training," Resolution A/RES/66/137, 19 December 2011; available at Office of the United Nations High Commissioner for Human Rights: http://daccess-dds-ny.un.org/doc/UNDOC/GEN/N11/467/04/PDF/N1146704.pdf?OpenElement.

18. John Vidal, "Ecological Web Is Badly Tangled," *Guardian Weekly*, 15–21 June 2012, p. 2.

19. Andrew Fagan, "Human Rights" (last updated 5 July 2005), *Internet Encyclopedia of Philosophy*, ed. James Fieser and Bradley Dowden; http://www.iep.utm.edu/humrts/#SH3d.

20. Carl Wellman, "Rights," in *The Cambridge Dictionary of Philosophy*, ed. Robert Audi, 2nd ed. (Cambridge, UK: Cambridge University Press, 1999), p. 796.

21. Attinà, *Global Political System*, p. 156.

22. Wellman, "Rights," p. 796.

23. US Peace Council, "Santiago Declaration on the Human Right to Peace," 10 December 2010; http://uspeacecouncil.org/?p=861; United Nations Office of the High Commissioner for Human Rights, United Nations Human Rights Council, "Open-ended Intergovernmental Working Group on the Draft United Nations Declaration on the Right to Peace"; http://www.ohchr.org/EN/HRBodies/HRC/RightPeace/Pages/WGDraftUNDeclarationontheRighttoPeace.aspx. See also Douglas Roche, *The Human Right to Peace* (Ottawa: Novalis Press, 2003); Anwarul K. Chowdhury, "Time is Right for the Human Right to Peace," *Other News*, 23 January 2012; http://www.other-news.info/2012/01/time-is-right-for-the-human-right-to-peace.

24. See Leif Wenar, "Rights," in *Stanford Encyclopedia of Philosophy*, ed. Edward N. Zalta, Fall 2011 ed., sec. 3; http://plato.stanford.edu/archives/fall2011/entries/rights.

25. Fagan, "Human Rights."

26. For an extensive list, see http://dir.yahoo.com/Society_and_Culture/Issues_and_ Causes/Human_Rights/Organizations.

27. Neier, *International Human Rights Movement*, pp. 115, 131.

28. Richard Wilkinson and Kate Pickett, *The Spirit Level: Why Greater Equality Makes Societies Stronger* (New York: Bloomsbury Press, 2010); for a summary of the evidence, see: http://www.equalitytrust.org.uk.

29. See, for example, the Earth Charter Initiative (http://www.earthcharterinaction.org/ content/pages/What-is-the-Earth-Charter%3F.html); James O'Dea, *Cultivating Peace: Becoming a 21st Century Peace Ambassador* (San Rafael, CA: Shift Books, 2012).

30. See, for example, Rosalind Hursthouse, *Ethics, Humans and Other Animals: An Introduction with Readings* (London: Routledge, 2000); Catharine Grant, *The No-Nonsense Guide to Animal Rights* (Oxford: New Internationalist, 2006); Angus Taylor, *Animals and Ethics: An Overview of the Philosophical Debate*, 3rd ed. (Peterborough, ON, Canada: Broadview Press, 2009); Michael Allen Fox, "Anthropocentrism," in *Encyclopedia of Animal Rights and Animal Welfare*, ed. Marc Bekoff, 2nd ed. (Santa Barbara: Greenwood Press, 2010), vol. 1, pp. 66–8.

31. See, for example, Joseph R. Des Jardins, *Environmental Ethics: An Introduction to Environmental Philosophy*, 5th ed. (Boston: Wadsworth, 2013); "Sustainability," http:// en.wikipedia.org/wiki/Sustainability.

32. See Michael Allen Fox, "Vegetarianism and Veganism," in *International Encyclopedia of Ethics*, ed. Hugh LaFollette (Malden, MA: Wiley-Blackwell, 2013), pp. 5310–16; Michael Allen Fox, "Vegetarianism and Treading Lightly on the Earth," in *Environmental Ethics*, ed. Louis P. Pojman and Paul Pojman, 5th ed. (Belmont, CA: Thomson Wadsworth, 2008), pp. 496–504; Michael Allen Fox, "Why We Should Be Vegetarians," *International Journal of Applied Philosophy* 20 (2006), pp. 295–310.

33. Will Tuttle, *The World Peace Diet: Eating for Spiritual Health and Social Harmony* (New York: Lantern Books, 2005), p. 221 (emphasis in original).

34. Michael and D'Neil Duffy, *Children of the Universe: Cosmic Education in the Montessori Elementary Classroom* (Hollidaysburg, PA: Parent Child Press, 2002), pp. 115, 128. See also Maria Montessori, *Education and Peace*, trans. Helen R. Lane (New York: Henry Regnery, 1972). My thanks to Peter Erskine for bringing these books to my attention.

35. See, for example, http://the-peaceful-educator.com; http://nonviolentsolutuions.org; http://www.preaceeducators.org.

36. Nel Noddings, *Peace Education: How We Come to Love and Hate War* (Cambridge, UK: Cambridge University Press, 2012), pp. 139, 141, 150.

37. Neil Postman and Charles Weingartner, *Teaching as a Subversive Activity* (New York: Delta Books, 1969), p. 218.

38. Joel Andreas, *Addicted to War: Why the U.S. Can't Kick Militarism*, 3rd ed. (Oakland, CA: AK Press, 2004). For details on the use of this publication in American schools, see Office of the Americas for the Cause of Justice and Peace, "Addicted to War Books-to-Schools Project"; http://www.officeoftheamericas.org/addictedtowar_schools.html.

39. Noddings, *Peace Education*, p. 154.

40. Elliot Aronson, "Reducing Hostility and Building Compassion: Lessons from the Jigsaw Classroom," in *The Social Psychology of Good and Evil*, ed. Arthur G. Miller (New York: Guilford Press, 2004), pp. 479, 481–2 (emphasis in original).

41. Douglas Fuchs et al., "Peer-Assisted Learning Strategies in Reading: Extensions for Kindergarten, First Grade, and High School," *Remedial and Special Education* 22 (2001), pp. 15–21; available at: http://rse.sagepub.com/content/22/1/15.full.pdf+html. My appreciation to Brian Byrne for directing my attention to this research.

42. Ingrid Wickelgren, "The Education of Character," *Scientific American Mind*, September/October 2012, pp. 49–58.

43. World Animal Net, "Humane Education"; http://www.worldanimal.net/resources/humane-education-resources.

44. TEACHkind, "Why Humane Education?" (emphases in original); http://www.teach kind.org/humaneEducation.asp.

45. TEACHkind, "Laws Mandating Humane Education"; http://www.teachkind.org/laws. asp.

46. Mary Louise Peterson and David P. Farrington, "Types of Cruelty: Animals and Child Cruelty, Domestic Violence, Child and Elder Abuse," in *The Link between Animal Abuse and Human Violence*, ed. Andrew Linzey (Brighton, UK: Sussex Academic Press, 2009), p. 30 (emphases in original).

47. Peterson and Farrington, "Types of Cruelty," p. 30.

48. American Humane Association, "Facts about Animal Abuse and Domestic Violence"; http://www.americanhumane.org/interaction/support-the-bond/fact-sheets/animal-abuse-domestic-violence.html.

49. National Association for Humane and Environmental Education, "An Annotated Bibliography of Research Relevant to Humane Education, vol. II (1984–2003)," compiled by Heidi O'Brien; available at: http://www.humanesociety.org/assets/pdfs/parents_educators/bibliography_humane_ed_research_volume2.pdf; Bernard Unti and Bill DeRosa, "Humane Education: Past, Present, and Future," in *The State of the Animals II, 2003*, ed. Deborah J. Salem and Andrew N. Rowan (Washington, DC: Humane Society Press, 2003), pp. 27–50; available at: http://www.humanesociety.org/assets/pdfs/hsp/soa_ii_chap03.pdf. See also Charles Siebert, "The Animal-cruelty Syndrome," *New York Times Magazine*, 11 June 2010; available at: http://www.nytimes.com/2010/06/13/magazine/13dogfighting-t.html?_r=1&ref=magazine.

50. Andrea M. Beetz, "Empathy as an Indicator of Emotional Development," in *Link Between Animal Abuse and Human Violence*, ed. Linzey, pp. 63–74.

51. Samuel P. Oliner assisted by Piotr Olaf Zylicz, *Altruism, Intergroup Apology, Forgiveness, and Reconciliation* (St. Paul, MN: Paragon House, 2008), pp. 229, 231.

52. James W. Messerschmidt, "Men, Masculinities, and Crime," in *Handbook of Studies on Men and Masculinities*, ed. Michael S. Kimmel, Jeff Hearn, and R. W. Connell (Thousand Oaks, CA: Sage, 2005), p. 198.

53. Walter S. DeKeseredy and Martin D. Schwartz, "Masculinities and Interpersonal Violence," in *Handbook of Studies on Men and Masculinities*, ed. Kimmel et al., p. 354.

54. DeKeseredy and Schwartz, "Men, Masculinities, and Crime," p. 361.

55. R. W. Connell, *The Men and the Boys* (Cambridge, UK: Polity Press, 2000), p. 225.

56. Gabriel Moran, *Living Nonviolently: Language for Resisting Violence* (Lanham, MD: Lexington Books, 2011), p. 172.

57. Karl Marx, *Theses on Feuerbach* (1845), sec. III.

58. This account and the quotations in it are taken from Kazu Haga, "Chicago's Peace Warriors," *Rethinking Schools* 26/2 (Winter 2001–12); available at: http://www.re thinkingschools.org/archive/26_02/26_02_haga.shtml. Information about the Kingian Nonviolence training program can be found at: http://positivepeacewarriornetwork. wordpress.com. See also Mariame Kaba, J. Cyriac Mathew, and Nathan Haines, eds., *Something Is Wrong: Exploring the Roots of Youth Violence* (Chicago: Chicago Freedom School Project, Project NIA, and Teachers for Social Justice, n.d.); http://project-nia. org/docs/Something_Is_Wrong-Curriculum.pdf. For other impressive examples of schools taking charge of their violent environment, see Katy Tur, "Principal Fires Se-curity Guards to Hire Art Teachers—And Transforms Elementary School," NBC News, 1 May 2013; http://dailynightly.nbcnews.com/_news/2013/05/01/18005192-principal-fires-security-guards-to-hire-art-teachers-and-transforms-elementary-school; Ann Schnoebelen, "After Shootings, Morgan State U. Trains Students in Conflict Resolu-tion," *Chronicle of Higher Education,* 6 May 2013; http://chronicle.com/article/After-Shootings-Morgan-State/139051; Jeff Deeney, "A Philadelphia School's Big Bet on Nonviolence," *The Atlantic,* 18 July 2013; http://www.theatlantic.com/national/archive/2013/07/a-philadelphia-schools-big-bet-on-nonviolence/27789F.

59. John Hunter, *World Peace and Other 4th Grade Achievements* (New York: Houghton Mifflin Harcourt, 2013); see press release at: http://www.worldpeacegame.org.

60. Daniel M. Mayton II, *Nonviolence and Peace Psychology: Intrapersonal, Interpersonal, Societal, and World Peace* (New York: Springer, 2009), p. 232.

61. Leah Witcher Jackson, "Educate the Women and You Change the World: Investing in the Education of Women Is the Best Investment in a Country's Growth and Devel-opment," *Forum on Public Policy,* Summer 2009, p. 1; available at: http://forumonpub licpolicy.com/summer09/archivesummer09/jackson.pdf.

62. Valerie M. Hudson, "What Sex Means for World Peace," *Foreign Policy,* 24 April 2012; available at: http://www.foreignpolicy.com/articles/2012/04/24/what_sex_ means_for_world_peace. See also Valerie M. Hudson, Bonnie Ballif-Spanvill, Mary Caprioli, and Chad F. Emmett, *Sex and World Peace* (New York: Columbia University Press, 2012).

63. Kieran Egan, *Educational Development* (New York: Oxford University Press, 1979), p. 10.

64. Kimberly Hutchings, *Global Ethics: An Introduction* (Cambridge, UK: Polity Press, 2010), p. 4.

65. Defense Manpower Data Center, US Department of Defense, "Active Military Person-nel Strengths by Regional Area and by Country," 31 December 2011; http://siadapp. dmdc.osd.mil/personnel/MILITARY/history/hst1112.pdf.

66. At the time of writing, the United Nations has begun investigating the use of drones against alleged terrorist targets: see "UN Launches Inquiry into Drone Killings," BBC News, 24 January 2013; http://www.bbc.co.uk/news/world-21176279; see also Mi-chael J. Boyle, "The Costs and Consequences of Drone Warfare," *International Affairs*

89 (2013), pp. 1–29. The US Senate has also conducted an inquiry into the justification for using drones; see "Dems, GOP Press Obama Administration on Authority
for Use of Drones for Targeted Killings," *Washington Post*, 24 April 2013; http://www.
washingtonpost.com/politics/congress/senates-no-2-democrat-presses-obama-ad
ministration-on-use-of-drones-for-targeted-killings/2013/04/23/032c569a-ac54–
11e2–9493–2ff3bf26c4b4_story.html.

67. Friends Committee on National Legislation, "Development: Flexible Funding for State
and USAID"; http://fcnl.org/issues/ppdc/diplomacy_flexible_funding_for_state/#Q1.

68. US Department of State, "Bureau of Conflict and Stabilization Operations"; http://
www.state.gov/j/cso.

69. The White House, Office of the Press Secretary, "Fact Sheet: A Comprehensive Strategy and New Tools to Prevent and Respond to Atrocities," 23 April 2012; http://www.
whitehouse.gov/the-press-office/2012/04/23/fact-sheet-comprehensive-strategy-and-
new-tools-prevent-and-respond-atro (emphasis in original).

70. Wilbert van der Zeijden, "Foreign Military Bases and the Global Campaign to Close
Them: A Beginner's Guide," Transnational Institute, July 2009; http://www.tni.org/
primer/foreign-military-bases-and-global-campaign-close-them#basesproblem. See
also David Vine, "U.S. Empire of Bases Grows," 15 July 2012; http://www.tomdispatch.
com/archive/175568.

71. Craig Whitlock, "US Expands Covert Operations in Africa," *Guardian Weekly*, 22–28
June 2012, p. 7.

72. Mudher Nizar Hassib, "An Insider's View on the Future of Peace in Iraq," talk delivered to School of Humanities Research Seminar, University of New England, Armidale,
NSW, Australia, 11 November 2011.

73. Van der Zeijden, "Foreign Military Bases."

74. Of interest and relevance for pursuing the topics of this section further are the following books: James O'Dea, *Cultivating Peace: Becoming a 21st-Century Peace Ambassador*
(San Rafael, CA: Shift Books, 2012); Carne Ross, *The Leaderless Revolution: How Ordinary People Will Take Power and Change Politics in the 21st Century* (London: Simon &
Schuster, 2011).

75. Nigel Dower, *The Ethics of War and Peace: Cosmopolitan and Other Perspectives* (Cambridge, UK: Polity Books, 2009), p. 60.

76. Kwame Anthony Appiah, *Cosmopolitanism: Ethics in a World of Strangers* (New York:
W.W. Norton, 2006), p. xv.

77. Soran Reader, "Cosmopolitan Pacifism," *Journal of Global Ethics* 3 (2007), pp. 87, 101 n. 1.

78. See, for example, Martin Ceadel, *Thinking about War and Peace* (Oxford: Oxford University Press, 1987), p. 5.

79. Rodrigue Tremblay, *The Code for Global Ethics: Ten Humanist Principles* (Amherst, NY:
Prometheus Books, 2010), p. 206.

80. Nigel Dower, *World Ethics: The New Agenda*, 2nd ed. (Edinburgh: Edinburgh University
Press, 2007), p. 8.

81. Dower, *World Ethics*, p. 2.

82. David Wong, "Relativism," in *A Companion to Ethics*, ed. Peter Singer (Oxford: Blackwell, 1993), p. 446.

83. Louis P. Pojman, "Relativism," in *The Cambridge Dictionary of Philosophy*, ed. Audi, p. 790.

84. Wong, "Relativism," p. 446.

85. Pojman, "Relativism," p. 790.

86. Hutchings, *Global Ethics*, p. 14.

87. Hutchings, *Global Ethics*, pp. 217–8.

88. Advertisement for Hilary French, *Vanishing Borders: Protecting the World in the Age of Globalization* (Washington, DC: Worldwatch Institute, 2000); http://www.worldwatch.org/bookstore/publication/vanishing-borders-protecting-planet-age-globalization.

89. Michael Renner, *Budgeting for Disarmament: The Costs of War and Peace*, Worldwatch Paper 122 (Washington, DC: Worldwatch Institute, November 1994), p. 7.

90. Attinà, *Global Political System*, p. 56.

91. Thomas Weber, "World Governance," *The Oxford International Encyclopedia of Peace*, ed. Nigel Young (Oxford: Oxford University Press, 2010), e-reference edition; http://www.oxford-peace.com/entry?entry=t296.e790.

92. Amartya Sen, *The Idea of Justice* (London: Penguin, 2010), p. 141.

93. "Global Directory of Peace Studies and Conflict Resolution Programs," *Peace Chronicle: Newsletter of the Peace and Justice Studies Association* (Spring-Summer 2012), p. 12; http://www.peacejusticestudies.org/globaldirectory.

94. George Lakey, "Update: Global Nonviolent Action Database," *Peace Chronicle: Newsletter of the Peace and Justice Studies Association* (Spring-Summer 2012), p. 22; http://www.nvdatabase.swarthmore.edu.

95. Vision of Humanity (http://www.visionofhumanity.org).

96. "What Is the GPI All About?"; http://www.visionofhumanity.org/about.

97. "About the U.S. Peace Index"; http://www.visionofhumanity.org/unitedstatespeaceindex/2012.

98. Bonn International Center for Conversion, *Annual Report 2010/2011* (Bonn: BICC, 2011), pp. 12–13; available at: http://www.bicc.de/uploads/pdf/publications/jahresbericht/2011/BICC_Jahresbericht_2010–2011-E.pdf.

99. United Nations Development Programme, "Human Development Reports"; http://hdr.undp.org/en.

100. See http://www.happyplanetindex.org.

101. Jean-Paul Sartre, *Being and Nothingness*, trans. Hazel Barnes (New York: Philosophical Library, 1956), p. 571. Sartre uses this expression to describe the "original project," or the way of being in the world each person fundamentally and uniquely chooses, from which his or her actions derive, and which always hovers in consciousness.

102. Walter Russell Mead, "Peace Myth," *Australian Financial Review*, 14 December 2012, p. 7.

Bibliography

Ackerman, Peter and Jack Duvall. *A Force More Powerful: A Century of Nonviolent Conflict.* New York: Palgrave, 2000.

Adler, Mortimer. *How to Think about War and Peace.* New York: Fordham University Press, 1995.

Adolf, Antony. *Peace: A World History.* Cambridge, UK: Polity Press, 2009.

Albert, David H. *People Power: Applying Nonviolence Theory.* Philadelphia: New Society, 1985.

Allan, Pierre and Alexis Keller, eds. *What Is a Just Peace?* New York: Oxford University Press, 2006.

Almond, Brenda, ed. *The Case for Pacifism in Applied Philosophy.* New York: Routledge, 1992.

Alonso, Harriet Hyman. *Peace as a Women's Issue: A History of the U.S. Movement for World Peace and Women's Rights.* Syracuse: Syracuse University Press, 1993.

Amster, Randall and Elavie Ndura. *Exploring the Power of Nonviolence: Peace, Politics, and Practice.* Syracuse, NY: Syracuse University Press, 2013.

Anderson, Mary B. and Marshall Wallace. *Opting Out of War: Strategies to Prevent Violent Conflict.* Boulder, CO: Lynne Rienner, 2012.

Andreas, Joel. *Addicted to War: Why the U.S. Can't Kick Militarism.* 3rd ed. Oakland, CA: AK Press, 2004.

Appiah, Kwame Anthony. *Cosmopolitanism: Ethics in a World of Strangers.* New York: W. W. Norton, 2006.

Appy, Christian G. *Working-Class War: American Combat Soldiers and Vietnam.* Chapel Hill: University of North Carolina Press, 1993.

Arbinger Institute. *The Anatomy of Peace: Resolving the Heart of Conflict.* San Francisco: Berrett-Koehler, 2006.

Archer, Dane. *Violence and Crime in Cross-National Perspective.* New Haven, CT: Yale University Press, 1984.

Arendt, Hannah. *On Violence.* San Diego: Harvest Books/Harcourt Brace, 1970.

Arkin, Ronald C. *Governing Lethal Behavior in Autonomous Robots*. Boca Raton, FL: Chapman & Hall/CRC, 2009.

Arment, J. Frederick. *The Elements of Peace: How Nonviolence Works*. Jefferson, NC: McFarland, 2012.

Arnold, Johann Christoph. *Seeking Peace: Notes and Conversations along the Way*. Farmington, PA: Plough, 1998.

Arnold, John H. *History: A Very Short Introduction*. New York: Oxford University Press, 2000.

Atack, Iain. *The Ethics of Peace and War: From State Security to World Community*. Edinburgh: Edinburgh University Press, 2005.

Attinà, Fulvio. *The Global Political System*. Trans. Antoinette Groom, with A. J. R. Groom. New York: Palgrave Macmillan, 2012.

Austin, Jay E. and Carl E. Bruch, eds. *The Environmental Consequences of War: Legal, Economic, and Scientific Perspectives*. Cambridge, UK: Cambridge University Press, 2000.

Bachevich, Andrew J. *Washington Rules: America's Path to Permanent War*. New York: Metropolitan Books, 2010.

Ball, Olivia and Paul Gready. *The No-Nonsense Guide to Human Rights*. Oxford: New Internationalist, 2006.

Barak, Gregg. *Violence and Nonviolence: Pathways to Understanding*. Thousand Oaks, CA: Sage, 2003.

Barash, David P., ed. *Approaches to Peace: A Reader in Peace Studies*. 2nd ed. New York: Oxford University Press, 2009.

Barash, David P., and Charles P. Webel. *Peace and Conflict Studies*. 2nd ed. Thousand Oaks, CA: Sage, 2009.

Baron, Robert A. and Deborah R. Richardson. *Human Aggression*. New York: Plenum Press, 1994.

Baron-Cohen, Simon. *Zero Degrees of Empathy: A New Theory of Human Cruelty*. London: Allen Lane, 2011.

Barry, Kathleen. *Unmaking War, Remaking Men: How Empathy Can Reshape Our Politics, Our Soldiers and Ourselves*. Santa Rosa, CA: Phoenix Rising Press of Santa Rosa, 2011.

Bartkowski, Maciej, ed. *Recovering Nonviolent History: Civil Resistance in Liberation Struggles*. Boulder, CO: Lynne Rienner, 2013.

Bauman, Zygmunt. *Modernity and the Holocaust*. Ithaca, NY: Cornell University Press, 2001.

Bekerman, Zvi and Claire McGlynn, eds. *Addressing Ethnic Conflict Through Peace Education: International Perspectives*. New York: Palgrave Macmillan, 2007.

Beller, Ken and Heather Chase. *Great Peacemakers: True Stories from Around the World*. Sedona, AZ: LTS Press, 2008.

Benjamin, Medea. *Drone Warfare: Killing by Remote Control*. London: Verso Books, 2013.

Benjamin, Medea and Jodie Evans, eds. *Stop the Next War Now: Effective Responses to Violence and Terrorism*. Makawao, Maui, HI: Inner Ocean, 2005.

Bickerton, Ian. *The Illusion of Victory: The True Costs of War*. Melbourne: Melbourne University Press, 2011.

Bickmore, Kathy and the Northeast Ohio Alternative to Violence Committee. *Alternatives to Violence: A Manual for Teaching Peacemaking to Youth and Adults.* Cleveland: Alternatives to Violence, Cleveland Friends Meeting, 1984.

Black, Jeremy. *Why Wars Happen.* London: Reaktion Books, 1998.

Black Elk. *The Sacred Pipe: Black Elk's Account of the Seven Rites of the Oglala Sioux.* Recorded and ed. Joseph Epes Brown. Norman: University of Oklahoma Press, 1989.

Blainey, Geoffrey. *The Causes of War.* 3rd ed. New York: Free Press, 1988.

Blumberg, Herbert H., A. Paul Hare, and Anna Costin. *Peace Psychology: A Comprehensive Introduction.* New York: Cambridge University Press, 2006.

Bonn International Center for Conversion. *Annual Report 2010/2011.* Bonn: BICC, 2011.

———. *Conversion Survey 2005: Global Disarmament, Demilitarization and Demobilization.* Baden-Baden: Nomos, 2005.

Bonta, Bruce D. *Peaceful Peoples: An Annotated Bibliography.* Metuchen, NJ: Scarecrow Press, 1993.

Boulding, Elise. *Building a Global Civic Culture: Education for an Interdependent World.* New York: Teachers College Press, 1988.

———. *Cultures of Peace: The Hidden Side of History.* Syracuse: Syracuse University Press, 2000.

Boulding, Elise, and Daisaku Ikeda. *Into Full Flower: Making Peace Cultures Happen.* Cambridge, MA: Dialogue Path Press, 2010.

Boulding, Kenneth. *Stable Peace.* Austin: University of Texas Press, 1978.

Braddon, Derek. *Exploding the Myth? The Peace Dividend, Regions and Market Adjustment.* London: Routledge, 2000.

Brand, Dione. *A Map to the Door of No Return.* Toronto: Random House Canada, 2001.

Brauer, Jurgen. *War and Nature: The Environmental Consequences of War in a Globalized World.* Lanham, MD: AltaMira Press, 2009.

Brock, Peter. *Varieties of Pacifism.* Syracuse: Syracuse University Press, 1981.

Brooks, Elaine and Len Fox. *Making Peace: A Reading/Writing/Thinking Text on Global Community.* Cambridge, UK: Cambridge University Press, 1998.

Brough, Michael, John W. Lango, and Harry Van der Linden, eds. *Rethinking the Just War Tradition.* Albany: State University of New York Press, 2007.

Brown, Donald E. *Human Universals.* Philadelphia: Temple University Press, 1991.

Brown, Ina Corinne. *Understanding Other Cultures.* Englewood Cliffs, NJ: Prentice-Hall, 1963.

Brown, Robert McAfee. *Making Peace in the Global Village.* Philadelphia: Westminster Press, 1981.

Brown, Seyom. *The Causes and Prevention of War.* New York: St. Martin's Press, 1987.

Bstan-'dzin-rgya-mtsho, Dalai Lama XIV. *Ethics for the New Millennium.* New York: Riverhead Books, 1999.

Burgess, Heidi and Guy M. Burgess. *Encyclopedia of Conflict Resolution.* Santa Barbara, CA: ABC/CLIO, 1997.

Burgess, Parke. *Our Tragic Flaw: A Case for Nonviolence.* San Francisco: Lulu.com/Creative Commons, 2008.

Burleigh, Michael. *Moral Combat: A History of World War II*. London: HarperPress, 2010.

Burrowes, Robert J. *The Strategy of Nonviolent Defense: A Gandhian Defense*. Albany: State University of New York Press, 2007.

Butler, Christopher. *Postmodernism: A Very Short Introduction*. Oxford: Oxford University Press, 2002.

Butler, Judith. *Frames of War: When Is Life Grievable?* London: Verso, 2009.

Byers, Michael. *War Law: Understanding International Law and Armed Conflict*. New York: Grove Press, 2006.

Cady, Duane L. *From Warism to Pacifism: A Moral Continuum*. 2nd ed. Philadelphia: Temple University Press, 2010.

Calvocoressi, P. *A Time for Peace*. London: Hutchinson, 1987.

Camus, Albert. *Neither Victims Nor Executioners*. Trans. Dwight Macdonald. Philadelphia: New Society, 1986.

Canadian Council for Peace in Freedom. *Peace and the Management of Fear: The Conversion of Fear into Understanding and Appropriate Actions*. Ottawa: Canadian Council for Peace in Freedom, 1987.

Cannon, Susan Gelber. *Think, Care, Act: Teaching for a Peaceful Future*. Charlotte, NC: Information Age, 2011.

Cantwell, John. *Exit Wounds: One Australian's War on Terror*. Melbourne: Melbourne University Press, 2012.

Caputo, Philip. *A Rumor of War*. New York: Holt, Rinehart and Winston, 1977.

Carter, Candice C. and Ravindra Kumar. *Peace Philosophy in Action*. New York: Palgrave Macmillan, 2010.

Cashman, Greg. *What Causes War?* New York: Macmillan/Lexington, 1993.

Ceadel, Martin. *Thinking about Peace and War*. New York: Oxford University Press, 1987.

Center on International Cooperation. *Annual Review of Global Peace Operations, 2012*. Boulder, CO: Lynne Rienner, 2012.

Chagnon, Napoleon. *Noble Savages: My Life among Two Dangerous Tribes—the Yanomamö and the Anthropologists*. New York: Simon & Schuster, 2013.

Chanteur, Janine. *From War to Peace*. Trans. Shirley Ann Weisz. Boulder, CO: Westview Press, 1992.

Chappell, David W., ed. *Buddhist Peacework: Creating Cultures of Peace*. Somerville, MA: Wisdom Publications/Boston Research Center for the 21st Century, 1999.

Chappell, Paul K. *The Art of Waging Peace: A Strategic Approach to Improving Our Lives and the World*. Westport, CT: Prospecta Press, 2013.

———. *The End of War: How Waging Peace Can Save Humanity, Our Planet, and Our Future*. Westport, CT: Easton Studio Press, 2010.

Chary, Frederick B. *The Bulgarian Jews and the Final Solution (1940–1944)*. Pittsburgh: University of Pittsburgh Press, 1972.

Chatfield, Charles and Ruzanna Ilukhina. *Peace/Mir: An Anthology of Historic Alternatives to War*. Syracuse, NY: Syracuse University Press, 1994.

Chayes, Antonia and Martha Minow, eds. *Imagine Coexistence: Restoring Humanity after Violent Ethnic Conflict*. San Francisco: Jossey-Bass, 2003.

Chenoweth, Erica and Maria J. Stephan. *Why Civil Resistance Works: The Strategic Logic of Nonviolent Conflict*. New York: Columbia University Press, 2011.

Christie, Daniel J., ed. *The Encyclopedia of Peace Psychology*. Hoboken: Wiley-Blackwell, 2012.

Christie, Daniel J. and Joám Evans Pim, eds. *Nonkilling Psychology*. Honolulu: Center for Global Nonkilling, 2012.

Christie, Daniel J., Richard V. Wagner, and Deborah Du Nann Winter, eds. *Peace, Conflict, and Violence: Peace Psychology for the 21st Century*. Upper Saddle River, NJ: Prentice-Hall, 2001.

Christman, Kristin Y. *The Taxonomy of Peace: A Comprehensive Classification of the Roots and Escalators of Violence and 650 Solutions for Peace, with a particular emphasis on peace within and between the Middle East and the United States*, 2011. https://sites.google.com/site/paradigmforpeace.

Clark, Anna. *History's Children: History Wars in the Classroom*. Sydney: University of New South Wales Press, 2008.

Clark, Howard, ed. *People Power: Unarmed Resistance and Global Solidarity*. London: Pluto Press, 2009.

Clark, Mary E. *In Search of Human Nature*. New York: Routledge, 2002.

Clarke, Richard A. and Robert K. Knake. *Cyber War: The Next Threat to National Security and What to Do About It*. New York: HarperCollins, 2010.

Coady, C. A. J. *Morality and Political Violence*. Cambridge: Cambridge University Press, 2008.

Coates, A. J. *The Ethics of War*. Manchester: Manchester University Press, 1997.

Cochrane, Feargal. *Ending Wars*. Cambridge, UK: Polity Press, 2008.

Cockburn, Cynthia. *From Where We Stand: War, Women's Activism, and Feminist Analysis*. London: Zed Books, 2007.

Codevilla, Angelo M. *A Student's Guide to International Relations*. Wilmington, DE: ISI Books, 2010.

Coker, Christopher. *Barbarous Philosophers: Reflections on the Nature of War from Heraclitus to Heisenberg*. New York: Columbia University Press, 2010.

———. *War and the 20th Century: A Study of War and Modern Consciousness*. London: Brassey's 1994.

Collyer, Charles E. and Ira G. Zepp, Jr. *Nonviolence: Origins and Outcomes*. 2nd ed. Victoria, BC, Canada: Trafford, 2006.

Connadine, David. *The Undivided Past: Humanity beyond Our Differences*. New York: Alfred A. Knopf, 2013.

Connell, R. W. *The Men and the Boys*. Cambridge, UK: Polity Press, 2000.

Coppieters, B. and N. Fotion, eds. *Moral Constraints on War: Principles and Cases*. Lanham, MD: Lexington Books, 2002.

Cortright, David. *Gandhi and Beyond: Nonviolence for an Age of Terrorism*. Boulder, CO: Paradigm, 2006.

———. *Peace: A History of Movements and Ideas*. Cambridge, UK: Cambridge University Press, 2008.

Cox, J. Gray. *The Ways of Peace: A Philosophy of Peace as Action*. New York: Paulist Press, 1986.

Cranna, Michael, ed. *The True Cost of Conflict*. London: Earthscan, 1994.

Curle, Adam. *Tools for Transformation: A Personal Study*. Stroud, UK: Hawthorn, 1990.

Danesh, H. B. and Sara Clarke-Habibi. *Education for Peace Curriculum Manual: A Conceptual and Practical Guide*. Vancouver: EFP Press, 2007.

Dator, James A. and Joám Evans Pim, eds. *Nonkilling Futures: Visions*. Honolulu: Center for Global Nonkilling, 2013.

Decade for a Culture of Peace Youth Team. *Report on the Decade for a Culture of Peace: Final Civil Society Report on the United Nations International Decade for a Culture of Peace and Non-violence for the Children of the World (2001- 2010)*. http://decade-culture-of peace.org/2010_civil_society_report.pdf.

DeGarmo, Denise and E. Duff Wrobbel. *Thinking about War and Peace*. New York: Routledge, 2010.

Demenchonok, Edward, ed. *Between Global Violence and the Ethics of Peace: Philosophical Perspectives*. Malden, MA: Wiley-Blackwell, 2009.

De Rivera, Joseph. *Handbook on Building Cultures of Peace*. New York: Springer, 2009.

Deveson, Anne. *Waging Peace: Reflections on Peace and War from an Unconventional Woman*. Sydney: Allen & Unwin, 2013.

De Waal, Frans. *The Age of Empathy: Nature's Lessons for a Kinder Society*. New York: Harmony Books, 2009.

———. *Good Natured: The Origins of Right and Wrong in Humans and Other Species*. Cambridge, MA: Harvard University Press, 1997.

———. *Peacemaking among Primates*. Cambridge, MA: Harvard University Press, 1989.

Diamandis, Peter H. and Steven Kotler. *Abundance: The Future Is Better Than You Think*. New York: Free Press, 2012.

Dinstein, Yoram. *The Conduct of Hostilities under the Law of International Armed Conflict*. 2nd ed. Cambridge, UK: Cambridge University Press, 2010.

———. *War, Aggression and Self-Defence*. 5th ed. Cambridge, UK: Cambridge University Press, 2011.

Dower, John W. *Cultures of War: Pearl Harbor/Hiroshima/9–11/Iraq*. New York: W. W. Norton/The New Press, 2010.

Dower, Nigel. *The Ethics of War and Peace: Cosmopolitan and Other Perspectives*. Cambridge, UK: Polity Press, 2009.

———. *Introduction to Global Citizenship*. Edinburgh: Edinburgh University Press, 2003.

———. *World Ethics: The New Agenda*. 2nd ed. Edinburgh: Edinburgh University Press, 2007.

——— and J. Williams, eds. *Global Citizenship: A Critical Reader*. Edinburgh: Edinburgh University Press, 2002.

Du Bois, J. Robert. *Powerful Peace: A Navy SEAL's Lessons on Peace from a Lifetime at War*. New York: Morgan James, 2013.

Duclos, Denis. *The Werewolf Complex: America's Fascination with Violence*. Trans. Amanda Pingree. Oxford: Berg, 1998.

Duffy, Michael and D'Neil Duffy. *Children of the Universe: Cosmic Education in the Montessori Elementary Classroom*. Hollidaysburg, PA: Parent Child Press, 2002.

Dundervill, Robert F., Jr. et al., eds. *Defense Conversion Strategies*. Proceedings of the NATO Advanced Study Institute on Defense Conversion Strategies, Pitlochry, Perthshire, Scotland, 2–14 July 1995. NATO ASI Series 1. Disarmament Technologies, Vol. 9. Dordrecht: Kluwer Academic, 2010.

Easwaran, Eknath. *Gandhi, the Man: How One Man Changed Himself to Change the World*. 4th ed. Tomales, CA: Nilgiri Press, 2011.

Egan, Kieran. *Educational Development*. New York: Oxford University Press, 1979.

Eibl-Eibesfeldt, Irenäus. *Biology of Peace and War: Men, Animals, and Aggression*. Trans. Eric Mosbacher. New York: Viking Press, 1979.

Eisler, Riane. *The Chalice and the Blade: Our History, Our Future*. New York: HarperOne, 1988; Gloucester, MA: Peter Smith, 1994.

Elfstrom, D. *Ethics in a Shrinking World*. London: Macmillan, 1990.

Elias, Norbert. *The Civilizing Process*. 2 vols. Trans. Edmund Jephcott. Oxford: Basil Blackwell, 1978, 1982.

Elias, Robert and Jennifer Turpin, eds. *Rethinking Peace*. Boulder, CO: Lynne Rienner, 1994.

Elshtain, Jean Bethke, ed. *Just War Theory*. Oxford: Blackwell, 1992.

—— and Sheila Tobias, eds. *Women, Militarism, and War: Essays in History, Politics, and Social Theory*. Lantham, MD: Rowman and Littlefield, 1990.

Elsner, Wolfram, ed. *International Restructuring and Conversion of Arms: Industries and the Military Sector* (Bremer Schriften Zur Konversion, Band 11). Berlin: Lit Verlag, 2002.

Engdahl, F. William. *Full Spectrum Dominance: Totalitarian Democracy in the New World Order*. Wiesbaden: edition.engdahl, 2009.

English, Richard. *Modern War: A Very Short Introduction*. New York: Oxford University Press, 2013.

Evan, William M., ed. *War and Peace in an Age of Terrorism: A Reader*. Boston: Pearson Education/Allyn and Bacon, 2006.

Evans, Mark. *Just War Theory: A Reappraisal*. Edinburgh: Edinburgh University Press, 2005.

Fahey, Joseph J. and Richard Armstrong, eds., *A Peace Reader: Essential Readings on War, Justice, Non-Violence and World Order*. Rev. ed. New York: Paulist Press, 1992.

Faure-Brac, Russell. *Transition To Peace: A Defense Engineer's Search For An Alternative To War*. Bloomington, IN: iUniverse, 2012.

Fava, Maurizio, ed. *The Psychiatric Clinics of North America*, Vol. 20, No. 2: *Anger, Aggression, and Violence*. Philadelphia: W.B. Saunders, June 1997.

Feldman, Christina. *Compassion: Listening to the Cries of the World*. Berkeley, CA: Rodmell Press, 2005.

Ferguson, John. *Disarmament: The Unanswerable Case*. London: Heinemann, 1982.

Ferrill, Arther. *The Origins of War: From the Stone Age to Alexander the Great*. Boulder, CO: Westview Press, 1997.

Fiala, Andrew. *Practical Pacifism*. New York: Algora, 2004.

Fish, Larry and John Schellenberg. *Patterns of Conflict, Paths to Peace*. Toronto: University of Toronto Press, 2009.

Fisher, Roger Fisher, William L.. Ury, and Bruce Patton, *Getting to Yes: Negotiating Agreement Without Giving In*. 2nd ed. New York: Penguin, 1991.

Fiske, Susan T. *Social Beings: A Core Motives Approach to Social Psychology*. New York: Wiley, 2004.

Fixdal, Mona. *Just Peace: How Wars Should End*. New York: Palgrave Macmillan, 2012.

Flannery, Tim. *Here on Earth: An Argument for Hope*. Melbourne: Text Publishing, 2010.

Flood, Michael, Judith Kegan Gardiner, Bob Pease, and Keith Pringle, eds. *International Encyclopedia of Men and Masculinities*. London: Routledge, 2007.

Foner, Eric. *Who Owns History? Rethinking the Past in a Changing World*. New York: Hill and Wang, 2003.

Forcey, Linda Rennie. *Peace: Meanings, Policies, Strategies*. New York: Praeger, 1989.

Fox, Michael Allen and Leo Groarke, eds. *Nuclear War: Philosophical Perspectives*. 2nd ed. New York: Peter Lang, 1987.

Francis, Diana. *People, Peace, and Power: Conflict Transformation in Action*. London: Pluto Press, 2002.

———. *Rethinking War and Peace*. London: Pluto Press, 2004.

Freire, Paulo. *Pedagogy of the Oppressed*. Trans. Myra Bergman Ramos. New York: Continuum, 1989.

French, Hilary. *Vanishing Borders: Protecting the World in the Age of Globalization*. Washington, DC: Worldwatch Institute, 2000.

Freud, Sigmund. *Why War?* (1933). Trans. James Strachey. In James Strachey, ed., *Standard Edition of the Complete Psychological Works of Sigmund Freud*, Vol. 22. London: Hogarth Press and Institute of Psycho-Analysis, 1964. Pp. 197–215.

Frowe, Helen. *The Ethics of War and Peace: An Introduction*. New York: Routledge, 2011.

Fry, Douglas P. *Beyond War: The Human Potential for Peace*. New York: Oxford University Press, 2007.

———, ed. *War, Peace, and Human Nature: The Convergence of Evolutionary and Cultural Views*. New York: Oxford University Press, 2013.

Gaddis, John Lewis. *The Landscape of History: How Historians Map the Past*. New York: Oxford University Press, 2004.

Gallie, W. B. *Philosophers of Peace and War*. Cambridge, UK: Cambridge University Press, 1978.

———. *Understanding War*. London: Routledge, 1991.

Galtung, John. *Peace by Peaceful Means: Peace and Conflict, Development and Civilization*. Oslo: International Peace Research Institute; Thousand Oaks, CA: Sage, 1996.

Gan, Barry L. *Violence and Nonviolence: An Introduction*. Lanham, MD: Rowman & Littlefield, 2013.

Gandhi, Mohandas Karamchand. *An Autobiography: The Story of My Experiments with Truth*. Trans. Mahadev Desai. Boston: Beacon Press, 1957.

———. *The Moral and Political Writings of Mahatma Gandhi*. 3 vols. Ed. Raghavan Iyer. Oxford: Clarendon Press, 1986–7.

———. *Non-violence in Peace and War*. Ahmedabad: Navajivan, 1942.

Gansler, J. *Defense Conversion*. Cambridge, MA: MIT Press, 1995.

Gat, Azar. *War in Human Civilization.* New York: Oxford University Press, 2006.

Gelderloos, Peter. *The Failure of Nonviolence: From the Arab Spring to Occupy.* Seattle: Left Bank Books, 2013.

———. *How Nonviolence Protects the State.* Boston: South End Press, 2007.

Gelsey, Rudolf C. *Mending Our Broken World: A Path to Perpetual Peace.* Denver: PlanDocs Press, 2012.

George, Mike. *Discover Inner Peace: A Guide to Spiritual Well-Being.* San Francisco: Chronicle Books, 2000.

Gilbert, Paul H. *New Terror, New Wars.* Washington, DC: Georgetown University Press, 2003.

Gittings, John. *The Glorious Art of Peace: From the Iliad to Iraq.* New York: Oxford University Press, 2012.

Glasser, Ronald. *Broken Bodies, Shattered Minds: A Medical Odyssey from Vietnam to Afghanistan.* Palisades, NY: History Publishing, 2011.

Glassman, Bernie. *Bearing Witness: A Zen Master's Lessons in Making Peace.* New York: Bell Tower, 1998.

Global Campaign for Peace Education Monthly Newsletter. http://www.peace-ed-campaign. org/newsletter/index.html.

Glossop, Ronald J. *Confronting War: An Examination of Humanity's Most Pressing Problem.* 4th ed. Jefferson, NC: McFarland, 2001.

Glover, Jonathan. *Humanity: A Moral History of the Twentieth Century.* London: Jonathan Cape, 1999.

Goldstein, Joshua S. *Winning the War on War: The Decline of Armed Conflict Worldwide.* New York: Dutton, 2011.

Goodman, Amy, with David Goodman. *The Exception to the Rulers: Exposing Oily Politicians, War Profiteers, and the Media That Love Them.* New York: Hyperion Books, 2004.

Govier, Trudy. *Forgiveness and Revenge.* New York: Routledge, 2002.

Gray, J. Glenn. *The Warriors: Reflections on Men in Battle.* New York: Harcourt, Brace, 1970.

Gregg, Richard B. *The Power of Nonviolence.* 2nd rev. ed. London: James Clarke, 1960.

———. *The Psychology and Strategy of Gandhi's Nonviolent Resistance.* New York: Garland, 1972.

Gregor, Thomas, ed. *A Natural History of Peace.* Nashville: Vanderbilt University Press, 1996.

Gribbin, John. *In Search of the Multiverse.* London: Allen Lane, 2009.

Griswold, Charles. *Forgiveness: A Philosophical Exploration.* New York: Cambridge University Press, 2007.

Guilaine, Jean and Jean Zammit. *The Origins of War: Violence in Prehistory.* Trans. Melanie Hersey. Malden, MA: Blackwell, 2005.

Guthrie, Charles and Michael Quinlan. *Just War: The Just War Tradition—Ethics in Modern Warfare.* London: Bloomsbury, 2007.

Hague Appeal for Peace. *Peace Lessons from around the World.* http://www.haguepeace.org/ resources/PEACE_LESSONS_FINAL.pdf.

Halverson, Jeffrey R. *Searching for a King: Muslim Nonviolence and the Future of Islam.* Dulles, VA: Potomac Books, 2012.

Hamilton, W. D. *Narrow Roads of Gene Land: The Collected Papers of W. D. Hamilton.* 3 vols. New York: Oxford University Press, 1996–2005.

Hampson, Fen Osler. *Nurturing Peace: Why Peace Settlements Succeed or Fail.* Washington, DC: United States Institute of Peace, 1996.

Hanh, Thich Nhat. *Peace Is Every Step: The Path of Mindfulness in Everyday Life.* New York: Bantam Books, 1991.

———. *The Sun My Heart.* Berkeley, CA: Parallax Press, 1988.

Harris, Ian M. and Mary Lee Morrison, eds. *Peace Education,* 3rd ed. Jefferson, NC: McFarland, 2012.

Hart, Donna and Robert W. Sussman. *Man the Hunted: Primates, Predators, and Human Evolution.* Exp. ed. Boulder, CO: Westview Press, 2008.

Harvey, A.E. *Demanding Peace: Christian Responses to War and Violence.* London: SCM Press, 1999.

Harvey, Peter. *An Introduction to Buddhist Ethics: Foundations, Values and Issues.* Cambridge, UK: Cambridge University Press, 2000.

Hastings, Tom H. *Nonviolent Response to Terrorism.* Jefferson, NC: McFarland, 2004.

———. *Power: Nonviolent Transformation from the Transpersonal to the Transnational.* Dallas: Hamilton Books, 2005.

Heater, Derek. *World Citizenship: Cosmopolitan Thinking and its Opponents.* New York: Continuum, 2002.

Hedges, Chris. *War Is a Force That Gives Us Meaning.* New York: Anchor Books, 2003.

———. *What Every Person Should Know about War.* New York: Free Press, 2003.

Heineman, Elizabeth, ed. *Sexual Violence in Conflict Zones: From the Ancient World to the Era of Human Rights.* Philadelphia: University of Pennsylvania Press, 2011.

Heinze, Eric A. and Brent J. Steele, eds. *Ethics, Authority, and War: Non-State Actions and the Just War Tradition.* New York: Palgrave Macmillan, 2009.

Heitmeyer, Wilhelm and John Hagan, eds. *International Handbook of Violence Research.* New York: Kluwer Academic, 2005.

Helfand, Ira, on behalf of International Physicians for the Prevention of Nuclear War and Physicians for Social Responsibility. *Nuclear Famine: A Billion People at Risk—Global Impacts of Limited Nuclear War on Agriculture, Food Supplies, and Human Nutrition.* Somerville, MA: IPPNW; Washington, DC: PSR, 2012.

Henderson, Michael. *No Enemy to Conquer: Forgiveness in an Unforgiving World.* Waco, TX: Baylor University Press, 2009.

Herman, Edward S. and Noam Chomsky. *Manufacturing Consent: The Political Economy of the Mass Media.* New York: Pantheon Books, 1988.

Himes, Joseph S. *Conflict and Conflict Management.* Athens: University of Georgia Press, 1980.

Hinde, Robert and Joseph Rotblat. *War No More: Eliminating Conflict in the Nuclear Age.* London: Pluto Press, 2003.

Holloway, Richard. *Between the Monster and the Saint: Reflections on the Human Condition.* Edinburgh: Canongate Books, 2008.

Holmes, Robert L., ed. *Nonviolence in Theory and Practice*. Belmont, CA: Wadsworth, 1990.
———. *On War and Morality*. Belmont, CA: Wadsworth, 1990.
Holsti, Kalevi J. *The State, War, and the State of War*. Cambridge, UK: Cambridge University Press, 1996.
Holzgrefe, J. L. and Robert O. Keohane, eds. *Humanitarian Intervention: Ethical, Legal, and Political Dilemmas*. Cambridge, UK: Cambridge University Press, 2003.
Horgan, John. *The End of War*. San Francisco: McSweeney's Books, 2012.
Horowitz, Irving. *The Idea of War and Peace: The Experience of Western Civilization*. 3rd ed. Piscataway, NJ: Transaction, 2006.
Horsburgh, H. J. N. *Non-Violence and Aggression: A Study of Gandhi's Moral Equivalent of War*. London: Oxford University Press, 1968.
Howard, Michael. *The Invention of Peace: Reflections on War and International Order*. New Haven: Yale University Press, 2000.
———, George Andreopoulos, and Mark R. Shulman. *The Laws of War: Constraints on Warfare in the Western World*. New Haven, CT: Yale University Press, 1997.
Howell, Martha C. and Walter Prevenier. *From Reliable Sources: An Introduction to Historical Methods*. Ithaca, NY: Cornell University Press, 2001.
Howell, Signe and Roy Willis, eds. *Societies at Peace: Anthropological Perspectives*. New York: Routledge, 1989.
Hudson, Valerie M., Bonnie Ballif-Spanvill, Mary Caprioli, and Chad F. Emmett. *Sex and World Peace*. New York: Columbia University Press, 2012.
Human Security Report Project. *Human Security Report 2009/2010: The Causes of Peace and the Shrinking Costs of War*. New York: Oxford University Press, 2010. http://www.hsrgroup.org/human-security-reports/20092010/text.asp.
———. *Human Security Report 2012: Sexual Violence, Education, and War—Beyond the Mainstream Narrative*. Vancouver, BC, Canada: Human Security Research Group/ Human Security Press, 2012. http://hsrgroup.org/human-security-reports/2012/text.aspx.
Hunt, Scott. *The Future of Peace: On the Front Lines with the World's Great Peacemakers*. New York: HarperCollins, 2004.
Hunter, John. *World Peace and Other 4th Grade Achievements*. New York: Houghton Mifflin Harcourt, 2013.
Hutchings, Kimberly. *Global Ethics: An Introduction*. Cambridge, UK: Polity Press, 2010.
Ife, Jim. *Human Rights From Below: Achieving Rights Through Community Development*. Cambridge, UK: Cambridge University Press, 2009.
Ikeda, Daisaku. *For the Sake of Peace: Seven Paths to Global Harmony—A Buddhist Perspective*. Santa Monica, CA: Middleway Press, 2001.
———. *Human Security and Sustainability: Sharing Reverence for the Dignity of Life*. Tokyo: Soka Gakkai International, 26 January 2012.
International Center on Nonviolent Conflict. Learning Resources. http://www.nonviolent-conflict.org/index.php/learning-and-resources/resources-on-nonviolent-conflict.
International Commission on Intervention and State Sovereignty (ICISS). *The Responsibility to Protect*. Ottawa: International Development Research Centre, 2001.

Ives, Susan. *Facilitator's Manual for the Class of Nonviolence.* San Antonio: peaceCENTER, 2007.

Jacoby, Tim. *Understanding Conflict and Violence: Theoretical and Interdisciplinary Approaches.* London: Routledge, 2008.

James, William. *The Will to Believe: And Other Essays in Popular Philosophy.* Charleston, SC: Nabu Press, 2010.

———. *William James: Writings 1902–1910.* Ed. Bruce Kuklick. New York: Library of America, 1987.

Janson, Susan and Stuart Macintyre, eds. *Through White Eyes.* Sydney: Allen & Unwin, 1990.

Jenkins, Keith, ed. *The Postmodern History Reader.* London: Routledge, 1997.

Jeong, Ho-Won. *Peace and Conflict Studies: An Introduction.* Aldershot, Hants, UK: Ashgate, 2000.

Johansen, Bruce E. *The Encyclopedia of Native American Legal Tradition.* Westport, CT: Greenwood Press, 1998.

Johnson, James Turner. *Can Modern War Be Just?* New Haven: Yale University Press, 1984.

———. *The Quest for Peace: Three Moral Traditions in Western Cultural History.* Princeton: Princeton University Press, 1987.

Jones, Ann. *War Is Not Over When It's Over: Women Speak Out from the Ruins of War.* New York: Metropolitan Books, 2010.

Juhnke, James C. and Carol M. Hunter. *The Missing Peace: The Search for Nonviolent Alternatives in United States History.* 2nd ed. Kitchener, ON, Canada: Pandora Press, 2004.

Kaba, Mariame, J. Cyriac Mathew, and Nathan Haines, eds. *Something Is Wrong: Exploring the Roots of Youth Violence.* Chicago: Chicago Freedom School Project, Project NIA, and Teachers for Social Justice, n.d. http://project-nia.org/docs/Something_Is_Wrong-Curriculum.pdf.

Kahane, Adam. *Power and Love: A Theory and Practice of Social Change.* San Francisco: Berrett-Koehler, 2010.

Kainz, Howard P. *Philosophical Perspectives on Peace.* Athens, OH: Ohio University Press, 1987.

Kaldor, Mary. *New and Old Wars: Organized Violence in a Global Era.* New ed. Cambridge, UK: Polity Press, 2001.

Kant, Immanuel. *Perpetual Peace and Other Essays on Politics, History, and Morals.* Trans. Ted Humphrey. Indianapolis: Hackett, 1983.

Kapuscinski, Ryszard. *The Other.* London: Verso, 2008.

Karlberg, Michael. *Beyond the Culture of Contest: From Adversarialism to Mutualism in an Age of Interdependence.* Oxford: George Ronald, 2004.

Kaza, Stephanie. *Mindfully Green: A Personal and Spiritual Guide to Whole Earth Thinking.* Boston: Shambhala, 2008.

Keane, John. *Violence and Democracy.* Cambridge, UK: Cambridge University Press, 2004.

Keegan, John. *A History of Warfare.* London: Pimlico, 1994.

Keeley, Lawrence H. *War before Civilization: The Myth of the Peaceful Savage.* New York: Oxford University Press, 1996.

Kegley, Charles W., Jr. and Gregory A. Raymond. *How Nations Make Peace*. New York: St. Martin's/WORTH, 1999.

Kelly, Amy S., ed. *On the Fate of the Earth: Peace on and with the Earth for All Its Children*. Proceedings of the Second Biennial Conference, 1984. San Francisco: Earth Island Institute, 1985.

Kelly, Raymond C. *Warless Societies and the Origin of War*. Ann Arbor: University of Michigan Press, 2000.

Keltner, Dacher, Jason Marsh, and Jeremy Adam Smith, eds. *The Compassionate Instinct: The Science of Human Goodness*. New York: W.W. Norton, 2010.

Kemp, Graham and Douglas Fry. *Keeping the Peace: Conflict Resolution and Peaceful Societies Around the World*. New York: Routledge, 2004.

Kempf, Hervé. *How the Rich Are Destroying the Earth*. Trans. Leslie Thatcher. Foxhole, Dartington, Totnes, Devon, UK: Green Books, 2008.

Keown, Damien. *Buddhist Ethics: A Very Short Introduction*. New York: Oxford University Press, 2005.

Kernan, Thomas P. *The Future of Peace*. New York: Philosophical Library, 1980.

Kim, Y. *A Common Framework for the Ethics of the 21st Century*. Paris: UNESCO, 1999.

Kimmel, Michael S., Jeff Hearn, and R. W. Connell, eds. *Handbook of Studies on Men and Masculinities*. Thousand Oaks, CA: Sage, 2005.

King, Martin Luther, Jr. "Letter from a Birmingham Jail." http://www.africa.upenn.edu/Articles_Gen/Letter_Birmingham.html.

———. *Strength to Love*. New York: Harper & Row, 1964.

Klein, Kenneth H., ed. *In the Interest of Peace: A Spectrum of Philosophical Views*. Longwood: Wolfeboro, 1990.

Knudsen-Hoffman, Gene, ed. *Ways Out: The Book of Changes for Peace*. Santa Barbara: John Daniel, 1988.

Kohn, Alfie. *The Brighter Side of Human Nature: Altruism and Empathy in Everyday Life*. New York: Basic Books, 1990.

Korten, David. *Agenda for a New Economy: From Phantom Wealth to Real Wealth*. 2nd ed. San Francisco: Berrett-Koehler, 2010.

Kraft, Kenneth, ed. *Inner Peace, World Peace: Essays on Buddhism and Nonviolence*. Albany: State University of New York Press, 1992.

Krall, Ruth. *Human Violence and Its Alternatives: An Annotated Bibliography*. Enduring Space, January 2007. http://ruthkrall.com.

Kropotkin, Peter. *Mutual Aid: A Factor of Evolution*. New York: New York University Press, 1972.

Kunkel, Joseph C. and Kenneth H. Klein, eds. *Issues in War and Peace: Philosophical Inquiries*. Wolfeboro, NH: Longwood Academic, 1989.

Kupchan, Charles. *How Enemies Become Friends: The Sources of Stable Peace*. Princeton, NJ: Princeton University Press, 2010.

Kurlansky, Mark. *Nonviolence: The History of a Dangerous Idea*. New York: Modern Library/Random House; London: Jonathan Cape, 2006.

Kurtz, Lester R. and Jennifer Turpin, eds. *Encyclopedia of Violence, Peace, and Conflict.* 3 vols. San Diego: Academic Press, 1999. 2nd ed. 2008.

Lackey, Douglas P. *The Ethics of War and Peace.* Englewood Cliffs, NJ: Prentice-Hall, 1989.

LaFollette, Hugh, ed. *International Encyclopedia of Ethics.* Malden. MA: Wiley-Blackwell, 2013.

Lake, Marilyn and Henry Reynolds. *What's Wrong with Anzac? The Militarisation of Australian History.* Sydney: University of New South Wales Press, 2010.

Lakoff, George and Mark Johnson. *Metaphors We Live By.* Chicago: University of Chicago Press, 2003.

Lamey, Andy. *Frontier Justice: The Global Refugee Crisis and What to Do About It.* St. Lucia: University of Queensland Press, 2011.

Lane, Patty. *A Beginner's Guide to Crossing Cultures: Making Friends in a Multicultural World.* Downers Grove, IL: InterVarsity Press, 2002.

Langille, H. P. *Bridging the Commitment-Capacity Gap: Existing Arrangements and Options for Enhancing UN Rapid Deployment Capabilities.* Wayne, NJ: Center for UN Reform Education, 2002.

Lankford, Adam. *The Myth of Martyrdom: What Really Drives Suicide Bombers, Rampage Shooters, and Other Self-Destructive Killers.* New York: Palgrave Macmillan, 2013.

Lantieri, Linda and Janet Patti. *Waging Peace in Our Schools.* Boston: Beacon Press, 1996.

Leahey, Christopher R. *Whitewashing War: Historical Myth, Corporate Textbooks, and Possibilities for Democratic Education.* New York: Teachers College Press, 2010.

Leavitt, Lewis A. and Nathan A. Fox. *The Psychological Effects of War and Violence on Children.* Hillsdale, NJ: Lawrence Erlbaum Associates, 1993.

Le Blanc, Steven and Katherine E. Register. *Constant Battles: Why We Fight.* New York: St. Martin's Press, 2003.

Lebow, Richard Ned. *Why Nations Fight: Past and Future Motives for War.* Reissue ed. Cambridge, UK: Cambridge University Press, 2010.

Lederach, John Paul. *Building Peace: Sustainable Reconciliation in Divided Societies.* Washington, DC: United States Institute of Peace Press, 1997.

———. *The Little Book of Conflict Transformation.* Intercourse, PA: Good Books, 2003.

———. *The Moral Imagination: The Art and Soul of Building Peace.* New York: Oxford University Press, 2005.

———. *Preparing for Peace: Conflict Transformation across Cultures.* Syracuse: Syracuse University Press, 1995.

——— and Janice Moomaw Jenner, eds. *A Handbook of International Peacebuilding: Into the Eye of the Storm.* San Francisco: Jossey-Bass, 2002.

LeShan, Lawrence. *The Psychology of War: Comprehending Its Mystique and Its Madness.* Enl. ed. New York: Helios Press, 2002.

Lind, Nancy S. and Manfred B. Steger, eds. *Violence and Its Alternatives.* New York: Palgrave Macmillan, 1999.

Lindemann, Thomas. *Causes of War: The Struggle for Recognition.* Colchester, Essex: European Consortium for Political Research Press, 2011.

Linzey, Andrew, ed. *The Link Between Animal Abuse and Human Violence.* Brighton, UK: Sussex Academic Press, 2009.

Listenbee, Robert J., Jr., Joe Torre et al. *Report of the Attorney General's National Task Force on Children Exposed to Violence*. Washington, DC: U.S. Department of Justice, Office of the Attorney General, 12 December 2012.

Loewen, James W. *Lies My Teacher Told Me: Everything Your American History Textbook Got Wrong*. Rev. ed. New York: Touchstone, 2007.

———. *Teaching What Really Happened: How to Avoid the Tyranny of Textbooks and Get Students Excited about Doing History*. New York: Teachers College Press, 2009.

Lollis, Edward W. "Peace Monuments [and Museums of Peace] around the World (& Notable Peacemakers)." http://peace.maripo.com.

Lorentzen, Lois Ann and Jennifer Turpin, eds. *The Women and War Reader*. New York: New York University Press, 1998.

Lynd, Staughton. *Nonviolence in America: A Documentary History*. Indianapolis: Bobbs-Merrill, 1966.

Macintyre, Stuart, ed. *The Historian's Conscience: Australian Historians on the Ethics of History*. Melbourne: Melbourne University Press, 2004.

——— and Anna Clark. *The History Wars*. Melbourne: Melbourne University Press, 2003.

MacNair, Rachel M. *The Psychology of Peace: An Introduction*. 2nd ed. Santa Barbara, CA: Praeger, 2012.

Macquarrie, John. *The Concept of Peace*. New York: Harper & Row, 1973.

Malley-Morrison, Kathleen Andrea Mercurio, and Gabriel Twose, eds. *International Handbook of Peace and Reconciliation*. New York: Springer, 2013.

Margolis, Joseph. *Moral Philosophy after 9/11*. University Park: Pennsylvania State University Press, 2004.

Markusen, Ann and Joel Yudken. *Dismantling the Cold War Economy*. New York: Basic Books, 1992.

———, Sean DiGiovanna, and Michael C. Leary, eds. *From Defense to Development? International Perspectives on Realizing the Peace Dividend*. London: Routledge, 2003.

Martel, Gordon, ed. *The Encyclopedia of War*. 5 vols. Hoboken, NJ: Wiley-Blackwell, 2012.

Martin, Brian. *Nonviolence Versus Capitalism*. London: War Resisters' International, 2001.

Martin, Debra and David Frayer, eds. *Troubled Times: Violence and Warfare in the Past*. Amsterdam: Gordon and Breach, 1997.

Marwick, Arthur. *The Nature of History*. London: Macmillan, 1973.

Mayer, P., ed. *The Pacifist Conscience*. Harmondsworth, Middlesex: Penguin, 1966.

Mayton, Daniel II. *Nonviolence and Peace Psychology*. New York: Springer, 2009.

McCarthy, Colman. *I'd Rather Teach Peace*. Maryknoll, NY: Orbis Books, 2007.

McKay, Ian and Jamie Swift. *Warrior Nation: Rebranding Canada in an Age of Anxiety*. Toronto: Between the Lines, 2012.

McMahan, Jeff. *Killing in War*. Oxford: Oxford University Press, 2009.

McMurtry, John. *Understanding War*. Buffalo: University of Toronto Press, 1989.

Mead, Margaret. "Warfare Is Only an Invention—Not a Necessity," *Asia* 40 (1940), pp. 415–21. http://acme.highpoint.edu/~msetzler/IntlSec/IntlSecReads/MeadeWarCreated.pdf.

Melko, Matthew. *52 Peaceful Societies*. Oakville, ON: Canadian Peace Research Institute Press, 1973.

Melman, Seymour. *The Defense Economy: Conversion of Industries and Occupations to Civilian Needs*. New York: Praeger, 1970.

Mendlovitz, Saul H. and R. B. J. Walker, eds. *Towards Just World Peace*. London: Butterworths, 1987.

Middleton, DeWight R. *The Challenge of Human Diversity: Mirrors, Bridges, and Chasms*. 3rd ed. Waveland Press, 2011.

Miller, Arthur G., ed. *The Social Psychology of Good and Evil*. New York: Guildford Press, 2004.

Miller, Christopher E. (Ed. Mary E. King.) *A Glossary of Terms and Concepts in Peace and Conflict Studies*. 2nd ed. Addis Ababa: University for Peace, Africa Program, 2005. http://www.upeace.org/pdf/glossaryv2.pdf.

Moix, Bridget and Trevor Keck. *The Responsibility to Prevent: A Report to Congress from the Friends Committee on National Legislation (Quakers)*. Washington, DC: Friends Committee on National Legislation, October 2008.

———, Daniel Smith, and Anna Staab. *Peaceful Prevention of Deadly Conflict*. 3rd ed. Washington, DC: Friends Committee on National Legislation Education Fund, July 2004.

Montagu, Ashley, ed. *Learning Non-Aggression: The Experience of Non-Literate Societies*. New York: Oxford University Press, 1978.

———. *The Nature of Human Aggression*. New York: Oxford University Press, 1976.

———. *The Peace of the World*. Tokyo: Kenyusha, 1987.

Montessori, Maria. *Education and Peace*. Trans. Helen R. Lane. New York: Henry Regnery, 1972.

Moran, Gabriel. *Living Nonviolently: Language for Resisting Violence*. Lanham, MD: Lexington Books, 2011.

Morsink, Johannes. *The Universal Declaration of Human Rights: Origins, Drafting, and Intent*. Philadelphia: University of Pennsylvania Press, 1999.

Mosley, Alexander. *A Philosophy of War*. New York: Algora, 2002.

Mosse, George L. *Fallen Soldiers: Reshaping the Memory of the World Wars*. New York: Oxford University Press, 1990.

Muchembled, Robert. *A History of Violence: From the End of the Middle Ages to the Present*. Cambridge, UK: Polity Press, 2011.

Mueller, John E. *The Remnants of War*. Ithaca, NY: Cornell University Press, 2004.

———. *Retreat from Doomsday: The Obsolescence of Major War*. New York: Basic Books, 1990.

———. "War has almost ceased to exist." *Political Science Quarterly* 124 (2009): 297–321.

Münkleer, Herfried. *The New Wars*. Cambridge, UK: Polity, 2005.

Munslow, Alun. *Deconstructing History*. London: Routledge, 1997.

Murithi, Tim. *The Ethics of Peacebuilding*. Edinburgh: Edinburgh University Press, 2009.

Murphy, Jeffrie G. and Jean Hampton. *Forgiveness and Mercy*. New York: Cambridge University Press, 1988.

Myers, Winslow. *Living Beyond War: A Citizen's Guide*. Maryknoll, NY: Orbis Books, 2009.

Nagler, Michael N. *The Search for a Nonviolent Future: A Promise of Peace for Ourselves. Our Families, and Our World*. Novato, CA: New World Library, 2004.

Nardin, Terry, ed. *The Ethics of War and Peace: Religious and Secular Perspectives*. Princeton, NJ: Princeton University Press, 1996.

Nash, Gary B., Charlotte Crabtree, and Ross E. Dunn. *History on Trial: Culture Wars and the Teaching of the Past*. New York: Alfred A. Knopf, 1997.

Neier, Aryeh. *The International Human Rights Movement: A History*. Princeton, NJ: Princeton University Press, 2012.

Neitzel, Sönke and Harald Welzer. *Soldaten: On Fighting, Killing, and Dying—The Secret WW II Transcripts of German POWs*. Trans. Jefferson Chase. New York: Alfred A. Knopf, 2012.

Nelson-Pallmeyer, Jack. *Brave New World Order: Must We Pledge Allegiance?* Maryknoll, NY: Orbis Books, 1992.

Newman, Graeme. *Understanding Violence*. New York: J.B. Lippincott, 1979.

Noddings, Nel. *Peace Education: How We Come to Love and Hate War*. Cambridge, UK: Cambridge University Press, 2012.

Noltner, John. *A Peace of My Mind: Exploring the Meaning of Peace, One Story at a Time*. Minneapolis: http://www.apeaceofmymind.net, 2011.

Nordstrom, Carolyn. *A Different Kind of War Story*. Philadelphia: University of Pennsylvania Press, 1997.

Norman, Richard. *Ethics, Killing and War*. Cambridge, UK: Cambridge University Press, 1995.

Norton, Brian G. *The Preservation of Species: The Value of Biological Diversity*. Princeton, NJ: Princeton University Press, 1986.

Nowak, Martin A., with Roger Highfield. *SuperCooperators: Altruism, Evolution, and Why We Need Each Other to Succeed*. New York: Free Press, 2012.

O'Dea, James. *Cultivating Peace: Becoming a 21st-Century Peace Ambassador*. San Rafael, CA: Shift Books, 2012.

O'Donovan, Oliver. *The Just War Revisited*. Cambridge, UK: Cambridge University Press, 2003.

Oldfield, Sybil. *Women against the Iron Fist: Alternatives to Militarism 1900–1989*. Oxford: Basil Blackwell, 1989.

Oliner, Samuel P., assisted by Piotr Olaf Zylicz. *Altruism, Intergroup Apology, Forgiveness, and Reconciliation*. St. Paul, MN: Paragon House, 2008.

Olmsted, Sterling P, Mike Heller, and Ruth Olmsted, eds. *Mohandas K. Gandhi: The Last Eighteen Years*. Wilmington, OH: Wilmington College Peace Resource Center, 2012.

Orend, Brian. *The Morality of War*. Peterborough, ON: Broadview, 2006.

Page, James. *Peace Education: Exploring Ethical and Philosophical Foundations*. Charlotte, NC: Information Age Press, 2008.

Paige, Glenn D. *Nonkilling Global Political Science*. 2nd rev. English ed. Honolulu: Center for Global Nonkilling, 2009. Creative Commons access: http://nonkilling.org/pdf/nkgps.pdf (2007 ed.).

Pape, Robert Anthony. *Dying to Win: The Strategic Logic of Suicide Terrorism*. New York: Random House, 2005.

Parekh, Bhikhu. *Gandhi*. Oxford: Oxford University Press, 1997.

Paris, Erna. *Long Shadows: Truth, Lies, and History*. New York: Bloomsbury USA, 2002.

Paskins, B. and M. Dockrill. *The Ethics of War*. London: Duckworth, 1979.

Patfoort, Pat. *An Introduction to Nonviolence: A Conceptual Framework*. Nyack, NY: Fellowship of Reconciliation, 1987.

Patterson, Eric, ed. *Ethics Beyond War's End*. Washington, DC: Georgetown University Press, 2011.

Peace Philosophy Centre (Vancouver, Canada). http://peacephilosophy.blogspot.com.

Peavey, Fran, with Myra Levy and Charles Varon. *Heart Politics*. Philadelphia: New Society, 1986.

The People's Charter to Create a Nonviolent World. http://thepeoplesnonviolencecharter. wordpress.com/about.

Perez de Cuellar, Javier and Young Seek Choue, eds. *World Encyclopedia of Peace*. 2nd ed. 8 vols. Dobbs Ferry, NY: Oceana, 1999.

Petit, Patrick U., ed. *Shaping the Culture of Peace in a Multilateral World*. New Brunswick, NJ: Transaction, 2011.

Phillips, Adam and Barbara Taylor. *On Kindness*. New York: Farrar, Straus and Giroux, 2009.

Pilisuk, Marc, with Jennifer Achord Rountree. *Who Benefits from Global Violence and War: Uncovering a Destructive System*. Westport, CT: Greenwood/Praeger, 2008.

Pim, Joám Evans, ed. *Nonkilling Societies*. Honolulu: Center for Global Nonkilling, 2010.

———. *Toward a Nonkilling Paradigm*. Honolulu: Center for Global Nonkilling, 2009.

Pinker, Steven. *The Better Angels of Our Nature: Why Violence Has Declined*. New York: Viking/Penguin, 2011.

Popovic, Srdja, Andrej Milivojevic, and Slobodan Djinovic. *Nonviolent Struggle: 50 Crucial Points—A Strategic Approach to Everyday Tactics* (Belgrade: Centre for Applied NonViolent Action and Strategies [CANVAS], 2006. http://www.canvasopedia.org/legacy/files/ various/Nonviolent_Struggle-50CP.pdf

Porter, Bruce D. *War and the Rise of the State: The Military Foundations of Modern Politics*. New York: The Free Press, 1994.

Postman, Neil and Charles Weingartner. *Teaching as a Subversive Activity*. New York: Delta Books, 1969.

Powers, Roger S. and William B. Vogele, eds. *Protest, Power and Change: An Encyclopedia of Nonviolent Action from ACT-UP to Women's Suffrage*. New York: Garland, 1997.

Presby, Gail M., ed. *Philosophical Perspectives on the "War on Terrorism."* New York: Rodopi, 2007.

Presler, Judith and Sally J. Scholz, eds. *Peacemaking: Lessons from the Past, Visions for the Future*. Atlanta: Rodopi, 2000.

Priest, Dana and William M. Arkin. *Top Secret America: The Rise of the New American Security State*. New York: Little, Brown, 2011.

Purnell, David. *Creative Conflict*. The Twenty-Fourth James Backhouse Lecture. O'Connor, ACT: The Religious Society of Friends (Quakers) in Australia, 1988.

Quigley, John B. *The Ruses for War: American Interventionism Since World War II*. Amherst, NY: Prometheus Books, 2007.

Quinn, Robert E. *Change the World: How Ordinary People Can Achieve Extraordinary Results*. San Francisco: Jossey-Bass, 2000.

Ram, Senthil and Ralph Summy, eds. *Nonviolence: An Alternative for Defeating Global Terror(ism)*. New York: Nova Science, 2008.

Ramsbotham, Oliver, Tom Woodhouse, and Hugh Miall. *Contemporary Conflict Resolution*, 2nd ed. London: Polity Press, 2005.

Rapoport, Anatol. *The Origins of Violence: Approaches to the Study of Conflict*. New Brunswick, NJ: Transaction, 1995.

———. *Peace: An Idea Whose Time Has Come*. Ann Arbor: University of Michigan Press, 1992.

Reardon, Betty A. *Sexism and the War System*. Syracuse: Syracuse University Press, 1996.

———. *Women and Peace: Feminist Visions of Global Security*. Albany: State University of New York Press, 1993.

Reed, Charles, David Ryall, eds. *The Price of Peace: Just War in the Twenty-First Century*. Cambridge, UK: Cambridge University Press, 2007.

Rees, Stuart. *Passion for Peace: Exercising Power Creatively*. Sydney: University of New South Wales Press, 2003.

Regan, Richard J. *Just War: Principles and Cases*. Washington, DC: Catholic University of America Press, 1996.

Reilly, Richard. *Ethics of Compassion: Bridging Ethical Theory and Religious Moral Discourse*. Lanham, MD: Lexington, 2008.

Reisman, Michael and Chris T. Antoniou, eds. *The Laws of War: A Comprehensive Collection of Primary Documents on International Laws Governing Armed Conflict*. New York: Vintage Books, 1994.

Renner, Michael. *Budgeting for Disarmament: The Costs of War and Peace*. Worldwatch Paper 122. Washington, DC: Worldwatch Institute, 1994.

———. *Small Arms, Big Impact: The Next Challenge of Disarmament*. Worldwatch Paper 137. Washington, DC: Worldwatch Institute, 1997.

———. *Swords into Plowshares: Converting to a Peace Economy*. Worldwatch Paper 96. Washington, DC: Worldwatch Institute, June 1990.

Richards, Jesse. *The Secret Peace: Exposing the Positive Trend of World Events*. New York: Book & Ladder Press, 2011.

Riches, David. *The Anthropology of Violence*. Oxford: Basil Blackwell, 1986.

Richler, Noah. *What We Talk about When We Talk about War*. Fredericton, NB, Canada: Goose Lane Editions, 2012.

Richmond, Oliver P. *Peace: A Very Short Introduction*. New York: Oxford University Press, 2013.

———. *The Transformation of Peace*. New York: Palgrave Macmillan, 2005.

Richerson, P. J. and R. Boyd. *Not by Genes Alone: How Culture Transformed Human Evolution*. Chicago: University of Chicago Press. 2005.

Ridley, Matt. *The Rational Optimist: How Prosperity Evolves*. London: Fourth Estate, 2010.

Rieff, David. *Against Remembrance*. Melbourne: Melbourne University Press, 2011.

Riegle, Rosalie G. *Crossing the Line: Nonviolent Resisters Speak Out for Peace*. Eugene, OR: Wipf and Stock, 2013.

Rifkin, Jeremy. *The Empathetic Civilization: The Race to Global Consciousness in a World in Crisis*. Cambridge, UK: Polity Press, 2010.

Rigby, Andrew. *Justice and Reconciliation: After the Violence*. Boulder, CO: L. Rienner, 2001.

Roberts, Adam and Timothy Garton Ash. *Civil Resistance and Power Politics: The Experience of Non-violent Action from Gandhi to the Present*. New York: Oxford University Press, 2009.

Roche, Douglas. *The Human Right to Peace*. Ottawa: Novalis Press, 2003.

Rodin, D. *War and Self-Defense*. Oxford: Clarendon Press, 2003.

Rosenberg, Marshall B. *Nonviolent Communication: A Language of Life*. Encinitas, CA: PuddleDancer Press, 2003.

Ross, Carne. *The Leaderless Revolution: How Ordinary People Will Take Power and Change Politics in the 21st Century*. London: Simon & Schuster, 2011.

Roth, John K. and Carol Rittner. *Rape: Weapon of War and Genocide*. St. Paul, MN: Paragon House, 2012.

Rouner, Leroy S., ed. *Celebrating Peace*. Notre Dame, IN: University of Notre Dame Press, 1990.

Rowe, Martin, ed. *The Way of Compassion*. New York: Stealth Technologies, 1999.

Ruddick, Sara. *Maternal Thinking: Toward a Politics of Peace, with a New Preface*. Boston: Beacon Press, 1995.

Rummel, R. J. *In the Minds of Men: Principles Toward and Waging Peace*. Seoul: Sogang University Press, 1984.

——. *Understanding Conflict and War*. Beverly Hills, CA: Sage, 1975.

Russell, Bertrand. *Why Men Fight: A Method of Abolishing the International Duel*. New York: Century, 1917.

Salem, Deborah J. and Andrew N. Rowan, eds. *The State of the Animals II, 2003*. Washington, DC: Humane Society Press, 2003.

Salomon, Gavriel and Edward Cairns, eds. *Handbook on Peace Education*. New York: Psychology Press, 2010.

Sanders, Barry. *The Green Zone: The Environmental Costs of Militarism*. Oakland, CA: AK Press, 2009.

Sandler, Todd and Keith Hartley. *The Economics of Defense*. Cambridge, UK: Cambridge University Press, 1995.

Sandole, Dennis J.D. *Peacebuilding Preventing Violent Conflict in a Complex World*. Cambridge, UK: Polity Press, 2010.

Sapolsky, Robert M. "A Natural History of Peace." *Foreign Affairs*, January/February 2006. http://opim.wharton.upenn.edu/˜sok/papers/s/sapolsky-foreignaffairs-2006.pdf.

Savir, Uri. *Peace First: A New Model to End War*. San Francisco: Berrett-Koehler, 2008.

Sawatsky, Jarem and Howard Zehr. *Justpeace Ethics: A Guide to Restorative Justice and Peacebuilding*. Eugene, OR: Cascade Books, 2009.

Scarry, Elaine. *The Body in Pain: The Making and Unmaking of the World*. New York: Oxford University Press, 1985.

Schäffner, Christina and Anita L. Wenden, eds. *Language and Peace*. Aldershot, Hants, UK: Dartmouth, 1995.

Schell, Jonathan. *The Unconquerable World: Power, Nonviolence, and the Will of the People*. New York: Metropolitan Books, 2003.

Schirch, Lisa. *Civilian Peacekeeping: Preventing Violence and Making Space for Democracy.* Uppsala: Life & Peace Institute, 2006.

———. *The Little Book of Strategic Peacebuilding.* Intercourse, PA: Good Books, 2004.

Schock, Kurt. *Unarmed Insurrections: People Power Movements in Nondemocracies.* Minneapolis: University of Minnesota Press, 2005.

Sémelin, Jacques. *Unarmed against Hitler: Civilian Resistance in Europe, 1939- 1943.* Trans. Suzan Husserl-Kapit. Westport, CT: Praeger, 1993.

Sen, Amartya. *The Idea of Justice.* London: Penguin Books, 2010.

———. *Identity and Violence: The Illusion of Destiny.* London: Penguin, 2006.

Shanley, Brayton. *The Many Sides of Peace: Christian Nonviolence, the Contemplative Life, and Sustainable Living.* Eugene, OR: Resource Publications, 2013.

Sharp, Gene. *From Dictatorship to Democracy: A Conceptual Framework for Liberation.* 4th US ed. East Boston, MA: The Albert Einstein Institution, 2010.

———. *The Politics of Nonviolent Action.* Boston: Extending Horizons Books, 1973.

———. *Waging Nonviolent Struggle: 20th Century Practice and 21st Century Potential.* Westford, MA: Porter Sargent, 2005.

Sheehan, James. *The Monopoly of Violence: Why Europeans Hate Going to War.* London: Faber and Faber, 2008.

Sherman, Nancy. *The Untold War: Inside the Hearts, Minds, and Souls of Our Soldiers.* New York: W.W. Norton, 2010.

Shifferd, Kent D. *From War to Peace: A Guide to the Next Hundred Years.* Jefferson, NC: McFarland, 2011.

Sider, Ronald J. *Non-Violence: The Invincible Weapon?* Dallas: Word Publishing, 1989.

Silverberg, James and J. Patrick Gray. *Aggression and Peacefulness in Humans and Other Primates.* New York: Oxford University Press, 1992.

Singer, Peter, ed. *Ethics.* New York: Oxford University Press, 1994.

Sites, Kevin. *The Things They Cannot Say: Stories Soldiers Won't Tell You about What They've Seen, Done or Failed to Do in War.* New York: Harper Perennial, 2013.

Slattery, Laura et al. *Engage: Exploring Nonviolent Living.* Oakland, CA: Pace e Bene Press, 2005

Smith, David Livingstone. *The Most Dangerous Animal: Human Nature and the Origins of War.* New York: St. Martin's Griffin, 2007.

Smolin, Lee. *The Life of the Cosmos.* New York: Oxford University Press, 1997.

Sobek, David. *Causes of War.* Cambridge, UK: Polity Press, 2008.

Solis, Gary D. *The Law of Armed Conflict: International Humanitarian Law in War.* Cambridge, UK: Cambridge University Press, 2010.

Sontag, Susan. *Regarding the Pain of Others.* New York: Farrar, Straus and Giroux, 2003.

Sowell, Thomas. *The Quest for Cosmic Justice.* New York: The Free Press, 1999.

Sparrow, Jeff. *Killing: Misadventures in Violence.* Melbourne: Melbourne University Press, 2009.

Sponsel, Leslie E. and Thomas Gregor, eds. *The Anthropology of Peace and Nonviolence.* Boulder, CO: L. Rienner, 1994.

Stafford, William. *Every War Has Two Losers: William Stafford on Peace and War.* Ed. Kim Stafford. Minneapolis: Milkweed Editions, 2003.

Stassen, Glen H., ed. *Just Peacemaking: The New Paradigms for the Ethics of Peace and War.* New ed. Cleveland: Pilgrim Press, 2008.

Staub, Ervin. *The Psychology of Good and Evil: Why Children, Adults, and Groups Help and Harm Others.* Cambridge, UK: Cambridge University Press, 2003.

Stedjan, Scott and Laura Weis. *Building Structures for Peace: Strategies for Filling a Peace Toolbox.* Washington, DC: Friends Committee on National Legislation Education Fund, 2007.

Steger, Manfred B. *Judging Nonviolence: The Dispute between Realists and Idealists.* New York: Routledge, 2003.

—— and Nancy S. Lind, eds. *Violence and Its Alternatives: An Interdisciplinary Reader.* New York: St. Martin's Press, 1999.

Stone, Oliver and Peter Kuznick. *The Untold History of the United States.* New York: Gallery Books, 2012.

Suganami, Hidemi. *On the Causes of War.* New York: Oxford University Press, 1996.

Suter, Keith. *Alternative to War: Conflict Resolution and the Peaceful Settlement of International Disputes.* Sydney: Women's International League for Peace and Freedom, 1986.

Swanson, David. *War Is a Lie.* Charlottesville, VA: davidswanson.org, 2010.

——. *When the World Outlawed War.* Charlottesville, VA: davidswanson.org, 2011.

——, ed. *The Military Industrial Complex at 50.* Charlottesville, VA: davidswanson.org, 2011.

Teichman, Jenny. *Pacifism and the Just War: A Study in Applied Philosophy.* New York: Blackwell, 1986.

——. *The Philosophy of War and Peace.* Charlottesville, VA: Imprint Academic/Philosophy Documentation Center, 2006.

Terkel, Susan. *People Power: A Look at Nonviolent Action and Defense.* New York: Lodestar, 1996.

Thalhammer, Kristina E. et al. *Courageous Resistance: The Power of Ordinary People.* New York: Palgrave Macmillan, 2007.

Thomas, Claude Anshin. *At Hell's Gate: A Soldier's Journey from War to Peace.* Boston: Shambhala, 2004.

Thomas, William. *Scorched Earth: The Military's Assault on the Environment.* Philadelphia: New Society, 1995.

Tollefson, Lowell. *What Is War? Philosophical Reflections about the Nature, Causes, and Persistence of Wars.* Lincoln, NE: iUniverse, 2007.

Tomasello, Michael. *Why We Cooperate.* Cambridge, MA: Boston Review, 2009.

Tremblay, Rodrigue. *The Code for Global Ethics: Ten Humanist Principles.* Amherst, NY: Prometheus Books, 2010.

Trivers, Robert. *Social Evolution.* Upper Saddle River, NJ: Benjamin-Cummings, 1985.

Troup, Kathleen and Anna Green, eds., *The Houses of History: A Critical Reader in Twentieth-Century History and Theory.* New York: New York University Press, 1999.

Turney, Jon. *The Rough Guide to the Future.* London: Rough Guides, 2010.

Turse, Nick. *The Complex: How the Military Invades Our Everyday Lives.* New York: Metropolitan Books, 2008.

Tuttle, Will. *The World Peace Diet: Eating for Spiritual Health and Social Harmony*. New York: Lantern Books, 2005.

Tutu, Desmond. *No Future without Forgiveness*. London: Rider, 1999.

Tyner, James A. *Military Legacies: A World Made by War*. New York: Routledge, 2010.

United Nations. *Declaration and Programme of Action on a Culture of Peace*. UN Ref. GA/A/Res/53/243. 53rd Session (1999), Agenda Item 31. http://www.unesco.org/cpp/uk/declarations/2000.htm.

——. *The Hague Agenda for Peace and Justice for the 21st Century*. UN Ref. A/54/98. http://www.vmpeace.org/pages/hague_agenda_for_peace.htm.

——. *Responsibility to Protect*. UN Ref. A/RES/60/1. New York: United Nations, 2005.

——. *The Universal Declaration of Human Rights*. Illustrated by Michel Streich. Crows Nest, NSW, Australia: Allen & Unwin, 2008.

Ury, William L., ed. *Must We Fight? From the Battlefield to the Schoolyard, a New Perspective on Violent Conflict and Its Prevention*. San Francisco: Jossey-Bass, 2002.

US Peace Memorial Foundation. *US Peace Registry*. 19 June 2013 ed. http://www.uspeacememorial.org/Registry.htm.

Van Creveld, Martin. *The Culture of War*. New York: Presidio Press, 2008.

Van der Dennen, Johan M. G. *The Origin of War: The Evolution of a Male-Coalitional Reproductive Strategy*. 2 vols. Groningen: Origin Press, 1995. http://rint.rechten.rug.nl/rth/dennen/dennen6.htm.

Vanderhaar, Gerard and Mary Lou Kownacki, eds. *Way of Peace: A Guide to Nonviolence*. Erie, PA: Pax Christi USA, 1987.

Vanier, Jean. *Finding Peace*. Toronto: House of Anansi Press, 2003.

Vasquez, John A. *The War Puzzle*. Cambridge, UK: Cambridge University Press, 1993.

Wallensteen, Peter. *Peace Research: Theory and Practice*. New York: Routledge, 2011.

Walzer, Michael. *Arguing about War*. New Haven: Yale University Press, 2004.

Ware, Helen, ed. et al. *The No-Nonsense Guide to Conflict and Peace*. Oxford: New Internationalist, 2006.

Waters, Kerry and Robin Jarrell. *Blessed Peacemakers: 365 Extraordinary People Who Changed the World*. Eugene, OR: Wipf and Stock, 2013.

Webel, Charles P. and John A. Arnaldi, eds. *The Ethics and Efficacy of the Global War on Terrorism*. New York: Palgrave Macmillan, 2011.

—— and Johan Galtung, eds. *Handbook of Peace and Conflict Studies*. New York: Routledge, 2007.

—— and Jorgen Johansen, eds. *Peace and Conflict Studies: A Reader*. New York: Routledge, 2011.

Weil, Pierre. *The Art of Living in Peace: Guide to Education for a Culture of Peace*. Paris: UNESCO/Unipaix, 2002.

Weisberg, Barry. *Ecocide in Indochina: The Ecology of War*. San Francisco: Canfield Press, 1970.

Welch, Sharon D. *Real Peace, Real Security: The Challenges of Global Citizenship*. Minneapolis: Fortress Press, 2008.

Wenden, Anita L. ed. *Educating for a Culture of Social and Ecological Peace*. Albany: State University of New York Press, 2004.

Wheatley, Margaret and Deborah Frieze. *Walk Out Walk On: A Learning Journey into Communities Daring to Live the Future Now*. San Francisco: Berrett-Koehler, 2011.

Whitman, Jim. *The Fundamentals of Global Governance*. New York: Palgrave Macmillan, 2009.

Wilkinson, Richard and Kate Pickett. *The Spirit Level: Why Greater Equality Makes Societies Stronger*. New York: Bloomsbury Press, 2010.

Wineberg, Samuel S. *Historical Thinking and Other Unnatural Acts: Charting the Future of Teaching the Past*. Philadelphia: Temple University Press, 2001.

Woocher, Lawrence. *Preventing Violent Conflict: Assessing Progress, Meeting Challenges*. Special Report 231. Washington, DC: United States Institute of Peace, September 2009.

Wright, Cyril and Tony Augarde, eds., for the Peace Pledge Union. *Peace Is the Way: A Guide to Pacifist Views and Actions*. Cambridge, UK: Lutterworth Press, 1990.

Wright, Quincy. *A Study of War*. Chicago: University of Chicago Press, 1965.

Wright, Robert. *Nonzero: The Logic of Human Destiny*. New York: Vintage Books, 2001.

Yalman, Nur and Daisaku Ikeda. *A Passage to Peace: Global Solutions from East and West*. London: I. B. Tauris, 2009.

Yoder, John Howard. *Non-Violence: A Brief History*. Waco, TX: Baylor University Press, 2009.

———. *When War Is Unjust: Being Honest in Just-War Thinking*. Minneapolis: Augsburg, 1984.

Young, Nigel, ed. *The Oxford International Encyclopedia of Peace*. 4 vols. Oxford: Oxford University Press, 2010.

Zelizer, Craig. *Integrated Peacebuilding: Innovative Approaches to Transforming Conflict*. Boulder, CO: Westview Press, 2013.

———. and Robert A. Rubinstein, eds. *Building Peace: Practical Reflections from the Field*. Sterling, VA: Kumarian Press, 2009.

Zimbardo, Philip. *The Lucifer Effect: How Good People Turn Evil*. New York: Random House, 2007.

Zinn, Howard. *A People's History of the United States*. New York: Harper Perennial, 2010.

Žižek, Slavoj. *Violence: Six Sideways Reflections*. London: Profile Books, 2009.

Zournazi, Mary. *Keywords to War: Reviving Language in an Age of Terror*. Carlton North, VIC, Australia: Scribe, 2007.

Zunes, Stephen, Lester R. Kurtz, and Sarah Beth Asher, eds. *Nonviolent Social Movements: A Geographical Perspective*. Malden, MA: Blackwell, 1999.

Sources for Epigraphs

FRONT MATTER

"The earth is too small a planet and we too brief visitors for anything to matter more than the struggle for peace." From Coleman McCarthy, *I'd Rather Teach Peace* (Maryknoll, NY: Orbis Books, 2007), p. xx.

"I am certain that after the dust of centuries has passed over our cities, we, too, will be remembered not for victories or defeats in battle or in politics, but for our contribution to the human spirit." From John F. Kennedy, remarks on behalf of National Cultural Center which would come to bear his name, 29 November 1962; inscribed on wall of John F. Kennedy Center for the Performing Arts, Washington, D.C.

INTRODUCTION

"The only alternative to coexistence is codestruction." From Jawaharlal Nehru, as quoted in *The Observer* (London), 29 August 1954.

"You can no more win a war than you can win an earthquake." From Jeannette Rankin, as quoted in Hannah Josephson, *Jeanette Rankin, First Lady in Congress: A Biography*, Chapter 8. (Indianapolis: Bobbs-Merrill, 1974; republished New York: Margaret K. McElderry Books, 2006).

"We seem always ready to pay the price for war. Almost gladly we give our time and our treasure—our limbs and even our lives—for war. But we expect to get peace for nothing." From Peace Pilgrim (Mildred Norman Ryder), *Peace Pilgrim: Her Life and Work in Her Own Words* (Santa Fe, NM: Ocean Tree Books, 1992), p. 110.

CHAPTER 1

"There was never a good war, or a bad peace." From Benjamin Franklin, letter to Sir Joseph Banks, president of the Royal Society, 27 July 1783; also contained in letter to Josiah Quincy, 8 September 1783; in Benjamin Franklin, *The Complete Works of Benjamin Franklin: Including His Private as Well as His Official and Scientific Correspondence, and Numerous Letters and Documents Now for the First Time Printed, With Many Others Not Included In Any Former Collection: Also the Unmutilated and Correct Version of His Autobiography*, vol. 8, compiled and ed. John Bigelow in 10 vols. (New York: G. P. Putnam's Sons, 1887–8).

"Peace has its victories no less than war, but it doesn't have as many monuments t' unveil." From Frank McKinney ("Kin") Hubbard, *The Best of Kin Hubbard: Abe Martin's Sayings and Wisecracks, Abe's Neighbors, His Almanack, Comic Drawings*, ed. David S. Hawes (Bloomington: Indiana University Press, 1984), p. 139.

This quotation has presumably been borrowed and developed from the following:

"Peace hath her victories no less renowned than war." From John Milton, "Sonnet 16" (1652).

"[I]t is the lot of all myths to creep gradually into the confines of a supposedly historical reality, and to be treated by some later age as unique fact with claims to historical truth. . . ." From Friedrich Nietzsche, *The Birth of Tragedy out of the Spirit of Music*, trans. Shaun Whiteside, ed. Michael Tanner (London: Penguin, 2005), sec. 10, p. 53.

CHAPTER 2

"Don't tell me peace has broken out. . . ." From Bertolt Brecht, *Mother Courage and Her Children: A Chronicle of the Thirty Years' War*, trans. Eric Bentley; in Bertolt Brecht, *Plays*, vol. II (London: Methuen, 1962), p. 57.

"To jaw-jaw is always better than to war-war." From Winston Churchill, remarks at a White House luncheon, 26 June 1954.

"War is not a primordial biological 'curse'. It is a cultural innovation, an especially vicious, persistent meme, which culture can help us transcend." From John Horgan, "No, War Is Not Inevitable," *Discover*, June 2012; available at: http://discovermagazine.com/2012/jun/02-no-war-is-not-inevitable#.UYCaOBzvLLI.

CHAPTER 3

"War, by its very nature, embodies the tyranny that it claims to address. . . . The worst effect of any war . . . is that it destroys the ground of peace, erodes its culture and wrecks its institutions, so preparing the way for new wars. . . . For us to live together in any kind of safety or to meet the real needs of human beings, like eliminating poverty or dealing with disease, the eradication of war is a prerequisite." From Diana Francis, *Rethinking War and Peace* (London: Pluto Press, 2004), pp. 52–3.

CHAPTER 4

"Nothing enduring can be built on violence." From Mohandas K. Gandhi, *Young India*, 15 November 1928.

"Nonviolence seeks to "win" not by destroying or even by humiliating the adversary, but by convincing him that there is a higher and more certain common good than can be attained by bombs and blood." From Thomas Merton, *Faith and Violence* (Notre Dame, IN: University of Notre Dame Press, 1968), p. 12.

CHAPTER 5

"Peace comes from within. Do not seek it without." From Siddhārtha Gautama (the Buddha). Widely quoted on the Internet, for example at: http://sourceso finsight.com/buddha-quotes; authenticity disputed by Bodhipaksa at http://www.fakebuddhaquotes.com.

"But why . . . do we still think of peace as the resolution of war, not as the way to prevent war?" From Anne Deveson, *Waging Peace: Reflections on Peace and War from an Unconventional Woman* (Sydney: Allen & Unwin, 2013), p. 98.

"Peace . . . is the struggle to solve concrete problems in ways that enable us to agree to work together in the future." From J. Gray Cox, *The Ways of Peace: A Philosophy of Peace as Action* (Mahwah, NJ: Paulist Press, 1986), p. 11.

CHAPTER 6

"Your worst enemy cannot harm you as much as your own thoughts, un-guarded. But once mastered, no one can help you as much, not even your father or your mother." from Siddhārtha Gautama (the Buddha), *Dhammapada*.

"If we desire peace, we must prepare for peace. The most important thing is to build a culture of peace." From Anwarul K. Chowdhury, as quoted at http://www.changemakrs.com/anwarulchowdhury/quotes.

"Establishing lasting peace is the work of education; all politics can do is keep us out of war." From Maria Montessori, *Education and Peace*, trans. Helen R. Lane (Chicago: Henry Regnery, 1972), p. viii. (Reprinted Santa Barbara, CA: ABC-CLIO, 1992).

CHAPTER 7

"All thinking about peace must now be global." From Kent D. Shifferd, *From War to Peace: A Guide to the Next Hundred Years* (Jefferson, NC: McFarland, 2011), p. 108.

"Peace is development in the broadest sense of the term." From Edward Azar, *The Management of Protracted Social Conflict: Theory and Cases* (Aldershot: Dartmouth, 1990), p. 155.

"The greatest gift we can give to our children is to raise them in a culture of peace." From Louise Diamond, as quoted in Michele A. Paludi, ed., *Women and Management: Global Issues and Promising Solutions, Volume Two—Signs of Solutions* (Santa Barbara, CA: ABC-CLIO, 2013), p. v.

Index